THE PROSPECT
OF PRESIDENTIAL RHETORIC

NUMBER EIGHTEEN
Presidential Rhetoric Series
   Martin J. Medhurst, General Editor

THE PROSPECT OF

Presidential Rhetoric

edited by

JAMES ARNT AUNE AND MARTIN J. MEDHURST

Texas A&M University Press • *College Station*

Copyright © 2008
Texas A&M University Press
Manufactured in the
United States of America
All rights reserved
First edition

The paper used meets the requirements
of ANSI/NISO Z39.48–1992
(Permanence of Paper)

Library of Congress Cataloging-in-Publication Data

  The prospect of presidential rhetoric / edited by James Arnt Aune and
Martin J. Medhurst. — 1st ed.
     p. cm. — (Presidential rhetoric series ; no. 18)
  Includes bibliographical references and index.
  ISBN-13: 978-1-58544-626-1 (cloth : alk. paper)
  ISBN-10: 1-58544-626-2 (cloth : alk. paper)
  ISBN-13: 978-1-58544-627-8 (pbk. : alk. paper)
  ISBN-10: 1-58544-627-0 (pbk. : alk. paper)
   1. Presidents—United States—History. 2. Presidents—United
States—Language. 3. Rhetoric—Political aspects—United States.
4. Rhetoric—Study and teaching—United States. 5. English
language—Rhetoric—Study and teaching—United States. 6. United
States—Politics and government. 7. Communication in politics—United
States. 8. Political leadership—United States. 9. Bush, George W.
(George Walker), 1946– —Language. 10. United States—Politics and
government—2001–   I. Aune, James Arnt. II. Medhurst, Martin J.
  E176.1.P974   2008
  973.09'9—dc22   2007026470

To the memory of

HERMAN GIESEN AND TED J. SMITH III

CONTENTS

Acknowledgments — xi

PART 1.
READINGS IN PRESIDENTIAL RHETORIC

1. From Retrospect to Prospect: The Study of Presidential Rhetoric, 1915–2005 — 3
   Martin J. Medhurst, Baylor University
2. Power and Authority in a Postmodern Presidency — 28
   John M. Murphy, University of Georgia
3. The Econo-Rhetorical Presidency — 46
   James Arnt Aune, Texas A&M University
4. The Return of the Imperial Presidency — 69
   Marouf Hasian Jr., University of Utah
5. To Produce a "Judicious Choice": Presidential Responses to the Exercise of Advice and Consent by the U.S. Senate on Supreme Court Nominations — 99
   Trevor Parry-Giles, University of Maryland
6. The Rhetorical Presidency and the Myth of the American Dream — 130
   Leroy Dorsey, Texas A&M University
7. Of Allies and Enemies: Old Wine in New Bottles or New Wine in an Old Jug? — 160
   Marilyn J. Young, Florida State University
8. Revising the Cold War Narrative to Encompass Terrorist Threats: Vietnam and Beyond — 182
   Carol Winkler, Georgia State University
9. George W. Bush, Public Faith, and the Culture War over Same-Sex Marriage — 209
   Martin J. Medhurst, Baylor University
10. Thinking Harder about Presidential Discourse: The Question of Efficacy — 238
    Roderick P. Hart, University of Texas at Austin

PART 2.
TASK FORCE REPORTS

11. Report of the National Task Force on the Presidency   251
    and Deliberative Democracy
    Chair: Vanessa B. Beasley, Southern Methodist University
    Robert B. Asen, University of Wisconsin, Madison
    Diane M. Blair, California State University, Fresno
    Stephen J. Hartnett, University of Illinois, Champaign-Urbana
    Karla K. Leeper, Baylor University
    Jennifer R. Mercieca, Texas A&M University, College Station

12. Report of the National Task Force on Presidential   272
    Communication to Congress
    Chair: Mary E. Stuckey, Georgia State University
    Michael A. Genovese, Loyola Marymount University
    Sharon E. Jarvis, University of Texas, Austin
    Craig Allen Smith, North Carolina State University
    Craig R. Smith, California State University, Long Beach
    Robert Spitzer, State University of New York, Cortland
    Susan M. Zaeske, University of Wisconsin, Madison

13. Report of the National Task Force on the Presidency   293
    and Public Opinion
    Chair: J. Michael Hogan, Pennsylvania State University, University Park
    George C. Edwards III, Texas A&M University, College Station
    Wynton C. Hall, Bainbridge College
    Christine L. Harold, University of Georgia, Athens
    Gerard A. Hauser, University of Colorado, Boulder
    Susan Herbst, Temple University
    Robert Y. Shapiro, Columbia University
    Ted J. Smith III, Virginia Commonwealth University

14. Report of the National Task Force on the Ethical   317
    Responsibilities of Presidential Rhetoric
    Chair: Steven R. Goldzwig, Marquette University
    Karrin Vasby Anderson, Colorado State University
    Frederick J. Antczak, Grand Valley State University

	Thomas W. Benson, Pennsylvania State University, University Park	
	Rita Kirk Whillock, Southern Methodist University	
15.	Report of the National Task Force on the Theory and Practice of the Rhetorical Presidency	340
	Chair: David Henry, University of Nevada, Las Vegas	
	Philip Abbott, Wayne State University	
	Davis W. Houck, Florida State University	
	Mel Laracey, University of Texas, San Antonio	
	Stephen E. Lucas, University of Wisconsin, Madison	
	Shawn J. Parry-Giles, University of Maryland	
16.	Report of the National Task Force on Presidential Rhetoric in Times of Crisis	355
	Chair: Denise M. Bostdorff, College of Wooster	
	Martin Carcasson, Colorado State University	
	James M. Farrell, University of New Hampshire	
	Robert L. Ivie, Indiana University, Bloomington	
	Amos Kiewe, Syracuse University	
	Kathleen B. Smith, Wake Forest University	

Contributors	379
Index	381

ACKNOWLEDGMENTS

The chapters in this volume were first presented at the tenth annual conference on presidential rhetoric held at Texas A&M University's Presidential Conference Center, March 4–7, 2004. The conference was sponsored by the Program in Presidential Rhetoric, a research arm of the Department of Communication at Texas A&M University. As the director of the 2004 conference, I am grateful for financial and logistical support from several departments and units at Texas A&M University, notably the Department of Communication and the George Bush Presidential Library Foundation. In addition, the Program in Presidential Rhetoric was supported by financial gifts from Linda and Herman Giesen of Dallas, Texas, and Clementine and Emil Ogden of College Station, Texas.

While planning the conference, I was fortunate to have the help of my colleagues at Texas A&M, including Kurt Ritter, Leroy Dorsey, Jennifer Mercieca, and Rick Rigsby. Martin J. Medhurst, now at Baylor University, provided the vision and leadership that made this conference possible for ten years. I especially thank my conference assistant Paul Stob, now a doctoral candidate at the University of Wisconsin–Madison, for his sheer wizardry in helping organize the details for the 2004 conference, and my current research assistant Yogita Sharma, for helping complete the manuscript. As always, the Texas A&M University Press was a model of professionalism and efficiency. Special thanks to Mary Lenn Dixon, without whom this series would not have been possible, and to Sally Antrobus, for her expert copyediting.

The volume is dedicated to two men who died shortly after the conference: Herman Giesen, long-time supporter of the Program in Presidential Rhetoric, and Ted J. Smith III, professor of Communication at Virginia Commonwealth University, whose tragically early death deprived our field of one of its most eloquent conservative voices.

James Arnt Aune

THE PROSPECT OF

PRESIDENTIAL RHETORIC

PART 1
Readings in Presidential Rhetoric

CHAPTER 1

FROM RETROSPECT TO PROSPECT

The Study of Presidential Rhetoric, 1915–2005

Martin J. Medhurst, Baylor University

The field formerly known as speech has contributed substantially to our knowledge about presidential rhetoric. For the past ninety years, scholars of speech and communication have analyzed how language functions to achieve particular goals for speakers. Until quite recently, speech scholars thought of the primary object of their studies as rhetorical discourse, and the presidency as merely one site among many where the practice of rhetoric could be studied with profit.

It was not until the 1980s that communication scholars began to recognize and articulate a specific interest in the presidency and in presidential rhetoric as a specialization within the larger world of rhetorical studies. This recognition and articulation first occurred publicly in 1984 when Theodore Otto Windt Jr., writing in the *Central States Speech Journal*, identified presidential rhetoric as a distinct subfield within the discipline. Drawing on the previous seventy years of scholarship in speech and communication studies, Windt identified four broad categories of research in presidential rhetoric.[1] Also in 1984, two communication scholars, Kathleen Hall Jamieson and Roderick P. Hart, published books focused on the presidency.[2] This proved to be the beginning of what would grow into a strong line of books focusing on presidential discourse.

In 1989, David Zarefsky announced the conceptual breakthrough that allowed scholars of speech and rhetoric to break away from the analytical approach that had characterized the field for most of its existence. Zarefsky wrote: "To start with, we have enlarged the meaning of 'public address' from a mode to a function of discourse. It seems self-evident that any rhetorical act is 'addressed' and hence evokes a 'public.' . . . By embracing a broader conception of public address and not reducing the term to formal oratory, our studies have enhanced the potential for understanding historical or rhetorical situations and for formulating theoretical generalizations."[3]

Henceforth, scholars of speech and communication began to think of themselves not just as students of public address but more importantly as students of public affairs and public culture, the analysis of which still included study of public addresses but also transcended the somewhat narrow boundaries, both conceptually and methodologically, within which the traditional study of public address had been practiced. Moreover, it soon came to be realized that rhetoric, which had always been the *object* of public address studies, could also function as a *mode of inquiry*—a way of knowing, understanding, and interpreting.[4]

This expansion of both the conceptualization and the domain of public address opened the way for a rhetorical renaissance. One of the beneficiaries of this renaissance of interest in all things rhetorical has been the study of presidential rhetoric. But before examining the fruits of the past twenty years, I want to sketch the first three phases through which the study of presidential rhetoric came into being, matured, and set the stage for the current renaissance.

PHASE ONE: IN THE BEGINNING, 1914–44

When the scholarly organization calling itself the National Association of Academic Teachers of Public Speaking came into being in 1914, there were no scholars of presidential rhetoric within its ranks. This was to be a practical and pedagogical association, devoted to the teaching of oral performance in its many modes, particularly public speaking, oral reading, debate, and drama. The primary concern was in establishing public speaking or speech as a recognized academic discipline within American colleges and universities, sometimes in conjunction with departments of English and sometimes separately.[5] Having a separate organizational structure, publishing a separate journal soon to be called the *Quarterly Journal of Speech* (*QJS*), and establishing both graduate and undergraduate programs across the country became the driving forces. There was no particular intellectual agenda, though there was much debate about what that agenda should be. Some were scholars of classical rhetoric; others were teachers of various performance skills, psychologists of language use, and scholars of persuasion or of speech science; and many were primarily interested in dramatic performance and oral reading. All came together to form departments or divisions of speech.

Within this barnyard of competing voices and agendas was one group of scholars who believed that part of teaching public speaking skills involved the study of great speakers.[6] In early twentieth-century America, most of those considered great speakers were British parliamentarians (Burke, Pitt, Disraeli), religious personalities (Edwards, Whitefield, Beecher, Fosdick), or legislative leaders (Henry, Webster, Clay, Calhoun). Presidents were not high on the list of those to be studied or emulated as models. Throughout the first decade of publication, not a single article in the *Quarterly Journal of Speech* focused on a president. For the entire decade of the 1920s, only four such articles appeared. In 1925, Marvin Bauer published the first article on presidential rhetoric when he examined "The Influence of Lincoln's Audience on His Speeches." In that article, derived from his M.A. thesis, Bauer argued that Lincoln was shaped by the forces of his time more than he was himself a shaper of those forces.[7]

In 1927, Gladys Murphy Graham published a substantial article "Concerning the Speech Power of Woodrow Wilson." Here, speech was identified as a form of power. Graham was particularly interested in the sources of that power and how they had evolved into the presidential orator. She wrote: "The war president is only half-understandable without a knowledge of the studies of the university professor and president. There is a basic interrelationship of parts which cannot be overlooked. And for a speech study the time-sequence arrangement is particularly significant. To watch a style and method establish itself in basic theory, develop, adapt, move from one stage to another, ever larger one until half a world is audience; to note, if possible, the progressively intensifying elements and factors of its powers. . . . It is an intriguing and a challenging possibility."[8]

Graham proceeded to accept this challenge and in so doing produced one of the first—and best—analyses of the development of Wilson's style and method of speaking. Having read for herself the recently released Wilson corpus, Graham could reach critical judgments that today's best scholarship still confirms—that "the speeches on the Western tour are, in general, far inferior to those of the war time and pre-defence-of-the-treaty period."[9]

Graham's focus on the development of style and method would soon become the preferred mode of rhetorical analysis. Two years later, in 1929, Edwin Paget isolated eight distinct methods Wilson used in his role as presidential persuader.[10] And in 1930, Dayton McKean analyzed the logic and method behind the rhetorical changes that Wilson made to two of his most famous speeches—the First Inaugural and "The Lawyer and the Community"—by comparing Wilson's own typewritten manuscripts with the changes he made by hand. McKean concluded that Wilson's changes in the manuscripts "show a nice sense of the meaning of words, the proper order for phrases and clauses; they show a desire to be exact, and an effort to express meaning precisely and forcefully."[11] It is important to note that both Graham and McKean were working directly from primary source materials and bringing their expertise in rhetoric to bear on those materials in order to reach critical judgments about style and method.

These earliest studies on Lincoln and Wilson represent almost all of what would follow between 1930 and 1944. In addition to Bauer's study, speech scholars produced seven more studies on Lincoln, including a long two-part article on "Lincoln—The Speaker" by Mildred Freburg Berry in 1931, and a series of four articles on Lincoln by Earl W. Wiley, making a total of eight studies from 1925 through 1944.[12] Likewise, in addition to the studies of Graham, Paget, and McKean, speech scholars produced four more studies of Woodrow Wilson, making a total of seven articles over this first phase of development.[13] The only other president written about during this period was Franklin D. Roosevelt, who was the subject of three studies—a "phonetic study" of his speech patterns in 1936, a study of the "textual authenticity" of FDR's Second Inaugural in 1937, and an examination of "rhythm" as an element of FDR's style in 1942.[14] The only article on presidential rhetoric that did not deal with Lincoln, Wilson, or Roosevelt was a 1930 study by Donald Hayworth that surveyed 145 presidential campaign speeches from 1884 to 1920, a study derived from his 1929 doctoral dissertation at the University of Wisconsin—the first dissertation on presidential rhetoric and one of only six such dissertations completed between 1915 and 1944.[15]

There are several important aspects to this early phase of development. Presidents were studied not so much because they were presidents but because they were thought to be good role models for rhetorical style and method. Of the thirteen scholars who published essays during this period, only three—Berry, Wiley, and McKean—could be said to be consistently interested in their subjects over a sustained period. In addition to publishing in the early 1930s, these three scholars continued to publish on Lincoln or Wilson. All three contributed chapters on these presidents to *A History and Criticism of American Public Address,* published in 1943, and Wiley continued to publish on Lincoln well into the 1950s.[16] Even though the pool of scholars interested in presidential rhetoric was quite shallow, a handful of experts on particular presidencies began to emerge. That emergence would not become clear until the second phase of development, from 1945 to 1964, but its seeds were sown in the first phase, particularly in the completion of master's theses and doctoral dissertations on presidential rhetoric between 1935 and 1944. According to the Knower Index, some twenty-four theses and five dissertations on presidential rhetoric were completed during this ten-year span.[17] The results of that research helped to make the second phase of development far more diverse.

PHASE TWO: THE HISTORICAL-RHETORICAL METHOD MATURES, 1945–64

It is clear that something was happening by the end of phase one, because the corpus of studies on presidential rhetoric suddenly exploded between 1945 and 1955. Whereas only three presidents had been the subject of published research during the preceding thirty years, from 1945 to 1955 eight different presidents were the subjects of critical analysis—Franklin Roosevelt (1945), Lincoln (1945), James Madison (1945), Wilson (1946, 1947), Theodore Roosevelt (1945, 1947), John Quincy Adams (1946), Thomas Jefferson (1947), and Harry S. Truman (1948).[18] It is clear that part of this expansion was fueled by publications arising from doctoral dissertations. Both of the articles on Theodore Roosevelt, for example, came from the 1942 dissertation of William A. Behl, completed at Northwestern University; Clair Henderlider's 1946 study of Woodrow Wilson originated in his dissertation completed at the University of Iowa in 1945. Throughout this second phase of development, dissertations would prove to be a primary source for the study of presidential rhetoric. Several of these dissertations were completed at the University of Iowa, under the direction of A. Craig Baird. In addition to Henderlider's study of Wilson, pathbreaking essays on Franklin D. Roosevelt by Earnest Brandenburg (1949 [two], 1952) and Laura Crowell (1952, 1955, 1958) originated in or grew out of their dissertation work under Baird.[19]

However, Baird's influence on the study of presidential rhetoric was more than pedagogical. As the coauthor of *Speech Criticism* (1948), and one who had published on orators, argument, and critical method since the mid-1920s, Baird exerted a powerful influence on the method used in all analyses of public rhetoric, presidential and otherwise.[20] That method, broadly construed as historical-rhetorical in orientation, resulted in a standard pattern followed by virtually all analysts of presidential rhetoric from 1945 to 1964. The main headings in Henderlider's study are representative of the approach:

I. The Speaker's Background
II. The Speaker's Ideas and Their Support
    A. Premises and Lines of Argument
    B. Proofs and Refutation
III. Speech Composition
    A. Speech Preparation
    B. Organization
    C. Language
IV. Delivery

The widespread adoption of this method of analyzing rhetorical discourse had mixed results. On the one hand, it produced a great deal of information and, if properly pursued, virtually guaranteed that the researcher would be well versed in the topic at hand. Those earning degrees under Baird at Iowa—or James McBurney and Ernest Wrage at Northwestern, or Henry Lee Ewbank at Wisconsin, or James M. O'Neill at Minnesota, or Louis Eich and Kenneth Hance at Michigan—were well-educated people, many of whom went on to distinguish themselves through their scholarship. On the other hand, in less well-trained hands, the historical-rhetorical method could become mechanical, categorical, and wooden. It could come to substitute for thought and to discourage innovation and insight by limiting the kinds of questions one might ask about a speaker, or text, or situation. This focus on a single method was seldom questioned during the second phase of development, but it would become a central focal point by the mid-1960s.

Another development of note was the explicit recognition of the importance of primary source materials when studying presidential rhetoric. While Graham, Berry, Wiley, and McKean had pioneered the use of such materials in the 1920s and '30s, it was not until the 1940s that articles begin to appear touting the availability of particular sources. In 1948 alone, two articles appeared in *QJS*, one on "The Roosevelt Papers" by the director of the Roosevelt Library in Hyde Park, and one on "The National Archives" by the head of Photographic Records at the Archives.[21] Indeed, many of the studies completed in this second phase of development did use primary sources beyond the speech texts themselves. The problem was not so much the lack of sources as the lack of good research questions by which to interrogate those sources. The

Thonssen-Baird method of criticism encouraged scholars to think primarily in terms of argumentative topics, sources of support, style, delivery, and general background information. In short, it focused rather narrowly on the speaker, the speech, and the speaking occasion, with the speech itself often receiving less than detailed treatment. Consequently, many of the studies seemed more heavily weighted toward the historical than the rhetorical.

Although interest in presidential campaign rhetoric can be traced to Hayworth's 1929 dissertation, it was not until 1948 that Harold Harding, editor of the *Quarterly Journal of Speech,* decided to feature a symposium on that year's presidential campaign, with Jennings Randolph writing about Truman and the Democratic campaign, and William Behl about Thomas Dewey and the Republicans. This symposium would continue to be a quadrennial feature in *QJS* until 1976, when it was picked up by *Speech Monographs* for the 1976 election cycle. It was then discontinued altogether in 1980. But by instituting the campaign symposium, Harding assured that campaign rhetoric could never totally disappear from the intellectual radar. He also legitimized campaign discourse by both incumbents and challengers as fertile ground for rhetorical analysis. Not surprisingly, articles such as "Franklin D. Roosevelt's Audience Persuasion in the 1936 Campaign" (1950), "Harry Truman at the Whistle Stops" (1952), and "An Analysis and Criticism of the 1940 Campaign Speeches of Wendell L. Willkie" (1954) followed in short order.[22]

Clearly the interest in presidential rhetoric dramatically increased in the second phase. From only nineteen published studies in 1925–44, the speech literature grew to fifty-seven studies in 1945–64, almost a threefold increase. Part of this increase is accounted for by the expansion of interest beyond Lincoln, Wilson, and FDR (though FDR still accounted for fourteen of the fifty-seven studies completed), but an even greater part of the increase is represented by the expansion of topics beyond individual speeches or groups of speeches to include such topics as presidential ghostwriting, the influence of radio and television on election campaigns, various types of presidential discourse, issues of textual authenticity, interviews with presidents and their aides, political conventions, presidential debates, and the role of presidential advance.

Encouraging as this numerical increase and topic expansion were, the commitment of scholars to sustained programs of research in presidential rhetoric remained limited. Once one moves beyond William Behl, Earnest Brandenburg, Laura Crowell, and Russel Windes, one is hard pressed to find research programs being pursued on anything like a systematic basis during phase two.[23] This is not to say that some of the individual essays were not good work. In fact, some of them were excellent exemplars of the period: Gregg Phifer on

"'Not for the Purpose of Making a Speech': Andrew Johnson's Swing around the Circle" (1954), John F. Wilson's "Rhetorical Echoes of a Wilsonian Idea" (1957), Ernest G. Bormann's "Ghostwriting and the Rhetorical Critic" (1960), William R. Underhill's "Harry S. Truman: Spokesman for Containment" (1961), Donald L. Wolfarth's "John F. Kennedy in the Tradition of Inaugural Speeches" (1961), and Anthony Hillbruner's "Word and Deed: Jefferson's Addresses to the Indians" (1963) are all worth reading even to this day.[24] But one isolated essay does not a research program make.

Phase two did produce one notable first. Robert G. Gunderson published the first book on presidential rhetoric, *The Log Cabin Campaign* (1957), which examined the presidential election of 1840. It had taken forty-three years, but the first book was out—and a very good book at that, one that is still considered authoritative nearly a half century after it was written.[25] It would be twenty more years before another communication scholar would write a book about presidential rhetoric. Speech was almost entirely an article-based discipline as phase two came to a close in 1964. It would remain so for many years to come.

PHASE THREE: THE ERA OF CRITICAL PLURALISM, 1965–84

The third phase of development in presidential rhetoric as a research field commenced in 1965, not with a bang but with a faint echo. The only article published that year on presidential rhetoric was Robert N. Hall's "Lyndon Johnson's Speech Preparation."[26] I describe it as a faint echo only to underscore that it was a relic from phase two, even as it appeared at the dawn of phase three. Indeed, never again in a major speech journal would an article appear with the term *speech preparation* in the title. That terminology was a sign of the old critical paradigm championed by Thonnsen and Baird and their many students and followers. Instead, phase three was to be the era of critical pluralism. Led by the searing indictment of "neo-Aristotelianism" issued by Edwin Black in *Rhetorical Criticism: A Study in Method* (1965), those who had thought of themselves as public address scholars suddenly found themselves in a world where not only the historical-rhetorical method was challenged, but the very assumptions about language, thought, discourse, and audiences upon which that method had been erected were challenged as well. The results of this change included a movement from speech to rhetoric (as controlling term), from history to criticism (as type of scholarly activity), from one monolithic method to multiple methods (each with equal credibility), from conscious attempts to achieve critical objectivity to conscious celebration of critical subjectivity (as acknowledgment of the radical situatedness of all knowledge claims), from reporters and compilers of data to interpreters and analyzers of data (with a radical expansion of what counts as "data" for the rhetorical critic), and from a predominant emphasis on style and delivery to a primary focus on strategy (or movement from a focus on the text or speaker to a focus on the critic and his or her interpretive powers).[27]

This sea change in the intellectual presumptions of speech scholars affected all areas of the discipline. In so doing it set in motion a series of forces that would culminate, some twenty years later, in a remarkable renaissance of all things rhetorical, including presidential rhetoric. One such force was the impetus toward textual criticism. While scholars of rhetoric had always claimed to be interested in speeches, the plain fact was that whether examining presidential rhetoric or any other kind of discourse, speech scholars had been wholly remiss in taking seriously the rhetorical dynamics within the speech text. From 1914 to 1964, one could count on both hands the total number of studies that had examined in detail a discrete presidential speech, for there were only seven such studies published.[28] Speech scholars simply did not do much textual analysis prior to phase three. But by drawing on the theories of such literary scholars as I. A. Richards, Kenneth Burke, Richard Weaver, Northrop Frye, Wayne Booth, and others, scholars of presidential rhetoric soon began to produce a series of outstanding studies, including:

1966: Hermann G. Stelzner, "'War Message,' December 8, 1941: An Approach to Language"
1967: Robert W. Smith, "The 'Second' Inaugural Address of Lyndon Baines Johnson: A Definitive Text"
1968: Robert N. Bostrom, "'I Give You a Man'—Kennedy's Speech for Adlai Stevenson"
1969: Thomas W. Benson, "Inaugurating Peace: Franklin D. Roosevelt's Last Speech"
1970: Robert P. Newman, "Under the Veneer: Nixon's Vietnam Speech of November 3, 1969"
1971: Hermann G. Stelzner, "The Quest Story and Nixon's November 3, 1969 Address"
1972: Forbes Hill, "Conventional Wisdom—Traditional Form—The President's Message of November 3, 1969"
1973: Stephen E. Lucas, "Theodore Roosevelt's 'The Man with the Muck-Rake': A Reinterpretation"

1973: Richard B. Gregg and Gerard A. Hauser, "Richard Nixon's April 30, 1970 Address on Cambodia: A 'Ceremony' of Confrontation"

1974: Michael C. Leff and Gerald P. Mohrmann, "Lincoln at Cooper Union: A Rhetorical Analysis of the Text"

In less than a decade, the field produced more analyses of single presidential texts than in all of its previous history combined. Paradoxically, at the very moment that some critics of presidential rhetoric were turning inward toward the text, others were turning outward toward the larger arenas of campaigns and movements. Some examined campaign strategies, or degradation rituals, or the use of rhetorical icons in campaigns.[29] Others extended the considerable theorizing about social movements to the study of presidential campaigns and initiatives.[30]

The phenomenon most characteristic of phase three was consistent experimentation in how best to study discourse rhetorically, and that experimentation extended to the study of presidential rhetoric. Some scholars explored the generic implications of presidential discourse.[31] Others focused on the linguistic and stylistic dimensions of presidential language.[32] Issues of presidential image and ethos received attention.[33] And another line of inquiry centered on the dramatistic and narrative qualities of presidential rhetoric.[34] There was also continuing exploration of the relationship between presidential rhetoric and the coverage of that rhetoric by the news media.[35] Several scholars tried to link the humanistic traditions of rhetoric with the newer social scientific means of investigating voters and political messages, with only limited success.[36]

With attention focused primarily on theories and methods of criticism, traditional rhetorical concerns with invention, style, and delivery fell by the wayside. So, too, did historical criticism, as emphasis switched from trying to discover the lessons of history to an attempt to reveal the creativity of the critic. It was almost as though scholars assumed that since the predominant method employed in historical-rhetorical studies had been discredited, history itself would have to be abandoned. These changes manifested themselves in several ways, most notably in the precipitous decline of historical studies of the presidency and in the ascendancy of studies focusing on the contemporary scene. Of the seventy-one studies of presidential rhetoric published in phase three, only eighteen dealt with a president or campaign before Lyndon Johnson. All the others were on Johnson, Nixon, Ford, Carter, or Reagan—the presidencies being enacted during the period covered by phase three. This heavy emphasis on the contemporary was interpreted by some as the death of rhetorical history generally and of public address studies particularly.[37]

But something odd happened on the way to the graveyard. Just as phase three was drawing to a close, rhetorical scholars started to publish books on presidential rhetoric. First it was Roderick P. Hart with *The Political Pulpit* (1977), then Lloyd F. Bitzer with *Carter vs. Ford: The Counterfeit Debates of 1976* (1980), Robert Underhill with *The Truman Persuasions* (1981), Kathleen Hall Jamieson with *Packaging the Presidency* (1984), and Hart again with *Verbal Style and the Presidency* (1984).[38] Some of these books had been anticipated by articles published during phase three, while others seemingly came out of nowhere. There had not been a book specifically on presidential rhetoric published in the speech communication field since 1957. Why the sudden increase? Was it just a fluke or had the turmoil brought about by the destruction of the reigning paradigm and the search for alternative methods started to bear intellectual fruit? The answer was not long in coming.

Phase Four: The Rise of the Rhetorical Renaissance, 1985–2005

It was perhaps merely coincidental that the appearance of the 1984 books by Jamieson and Hart happened at the same moment that Windt was proclaiming the existence of a recognized subfield called presidential rhetoric. At the very least, those books tended to support Windt's thesis, as did other books following in quick succession:

- 1985: Kathleen J. Turner, *Lyndon Johnson's Dual War: Vietnam and the Press*
- 1985: Paul D. Erickson, *Reagan Speaks: The Making of an American Myth*
- 1986: David Zarefsky, *Lyndon Johnson and the War on Poverty: Rhetoric and History*
- 1986: J. Michael Hogan, *The Panama Canal and American Politics*
- 1987: Theodore Windt and Beth Ingold, *Essays in Presidential Rhetoric, 2nd edition*
- 1987: Halford Ross Ryan, *Franklin D. Roosevelt's Rhetorical Presidency*
- 1987: L. Patrick Devlin, *Political Persuasion in Presidential Campaigns*
- 1988: Robert Underhill, *The Bully Pulpit: From Franklin Roosevelt to Ronald Reagan*
- 1988: Kathleen Hall Jamieson, *Eloquence in an Electronic Age*
- 1988: Robert E. Denton Jr., *The Primetime Presidency of Ronald Reagan*

1989: Brant Short, *Ronald Reagan and the Public Lands*
1990: Karlyn Kohrs Campbell and Kathleen Hall Jamieson, *Deeds Done in Words: Presidential Rhetoric and the Genres of Governance*
1990: Ruth M. Gonchar Brennan and Dan F. Hahn, *Listening for a President*
1990: Mary E. Stuckey, *Playing the Game: The Presidential Rhetoric of Ronald Reagan*
1990: David Zarefsky, *Lincoln, Douglas, and Slavery: In the Crucible of Debate*
1990: Theodore Otto Windt Jr., *Presidents and Protesters*
1990: Hal W. Bochin, *Richard M. Nixon: Rhetorical Strategist*
1990: Robert V. Friedenberg, *Theodore Roosevelt and the Rhetoric of Militant Decency*
1990: Kathleen Hall Jamieson and David Birdsell, *Presidential Debates: The Challenge of Creating an Informed Electorate*
1991: Patricia Dennis Witherspoon, *Within These Walls*
1991: Amos Kiewe and Davis W. Houck, *A Shining City on a Hill: Ronald Reagan's Economic Rhetoric, 1951–1989*
1991: Mary E. Stuckey, *The President as Interpreter-in-Chief*
1991: David E. Procter, *Enacting Political Culture*
1992: Kurt Ritter and David Henry, *Ronald Reagan: The Great Communicator*
1992: Kathleen Hall Jamieson, *Dirty Politics*
1992: Susan A. Hellweg et al., *Televised Presidential Debates*
1992: Lois J. Einhorn, *Abraham Lincoln the Orator*
1992: Rebecca S. Bjork, *The Strategic Defense Initiative: Symbolic Containment of the Nuclear Threat*
1992: Ryan J. Barilleau and Mary E. Stuckey, eds., *Leadership and the Bush Presidency*
1992: Michael Weiler and W. Barnett Pearce, eds., *Reagan and Public Discourse in America*
1992: Moya Ann Ball, *Vietnam-on-the-Potomac*
1993: Halford Ryan, *Harry S. Truman: Presidential Rhetoric*
1993: Martin J. Medhurst, *Dwight D. Eisenhower: Strategic Communicator*
1993: Joanne Morreale, *The Presidential Campaign Film*
1993: Edward A. Hinck, *Enacting the Presidency*
1993: Halford Ryan, ed., *The Inaugural Addresses of Twentieth-Century American Presidents*

1994: Denise M. Bostdorff, *The Presidency and the Rhetoric of Foreign Crisis*
1994: Martin J. Medhurst, ed., *Eisenhower's War of Words: Rhetoric and Leadership*
1994 James J. Kauffman, *Selling Outer Space: Kennedy, the Media, and Funding for Project Apollo, 1961–1963*
1994: Arthur H. Miller and Bruce E. Gronbeck, eds., *Presidential Campaigns and American Self Images*
1994: Robert V. Friedenberg, ed., *Rhetorical Studies of National Political Debates, 1960–1992*
1994: Craig Allen Smith and Kathy B. Smith, *The White House Speaks: Presidential Leadership as Persuasion*
1994: Amos Kiewe, ed., *The Modern Presidency and Crisis Rhetoric*
1994: Stephen A. Smith, ed., *Bill Clinton on Stump, State, and Stage*
1994: Diana B. Carlin and Mitchell S. McKinney, *The 1992 Presidential Debate in Focus*
1994: Robert E. Denton Jr., *The 1992 Presidential Campaign*
1995: Kathleen E. Kendall, ed., *Presidential Campaign Discourse*
1995: Robert P. Newman, *Truman and the Hiroshima Cult*
1995: Steven R. Goldzwig and George N. Dionisopoulos, *"In a Perilous Hour": The Public Address of John F. Kennedy*
1995: Halford Ryan, ed., *U.S. Presidents as Orators*

From 1984 through 1995, speech and communication scholars produced more than fifty books on presidential rhetoric, a number surpassing all other books on rhetoric, whether theoretical, pedagogical, historical, or critical in orientation.

From the outset of phase four, scholars began to recognize the emergence of what was soon labeled a rhetorical renaissance.[39] More and better scholarship was being produced, scholarship that often had its genesis in phase three but did not fully come to fruition until the onset of phase four. Indeed, it is interesting to look back at some of the articles produced toward the end of phase three. In 1982, Jamieson and Campbell had written about "Rhetorical Hybrids: Fusions of Generic Elements." This article followed from their 1978 anthology on generic analysis. In 1985, they wrote an article for *Presidential Studies Quarterly* titled "Inaugurating the Presidency." All of this thinking about genre culminated in their 1990 book *Deeds Done in Words*. Zarefsky had published articles on Johnson's War on Poverty, Lester Olson had published on the use of rhetorical iconology in a presidential campaign, and Philip Wander had set forth an outline of "The Rhetoric of American Foreign Policy" that focused on the Eisenhower and Kennedy administrations. Each of these essays represented research programs that ended up leading to books.[40] In retrospect, it is clear that the ferment of the late 1960s and '70s led to the development of new research programs and agendas that, in turn, ultimately led to the production of scholarly books, starting in the middle 1980s.

Whereas phase one featured only three researchers with anything like a sustained research program in presidential rhetoric (Mildred Freburg Berry, Dayton David McKean, and Earl W. Wiley), and phase two featured only four with sustained research agendas (William Behl, Earnest Brandenburg, Laura Crowell, and Russel Windes), beginning toward the middle of phase three and extending into the beginning of phase four, we a larger number of researchers who start by publishing articles and then proceed to develop those articles into book-length treatments. Researchers who made this transition from phase three articles to phase four books included Karlyn Kohrs Campbell, Robert E. Denton Jr., L. Patrick Devlin, Robert V. Friedenberg, Bruce E. Gronbeck, Roderick Hart, David Henry, J. Michael Hogan, Robert L. Ivie, Kathleen Hall Jamieson, Martin J. Medhurst, Kurt Ritter, Halford Ryan, Kathleen J. Turner, Theodore O. Windt Jr., and David Zarefsky. Several other researchers who would later become prominent scholars of presidential rhetoric—Thomas W. Benson, G. Thomas Goodnight, James R. Andrews, and Edwin Black, for example—spent most of this transitional period establishing research programs in other areas of the field, such as film (Benson), argumentation (Goodnight), British public address (Andrews), and criticism (Black) and only later turned their analytical powers to the subject of presidential rhetoric, though all had touched on the subject early in their careers.

Another explanation for the rise of a book culture in presidential rhetoric, one not inconsistent with these other factors, was the wider availability of publishing opportunities, starting in the mid-1980s and expanding substantially in the 1990s. While there had always been a few publishers willing to take a chance on an isolated monograph, until the 1980s there was only one university press that had an ongoing series in rhetorical studies—Southern Illinois University Press. Yet, SIU Press seldom published a title in presidential rhetoric. There were also some presses with a short list of titles in rhetoric/communication, including the University of Chicago Press and Oxford University Press, but neither had an established series. Both did, however, publish some very important books in presidential rhetoric in the 1980s and 1990s.[41] But the publishing landscape changed radically with the founding of book series at the University of South Carolina Press (1984), Praeger/Greenwood Press (1988), University of Alabama Press (1989), Michigan State University Press (1994), and Texas A&M University Press (1996). Of particular import for presidential studies was the founding of the Presidential Rhetoric Series at Texas A&M University Press in 1996, the present volume being part of it. By 2006, this series alone had issued seventeen books, including:

1996: Martin J. Medhurst, ed., *Beyond the Rhetorical Presidency*
2000: Martin J. Medhurst and H. W. Brands, eds., *Critical Reflections on the Cold War: Linking Rhetoric and History*
2001: Garth E. Pauley, *The Modern Presidency and Civil Rights*
2001: Davis W. Houck, *Rhetoric as Currency: Hoover, Roosevelt and the Great Depression*
2002: Leroy G. Dorsey, ed., *The Presidency and Rhetorical Leadership*
2003: Kurt Ritter and Martin J. Medhurst, eds., *Presidential Speechwriting*
2003: Davis W. Houck and Amos Kiewe, *FDR's Body Politics: The Rhetoric of Disability*
2003: Francis A. Beer, *The Meanings of War and Peace*
2004: Robert Alexander Kraig, *Woodrow Wilson and the Lost World of the Oratorical Statesman*
2004: Vanessa B. Beasley, *You, the People: American National Identity in Presidential Rhetoric*
2004: Tarla Rai Peterson, ed., *Green Talk in the White House: The Rhetorical Presidency Encounters Ecology*
2005: James Arnt Aune and Enrique D. Rigsby, eds., *Civil Rights Rhetoric and the American Presidency*
2005: William D. Harpine, *From the Front Porch to the Front Page: McKinley and Bryan in the 1896 Presidential Campaign*
2006: Vanessa B. Beasley, ed., *Who Belongs in America? Presidents, Rhetoric, and Immigration*
2006: Martin J. Medhurst, ed., *The Rhetorical Presidency of George Herbert Walker Bush*
2006: James J. Kimble, *Mobilizing the Home Front: War Bonds and Domestic Propaganda*
2006: Colleen J. Shogan, *The Moral Rhetoric of American Presidents*

In addition, a separate subseries titled the Library of Presidential Rhetoric, which focuses on detailed analysis of individual presidential texts, commenced publication in 2002. This monograph series, projected to be a fifty-volume set upon completion, has issued the following volumes through 2006:

2002: Davis W. Houck, *FDR and Fear Itself: The First Inaugural Address*
2002: Ira Chernus, *Eisenhower's Atoms for Peace*
2003: Stephen Howard Browne, *Jefferson's Call for Nationhood: The First Inaugural Address*
2004: Thomas W. Benson, *Writing JFK: Presidential Rhetoric and the Press in the Bay of Pigs Crisis*
2006: Mary E. Stuckey, *Slipping the Surly Bonds: Reagan's Challenger Address*
2006: J. Michael Hogan, *Woodrow Wilson's Western Tour: Rhetoric, Public Opinion, and the League of Nations*

Other important books were also published between 1996 and 2006, including:

1996: William L. Benoit and William T. Wells, *Candidates in Conflict: Persuasive Attack and Defense in the 1992 Presidential Debates*
1996: Robert E. Denton Jr. and Rachel L. Holloway, eds., *The Clinton Presidency*
1997: Jim A. Kuypers, *Presidential Crisis Rhetoric and the Press in the Post–Cold War World*
1997: Mary E. Stuckey, *Strategic Failures in the Modern Presidency*
1998: William L. Benoit et al., *Campaign '96*
1998: Robert E. Denton Jr., ed., *The 1996 Presidential Campaign*
1999: William L. Benoit, *Seeing Spots: A Functional Analysis of Presidential Television Advertising, 1952–1996*
2000: Roderick P. Hart, *Campaign Talk: Why Elections Are Good for Us*
2000: Vito N. Silvestri, *Becoming JFK: A Profile in Communication*
2000: Kathleen E. Kendall, *Communication in the Presidential Primaries*
2001: William L. Benoit et al., *The Primary Decision*
2001: Kathleen Hall Jamieson and Paul Waldman, *Electing the President, 2000: The Insiders' View*
2001: Joseph R. Blaney and William L. Benoit, *The Clinton Scandals and the Politics of Image Restoration*
2002: Robert E. Denton Jr., ed., *The 2000 Presidential Campaign*
2002: Robert V. Friedenberg, ed., *Notable Speeches in Contemporary Presidential Campaigns*

2003: Robert E. Denton and Rachel L. Holloway, eds., *Images, Scandals and Communication Strategies of the Clinton Presidency*
2004: Lloyd Rohler, *George Wallace: Conservative Populist*
2004: Mary E. Stuckey, *Defining Americans: The Presidency and National Identity*
2005: Roderick P. Hart et al., *Political Keywords: Using Language That Uses Us*
2005: Robert E. Denton Jr., ed., *The 2004 Presidential Campaign*
2005: Robert E. Denton Jr., *Moral Leadership and the American Presidency*
2006: Michael William Pfau, *The Political Style of Conspiracy: Chase, Sumner, and Lincoln*

As these lists clearly demonstrate, the study of presidential rhetoric from a communication-oriented perspective has expanded exponentially over the past twenty years. To these titles we might add works by scholars outside communication studies, particularly those working within the paradigm of the "rhetorical presidency"—Jeffrey Tulis, James Ceaser, Glen Thurow, Joseph Bessette, Mel Laracey, Richard Ellis, David Crockett, and others.[42] We could likewise add those exploring the phenomenon of "going public"—Samuel Kernell, George C. Edwards III, Reed Welch, and others.[43] When all these works are taken together, the universe of scholarship on rhetoric and the presidency begins to reveal itself in an amazing tapestry of interdisciplinary effort that includes scholars from English, history, journalism, law, American studies, and religious studies, as well as political science and communication.[44] This scholarship, as well, is a part of the rhetorical renaissance that has manifested itself in interdisciplinary conferences, anthologies drawn from multiple disciplines, and scholarly journals with an explicitly interdisciplinary mission. Among such journals, two stand out for their multiple contributions to this interdisciplinary dialogue—*Presidential Studies Quarterly* and *Rhetoric & Public Affairs* (*PSQ, R&PA*).

Space does not permit a detailed survey of the scholarship appearing in these two journals over the last two decades. Even so, it is an empirical fact that scholars of presidential rhetoric often appear in the pages of *PSQ*, while scholars who study the rhetorical presidency or the practice of going public often appear in *R&PA*. There is a mutual recognition of the scholarship on rhetoric and the presidency that transcends the various disciplinary divides, and it is precisely this recognition of the interdisciplinary nature of rhetoric that has fueled the current renaissance. Many of the essays appearing in *PSQ* and *R&PA* have contributed to this growing interdisciplinary dialogue.[45] Although it may be unfair to single out any individual or group of individuals for special recognition, the fact is that two scholars stand synecdochically for this wider interdisciplinary phenomenon. One holds a doctorate in political science and the other in communication. Both have published repeatedly in *PSQ* and *R&PA*, as well as in the major disciplinary journals of communication and political science. Both attend interdisciplinary conferences and promote interdisciplinary thinking and cooperation. And both have contributed to this book. I refer to Professors Mary E. Stuckey of Georgia State University and John M. Murphy of the University of Georgia.[46] Mary Stuckey has been the foremost ambassador of rhetorical studies to the larger world of political science. Her books and articles are deeply informed by both intellectual traditions. Her long-time service as book review editor of *R&PA* was marked by ever-increasing interdisciplinary reviews and an aggressive outreach to younger scholars. John Murphy is, perhaps, the finest rhetorical critic of the presidency writing today. His medium is the essay and his methods are wide-ranging, sensitive to context, and deeply informed by the larger interdisciplinary conversation represented in *PSQ* and *R&PA*. One need only read his opening chapter in this book, "Power and Authority in a Postmodern Presidency," to see a powerful, analytical mind at work. The scholarship of Murphy and Stuckey is representative of a much larger universe of scholarship that has come to maturity over the course of the last twenty years. Having now surveyed the past and described the present, it is time to turn toward the future.

The Prospect of Presidential Rhetoric is based on the essays and reports delivered at the Tenth Annual Texas A&M Conference on Presidential Rhetoric, held in 2004. As it turned out, the tenth conference was also the last, so this volume represents, in a sense, not only the report of that single conference but a culmination of a decade of scholarship, community building, and reflection on presidential rhetoric, the rhetorical presidency, going public, and their interrelationships. The volume has two goals. The first is to examine the current state of presidential rhetoric by focusing on some of the issues that George W. Bush, and presumably those who will follow him, has had to confront and will continue to confront for some years to come—religion in the public square, the articulation of the American Dream, the role of economics in policy making, the fight over Supreme Court nominations, the role of alliances in American foreign policy, how to confront terrorism rhetorically as well as militarily, and the interface of law and justice as manifested, for example, in the debate over military tribunals. And the second goal is to examine the current state of scholarship on six broad fronts—communication between the president and Congress, the theory and practice of deliberative democracy, the theory and practice of the rhetorical presidency, the presidency and public opinion, ethics and the presidency, and the presidency and crisis communication—in an effort to discern what is still to be done and to establish a research agenda for the future.

More than forty scholars contributed to the six national task force reports included in the volume. To all of them, and to the several hundred scholars who participated in one or more of the presidential rhetoric conferences, we express our thanks. The conference ends, but the work goes on. The study of presidential rhetoric, virtually nonexistent just seventy-five years ago, is now a vital force in the academy of the twenty-first century.

Notes

1. Theodore Otto Windt Jr., "Presidential Rhetoric: Definition of a Field of Study," *Central States Speech Journal* 35 (1984): 24–34.

2. See Kathleen Hall Jamieson, *Packaging the Presidency: A History and Criticism of Presidential Campaign Advertising* (New York: Oxford University Press, 1984); Roderick P. Hart, *Verbal Style and the Presidency* (Orlando: Academic Press, 1984).

3. David Zarefsky, "The State of the Art in Public Address Scholarship," in *Texts in Context: Critical Dialogues on Significant Episodes in American Political Rhetoric* (Davis, Calif.: Hermagoras Press, 1989), 15–16.

4. On rhetoric as a way of understanding and interpreting see David Zarefsky, "Four Senses of Rhetorical History," in *Doing Rhetorical History*, ed. Kathleen J. Turner (Columbia: University of South Carolina Press, 1998), 19–32; Martin J. Medhurst, "The Rhetorical Construction of History," in *Critical Reflections on the Cold War: Linking Rhetoric and History* (College Station: Texas A&M University Press, 2000), 3–19; Allan Megill and Donald N. McCloskey, "The Rhetoric of History," in *The Rhetoric of the Human Sciences*, ed. John S. Nelson, Allan Megill, and Donald N. McCloskey (Madison: University of Wisconsin Press, 1987).

5. On the early history of the speech field see Karl R. Wallace, ed., *History of Speech Education in America: Background Studies* (New York: Appleton-Century-Crofts, 1954).

6. Evidence of this belief was the production of "model" speech collections. See, for example, William Norwood Brigance, *Classified Speech Models of Eighteen Forms of Public Address* (New York: F. S. Crofts, 1928).

7. Marvin G. Bauer, "The Influence of Lincoln's Audience on His Speeches," *Quarterly Journal of Speech Education* 11 (1925): 225–29. Bauer's M.A. thesis was completed in 1924 at the University of Iowa.

8. Gladys Murphy Graham, "Concerning the Speech Power of Woodrow Wilson," *Quarterly Journal of Speech Education* 13 (1927): 412–24.

9. Graham, "Speech Power of Woodrow Wilson," 423.

10. Edwin Paget, "Woodrow Wilson: International Rhetorician," *Quarterly Journal of Speech* 15 (1929): 15–24.

11. Dayton D. McKean, "Notes on Woodrow Wilson's Speeches," *Quarterly Journal of Speech* 16 (1930): 176–84, quote at 179.

12. See Mildred Freburg Berry, "Lincoln—The Speaker (Part I)," *Quarterly Journal of Speech* 16 (1931): 25–40; Berry, "Lincoln—The Speaker (Part II)," *Quarterly Journal of Speech* 16 (1931): 177–90; Earl W. Wiley, "A Footnote on the Lincoln-Douglas Debates," *Quarterly Journal of Speech* 17 (1932): 216–24; Wiley, "Lincoln the Speaker: 1816–1830," *Quarterly Journal of Speech* 19 (1934): 1–15; Wiley, "Lincoln the Speaker: 1830–1837," *Quarterly Journal of Speech* 20 (1935): 305–22; Bert Emsley, "Phonetic Structure in Lincoln's Gettysburg Address," *Quarterly Journal of Speech* 23 (1938): 281–87; Wiley, "Motivation as a Factor in Lincoln's Rhetoric," *Quarterly Journal of Speech* 23 (1938): 615–21.

13. See V. E. Simrell, "Mere Rhetoric," *Quarterly Journal of Speech* 14 (1928): 359–74; Dayton D. McKean, "Woodrow Wilson as a Debate Coach," *Quarterly Journal of Speech* 16 (1930): 458–63; Howard L. Runion, "An Objective Study of the Speech Style of Woodrow Wilson," *Speech Monographs* 3 (1936): 75–94; and Robert T. Oliver, "Wilson's *Rapport* with His Audience," *Quarterly Journal of Speech* 27 (1941): 79–90.

14. Charles H. Voelker, "A Phonetic Study of Roosevelt," *Quarterly Journal of Speech* 22 (1936): 366–68; Robert D. King, "Franklin D. Roosevelt's Second Inaugural Address," *Quarterly Journal of Speech* 23 (1937): 439–44; Harold P. Zelko, "Franklin D. Roosevelt's Rhythm in Rhetorical Style," *Quarterly Journal of Speech* 28 (1942): 138–41.

15. These dissertations included Donald Hayworth, "An Analysis of Speeches in Presidential Campaigns from 1884 to 1920," Ph.D. diss., University of Wisconsin, 1929; Horace Rahskopf, "John Quincy Adams' Theory and Practice of Public Speaking," Ph.D. diss., University of Iowa, 1935; Howard L. Runion, "An Objective Study of the Speech Style of Woodrow Wilson," Ph.D. diss., University of Michigan, 1936; Joseph Baccus, "The Oratory of Andrew Johnson," Ph.D. diss., University of Wisconsin, 1941; William Behl, "The Rhetoric of Theodore Roosevelt," Ph.D. diss., Northwestern University, 1942; and Cyril Francis Hager, "Persuasion in the 1916 Presidential Campaign," Ph.D. diss., University of Wisconsin, 1942.

16. See Mildred Freburg Berry, "Abraham Lincoln: His Development in the Skills of the Platform," 828–58; Earl W. Wiley, "Abraham Lincoln: His Emergence as the Voice of the People," 859–77; and Dayton David McKean, "Woodrow Wilson," 968–92, all in *A History and Criticism of American Public Address*, vol. 2, ed. William Norwood Brigance (New York: McGraw-Hill, 1943). It is interesting to note that of the twenty-eight different orators covered in this two-volume set, only two were presidents. See also Earl W. Wiley, "Buckeye Criticism of the Gettysburg Address," *Speech Monographs* 23 (1956): 1–8.

17. All of the statistics concerning theses and dissertations are derived from the studies conducted by Franklin H. Knower and appearing in *Speech Monographs* from 1935 to 1969. The field owes a debt of gratitude to Professor Knower for maintaining this database for almost thirty-five years. The statistics concerning published research are based only on the research appearing in the *Quarterly Journal of Speech* or *Speech Monographs* from 1915 to 1964.

18. See Robert T. Oliver, "The Speech That Established Roosevelt's Reputation," *Quarterly Journal of Speech* 31 (1945): 274–82; W. A. Dahlberg, "Lincoln the Wit," *Quarterly*

Journal of Speech 31 (1945): 424–27; Wilbur E. Moore, "James Madison, the Speaker," *Quarterly Journal of Speech* 31 (1945): 155–62; Clair R. Henderlider, "Woodrow Wilson's Speeches on the League of Nations, September 4–25, 1919," *Speech Monographs* 13 (1946): 23–34; Robert D. Clark, "Lesson in Persuasion: Factors Leading to the Rejection of the League of Nations," *Quarterly Journal of Speech* 33 (1947): 265–73; William A. Behl, "Theodore Roosevelt's Principles of Speech Preparation and Delivery," *Speech Monographs* 12 (1945): 112–22; Behl, "Theodore Roosevelt's Principles of Invention," *Speech Monographs* 14 (1947): 93–110; Horace G. Rahskopf, "John Quincy Adams: Speaker and Rhetorician," *Quarterly Journal of Speech* 32 (1946): 435–41; Eleanor Davidson and E. C. McClintock, "Thomas Jefferson and Rhetoric," *Quarterly Journal of Speech* 33 (1947): 1–8; and Jennings Randolph, "Truman—A Winning Speaker," *Quarterly Journal of Speech* 34 (1948): 421–24.

19. See Earnest Brandenburg, "The Preparation of Franklin D. Roosevelt's Speeches," *Quarterly Journal of Speech* 35 (1949): 214–21; Brandenburg, "Franklin D. Roosevelt's International Speeches, 1939–1941," *Speech Monographs* 16 (1949): 21–40; Earnest Brandenburg and Waldo W. Braden, "Franklin D. Roosevelt's Voice and Pronunciation," *Quarterly Journal of Speech* 38 (1952): 23–30; Laura Crowell, "Franklin D. Roosevelt's Audience Persuasion in the 1936 Campaign," *Speech Monographs* 17 (1950): 48–64; Crowell, "Roosevelt the Grotonian," *Quarterly Journal of Speech* 38 (1952): 31–36; Crowell, "Building the 'Four Freedoms' Speech," *Speech Monographs* 22 (1955): 266–83; Crowell, "Word Changes Introduced *Ad Libitum* in Five Speeches by Franklin Delano Roosevelt," *Speech Monographs* 25 (1958): 229–42.

20. See A. Craig Baird, "Argumentation as a Humanistic Subject," *Quarterly Journal of Speech* 10 (1924): 258–64; Baird, "A Selected Bibliography of American Oratory," *Quarterly Journal of Speech* 12 (1926): 352–56; A. Craig Baird and Lester Thonssen, "Methodology in the Criticism of Public Address," *Quarterly Journal of Speech* 33 (1947): 134–38; Lester Thonssen and A. Craig Baird, *Speech Criticism* (New York: McGraw-Hill, 1948).

21. See Fred W. Shipman, "The Roosevelt Papers," *Quarterly Journal of Speech* 34 (1948): 137–42; Camilla Painter Luecke, "The National Archives," *Quarterly Journal of Speech* 34 (1948): 347–49.

22. Crowell, "Franklin D. Roosevelt's Audience Persuasion in the 1936 Campaign," 48–64; Cole S. Brembeck, "Harry Truman at the Whistle Stops," *Quarterly Journal of Speech* 38 (1952): 42–50; Carl Allen Pitt, "An Analysis and Criticism of the 1940 Campaign Speeches of Wendell L. Willkie," *Speech Monographs* 21 (1954): 64–72.

23. The work of Behl, Brandenburg, and Crowell is cited in notes 18 and 19. See also Russel Windes Jr. and James A. Robinson, "Public Address in the Career of Adlai E. Stevenson," *Quarterly Journal of Speech* 42 (1956): 225–33; Windes, "Adlai E. Stevenson's Speech Staff in the 1956 Campaign," *Quarterly Journal of Speech* 46 (1960): 32–43; Windes, "A Study in Effective and Ineffective Presidential Campaign Speaking," *Speech Monographs* 28 (1961): 39–49.

24. See Gregg Phifer, "'Not for the Purpose of Making a Speech': Andrew Johnson's Swing around the Circle," *Speech Monographs* 21 (1954): 285–93; John F. Wilson, "Rhetorical Echoes of a Wilsonian Idea," *Quarterly Journal of Speech* 43 (1957): 271–77; Ernest G. Bormann, "Ghostwriting and the Rhetorical Critic," *Quarterly Journal of Speech* 46 (1960): 284–88; William R. Underhill, "Harry S. Truman: Spokesman for Containment," *Quarterly Journal of Speech* 47 (1961): 268–74; Donald L. Wolfarth, "John F. Kennedy in the

Tradition of Inaugural Speeches," *Quarterly Journal of Speech* 47 (1961): 124–32; Anthony Hillbruner, "Word and Deed: Jefferson's Addresses to the Indians," *Speech Monographs* 30 (1963): 328–34.

25. See Robert G. Gunderson, *The Log Cabin Campaign* (Lexington: University of Kentucky Press, 1957). Gunderson is still quoted as an authority on the 1840 presidential campaign. See Sean Wilentz, "Election of 1840," in *Running for President: The Candidates and Their Images*, ed. Arthur M. Schlesinger Jr. (New York: Simon and Schuster, 1994), 148.

26. Robert N. Hall, "Lyndon Johnson's Speech Preparation," *Quarterly Journal of Speech* 51 (1965): 168–76. There were a few other articles on presidential rhetoric that appeared in the four regional speech journals, but none of them used the old nomenclature. An informal survey of what those regional journals published in presidential rhetoric from the time of their foundings through 1964 illustrates just how very little rhetorical scholars were concerned with the presidency: *Southern Speech Journal* (1935–64): seven articles; *Western Speech* (1937–64): nine articles; *Central States Speech Journal* (1949–64): seven articles; *Today's Speech* (1953–64): nine articles.

27. See Edwin Black, *Rhetorical Criticism: A Study in Method* (New York: Macmillan, 1965). I do not mean to suggest that Black necessarily intended all of the changes brought about by scholarly engagement with his book or that he would necessarily endorse my interpretation of those changes.

28. See King, "Franklin D. Roosevelt's Second Inaugural Address"; Bert Emsley, "Phonetic Structure in Lincoln's Gettysburg Address," *Quarterly Journal of Speech* 24 (1938): 281–87; Wayne N. Thompson, "A Case Study of Dewey's Minneapolis Speech," *Quarterly Journal of Speech* 31 (1945): 419–23; Gregg Phifer, "Andrew Johnson at Cleveland and St. Louis, 1866: A Study in Textual Authenticity," *Quarterly Journal of Speech* 37 (1951): 45–62; Crowell, "Building the 'Four Freedoms' Speech"; Wiley, "Buckeye Criticism of the Gettysburg Address"; Wolfarth, "John F. Kennedy in the Tradition of Inaugural Addresses."

29. See Robert J. Brake, "The Porch and the Stump: Campaign Strategies in the 1920 Presidential Election," *Quarterly Journal of Speech* 55 (1969): 256–7; W. Lance Bennett, "Assessing Presidential Character: Degradation Rituals in Political Campaigns," *Quarterly Journal of Speech* 67 (1981): 310–21; Lester C. Olson, "Portraits in Praise of a People: A Rhetorical Analysis of Norman Rockwell's Icons in Franklin D. Roosevelt's 'Four Freedoms' Campaign," *Quarterly Journal of Speech* 69 (1983): 15–24.

30. See Herbert W. Simons, James W. Chesebro, and C. Jack Orr, "A Movement Perspective on the 1972 Presidential Campaign," *Quarterly Journal of Speech* 59 (1973): 168–79; David Zarefsky, "President Johnson's War on Poverty: The Rhetoric of Three 'Establishment' Movements," *Communication Monographs* 44 (1977): 352–73.

31. See Lawrence W. Rosenfield, "George Wallace Plays Rosemary's Baby," *Quarterly Journal of Speech* 55 (1969): 36–44; G. P. Mohrmann and Michael C. Leff, "Lincoln at Cooper Union: A Rationale for Neo-Classical Criticism," *Quarterly Journal of Speech* 60 (1974): 459–67; Jackson Harrell, B. L. Ware, and Wil A. Linkugel, "Failure of Apology in American Politics: Nixon on Watergate," *Speech Monographs* 42 (1975): 245–61; Ellen Reid Gold, "Political Apologia: The Ritual of Self-Denial," *Communication Monographs* 45 (1978): 306–16; Robert L. Ivie, "Images of Savagery in American Justifications for War," *Communication Monographs* 47 (1980): 279–94; Kathleen Hall Jamieson and Karlyn Kohrs Campbell, "Rhetorical Hybrids: Fusions of Generic Elements," *Quarterly Journal of Speech* 68 (1982): 146–57.

32. See Hermann G. Stelzner, "'War Message,' December 8, 1941: An Approach to Language," *Speech Monographs* 33 (1966): 419–37; Roderick P. Hart, "Absolutism and Situation: Prolegomenon to a Rhetorical Biography of Richard M. Nixon," *Communication Monographs* 43 (1976): 204–28; Hermann G. Stelzner, "Ford's War on Inflation: A Metaphor That Did Not Cross," *Communication Monographs* 24 (1977): 284–97; Martha Solomon, "Jimmy Carter and *Playboy:* A Sociolinguistic Perspective on Style," *Quarterly Journal of Speech* 64 (1978): 173–82; Robert L. Ivie, "The Metaphor of Force in Prowar Discourse: The Case of 1812," *Quarterly Journal of Speech* 68 (1982): 240–53.

33. See Richard E. Crable, "Ike: Identification, Argument, and Paradoxical Appeal," *Quarterly Journal of Speech* 63 (1977): 188–96.

34. Ernest G. Bormann, "The Eagleton Affair: A Fantasy Theme Analysis," *Quarterly Journal of Speech* 59 (1973): 143–59; David L. Rarick et al., "The Carter Persona: An Empirical Analysis of the Rhetorical Visions of Campaign '76," *Quarterly Journal of Speech* 63 (1977): 258–73; John F. Cragan and Donald C. Shields, "Foreign Policy Communication Dramas: How Mediated Rhetoric Played in Peoria in Campaign '76," *Quarterly Journal of Speech* 63 (1977): 274–89; Ernest G. Bormann, Jolene Koester, and Janet Bennett, "Political Cartoons and Salient Rhetorical Fantasies: An Empirical Analysis of the '76 Presidential Campaign," *Communication Monographs* 45 (1978): 317–29; Ernest G. Bormann, "A Fantasy Theme Analysis of the Television Coverage of the Hostage Release and the Reagan Inaugural," *Quarterly Journal of Speech* 68 (1982): 133–45.

35. See Ronald F. Reid, "Newspaper Response to the Gettysburg Address," *Quarterly Journal of Speech* 53 (1967): 50–60; William R. Brown, "Television and the Democratic National Convention of 1968," *Quarterly Journal of Speech* 55 (1969): 237–46; David L. Swanson, "And That's the Way It Was? Television Covers the 1976 Presidential Campaign," *Quarterly Journal of Speech* 63 (1977): 239–48; Robert K. Tiemens, "Television's Portrayal of the 1976 Presidential Debates: An Analysis of Visual Content," *Communication Monographs* 45 (1978): 362–70; Paul H. Arntson and Craig R. Smith, "News Distortion as a Function of Organizational Communication," *Communication Monographs* 45 (1978): 371–81.

36. See Bill O. Kjeldahl, Carl W. Carmichael, and Robert J. Mertz, "Factors in a Presidential Candidate's Image," *Communication Monographs* 38 (1971): 129–31; David L. Swanson, "The New Politics Meets the Old Rhetoric: New Directions in Campaign Communication Research," *Quarterly Journal of Speech* 58 (1972): 31–40; Linda L. Swanson and David L. Swanson, "The Agenda-Setting Function of the Ford-Carter Debate," *Communication Monographs* 45 (1978): 347–53; James A. Anderson and Robert K. Avery, "An Analysis of Changes in Voter Perception of Candidates' Positions," *Communication Monographs* 45 (1978): 354–61.

37. See Bruce E. Gronbeck, "The Birth, Death, and Rebirth of Public Address," paper presented at the Speech Communication Association Convention, Denver, Colorado, November 1985.

38. See Roderick P. Hart, *The Political Pulpit* (West Lafayette: Purdue University Press, 1977); Lloyd F. Bitzer, *Carter vs. Ford: The Counterfeit Debates of 1976* (Madison: University of Wisconsin Press, 1980); Robert Underhill, *The Truman Persuasions* (Ames: Iowa State University Press, 1981); Jamieson, *Packaging the Presidency;* Hart, *Verbal Style and the Presidency.*

39. See Stephen E. Lucas, "The Renaissance of American Public Address: Text and Context in Rhetorical Criticism," *Quarterly Journal of Speech* 74 (1988): 241–60; Martin J. Medhurst,

"Public Address and Significant Scholarship: Four Challenges to the Rhetorical Renaissance," in *Texts in Context*, 29–42; Medhurst, "The Academic Study of Public Address: A Field in Transition," in *Landmark Essays on American Public Address*, ed. Martin J. Medhurst (Davis, Calif.: Hermagoras Press, 1993), xi–xliii; Medhurst, "The Rhetorical Renaissance: A Battlefield Report," *Southern Communication Journal* 63 (1998): 309–14; Medhurst, "The Contemporary Study of Public Address: Renewal, Recovery, and Reconfiguration," *Rhetoric & Public Affairs* 4 (2001): 495–511; Medhurst, "William Norwood Brigance and the Democracy of the Dead: Toward a Genealogy of the Rhetorical Renaissance," in *Rhetoric and Democracy: Essays in the Tradition of W. Norwood Brigance*, ed. David M. Timmerman and Todd McDorman (East Lansing: Michigan State University Press, 2008).

40. See Karlyn Kohrs Campbell and Kathleen Hall Jamieson, *Deeds Done in Words: Presidential Rhetoric and the Genres of Governance* (Chicago: University of Chicago Press, 1990); David Zarefsky, *Lyndon Johnson's War on Poverty: Rhetoric and History* (Tuscaloosa: University of Alabama Press, 1986); Lester C. Olson, *Emblems of American Community in the Revolutionary Era: A Study in Rhetorical Iconology* (Washington, D.C.: Smithsonian Institute Press, 1991); and Martin J. Medhurst, Robert L. Ivie, Philip Wander, and Robert L. Scott, *Cold War Rhetoric: Strategy, Metaphor, and Ideology* (Westport, Conn.: Greenwood Press, 1990).

41. These books included Kathleen J. Turner, *Lyndon Johnson's Dual War: Vietnam and the Press* (Chicago: University of Chicago Press, 1985); Roderick P. Hart, *The Sound of Leadership: Presidential Communication in the Modern Age* (Chicago: University of Chicago Press, 1987); Campbell and Jamieson, *Deeds Done in Words*; Jamieson, *Packaging the Presidency*; Kathleen Hall Jamieson, *Eloquence in an Electronic Age* (New York: Oxford University Press, 1988).

42. On the rhetorical presidency construct see James W. Ceaser, Glen E. Thurow, Jeffrey K. Tulis, and Joseph M. Bessette, "The Rise of the Rhetorical Presidency," *Presidential Studies Quarterly* 11 (1981): 158–71; Glen Thurow and Jeffrey D. Wallin, eds., *Rhetoric and American Statesmanship* (Durham, N.C.: Carolina Academic Press, 1984); Jeffrey K. Tulis, *The Rhetorical Presidency* (Princeton: Princeton University Press, 1987); Richard J. Ellis, ed., *Speaking to the People: The Rhetorical Presidency in Historical Perspective* (Amherst: University of Massachusetts Press, 1998); Mel Laracey, *Presidents and the People: The Partisan Story of Going Public* (College Station: Texas A&M University Press, 2002); David Crockett, "George W. Bush and the Unrhetorical Rhetorical Presidency," *Rhetoric & Public Affairs* 6 (2003): 465–86.

43. Samuel Kernell, *Going Public: New Strategies of Presidential Leadership* (Washington, D.C.: Congressional Quarterly Press, 1986); Karen S. Hoffman, "'Going Public' in the 19th Century: Grover Cleveland's Repeal of the Sherman Silver Purchase," *Rhetoric & Public Affairs* 5 (2002): 57–77; George C. Edwards III, *On Deaf Ears: The Limits of the Bully Pulpit* (New Haven: Yale University Press, 2003); Reed L. Welch, "Presidential Success in Communicating with the Public through Televised Addresses," *Presidential Studies Quarterly* 33 (2003): 347–65; Welch, "Was Reagan Really a Great Communicator? The Influence of Televised Addresses on Public Opinion," *Presidential Studies Quarterly* 33 (2003): 853–76.

44. For examples of scholarship from fields other than communication or political science see Wayne Fields, *Union of Words: A History of Presidential Eloquence* (New York: Free Press, 1996); H. W. Brands, "Politics as Performance Art: The Body English of

Theodore Roosevelt," in *The Presidency and Rhetorical Leadership*, ed. Leroy G. Dorsey (College Station: Texas A&M University Press, 2002), 115–28; Robert J. McMahon, "'By Helping Others, We Help Ourselves': The Cold War Rhetoric of American Foreign Policy," in *Critical Reflections on the Cold War: Linking Rhetoric and History*, ed. Martin J. Medhurst and H. W. Brands (College Station: Texas A&M University Press, 2000); McMahon, "Rationalizing Defeat: The Vietnam War in American Presidential Discourse, 1975–1995," *Rhetoric & Public Affairs* 2 (1999): 529–49; David Hoogland Noon, "Operation Enduring Analogy: World War II, the War on Terror, and the Uses of Historical Memory," *Rhetoric & Public Affairs* 7 (2004): 339–66; Peter C. Rollins and John E. O'Connor, eds., *Hollywood's White House: The American Presidency in Film and History* (Lexington: University Press of Kentucky, 2003); Ira Chernus, *Eisenhower's Atoms for Peace Speech* (College Station: Texas A&M University Press, 2003).

45. For examples of rhetorical scholarship appearing in *Presidential Studies Quarterly* see Denise M. Bostdorff and Daniel J. O'Rourke, "The Presidency and the Promotion of Domestic Crisis: John Kennedy's Management of the 1962 Steel Crisis," *Presidential Studies Quarterly* 27 (1997): 343–61; Robert L. Ivie, "Fire, Flood, and Red Fever: Motivating Metaphors of Global Emergency in the Truman Doctrine Speech," *Presidential Studies Quarterly* 29 (1999): 570–91; Martin J. Medhurst, "Text and Context in the 1952 Presidential Campaign: Eisenhower's 'I Shall Go to Korea' Speech," *Presidential Studies Quarterly* 30 (2000): 464–84; Robert C. Rowland and John M. Jones, "'Until Next Week': The Saturday Radio Addresses of Ronald Reagan," *Presidential Studies Quarterly* 32 (2002): 84–110. For examples of political science scholarship appearing in *Rhetoric & Public Affairs* see Bruce Miroff, "From 'Midcentury' to Fin-de-Siecle: The Exhaustion of the Presidential Image," *Rhetoric & Public Affairs* 1 (1998): 185–99; Timothy M. Cole, "Avoiding the Quagmire: Alternative Rhetorical Constructs for Post–Cold War American Foreign Policy," *Rhetoric & Public Affairs* 2 (1999): 367–93; Karen M. Hult, "Presidents, Policies and Influence," *Rhetoric & Public Affairs* 4 (2001): 145–53; Nancy Kassop, "The 2000 Presidential Election and Its Aftermath," *Rhetoric & Public Affairs* 5 (2002): 741–58; Crockett, "George W. Bush and the Unrhetorical Rhetorical Presidency"; Philip Abbott, "A 'Long and Winding Road': Bill Clinton and the 1960s," *Rhetoric & Public Affairs* 9 (2006): 1–20.

46. For some of their most recent work, see Mary E. Stuckey, *Slipping the Surly Bonds: Reagan's Challenger Address* (College Station: Texas A&M University Press, 2006); Stuckey, *Defining Americans: The Presidency and National Identity* (Lawrence: University Press of Kansas, 2004); Stuckey, "'The Domain of Public Conscience': Woodrow Wilson and the Establishment of a Transcendent Political Order," *Rhetoric & Public Affairs* 6 (2003): 1–24; John M. Murphy, "The Language of the Liberal Consensus: John F. Kennedy, Technical Reason, and the 'New Economics' at Yale University," *Quarterly Journal of Speech* 90 (2004): 133–62; Murphy, "'Our Mission and Our Moment': George W. Bush and September 11th," *Rhetoric & Public Affairs* 6 (2003): 607–32; Murphy, "Cunning, Rhetoric, and the Presidency of William Jefferson Clinton," in *The Presidency and Rhetorical Leadership*, 231–51; John M. Murphy and Mary E. Stuckey, "'Never Cared to Say Goodbye': Presidential Legacies and Vice Presidential Campaigns," *Presidential Studies Quarterly* 32 (2002): 46–66.

CHAPTER 2

POWER AND AUTHORITY

IN A POSTMODERN PRESIDENCY

John M. Murphy, University of Georgia

Dawn came grudgingly. Overcast skies and temperatures in the forties greeted presidents and protestors as they rolled out of bed and prepared for the Inauguration. Conditions worsened as the ceremony approached, with the temperature dipping into the low thirties, a nasty cold rain falling on the just and unjust alike, and southerly gusts of wind buffeting the president-elect and the chief justice as they took their places in the traditional ritual. The conditions, the *New York Times* reported, gave the television images a "sepia-toned look," hearkening back to an earlier age and visually highlighting the traditional values so dear to the new president. The images of that ritual—the oath, the twenty-one-gun salute, the speech—conferred, "more than anything else," wrote R. W. Apple Jr., "the mantle of authority and legitimacy" on a man "without an unchallenged, universally accepted title to office."[1]

Apple understood the occasion. In traditional usage, a mantle was a cloak or an outer garment that signified preeminence and authority. It granted one title to the office in question, title in turn meaning a legally just cause of exclusive possession or an appellation of dignity, honor, or preeminence attached to a person by virtue of rank, office, precedent, privilege, lands or a 5–4 Supreme Court decision. In other words, a mantle invested the bearer with the authority to exercise the powers of position symbolized by that token. In contemporary usage, mantle has become metaphor, signifying only by virtue of its similarity to or difference from other verbal tokens, its woven solidity melting into air. As metaphor, a mantle, and the authority it signifies, must now be performed through the languages and images of the cultures in which and through which it moves. Authority in turn rests less in those ranks, privileges, and lands and more on the words that accomplish the investiture of this person with that office—of George W. Bush with the presidency.

In an age in which mantle has become metaphor, at best a sign of a sign of authority, how does a leader establish the legitimacy to exercise the powers of the office? That is the question I address here and I do so through a close reading of George W. Bush's first Inaugural Address. The peculiar circumstances of Bush's election—only the third president to lose the popular vote and win the electoral count—offer an opportunity to explore the creation of presidential authority. He could hardly have been unaware of his plight. Protestors lined the streets chanting "Hail to the Thief," and a poll released on inauguration eve revealed that only 51 percent of Americans, a bare majority, considered his election legitimate—and that included only 19 percent of Democrats and 12 percent of African Americans.[2] As the president said, "Sometimes our differences run so deep, it seems we share a continent but not a country."[3] To make of himself a president, he would have to make of the continent a country. The Inaugural Address was a good place to start. Before we turn to that, however, I consider the prospects for presidential authority in a postmodern era, as my brazenly ambitious title suggests. I then explore the obstacles and resources confronting the president-elect and conclude by considering the text.

THE PRESIDENCY, AUTHORITY, AND POSTMODERNITY

Any discussion of authority inevitably begins with Hannah Arendt. She would probably have preferred that it end with her as well. "In order to avoid misunderstanding," she opens her famous essay, "it might have been wiser to ask in the title: What was—and not what is—authority? For it is my contention that . . . authority has vanished from the modern world."[4] Her claim is supported not by evidence but by definition. Tracing "our concept of authority" to Plato, Arendt argues that authority must be defined in "contradistinction" to force and persuasion. When "force is used," authority has failed because coercion has taken its place; when persuasion is used, "authority is left in abeyance" because rhetoric "presupposes equality and works through a process of argument," two qualities she believes to be incompatible with authority. She notes: "The authoritarian relation between the one who commands and the one who obeys rests neither on common reason nor on the power of one who commands; what they have in common is the hierarchy itself, whose rightness and legitimacy both recognize and where both have their predetermined place."[5] If the hierarchy is to possess rightness, in turn, it must have a foundation outside the range of human action. That is, for authority to possess an "unshaken cornerstone," its substance—or sub-stance, as Kenneth Burke would have it—must be indisputable.[6] Arendt offers religion and tradition as the two most prominent supports for the exercise of authority and turns to the Romans as her primary example.

"At the heart of Roman politics," she asserts, "stands the conviction of the sacredness of foundation, in the sense that once something has been founded, it remains binding for all future generations."[7] Indeed, religion or *re-ligare* literally meant to "be tied back, obligated, to the enormous, almost superhuman and hence always legendary effort to lay the foundations, to build the cornerstone, to found for eternity." Authority makes its appearance in this context; *auctoritas* evolves from *augere*, meaning to "augment." Authorities augment the foundation and draw the legitimacy to do so from the principles of the founding. Those principles need always to be adapted to new conditions, but those changes can only justify themselves through reference to the origin. The outline of Arendt's trivium is now clear. Religion establishes the supernatural foundation, tradition transmits those principles in an unbroken chain through generations, and authority derives its sub-stance, its support from outside itself and yet its very character, from that founding and its chain.[8]

William Connolly picks up the narrative in the late Middle Ages. He reveals a world in which God the Creator, the Designer, and the Sovereign was central. Such a world "was alive with God's purpose; it contained a majestic harmony, a *telos*, which humans could glimpse if they exerted themselves in the right ways, and these glimpses gave them support and guidance in governing their lives. Authority, then, permeated this world." In this place, authorities laid claim to a privileged access to that *telos*, whether through careful study, communion with God, divine inspiration, or, in some theories, victory in battle. Certainly, there was ambiguity and difficulty; God's purpose inevitably faded into mystery at the most inconvenient moments (think of Henry IV calling on the divine right of kings *after* he had committed regicide), but mystery, as

Kenneth Burke has taught us, has its rhetorical advantages. Whatever the role of mystery, however, there was confidence that "the signs were there to be read and they did provide a standard of appeal for authority beyond human deeds themselves."[9]

The signs, apparently, have disappeared even as the number of readers has increased exponentially. To a great extent, the story of modernity and postmodernity is a narrative of God's withdrawal from this world, his replacement by the transcendental human subject, and the eclipse of that subject by a "discursive formation." As God becomes Jim Carrey, Morgan Freeman, or one of us in the lyrics of Joan Osborne, authority trails in her wake. To follow the more scholarly language of Connolly, "One way to characterize the shift from medieval to modern life at the ontological level is to say that subjectivity, previously finding perfect expression in God and imperfectly manifested in words, things, events, and living beings, now withdraws from other spheres and migrates to the human self."[10] As a result, the world is transformed. Nature becomes not a sacred text but a set of unpredictable objects to be tamed and understood by human reason; words no longer manifest divine origin but rather human construction; knowledge shifts from traditional texts to scientific experimentation. To ground authority outside of human deeds in a modern world permeated with human reason and purpose would be an achievement, indeed. To do so in a postmodern world still void of God's *telos* (or Lyotard's metanarrative) *and* of the transcendental subject (Foucault's author) would seem almost impossible.[11]

The demise of the latter has had as profound an effect on the operations of authority as that of the former. Donald Pease illuminates the obvious etymological connection between author and authority: "The word 'author' derives from the medieval term *auctor*, which denoted a writer whose words commanded respect and belief." That word grew from at least four Latin and Greek verbs meaning to act or perform, to tie, to augment, or to have authority. In this time, disciplines possessed *auctores* who founded their rules and principles. Their continued authority derived from the scribes' ability to resolve problems in ways sanctioned by the founders' language.[12] As the world changed, authority flowed from the words of the founder to the originality and genius of the transcendental subject, the author—I give you the Romantics.

Foucault takes dead aim at that author. Although "What Is an Author?" is a complex work, Foucault writes with uncharacteristic clarity in the conclusion. As a result of his analysis, he wishes to "suspend the typical questions" such as "Who is the real author?" or "What has he revealed of his most profound self in his language?" Instead, Foucault turns to an exploration of the "author-function" and proposes to examine "under what conditions and through what forms can an entity like the subject appear in the order of discourse; what position does it occupy; what functions does it exhibit; and what rules does it follow in each type of discourse? In short, the subject (and its substitutes) must be stripped of its creative role and analysed as a complex and variable function of discourse."[13] Once stripped of creativity, à la the Romantics in particular and modernity in general, the author is also stripped of its authority—and, if the impersonal "it" is any indication, of its humanity as well. It assumes its place in the order of discourse.

Authority, however, does not quite follow this time. Absent the legitimacy provided by either the presence of God or the creativity of the author, authority becomes disciplinary power. Ironically, however, such power, like medieval authority, migrates out of the domain of human deeds. It "is expressed anonymously," to cite Raymie McKerrow's essay on critical rhetoric, "in nondeliberate ways, at a 'deep structure' level and may have its origins in the remoteness of our past (carried forward through a particularizing discursive formation)."[14] Even in our commonsense use of the terms, the difference between authority and power is profound. It is, in fact, the same gap between coercion and authority that concerned Arendt. Equally important, persuasion also comes under pressure. It hardly seems possible to "presuppose equality" and the processes of rational argument in such an order of things. Disciplinary power, it seems, encompasses both authority and persuasion in this version of postmodernity.

This may well be one of those moments in which theory outstrips our lived experiences. Most of us, for instance, fly to conferences such as the one that gave rise to this book. We obediently stand in line at security, certify that our bags have remained in our possession, and dispose of any liquids before boarding our flights by section only please, beginning with the back of the aircraft. If pressed, poststructuralists might lament the ways in which they have internalized these disciplinary practices, rationalists might note the good reasons for their freely given consent to these measures, and pragmatists might take heed of the possible consequences of disobedience. In general, however, we do not think about it. We know our place in the hierarchy, understand the role of authority in assuring a minimal order in our lives, and obey the commands. Authority lives.

That does not mean, however, that we should ignore the key insight offered by this narrative of authority. Whatever Foucault's excesses, the notion that authority has moved from the voice of God in the burning bush through the musings of Descartes as he sits in his study to the words and images that flow in an unending wave through and around us challenges even the most traditional of scholars to augment authority even as we remain true to its character. In the context of presidential studies, I suspect that I could refigure Mary Stuckey and Fred Antczak's superb review of research on the rhetorical presidency into a similar narrative of authority.[15] In the last fifty years, scholars shifted the locus of authority from the institution to the president's ability to develop a relationship with the American people. Despite the misgivings present on virtually every page of the book, Jeffrey Tulis's *The Rhetorical Presidency* is a Romantic document.[16] It posits a president able to leap tall Congresses in several bounds. And those presidents occasionally fall down, as Stuckey notes in her enjoyable *Strategic Failures in the Modern Presidency*. Yet even she writes, in words many of us would use: "Presidents define themselves as leaders in response to situations, events, and the interplay of those situations and events with the members of other institutions."[17] Caveats aside, the subject of that sentence, presidents, define themselves as leaders; they are not defined by others nor by the words that swirl around them. In fact, if presidents allow others to define them, that is, by many accounts, the reason for presidential failure. Whether we study the rhetorical presidency or presidential rhetoric, to invoke Martin Medhurst's distinction, we tend to assume a Romantic presidency. Presidents themselves generate their successes or failures as they strive for authority.

At least three recent works of presidential scholarship challenge that assumption. Stephen Skowronek's *The Politics Presidents Make* pays more attention to authority than is common in presidential studies. Skowronek acknowledges the ability of "successful leaders [to] control the political definition of their actions, the terms in which their places in history are understood." He also understands that the credibility of that interpretation rests to a large extent on the president's authority, which "hinges on the warrants that can be drawn from the moment at hand to justify action and secure the legitimacy of the changes effected."[18] Therein lies the rub. As Skowronek's book unfolds, a kind of historical determinism unfolds as well. Skowronek seems to believe that only "the moment at hand" can provide the warrants for action. For instance, absent the catastrophe of a disjunctive president, one who accompanies but does not cause the breakdown of political order, a reconstructive president, one who has drunk the elixir of authority, cannot emerge. Such determinism bodes ill for the possibilities of a democratic politics.

Nonetheless, Skowronek shifts the locus of authority from the occupant of the office to the discourses available in political life, as do Trevor and Shawn Parry-Giles in an essay on *The West Wing*. They coin the term "presidentiality," defined as "an ideological rhetoric that helps shape and order the cultural meaning of the institution of the presidency."[19] Through the use of this concept, they explore the symbolic charge of fictional accounts of the presidency, arguing that such stories help to define the institution. To borrow the terms of Michael McGee, however, they are concerned primarily with the synchronic, the current, conflicting, and multiple fields of discourse that energize the presidency rather than the diachronic, the past, conflicting, and multiple fields of discourse that shape the office.[20]

Karlyn Kohrs Campbell and Kathleen Hall Jamieson turn to the past, tracing the ways in which presidential genres speak the president in *Deeds Done in Words*. Significantly, they note: "The identity of the presidents as spokespersons for the institution, fulfilling constitutional roles and exercising their institutional power, gives this discourse a distinctive character. In turn, that identity—the institution of the presidency—arises out of such discourse. Moreover, we view the emergence of identifiable genres across time as creating a coherent sense of the presidency that transcends the idiosyncratic use of any of these genres by any single president."[21] In this view, the subjectivity of the office is enabled and constrained by the discursive typifications manifestly present in the rhetoric. Presidents shape, and are shaped by, the genres that craft their authority.

These three works offer a renewed sense of authority. Drawing on them and on Thomas Farrell and James Boyd White, I claim, with Farrell, that authority "may be considered as a variation of ethos, a grounded entitlement to offer a perspective on appearances based on some claim to a constituency."[22] The natural queries that result are: What are those grounds? And who is that constituency? Consistent with the premises I have laid down, I think it useful to conceive of them as linguistic interpretations of lived experience. As Murray Edelman notes, "language is the key creator of the social worlds people experience."[23] In such a context, authority, White argues, is a "way of talking and thinking." When faced with authority, we cannot choose only to resist or submit because "the authorities to which we respond often have a purchase in our own minds, partly because as we grow we find ourselves making authorities of our own: in reworking the languages we have inherited, from early childhood on, in making claims for the rightness of our conduct, or in arguing for the cogency of our reasons."[24] As presidents rework the languages they have inherited, from the early republic on, they make claims for the rightness or grounds of their conduct and the legitimacy or identity of their constituencies; to borrow from Arendt, they augment words that have long established political authority. In a powerful sense, our grounds and identities are linguistic. Those words, in turn, speak the presidents because such terms have a purchase in their minds and lives—and in the mind and life of the nation.

This process occurs through genre, but it also evolves, as James Jasinski and I claim, from the political languages that have charged the nation's debates. I have, for instance, explored the ways in which President Clinton generated authority through an orchestration of the idioms of the black church and classical liberalism; Jasinski has examined the reconstitution of the concept of "constitution" through the collision of languages in the Federalist Papers.[25] Critical to both of us are the textual dynamics that realize the *dynamis,* or capacity of these traditions. Languages live in a concrete engagement with the audience. If we are to understand the authority they generate, we must look to those texts. It is to one such moment that I now turn.

THE CALLING

To this point, I have constructed a grand narrative of the sort that poststructuralism denies us the ability to craft. I have argued that as the human view of the world has changed from one infused with God's purpose through one saturated with human reason to one permeated by language, so too has authority mutated. It rests less in those signs of God's favor and more in the performance of legitimacy. Naturally, in the way of all scholars, I have chosen the perfect case with which to prove my point. The Inaugural Address, Campbell and Jamieson explain, is a type of epideictic rhetoric, "a form of rhetoric that praises or blames on ceremonial occasions, invites the audience to evaluate the speaker's performance, recalls the past and speculates about the future while focusing on the present, employs a noble, dignified literary style, and amplifies or rehearses admitted facts." Given such constraints, epideictic rhetoric, including Inaugurals, relies on *memoria,* or recollection of a shared past, as a key source of invention. Their character, in turn, draws from the ceremony's purpose: "Inauguration is a rite of passage, a ritual of transition in which a newly elected president is invested with the office of the presidency." The generic elements evolve out of the need to achieve that end; they unify the audience, rehearse traditional values, set forth political principles, demonstrate the new president's understanding of the office, and perform these qualities through the appropriate epideictic style.[26] Each of these roads, as it were, leads us back to the Rome of this genre, the need to invest the president with the office.

This president-elect faced at least three challenges to his investiture. The procedural challenge is the one I alluded to earlier and is well known; Supreme Courts are not supposed to elect presidents. The lineal challenge is also familiar. Put simply, George W. Bush needed to demonstrate that he was not elected merely because of his last name and his father's judicial friends, a point made forcibly by Kevin Phillips's acerbic book *American Dynasty*.[27] Finally, the performative challenge should also be familiar. The man who said, "Is our children learning?" needed to diminish the stereotype that resulted in this pseudo-Inaugural that circulated on the Web: "My fallow Americans, As I stand here today, looking out at this magnificent Visa, I think we can all agree that during this last election, we saw Democracy in traction."

Yet George Bush also possessed resources he could bring to bear. Certainly the genre, enacted appropriately, would help establish authority. The scandals of Clinton's administration, and the widely discussed "Clinton Fatigue," emphasized by the string of dubious pardons that ended his term, combined to offer Bush the chance for a fresh start. Equally important, I argue today, was the president-elect's faith. Legend has it that Bush was born again during a walk with the Reverend Billy Graham in 1986. As Stephen Mansfield explains in *The Faith of George W. Bush*, the process was more fitful. He joined his wife's Methodist church, participated in weekly Bible study, spoke with Graham and others, and came to accept Jesus as his personal Savior.[28] More important for the rhetorical critic, however, is the process of translating what is, by all accounts, a private, ineffable experience into a public language of governance. When Bush tries to accomplish that task, he must grapple with inherited words that have traditionally made sense of such experiences for his culture. In this case, he collides with American civil religion.

As citizens of this nation, we can hardly help but be aware of the tenets of our civic faith. To borrow the words of a former president, it builds on the premise that "we are a special people placed between two great oceans for God's purpose." Beginning with the Puritan insistence on a typological interpretation that equated their settlements with the Chosen people of the Bible, Americans, like those people, are on a mission from God. Over time, American idols came to replace biblical prophets and our sacred texts replaced those sacred texts. In that sense, as Roderick Hart points out in *The Political Pulpit*, our civil religion is not quite a religion and America's God is a more distant figure than the Puritan God. Writing in 1977, however, Hart posits a less robust faith than the one animating this Inaugural.[29]

After the ritualistic acknowledgment of those present, Bush begins with an expression of American exceptionalism common to Inaugural Addresses: "The peaceful transfer of authority is rare in history, yet common in our country. With a simple oath, we affirm old traditions and make new beginnings" (1). With two simple statements, Bush sets in place the foundation for his interpretation of the American community—we are a special people because our common acts are rare in history—and signals the powerful relationship between past and future that will energize this speech.

The new president briefly thanks the exiting president and vice president and then hurries forward to develop his community. Indicating his awareness that the generic demand to define the office also requires of the president that he assure us he will not be a tyrant, Bush says, "I am honored and humbled to stand here where so many of America's leaders have come before me, and so many will follow" (1). His humility flows from his knowledge that he is but a small part of "a long story, a story we continue but whose end we will not see" (1). Bush shapes history as a "story" seven times in four sentences. We often think of history as a story, of course, but we should not forget that this is a metaphor. To craft history as "story" is to give it a form and coherence that the rush of events might otherwise obscure. It is also an unfolding story—we will not see its end—but, as the following lines suggest, a repetitive story: "It is a story of a new world that became a friend and liberator of the old, the story of a slaveholding society that became a servant of freedom, the story of a power that went into the world to protect, but not possess, to defend, but not to conquer" (1). Note the verb; America "became" a servant. It came into being, was transformed, born again, at these times. Such is "the American story, a story of a flawed and fallible people united across the generations by grand and enduring ideals" (1).

This sentence introduces a productive tension. The movement and change implied by a continuing story are arrested by the unity offered by the enduring ideals, the "grandest" of which "is an unfolding American promise that everyone belongs, that everyone deserves a chance, that no insignificant person was ever born"(1). The timeliness posited by the "unfolding" promise is checked by the timelessness of the grand idea. Recognizing his need to reconstitute the nation's citizens as witnesses so that they might ratify his authority, he unites—indeed, he subordinates—the "flawed and fallible people" to the perfect principle for which they strive. This is the president's effort to fuse past and future into what Campbell and Jamieson discuss as the "mythic time" of Inaugurals, the "time out of time." They write: "This time out of time allows one to experience a universe of eternal relationships."[30] The language accentuates that idea; never does the president refer to the United States. We are always "America," a place both of and not of this world.

The people of this place have a mission: "Americans are called to enact this promise in our lives and in our laws" (1). This line is the most important of the address and frames all that has come and all that is to follow. J. L. Houlden writes in *The Oxford Companion to the Bible* that a call marks a "turning to

God." He cautions against reading "modern individualism" into conversions. They represent a shift in community allegiance from one deity to another or "calls to deeper loyalty or a new phase in the relationship between God and his people." Houlden focuses initially on the prophets but then turns to the Apostle Paul. Given the paucity of Old Testament allusions—I found one—compared to New Testament allusions—I found seven—in Bush's fifteen-minute address, it seems appropriate to call on Paul.

Call, Houlden notes, is Paul's "most characteristic word for the summons of God both to himself and to others." There is little sign that Paul saw his call as a conversion; rather, he saw it as "the realization of God's plan for his people . . . a call from God to serve as his emissary of Jesus Christ whom God had sent for the purpose of drawing Jews and Gentiles alike into his people."[31] The call was a culmination, not a change, of God's plan, a move from old covenant to new. In his commentary on First Corinthians, Victor Furnish notes that Paul views the Corinth Church as called: "The underlying conception here draws from Paul's Jewish heritage . . . which represent[s] the elect of God as formed into an eschatological community of 'holy people' and called to remain faithful to God's covenant." Their true identity does not rest in the geographic place of Corinth, nor in their social status: "It derives, rather, from the holy God who has sanctified them—as Paul now believes—'in Christ Jesus,' and formed them into a community of faith that embraces believers everywhere."[32] Corinthians is, in fact, an irresistible analogy. The Corinth Church, much like Clinton's United States, was riven by claims of special knowledge and acts of sexual immorality, believing "everything is permissible for me" (I Corinthians 6:12). Paul chastises them: "For the wisdom of this world is folly with God. For it is written, 'He catches the wise in their craftiness'" (3:19) as surely as He caught Clinton and Gore in the view of those who elected the new president.

To say that "Americans are called," then, is to sanctify the nation, to make it eternal, and to realize its covenant with God. Nor is this call an isolated incident; variations of "call" appear six times in the text. As a result of that, the statement of American exceptionalism becomes more powerful because we are holy. Identity shifts ("a slaveholding society that became a servant of freedom") become comprehensible as types—events in sacred history that foreshadow worldly events, or antitypes, presumably the policies of this president.[33] Each of these events follows on the other in an eternal pattern of renewal. The story, then, does not so much change as remain the same. We are always a "flawed and fallible people" in service to a perfect ideal, just like the early church. The vaguely religious language becomes more dense. As a "servant" of freedom, America becomes, for instance, "my servant, whom I have chosen, the one I love, in whom I delight" (Matthew 12:17). As a "power that went out into the world," our nation becomes Paul who "came to you in weakness and fear, and with much trembling. My message and preaching were not with wise and persuasive words, but with a demonstration of the Spirit's power, so that your faith might not rest on men's wisdom but on God's power" (I Corinthians 2:3–5). Richard Lischer notes in his discussion of type and antitype in the black church that these strategies do not teach moral lessons to the community; rather, it "is *enrolled* in the world of the Bible." As a result, "the Bible and contemporary experience take the shape of a single, enormous tapestry whose figures are repeated in many locations with a variety of significations. The interpreter (preacher + community) decodes the pattern as it occurs in contemporary events by means of a divinely given spiritual discernment."[34] By figuring the American community as antitype to the type of the early Christian church, Bush crafts not only our place in the eternal present but also his place as the authoritative leader and teacher who decodes and continues the American story.

Lest I be accused of reading too much into this text, let us turn to the two subsequent metaphors. After he insists in the imperative that we "must follow no other course" than our call, Bush says: "Throughout much of the last century, America's faith in freedom and democracy was a rock in a raging sea. Now it is a seed upon the wind, taking root in many nations" (1). The first image comes from the familiar story of Matthew 7 (and Luke 6:47–49). Jesus says: "Every one then who hears these words of mine and does them will be like a wise man who built his house upon the rock; and the rain fell, and the floods came, and the winds blew and beat upon that house, but it did not fall, because it had been founded on the rock" (24–25). The second appears in all four gospels; Jesus says in Mark: "The Kingdom of God is as if a man should scatter seed upon the ground, and should sleep and rise night and day, and the seed should sprout and grow, he knows not how" (4:26–27). The parable of the mustard seed follows, the smallest of seeds, yet "when it is sown it grows up and becomes the greatest of all shrubs" (32). The juxtaposition of the two images is powerful. A new and weak America is safe in the raging sea because its people have heard those words of mine. As the nation sprouts and grows, it takes root in many nations, we know not how. As Bush then puts it, the mystery of "our democratic faith is more than the creed of our country. It is the inborn hope of our humanity, an ideal we carry, but do not own, a trust we bear and pass along" (1). We are the one church universal, the "inborn," planted at birth, hope of humanity. Hope, of course, echoes Lincoln's characterization of the nation as the "last, best hope of mankind" and weaves together traditional American civil religion with Bush's more robust version.

The notion of a church universal, united not by geography or ethnicity, is immediately reinforced. The president notes that many citizens doubt the promise of America and that our differences run deep, the line I quoted in the introduction. That line, the idea that continent is inferior to country, subordinates geography to ideal. He asserts that we will not accept doubt and, recalling Lincoln, says: "Our unity, our Union, is a serious work of leader and citizens and every generation." He pledges to "work to build a single nation of justice and opportunity." Such is a grand goal for a conservative president, but Bush believes he can meet this standard: "I know this is in our reach because we are guided by a power larger than ourselves, who creates us equal, in his Image, and we are confident in principles that unite us and lead us forward" (1). God not only grants us our rights, as the reference to the Declaration of Independence suggests, but He also continues to guide us from that moment forward and His guidance can be found in our principles. This paragraph also subtly invokes the complicated relationship between faith and works present in Paul's theology and in the letter of James. One is justified by faith alone, Paul argues, but at other points, he and James contend that faith must be enacted in our lives. James writes: "What does it profit, my brethren, if a man says he has faith but has not works?" (2:14). Paul, chastising the Corinthians, recognizes the place of faith but also demands good behavior: "Do you not know that your bodies are members of Christ? Shall I therefore take the members of Christ and make them members of a prostitute? Never!" (6: 15). In Bush's America, faith and works are required.

This is so because "America has never been united by blood or birth or soil. We are bound by ideals that move us beyond our backgrounds, lift us above our interests, and teach us what it means to be citizens" (1). Again, all is subordinate to these ideals in the creation of American citizenship. In a series of imperative sentences, Bush insists: "Every child must be taught these principles. Every citizen must uphold them. And every immigrant, by embracing these ideals, makes our country more, not less, American" (1). Ideals are transformative. In an almost syllogistic progression, the president argues that by "embracing" ideals, we are born into citizenship; as citizens, we must uphold ideals, and by upholding them, the nation itself becomes "more American." The intricate relationship between personal action and national destiny implicitly recalls Puritan culture.[35]

These ideals take the shape of four God-terms: civility, courage, compassion, and character. The terms organize the speech's body and each develops in a similar fashion. First, they are defined, what Richard Weaver terms the highest form of argument because definition "captures essence." It invokes "qualities that in Western civilization are usually expressed in the language of theism."[36] They exist throughout time and space, as do Bush's principles. Second, consistent with Paul's letters and Bush's admonition that our call must be enacted "in our lives and in our laws," the implications of each term are traced out both for our behavior as citizens and for the government's behavior as lawmaker. This move allows Bush to fulfill the Inaugural requirements to rehearse traditional values and forward political principles. Programs grow out of values that are sanctified by the call. For instance, faith-based programs are justified, naturally, by "that wounded traveler on the road to Jericho" (2). Programs, values, and sanctity are tightly interwoven; to oppose Bush's programs is to pass by on the other side of the road.

Finally, Bush says that it is not only God who judges us but also our ancestors. Filiopiety fills civil religious discourse, tracing back to the Puritan veneration for their founders, which elevated the original immigrants into "a mythical tribe of heroes—a race of giants in an age of miracles."[37] Bush asserts that American courage "has been clear in times of depression and war. . . . Now we must choose if the examples of our fathers and mothers will inspire or condemn us" (2). Founding principles flowed down to us through the traditions upheld by our mothers and fathers; we must now live up to them. Tradition matters, and filiopiety establishes not only the authority of father over son and son over us but also the anxiety that spurs us to such emulation. Much as this son of a president, now a president, has imitated his father, we, too, must imitate. Absent such emulation, the nation fails.[38]

The president concludes the body with his assurance that he, too, will "live and lead by these principles" (3). He repeats each, so that the lessons will not be lost, and assures us, in the first person, "I will bring the values of our history to the care of our times," a clear statement of the importance of tradition. In addition, his personal commitment echoes the injunction of Paul near the end of First Corinthians: "Be imitators of me, as I am of Christ" (11:1). When we do so, we demonstrate our worth, which exists "not because we believe in ourselves but because we hold beliefs beyond ourselves" (3). Such beliefs create the spirit of citizenship, a spirit so strong that "no power can stand against it" (3). This is so because it has always been so. Quoting the famous lines of Benjamin Page to Thomas Jefferson, Bush says: "We know the race is not to the swift nor the battle to the strong. Do you not think that an angel rides in the whirlwind and directs this storm?" (3). The anxiety produced by the allusion to Ecclesiastes 9:11, which ends with the fatalistic words, "time and chance happen to them all," is resolved by the "angel in the whirlwind" (God's voice appeared to Job in a whirlwind) who directs the storm. We are under His direction, as Bush then explicitly asserts: "We are not this story's author, who fills time and eternity with his purpose. Yet his purpose is achieved in our duty. And our duty is fulfilled in service to one another" (3). The author shapes the foundation, the president interprets tradition, and the people renew that foundation in our duty to each other and to the president. Arendt's trivium of religion, tradition, and authority finds a new home in a postmodern era. The president concludes: "This work continues, the story goes on, and an angel still rides in the whirlwind and directs this storm" (3).

Bruce Lincoln writes of Bush's war rhetoric: "Conversion of secular political speech into religious discourse invests otherwise human events with transcendent significance. By the end, America's adversaries have been redefined as enemies of God, and current events have been constituted as confirmation of Scripture."[39] So it is in this Inaugural. President George W. Bush constitutes his authority through a powerful version of civil religion. It positions him as apostle and teacher. It defines his people as flawed and fallible, but chosen of God, as were the early Christians. The story of America is the story of the early church, and this tale holds "transcendent significance" because, as Bush says, "The stakes for America are never small. If our country does not lead the cause of freedom, it will not be led" (2). Freedom, in turn, results from obedience to the author's purpose, a theological position that President Bush explains in his autobiography: "I build my life on a foundation that does not shift. My faith frees me. Frees me to put the problem of the moment in proper perspective. Frees me to make decisions that others might not like. Frees me to try to do the right thing, even though it may not poll well." Bush feels the importance of this freedom because "I could not be governor if I did not believe in a divine plan that supersedes all human plans."[40] Freedom means obedience to that plan. As the president translates this private view into a public language, he figures this religious authoritarian relationship as a political one, as he notes in the autobiography. After all, he could not be governor, and presumably president, without it. He defines his people, his followers, in turn. They, too, are free because they "must" learn and uphold each of those four principles.

This view of civil religion calls back less to American forebears and more to English conservatives such as one of Bush's heroes, Winston Churchill, and, of course, Edmund Burke. James Boyd White notes: "For Burke, the establishment of religion incorporates . . . a way in which the community can talk about right and wrong, better and worse, under a permanent standard of justice and humanity. It is the church that maintains a language of character and conduct . . . by which the actions of men [sic] in power can be defined, checked, and encouraged; it is a central language of motive and meaning." It frees leaders to act in accordance with those meanings, regardless of, well, polls; as Burke writes, religion says to authorities: "they should not look to the paltry pelf of the moment, nor to the temporary and transient praise of the vulgar, but to a solid, permanent existence, in the permanent part of their nature, and to a permanent fame and glory, in the example they leave as a rich inheritance to the world."[41] Religion, tradition, and authority come together in an organic view of an eternal national community.

I do not mean to say here that President Bush wishes an established church; I do mean to say that once he enters into this language, once he creates his authority in its terms, the language uses him as much as he uses the language. His policies, roles, and relationships are shaped as much by the words as by his intent, whatever that may be. His language has a purchase on his life and, given his position, on the life of the nation. That is a not an altogether reassuring prospect.

There is one final observation to be made here. The past two presidencies have revealed, as much as anything, two civil religions in the nation. One is the language of Being, of eternal principles, of religion, tradition, and authority, of the Republican Party and the Christian Right. The other is the language of Becoming, of change as we strive to understand the injunction that the arc of the universe is long but that it bends toward justice, of the revolutionary Jesus, of the Democratic Party and the civil rights movement. However much one may disdain the shallow metaphor of a Red and a Blue America, these differences constitute a powerful chasm in American politics.

Notes

1. R. W. Apple Jr., "Tradition and Legitimacy," *New York Times*, January 21, 2001, A1, A16; Frank Bruni and David E. Sanger, "Unity Is A Theme," *New York Times*, January 21, 2001, A1, A16.

2. Apple, "Tradition," A16.

3. George W. Bush, "Inaugural Address," *Public Papers of the Presidents of the United States: George W. Bush, 2001* (Washington, D.C.: U. S. Government Printing Office, 2002), 1. All subsequent citations are in the chapter text, with page number.

4. Hannah Arendt, "What Is Authority?" in *Between Past and Future* (New York: Penguin Books, 1993), 91.

5. Arendt, "Authority," 93.

6. Arendt, "Authority," 95; Kenneth Burke, *A Grammar of Motives* (Berkeley: University of California Press, 1969), 21–22.

7. Arendt, "Authority," 120.

8. Arendt, "Authority," 121–23.

9. William Connolly, *Politics and Ambiguity* (Madison: University of Wisconsin Press, 1987), 128–30.

10. Connolly, *Politics,* 129–30.

11. Jean-Francois Lyotard, *The Postmodern Condition,* trans. Geoff Bennington and Brian Massumi (Minneapolis: University of Minnesota Press, 1984); Michel Foucault, "What Is An Author?" in *Language, Counter-Memory, Practice* (Ithaca, N.Y.: Cornell University Press, 1977).

12. Donald E. Pease, "Author," in *Critical Terms for Literary Study,* 2nd edition, ed. Frank Lentricchia and Thomas McLaughlin (Chicago: University of Chicago Press, 1995), 106.

13. Foucault, "Author," 137–38.

14. Raymie E. McKerrow, "Critical Rhetoric: Theory and Praxis," *Communication Monographs* 56 (1989): 99.

15. Mary E. Stuckey and Frederick J. Antczak, "The Rhetorical Presidency: Deepening Vision, Widening Exchange," in *Communication Yearbook 21,* ed. Michael E. Roloff (Thousand Oaks, Calif.: Sage Publications, 1998): 405–41.

16. Jeffrey Tulis, *The Rhetorical Presidency* (Princeton: Princeton University Press, 1987).

17. Mary E. Stuckey, *Strategic Failures in the Modern Presidency* (Cresskill, N.J.: Hampton Press, 1997).

18. Stephen Skowronek, *The Politics Presidents Make: Leadership from John Adams to Bill Clinton* (Cambridge, Mass.: Belknap Press, 1997), 17–18.

19. Trevor Parry-Giles and Shawn J. Parry-Giles, "*The West Wing's* Prime-Time Presidentiality: Mimesis and Catharsis in a Postmodern Romance," *Quarterly Journal of Speech* 88 (2002): 209.

20. Michael Calvin McGee, "The 'Ideograph': A Link Between Rhetoric and Ideology," *Quarterly Journal of Speech* 66 (1980): 1–16.

21. Karlyn Kohrs Campbell and Kathleen Hall Jamieson, *Deeds Done in Words: Presidential Rhetoric and the Genres of Governance* (Chicago: University of Chicago Press, 1990), 4.

22. Thomas B. Farrell, *Norms of Rhetorical Culture* (New Haven: Yale University Press, 1993), 290.

23. Murray Edelman, *Constructing the Political Spectacle* (Chicago: University of Chicago Press, 1988), 103.

24. James Boyd White, *Acts of Hope: Creating Authority in Literature, Law, and Politics* (Chicago: University of Chicago Press, 1994), x–xi.

25. John M. Murphy, "Bill Clinton, Martin Luther King, Jr., and the Orchestration of Rhetorical Traditions," *Quarterly Journal of Speech* 83 (1997): 71–89; James Jasinski, "A Constitutive Framework for Rhetorical Historiography: Toward an Understanding of the Discursive (Re)constitution of 'Constitution' in the *Federalist Papers,*" in *Doing Rhetorical History: Concepts and Cases,* ed. Kathleen J. Turner (Tuscaloosa: University of Alabama Press, 1998): 72–92.

26. Campbell and Jamieson, *Deeds,* 14–15.

27. Kevin Phillips, *American Dynasty* (New York: Viking Press, 2004).

28. Stephen Mansfield, *The Faith of George W. Bush* (New York: Jeremy P. Tarcher–Penguin, 2003).

29. Roderick Hart, *The Political Pulpit* (West Lafayette, Ind.: Purdue University Press, 1977). An extraordinary number of writers have explored the issue of chosen people and sacred texts. My favorite is Sacvan Bercovitch. See his *The American Jeremiad* (Madison: University of Wisconsin Press, 1978) and *The Rites of Assent: Transformations in the Symbolic Construction of America* (New York: Routledge, 1993).

30. Campbell and Jamieson, *Deeds,* 27.

31. J. L. Houlden, "Conversion," in *The Oxford Companion to the Bible* (New York: Oxford University Press, 1993), 132–33.

32. Victor Paul Furnish, *The Theology of the First Letter to the Corinthians* (Cambridge: Cambridge University Press, 1999), 31–32.

33. Malinda Snow, "Martin Luther King's 'Letter from Birmingham Jail' as Pauline Epistle," *Quarterly Journal of Speech* 71 (1985): 319.

34. Richard Lischer, *The Preacher King* (New York: Oxford University Press, 1995), 201.

35. See John M. Murphy, "'A Time of Same and Sorrow': Robert F. Kennedy and the American Jeremiad," *Quarterly Journal of Speech* 76 (1990): 401–14.

36. Richard Weaver, "Language Is Sermonic," in *The Rhetorical Tradition,* 2nd edition, ed. Patricia Bizzell and Bruce Herzberg (New York: St. Martin's Press, 2001), 1351, 1355.

37. Bercovitch, *Jeremiad,* 67–68.

38. See also the analysis of Denise Bostdorff, who sees this pattern in the president's 9/11 rhetoric as well and nicely roots this language in Puritan culture. Denise M. Bostdorff, "George W. Bush's Post-September 11 Rhetoric of Covenant Renewal: Upholding the Faith of the Greatest Generation," *Quarterly Journal of Speech* 89 (2003): 293–319.

39. Bruce Lincoln, *Holy Terrors* (Chicago: University of Chicago Press, 2003), 31–32.

40. George W. Bush, *A Charge to Keep* (New York: William Morrow and Company, 1999), 6. The title comes from a favorite Methodist hymn and reflects Bush's belief in tradition.

41. James Boyd White, *When Words Lose Their Meaning* (Chicago: University of Chicago Press, 1984), 214.

CHAPTER 3

THE ECONO-RHETORICAL PRESIDENCY

James Arnt Aune, Texas A&M University

One of the most important moments in the history of the American presidency occurred in 1951, during what was perhaps Harry Truman's most difficult year in office. I would guess that almost no one in this room is able to name the event; it is not discussed at all in David McCullough's biography or in Truman's own memoirs.[1] The event is now referred to as the "Treasury-Federal Reserve Accord," a bureaucratic struggle that led to the functional independence of the Federal Reserve System in setting monetary policy.[2] I will proceed in extremely inductive fashion, telling the story of this accord, followed by a brief discussion of Fed-presidential relations from Eisenhower to George W. Bush. In the final, theoretical section of the paper I discuss implications of my narrative for our understanding of the rhetorical presidency and of the problem of what Jürgen Habermas calls the "colonization of the lifeworld," or the continuing displacement of political controversy by instrumental, economic forms of rationality.

TRUMAN AND THE FED: TOWARD THE 1951 ACCORD

The story begins after World War II. Central banks throughout the West had lost credibility because of their failure to stop the Great Depression. Social democratic governments in France and Great Britain nationalized central banks and mandated that the allocation of credit be consistent with national planning. The relationship of Congress and the president to the Federal Reserve in the United States, however, remained more or less undefined.

The Fed, then as now, had two specifically assigned roles to play in the economy: (1) it sets the discount rate, the rate the Fed charges banks for overnight loans (at that time the only publicly announced change, which had a psychological impact on the markets and the economy); and (2) most important, however, the law gives the Fed power to trade in the bond market. The Federal Open Market Committee (FOMC) can ease credit by having its trading desk in New York buy U.S. Treasury bonds, thus making it easier for businesses or consumers to borrow money. Easing credit is the standard move in averting recession. If there are inflationary pressures, however, the FOMC can tighten credit by selling Treasury bonds, making it more difficult to borrow. The FOMC consists of twelve voting members: all seven Fed governors plus five of the twelve presidents from Fed district banks throughout the country. The president makes appointments to the board as a whole, and the Senate confirms them. Board members are appointed for a fourteen-year term, while the chairman is appointed for a four-year term.[3]

After World War II, banks went on something of a lending spree, unconcerned about reserve requirements. They simply funded their loans by selling from their massive stock of government paper, the price of which was maintained by the Fed. In 1951, the Fed attempted to rein in the banks with a Voluntary Credit Restraint Program, but it was unsuccessful. One amusing incident illustrates the lack of independence of the Fed at this point in American history.

The state of West Virginia tried to float a bond issue to support a veterans' bonus approved by voters in 1950, but it failed to get any bids from investment bankers. George Moore of Citibank, one of the members of the Voluntary Credit Restraint Program, recalls a meeting with Governor Oakley Patterson in which he asked the governor what he thought the veterans would do with the money. "About a third will spend it on women," he said, "and a third will spend it on booze, and the rest I guess will just waste it." West Virginia congressmen complained to Truman that the Fed was interfering with the sale of state and municipal paper, and Truman sent a memo to the Fed telling them to stop it.[4]

In the meantime, however, the Korean War was causing tremendous inflationary pressures: for the three-month period ending in February 1951, Consumer Price Index inflation was running an annualized rate of 21 percent.[5] The Truman Administration wanted to continue funding the war the same way that World War II had been financed, keeping the rates for government issues artificially low. From 1917 to 1951, the Fed backed up every sale of Treasury paper and made sure that no bonds went unpurchased at the government's asking price. Mariner Eccles, the Fed chairman under FDR but later demoted to board member under Truman, began a campaign against Truman's return to wartime finance. Treasury Secretary John Snyder believed he could be successful in bullying the Fed into accepting the inflationary policy. Allan Sproul, head of the New York Fed, and Eccles began a quiet campaign in the business press to undermine the administration's position. Senator Robert Taft, chair of the Joint Economic Committee of Congress, began holding hearings. Thomas McCabe, Truman's appointee as head of the Fed, was reluctant to testify against the administration lest he lose his job. Mariner Eccles testified instead and contended that Truman's policies would cause inflation. The Fed's Open Market Committee was scheduled to meet on January 31, and Truman invited all the members to meet with him at the White House at four o'clock that afternoon. According to Governor M. R. Evans's account of the meeting, Truman discussed his frustration after WWI when he returned from France and had to sell his Liberty Bonds, bought out of soldier's pay, but could get only about eighty dollars for his hundred-dollar bonds. He also contended that maintaining the confidence of the public in government securities was necessary to present a unified front against communism.[6]

The next day the White House issued a press statement that "the Federal Reserve Board has pledged its support to President Truman to maintain the stability of Government securities," followed up by a Treasury press release: "The White House announcement means that the market for government securities will be established at present levels and that these levels will be maintained during the present emergency." Truman then wrote a letter to Chairman McCabe thanking him and the Board of Governors for their "cooperative attitude." The board voted to have McCabe schedule a meeting to straighten out Truman, but then Truman released the "private" letter to the press.[7] In response, Eccles released to the press Governor Evans's memorandum of what had actually happened. Eccles ends his memoirs with this leak and observes: "It is difficult to predict the long-run significance of bringing the controversy between the Treasury and the Federal Reserve out in the open for public and congressional discussion."[8]

Then on February 7, the Open Market Committee sent this letter to Truman: "You as President of the United States and we as members of the Federal Open Market Committee have unintentionally been drawn into a false position before the American public—you as if you were committing us to a policy which we believe to be contrary to what we all truly desire, and as if we were questioning you and defying your wishes as the chief executive of the country in this critical period."[9] McCabe and Sproul then met with members of the Senate Banking Committee and the Join Economic Committee. Senator Paul Douglas, solidly on the left of the Democratic Party and a former professor of economics, supported the Fed's position. He gave a speech before Congress in which he urged that "the Federal Reserve gird its legal loins and fulfill the responsibilities which I believe the Congress intended it to have."[10]

Treasury Secretary Snyder then entered the hospital for an operation, and William McChesney Martin, assistant secretary (and former president of the New York Stock Exchange) became chief negotiator for the White House. A meeting was called for February 26 at the White House. Martin and the Treasury staff had come to an agreement with the Federal Reserve Board staff, with only perfunctory consultation with the hospitalized Snyder, and an "Accord" was drafted. Truman earlier had asked his former Treasury secretary Fred Vinson, now chief justice of the Supreme Court, for advice, and Vinson had recommended that Truman listen to Robert Anderson, a Texas oilman and deputy chairman of the Dallas Fed. Anderson contends that he persuaded Truman to back off from his assault on the Fed, and on March 4, a joint announcement by the Fed and Treasury said that they "have reached full accord with respect to debt management and monetary policies."[11] The Open Market Committee would "reduce to a minimum the creation of bank reserves through monetization of the public debt, while assuring the financing of the government's needs."

Presidents and the Fed from Eisenhower to George W. Bush

The result was a clear commitment to central bank independence, maintained consistently through subsequent presidential administrations. The independence of the Fed was, for bankers at least, part of its original mission. As one banker remarked at the time of its founding in 1913: "We must establish some institution wholly free from politics or outside influence—as much respected for character and integrity as the Supreme Court—which shall be able to use government bonds or selected securities, as a basis for the issue of forms of lawful money which could be added to the reserves of banks."[12]

Independence, however, cuts both ways, and the decentralization of the bank's structure reflected both the ongoing Jacksonian distrust of centralized power and the Progressives' concern for countervailing power against big business and big finance. The Fed was rightly blamed for bungling monetary policy in the years leading up to the 1929 Crash and immediately afterward, and during the New Deal the Fed's control of monetary policy was subservient to the administration's fiscal policy. The Fed-Treasury Accord was the key moment at which the Fed went head to head with the presidency, and the presidency blinked. Some brief snapshots of president-Fed interaction illustrate the point.

Eisenhower

William McChesney Martin served as Fed chairman for more than eighteen years, until replaced by Arthur Burns during the Nixon Administration. Martin was both a Missourian and a Democrat, two facts that endeared him to Truman. Martin uttered perhaps the single most important line about the role of the Fed in American politics: "The function of the Federal Reserve is to take away the punch bowl just as the party is getting good."[13] During the Eisenhower Administration, the Fed sent the stock market into sharp decline on three occasions between 1956 and 1959, creating opportunities for the Democrats, but Eisenhower remained committed to the concept of central bank independence.

Kennedy-Johnson

Kennedy campaigned on the slogan of "getting the country moving again." As later with the Clinton Administration, Kennedy's relations with the Fed were unusually close. Martin frequently had breakfast with Douglas Dillon, JFK's Treasury secretary; met with Walter Heller, chair of the Council of Economic Advisers; and talked on the telephone with the president.[14] The Kennedy years are now rightly remembered as a time of economic prosperity. It is instructive to compare economic growth figures under Alan Greenspan's tenure as Fed chairman with Martin's. From 1987 to 2003 the Dow rose 219 percent (the Dow is an average of thirty stocks, and thus not always a precise measure of economic performance, but it is a useful one). Yet during Martin's first sixteen years (a time of high marginal tax rates and strong labor unions, one must remind today's born-again supply-siders), the Dow was up 264 percent. If we factor in the slump that occurred during the Johnson Administration, Martin's average declines to 200 percent, but Martin had to deal with an economic crisis in 1967 that was fueled by LBJ's insistence on having both "guns and butter" during the Vietnam War.[15] The United States was running a huge trade deficit with the rest of the world. Charles de Gaulle, resentful of the way that Americans could print money and then use it to buy French companies, began to buy gold from the American reserve stock with dollars the French had accumulated from their trade surpluses.[16] Inflation was running at 4 percent, further increasing the demand for cash. The Bretton Woods agreement of 1944 required the Fed to have 25 percent gold backing for U.S. currency, and it was obliged to sell gold to foreign buyers at $35 an ounce. Martin went to Congress to eliminate the gold-cover requirements from the law, and he successfully negotiated with European central bankers to segregate their stocks of monetary gold from the gold markets in Zurich and London, but the crisis would continue until Nixon's formal abrogation of Bretton Woods a few years later.[17]

Nixon-Ford

One might have expected Nixon to have a sound sense of strategy in dealing with his Fed chairman. Arthur Burns, whom he appointed in January 1970, had been a longtime adviser and friend of Nixon's. At the press conference when Nixon announced Burns's appointment he turned to Burns and said, "*Please*, Dr. Burns, give us some money."[18] On swearing in Burns he said: "I respect his independence. However, I hope that independently he will conclude that my views are the ones that should be followed." Nixon, characteristically, exerted intense pressure when Burns did not move as fast as the White House wanted. He planted stories in the press that the chairman had sought a 20 percent pay increase at the same time that he urged business and Congress not to allow wage hikes. It is fairly clear that Nixon's influence led to the single most obvious example of political collusion in the Fed's history: Burns, against the advice of other senior governors, allowed rapid money growth that reached 11 percent three months before the election. As William Greider writes, "the memory of 1972 lingered over the institution like an embarrassing odor."[19] Nonetheless, Nixon told an interviewer years later that "one of his greatest regrets was that he never mastered an understanding of what went on at the Federal Reserve."[20]

President Ford, of course, was left to pick up the pieces from the inflation generated by LBJ's and Nixon's policies. Industrial production shrank by 15 percent. Unemployment peaked at 9.1 percent. The economy's overall output declined by nearly 6 percent.[21] Democrats in Congress attacked Burns for not increasing money growth in response to the crisis, the worst since the 1930s, but Burns responded by tightening up Fed secrecy: he abolished the practice of keeping minutes of Federal Open Market Committee Meetings. It was not until Greenspan's tenure that the workings of the Fed were to become more "transparent."

Carter

Burns desperately wanted to be reappointed. A memo from one of his aides reads as follows: "Carter can be seduced.... reappointment would make Carter out to be a high-minded statesman.... Any seduction program would have to reassure the President that you won't criticize him publicly every six months."[22] As part of his campaign of ingratiation, Burns eased the money supply from late 1976 through 1977, leading to the renewed burst of inflation that was to hurt Carter in 1978. But Carter did not trust Burns and appointed G. William Miller, former CEO of Textron, as Fed chairman.

Miller served only eighteen months, resigning in the larger shakeup that occurred after Carter's famous "malaise" speech of July 15, 1979. Carter then appointed Paul Volcker as Fed chair, perhaps the most fateful appointment of his presidency, yet one that he does not mention in his memoirs. (This remarkable disconnect between the importance of the Fed chair in American politics and discussion of his role in standard political histories remains the clearest sign of an almost willful repression by political leaders and scholars.) Volcker, a late convert to Milton Friedman's monetarism, quietly began a campaign to eliminate inflation by throwing the country into a deep recession. He campaigned for his proposal with several of the twelve Reserve Bank presidents, but in general he did not have to, because they were almost universally enthusiastic about monetarism.

The Carter Administration, however, was completely in the dark. They were working up a new anti-inflation initiative, inviting labor and business leaders to the White House, and negotiating what they hoped would be a labor-management "accord" on wages. Under the law, Volcker was not required to tell the White House anything, but as a matter of politics he needed to know how they would respond. Volcker informally began discussions with Treasury and with Carter's economic advisers, several of whom encouraged Carter to resist the Fed's policy. Carter, however, declined on the grounds of his low approval ratings. The Fed, as CEA chairman Charles Schultze later said, "held all the cards."[23] What followed was unprecedented in American history: in a few short months the Fed doubled the price of money.[24] Liberal Democrats Senator William Proxmire and Congressman Henry Reuss of Wisconsin, the two most knowledgeable Democrats on financial policy, endorsed Volcker's initiatives, further undermining the position of the Carter Administration.

To digress for a moment, why did the Democrats acquiesce? According to Greider, there was a progressive decline in the number of working-class voters in the 1970s, an increase in contributions by financial institutions to the Democratic Party, and an increased dependency of members of Congress on financial enterprises (more than a quarter of the Congress in 1980 owned a direct stake in financial enterprises).[25]

Reagan

Reagan had endorsed Volcker's tight-money policies that jacked up interest rates to an unprecedented 19 percent, and Volcker was appointed for a second term in part because Wall Street was still jittery in the aftermath of the recession. Volcker, however, did not trust Reagan or his Treasury secretary James Baker (who knew each other from their days at Princeton). He feared another recession, but he did not want to tell the administration that he was going to lower interest rates, because he knew they would leak this information to the press. Volcker, of course, did lower rates, and Reagan was reelected by a landslide in November 1984. Baker, however, then seized the opportunity to stack the Federal Reserve Board with Republicans and appointed members who were committed to lower interest rates. By 1986 Volcker found himself outvoted for the first time, and he threatened to resign. Baker knew that a resignation would rattle the financial markets, and he attempted to mollify Volcker, but Volcker finally resigned in 1987, at which point Baker insisted that Reagan appoint Alan Greenspan as his replacement. On June 2, Reagan made a surprise announcement of Greenspan's appointment, and Greenspan was confirmed by a vote of 91 to 2 on August 3.[26]

Greenspan faced his first major test on October 19, 1987, when the stock market took its greatest plunge ever in a single day—down 22.6 percent, compared with the 11.7 percent drop in 1929. Greenspan went on an immediate offensive, negotiating carefully with the major players in the financial markets. The next day, Greenspan issued the following one-sentence statement at 8:41 A.M., before the markets opened: "The Federal Reserve, consistent with its responsibilities as the nation's central bank, affirmed today its readiness to support the economic and financial system." This simple "speech act" worked; the alternatives—having Reagan suspend securities trading, or having Congress hold hearings—would have drawn out the process and increased uncertainty. Baker and Reagan were extremely satisfied. The 1988 report by a government commission headed by Nicholas Brady suggested some important reforms to prevent the crash from happening again, especially an end to the computer-driven trading practices that automatically drop large amounts of stock when prices drop.[27]

Greenspan's honeymoon with the Reagan Administration, however, was not to last. In 1988 Baker pressured Greenspan to lower interest rates further, probably to benefit his friend George Bush's chances in the fall election. Greenspan refused and promised to "use a sledgehammer" to stop White House pressure. He made the conflict public in a February 24 Senate Banking Committee meeting, and the next day's *Washington Post* headline read: "Greenspan Tells Administration to Stop Pressure."[28] The conflict got worse under Bush.

Bush I

Bush appointed Richard G. Darman as budget director. Darman, an assistant to Baker under Reagan, began to urge Greenspan to lower interest rates to help the economy. Greenspan urged him to cut the inflationary federal deficit, something that Darman and Bush, after his famous "read my lips" speech at the Republican convention, were reluctant to do. Darman went on the offensive, contending on *Meet the Press* that Greenspan risked throwing the economy into a recession (Greenspan famously yelled "What!?" at the television set). Darman then flooded Greenspan's office with memos and faxes.

Greenspan believed that Friedman's monetarism had been thoroughly discredited during the Reagan and Thatcher administration, but Darman was a true believer. Greenspan knew that it was no longer possible even to measure the money supply, largely because so many people were moving money to mutual funds. As deficits headed up, the Bush Administration finally consented to a deficit-reduction package, including a jump in the top income tax rate from 28 to 31 percent. Darman and Treasury Secretary Nicholas Brady both pressured Bush to sign $500 deficit reduction package in October 1991, although Bush said later publicly that parts of it "made him gag."[29]

Greenspan was generally impressed with Bush, who held an undergraduate degree in economics from Yale; with characteristically Greenspanian litotes, he said he found Bush "not unknowledgeable," especially in comparison to Reagan, who never wanted to know anything about monetary policy.[30] Although Greenspan privately supported Bush's reelection, he resented pressure by Darman, Nicholas Brady, and finally Bush himself to lower interest rates. In August 1998, during a television interview, Bush blamed Greenspan for his 1992 defeat: "I think that if the interest rates had been lowered more dramatically that I would have been reelected president, because the recovery that we were in would have been more visible. . . . I reappointed him, and he disappointed me."[31]

Greenspan chose not to challenge Bush's comment, but he believed privately, according to Bob Woodward, that Bush's problem was failure to explain the fact that the United States was actually in economic recovery in 1992. Greenspan also believed that technical tinkering with the money supply was less important than an overall understanding of the psychology of inflation, something far more important than real inflation.[32] Greenspan again revealed himself to be more in tune with the rhetorical dimensions of politics and the economy than presidents often were.

Clinton

The Clinton Administration early on established a close working relationship with Greenspan. Greenspan was genuinely impressed with Clinton's intellect, especially as compared to Reagan and Bush, and he met regularly with the two main economic advisers to Clinton, Robert Rubin and Lawrence Summers, thanks to the efforts of Treasury Secretary Lloyd Bentsen, whom Greenspan considered more Republican than Nicholas Brady. Bentsen and Greenspan quickly persuaded Clinton that attacking the federal deficit was essential, and they silenced more populist advisers such as James Carville and Paul Begala. Clinton famously blew up at Rubin and at Alan Blinder, also on the Council of Economic Advisers: "You mean to tell me that the success of the program and my reelection hinges on the Federal Reserve and a bunch of fucking bond traders?"[33] But Clinton got the message.

Perhaps the most significant moment of "inartistic proof," in the Aristotelian sense, during Clinton's presidency (with the possible exception of Monica Lewinsky's stained dress) occurred when Hillary Clinton invited Greenspan to sit next to her during the president's first State of the Union Address on February 17, 1993. Within a week, Clinton was able to announce: "Just yesterday, due to increased confidence in the bond market, long-term interest rates fell to a 16-year low." Despite Republican opposition to Clinton's deficit reduction plan, it successfully passed Congress by a narrow margin, with Gore breaking a tie in the Senate. The only Republican support had come from Greenspan.[34]

Clinton gladly reappointed Greenspan to another term, commenting that if Greenspan died he would have to be stuffed and propped like the character in *Weekend at Bernie's*.[35] The result was sustained economic growth, low interest rates, and high employment levels that challenged the concept of NAIRU, the non-accelerating inflation rate of unemployment, which had contended that unemployment could not drop below 6 percent without triggering inflation. Greenspan argued that productivity growth from computing technology had been consistently unmeasured, accounting for the end of the NAIRU tradeoff. After careful negotiations with Rubin and Summers, the Clinton Administration successfully managed the successive crises of the Mexican and Asian economies (Greenspan even called Rush Limbaugh to enlist his aid in supporting the Mexican bailout), as well as the more controversial bailout of the Long Term Capital Hedge Fund.[36] Greenspan was actually quite glad when Clinton was reelected in 1996, although like all of Clinton's admirers, he remained puzzled at how a man of Clinton's intellectual and political gifts could get himself into such trouble in his second term.

Nonetheless, Greenspan, Rubin, and Summers were featured on the cover of *Time* magazine in February 1999 as "The Committee Who Saved the World." Despite the ominous collapse of the dot.com economy in 2000, the record of the Clinton years was clear: 20 million new jobs had been created, and there was a projected budget surplus of several trillion dollars.[37]

Bush II

It is, of course, too early to pass judgment on George W. Bush's years, but it is fairly obvious, both from press accounts and from Paul O'Neil's disturbing memoirs, that Bush is perhaps even more unengaged with economic policy than Reagan—a "blind man in a room of the deaf," as O'Neil writes. Bush, too, resurrected the supply-side attitude toward taxes and deficits that Greenspan had fought against since 1987. Despite signs of recovery (though without increased employment) in late 2003, the Bush Administration's economic legacy is poor; the U.S. went from a several-trillion-dollar budget surplus in 2000 to a 2006 deficit of 8 trillion dollars and rising. Even conservative stalwarts such as Grover Norquist and the American Conservative Union have blasted Bush for his runaway spending. No one would have predicted even ten years ago that the Democrats would emerge as the party of fiscal restraint, while the Republicans would emerge as the big spenders. As President Reagan said in 1984, the government is now spending money like drunken sailors, with the difference that at least drunken sailors only spend their own money.

The Economy and the Rhetorical Presidency

What follows is an attempt to make sense of my historical narrative in theoretical terms. I will hedge my bets by noting that this chapter is part of a larger project I am tentatively calling *The Federal Reserve in the American Imagination*. My first question is: What are the implications of White House–Fed relations for our understanding of presidential rhetoric and the rhetorical presidency?

I identify myself mainly as a rhetorical theorist, with special interests in the interaction of the technical discourses of law and the economy with democratic politics. The nearly ten years of my involvement with this conference have been among the most educational experiences in my life, but I remain surprised at the limited role that discussion of the economy has played in the formidable scholarship that has issued from this room. There are still only a handful of studies of presidential economic rhetoric, notably the work of Davis Houck and Amos Kiewe.[38] If one turns to work in political science on the presidency, there is an almost equal silence. For example, two influential textbooks on the presidency, George C. Edwards III and Stephen J. Wayne's *Presidential Leadership* and Lyn Ragsdale's *Presidential Politics*, only briefly mention White House–Fed relations. Ragsdale's brief comment—"[Fed] independence enlarges the economic policy complexity that presidents face and hampers their ability to manage it"—illustrates the relative shallowness of these accounts.[39]

From its inception, of course, this conference has dwelt in shadow of Jeffrey Tulis's *The Rhetorical Presidency*.[40] Although we now know, thanks to work by Mel Laracey and others who have attended this conference, that elements of the rhetorical presidency antedate Theodore Roosevelt and Woodrow Wilson, no one now would disagree that there was a qualitative increase in the direct communication between the president and the public in the twentieth century. As Tulis writes, "Direct popular appeal has been the central element of a political strategy that has produced a stunning string of partisan successes, including budget cuts, tax reform, a large military build-up and accompanying social and diplomatic policies. Beneath the differing policies of Democrats and Republicans and varying abilities to secure partisan objectives lies a common understanding of the essence of the modern presidency—rhetorical leadership."[41]

The normative dimensions of Tulis's construct remain ambiguous, to me at least, these many years later, perhaps partially because I have never been able to learn the secret Straussian handshake, but also, I believe, because Tulis's conception was founded on a faulty view of political history (the view that political philosophy drives history rather than the other way around) and on a faulty view of rhetoric (largely untheorized in his writings). The point I want to make here is a more limited one, however. It seems significant that the birth of the Federal Reserve accompanies the birth of the rhetorical presidency. Although Wilson was not particularly active in promoting the legislation that founded the Fed in 1913, the Fed was part of the same climate of high-minded Progressive legislation that, depending on your political point of view, either removed important public issues from partisan corruption or represented the triumph of the conservatism of big business, as in Gabriel Kolko's famous account.[42] The English economic historian James Forder, however, in the best recent account of the founding of the Fed, reminds us that the Federal Reserve Act was a compromise. Its decentralized structure was a compromise between "the Jacksonian suspicion of any bank and credit needs of a developing economy." Although the presence of bankers on the board reflects the banking community's desire for control, it also reflects Wilson's fear of the bankers' power and William Jennings Bryan's suspicion of the banks for creating rural economic crises.[43] Although the Fed originally was designed simply to avoid bank panics, it gradually became the nation's chief authority on economic matters, eventually displacing the president and Congress by the 1950s. If it is now a truism that presidents both communicate more to the public and thus are held more responsible for policy failures, especially economic failures—still the single best predictor of presidential election outcomes—then why did a succession of "rhetorical presidents" willingly cede control to the Fed?

There are probably several causes: first, the gradual detachment of economic controversy from public discussion and debate was part of the Progressive agenda. My immigrant forebears, populists, socialists, and Farmer-Laborites all, held spirited discussions at their farm dinner tables about free silver and the gold standard. Most Americans today, even or especially college-educated Americans, are unable to discuss basic questions of economic policy, except perhaps the state of the federal deficit or tax rates. Second, the increasing mathematization of the economics profession, while yielding definite benefits in microeconomics and in our understanding of the behavior of financial markets, has created a powerful disincentive for policy-oriented humanists and social scientists to engage macroeconomic theory.

Yet these facts do not explain the complete acquiescence of both political parties to Fed independence and to the virtual elimination of economic controversy from the public sphere. The last serious proposals for reforming the Federal Reserve came during the 1970s, from that remarkable Texas congressman Wright Patman of Texarkana, often rightly labeled the "last Populist." Patman consistently proposed legislation to make the Fed more responsive to political pressure: shorten the terms of the governors so that a single president would have more influence; remove the Reserve Bank presidents from the Federal Open Markets Committee so that only political appointees would decide monetary policy; force the Fed to open its books for regular audits; and there were other proposals.[44] All failed, despite being introduced year after year, even after Patman's death in 1975, with the single exception of the audit proposal passed in 1978, at a time of high Fed unpopularity, as we saw in the previous narrative.

Perhaps the simplest explanation is Roderick P. Hart's: presidents talk so much because they find it easier than governing. If, in fact, presidents tend to follow a kind of minimax rational choice strategy (i.e., seeking to minimize the maximum harm of their or their opponents' actions), then ceding independence to the Fed is the easy way out. Imagine, for example, a group of politicians operating under a James Buchanan– or John Rawls–like "veil of ignorance." They know simultaneously that they will be held responsible by the public for their decisions affecting the economy, yet they want an effective combination of good economic policies with maximum deniability in times of crisis. I would argue, provisionally at least, that the dynamic of the rhetorical presidency and the macroeconomy in the twentieth century follows two steps: first, Congress, seeking to maintain its own power, gradually cedes power and responsibility over the economy to the White House; second, the White House, recognizing both its heightened accountability and its general impotence to guide the macroeconomy, rationally cedes responsibility to the Fed, especially after recognizing the political power of Clinton's famous "fucking bond traders." A very important recent book by Constantine J. Spiliotes, *Vicious Cycle: Presidential Decision Making in the American Political Economy*, makes the related point that presidents have changed increasingly from being accountable to their political parties to being constrained by the chief executive's institutional mission.[45] Spiliotes does not discuss the Fed extensively, but any future discussion of presidential economic rhetoric will benefit from his careful timeline of presidential speeches and directives on the economy from Eisenhower through Reagan.

A second generalization I want to make from my account of president-Fed relations is that we need to incorporate presidential rhetoric into a larger theory of presidential *influence*. How do the rhetorical performances of presidents intersect with presidential bargaining in various institutional contexts? It seems possible to conclude, tentatively, that Presidents Kennedy, Nixon, Reagan, and Clinton exercised the greatest attempted political control over the Fed, while only Kennedy and Clinton maintained mutually beneficial relationships with the Fed.

A third generalization is that there is such a thing as the rhetorical Fed as well as the rhetorical presidency. William McChesney Martin and Alan Greenspan were arguably the most successful Fed chairmen in their prudent management of interest rates, in negotiating with the White House, and in communicating with the business and financial communities, if not necessarily with the general public.

We obviously need more extended case studies of presidential rhetoric and influence on economic matters beyond monetary policy, but I hope I have contributed something to such future research.

THE FEDERAL RESERVE CONSPIRACY AND THE COLONIZATION OF THE LIFEWORLD

In this final section of my paper, I want to raise more abstract and normative questions: (1) Should we have a more robust public debate on the problems with inflation? (2) How can we reconcile the independence and power of the Fed with American democracy?

What is wrong with inflation? An interesting content analysis of late twentieth century newspapers by Yale economist Robert Shiller revealed that *inflation* is the single most commonly used economic term; in fact, newspapers use the word *inflation* more than *sex*.[46] The term has gone through considerable rhetorical reframing in this century; one could argue that it is a more potent economic devil term than *unemployment*. The two most important defenders of inflationary policies in post–World War II America have been the aforementioned Congressman Wright Patman and the journalist William Greider, whose *Secrets of the Temple: How the Federal Reserve Runs the Country* hit the bestseller list in the 1980s. Greider and Patman contend that inflation benefits the working class while hurting the "rentier" class only. Simply put, inflation helps debtors by reducing the value of their debts. A similar argument was central to the debate over the gold standard in the 1890s; debtors, especially farmers, wanted to see free coinage of silver or unlimited printing of greenbacks to lower their debts after a period of grueling deflation. Most mainstream economists reject the pro-inflation thesis on the grounds that inflation eventually cuts corporate profits, leading to reduced investment, which in turn leads to unemployment. It is arguable, however, that the Fed might take a more balanced middle course between inflation and deflation, although the trend of the world's central banks has been toward the American independence model and away from the post–World War II political model of England and France.

Populist opponents of the Fed are not only "inflation doves." A number of commentators on the libertarian or traditionalist Right contend that the Fed is responsible for a secular rise in prices over the twentieth century, and they support a return to the classical gold standard. The Texas Republican Party, in addition to its proclamation that the United States is a Christian nation, also has proclaimed the need to return to the gold standard. At one point Greenspan himself supported this return, although it is doubtful that he currently does. Only Steve Forbes, among recent Republican presidential candidates, has supported a return to the gold standard.

I want to devote some brief space here to the persistent right-wing populist belief in the Federal Reserve conspiracy, because it illustrates the problem of democratic control of the Fed in a very powerful way. There are roughly four right-wing narratives about the Fed, differing only in their degree of paranoia and in their antisemitism. While the basic narrative line has been around since the days of populism, it has gained in strength and detail with the rise of globalization in the 1990s.

The purest form of the Fed and globalization narrative treats the Jewish people as the central characters. A group of Jewish leaders, the famed Elders of Zion, have conspired to do the following:

1. They have conspired to create money out of nothing, using the alchemy of fractional reserve banking (which allows banks to lend out money at interest without having 100 percent reserves of gold or silver to back up the money). In doing so, they usurp the divine power to create value; at this point conspiracy theorists remind their audience of the traditional Roman Catholic and Islamic ban on lending money at interest as well as the traditional association of Jews with moneylending.
2. Two prominent Jewish European investment banking families, the Rothschilds and the Warburgs, made a fortune through controlling central banks, especially by stirring up wars that would require national governments to go further into debt. (Part of this argument also appears currently on the antiwar right; see discussions on Justin Raimondo's antiwar.com.)
3. Under the direct guidance of Rothschild and Warburg, U.S. banking interests, notably Jacob Schiff of Kuhn, Loeb, and J. P. Morgan, Rothschild's "U.S. stooge," were able to convince Congress to create the Fed in 1913.

THE ECONO-RHETORICAL PRESIDENCY

4. The Jewish bankers proceeded to use their newfound power to finance the Bolshevik Revolution, and they supported Western political movements ostensibly opposed to communism: the Fabian socialists in England, the New Deal (Roosevelt's name, of course, was changed from the Jewish Rosenfeld), the United Nations, and the Eisenhower wing of the Republican Party.
5. The bankers have conspired to drive up prices (inflation is the "hidden tax" paid to the Fed), drive out small farmers, ranchers, and small businesspeople, and install a puppet regime in Washington, otherwise known as ZOG, "Zionist Occupied Government."[47]

A second, even more popular conspiracy narrative was devised by Pat Robertson in his 1991 book, *The New World Order,* which has sold millions of copies worldwide since 1991.[48] President George H. W. Bush's unfortunate use of the term *new world order* in a key Gulf War speech in January 1991 pricked Robertson's imagination. Robertson writes: "A single thread runs from the White House to the State Department to the Council on Foreign Relations to the Trilateral Commission to secret societies to extreme New Agers. There must be a new world order. It must eliminate national sovereignty. There must be world government, a world police force, world courts, world banking and currency, and a world elite in charge of it all." He continues: "Is George Bush merely an idealist or are there plans now under way to merge the interests of the United States and the Soviet Union in the United Nations—to substitute "world order power" for "balance of power," and install a socialist "world order" in place of a free market system?"[49]

Is Bush, finally, merely an instrument of Satan? Is Bush—the scion of an old Connecticut family, a "Yalie, preppy, and a sissy," as Reagan memorably called him in 1980, member of Skull and Bones, Texas oilman, head of the CIA—at best an idealist stooge or at worst a Satanic socialist? If you believe that (as G. K. Chesterton once said in another context), you will believe anything, and that is what Robertson wants his readers to do. The direct connection with the Federal Reserve, the Masons, and the earlier Illuminati that exercised the imagination of the Federalist clergy in the 1800 presidential election is demonstrated, according to Robertson, by the Great Seal of the United States. The designer of the seal, Charles Thompson, was a Mason who had served as secretary to the Continental Congress. The Great Seal's reverse depicts an unfinished pyramid, above which is set a shining eye. Below the pyramid is the Latin phrase *Novus Ordo Seclorum,* meaning "a new order of the ages," or, as Robertson puts it, in ominous italics, a *new world order*. Thus, for those in the know, the Great Seal encodes this message: the unfinished pyramid represents the unfinished work of building a one-world government under the all-seeing eye of Osiris, the Egyptian deity worshiped by the Masons. The appearance of the Great Seal on Federal Reserve notes clinches the evidence for the conspiracy.

Robertson later got into some trouble, when it was revealed by Michael Lind that his footnotes were all to openly antisemitic sources of the kind featured in my first narrative, although Robertson denied any antisemitism and blamed his research assistant.[50] In any case, despite George W. Bush's famous touchiness where his father is concerned, Robertson's swipe at Bush 41 didn't prevent Bush 43 from handing Robertson's organization several million dollars in faith-based charity money in the fall of 2001 via an executive order end-run around Congress. Robertson repaid the favor in December 2003 by proclaiming that the capture of Saddam Hussein revealed that God Himself wanted Bush to be reelected.[51]

The conspiracy narratives make fun (if somewhat scary fun) reading, but they are interesting as the only serious discourse in American politics about democracy and the Fed. Right-wing conspiracy discourse, to my view, is a kind of postmodernism for the masses. Fredric Jameson has written: "It is safest to grasp the concept of the postmodern as an attempt to think the present historically in an age that has forgotten to think historically in the first place."[52] In the absence of a credible counternarrative about monetary policy and globalization from the center and the left, it is not hard to imagine potentially fascist consequences from this enduring anti-Fed narrative if the world economy enters into serious, extended crisis. It is not hard to imagine what the presence of three Jews, Rubin, Greenspan, and Summers, on the cover of *Time* as "the committee that saved the world" in 1999 meant to the far Right.

A better way of accounting both for the econo-rhetorical presidency and the surprising persistence of the Fed conspiracy narratives lies in Jürgen Habermas's theory of the colonization of the lifeworld, as developed in the second volume of his *Theory of Communicative Action*.[53] Following Talcott Parsons, Habermas identified four microsystems within the larger social system, labeled by Parsons as A, G, I, and L.

>A stands for Adaptation of the system to the material environment
>G stands for Goal attainment, or management of resources
>I stands for Influence
>L (for latency) stands for value-commitments

To picture their role in the social system, draw an AGIL diagram, with A in the upper right, progressing counterclockwise. The four cells divide on horizontal and vertical axes. A and L represent the "private sphere," and G and I the "public sphere." Society requires certain boundaries between these spheres but also mutual interchange between them. Horizontally, G and A represent what Habermas calls systems of material reproduction, or the reproduction context of society. I and L represent what he calls the lifeworld, or the symbolic reproduction context of society. Each of the four social subsystems "communicates" with the others via a distinctive medium: money (for A), votes (for G), influence (for I), and value-commitments (for L).

Habermas contends that there are fundamental differences between two types of media. The A and G media, money and power (votes) are *quantitative*: both money and votes can be counted, and whoever has the most wins. The I and L media, by contrast, are *qualitative*: you cannot quantify influence or value-commitments, since these are only enacted in communication between persons.

"Colonization" thus means that in social settings that formerly operated by communicative media (I and L), the quantitative media (A and G) now dominate. Rather than communicative action—people talking about their differences and coming to a common understanding—one (person, party, or interest) dominates the other by having more money or votes. Colonization reduces the sphere in which communicative, qualitative media operate, and more of social life depends on noncommunicative, quantitative media.

Nonetheless, the legitimacy of the quantitative media depends on the qualitative media: the value of money and votes requires constant acts of influence and value-commitment, or the A and G media become worthless. Money and votes are, after all, only worth as much as shared understandings assert them to be worth. Money depends on mutual understandings that we will treat these pieces of paper a certain way for purposes of exchange, and at times in history that understanding has been withdrawn. Votes are only worth as much as a common understanding that we will abide by the final count, but that understanding can be withdrawn, as in military coups. *Legitimation crisis* in Habermas's specialized sense occurs when those qualitative media (influence and value-commitments) are too weak to generate the legitimacy of the quantitative media.

It is plausible to conclude, at least in part, that continued decline in voting participation in the Western democracies stems from the continued colonization of the qualitative media by the quantitative ones. If the promise of Enlightenment reason can be fulfilled only by democratic discussion and debate about all the subsystems of the social order, perhaps the most important task of critical social theory at the present time is to increase knowledge and controversy about the quantitative medium of money, a medium progressively isolated from the lifeworld and the public sphere by the United States since 1951—not coincidentally the precise time at which the United States began to back away from the goal of full employment as the key objective of the national economy. The anti-Fed narratives of the religious and far Right represent another kind of protest against lifeworld colonization, in the name of the medium of ultimate value-commitments. At minimum, a program of resistance would include:

- A commitment to continuing transparency on the part of financial and governmental institutions—a commitment that thus far Alan Greenspan has been more willing to promote than, say, the George W. Bush Administration, whose mania for secrecy exceeds even that of Richard Nixon's.
- An insistence on studying and debating economic issues in a number of academic disciplines, along with forthright resistance to the imperialism of mainstream economics and its continuing colonization of political science in the form of rational choice theory. Economic debate is too important to leave to the economics profession.
- Serious rethinking of what a democratic financial system might look like, after the failures of both the command economies of communism and of the new laissez-faire in both its monetarist and supply-side forms. If you read no other book on public policy this year, please try to read Yale economist Robert J. Shiller's 2003 *The New Financial Order: Risk in the Twenty-First Century*, in which he proposes some ingenious, market-based solutions to poverty and unemployment by enabling workers, professionals, and even urban home owners in transitional neighborhoods to "socialize risk" with new types of financial instruments. The Fed itself, like the stock market before it, were efforts by entrepreneurs and bankers to socialize risks by distributing potential losses widely. In Shiller's vision, we may be able to do so worldwide.
- A serious commitment to exposing the influence of special interests on monetary policy, and a serious debate on the question of the Fed's independence. I am personally agnostic on the question of whether the Fed should be independent; the evidence probably lies in favor of independence combined with reciprocal influence as it occurred during the Kennedy and Clinton administrations. Nonetheless, the populist right

remains convincing in its claim that the founding of the Fed represents an unconstitutional subversion of the constitutional requirement (Article I, section 8) that Congress "coin Money" and "regulate the Value thereof." If the "rhetorical presidency" represents a fundamental subversion of the original constitutional order, the econo-rhetorical presidency represents perhaps an even greater subversion, one that deserves at least another ten years of study by rhetoricians, historians, and political scientists.

Notes

1. David G. McCullough, *Truman* (New York: Simon and Schuster, 1992).

2. The fullest account of the accord is Robert L. Hetzel and Ralph F. Leach, "The Treasury-Fed Accord: A New Narrative Account," *Federal Reserve Bank of Richmond Economic Quarterly* 87, no. 1 (Winter 2001): 33–55. The most entertaining account is in Martin Mayer, *The Fed* (New York: Free Press, 2001), chap. 4.

3. See "The Board of Governors of the Federal Reserve System," *The Federal Reserve System: Purposes and Functions* (Washington, D.C.: U.S. Government Printing Office, 1994), 1–15. See also William Greider, *Secrets of the Temple: How the Federal Reserve Runs the Country* (New York: Simon and Schuster, 1987), 60–65.

4. George Moore, *The Banker's Life* (New York: W. W. Norton, 1987), 113, 115; see also Mayer, *The Fed*, 82–83.

5. Hetzel and Leach, "Treasury-Fed Accord," 40.

6. Cited in Mayer, *The Fed*, 89.

7. Hetzel and Leach, "Treasury-Fed Accord," 45.

8. Mariner Eccles, *Beckoning Frontiers* (New York: Alfred A. Knopf, 1951), 498. Eccles's commendable commitment to "transparency" renders some of the populist critiques of the Fed less persuasive.

9. The minutes of this meeting are now available online at http://www.rich.frb.org/research/specialtopics/treasury/primary/bog0206.html.

10. Cited in Mayer, *The Fed*, 91.

11. See the text of the statement at http://www.rich.frb.org/research/specialtopics/treasury/primary/statement.html.

12. Lawrence Laughlin, an active member of the American Bankers' Association at the time, cited in R. Timberlake, *Monetary Policy in the United States: An Intellectual and Institutional History* (Chicago: University of Chicago Press, 1993), 12.

13. Mayer, *The Fed*, 83.

14. Mayer, *The Fed*, 175.

15. Dan Ackman, "Alan Greenspan Is No William McChesney Martin," *Forbes*, April 23, 2003, available online at http://www.forbes.com/2003/04/23/cx_da0423topnews_print.html.

16. Mayer, *The Fed*, 181.

17. For a compelling account of this period, from a broadly Marxist perspective, see Fred L.

Block, *The Origins of International Economic Disorder* (Berkeley: University of California Press, 1977), chaps. 7 and 8.

18. Mayer, *The Fed*, 93.
19. Greider, *Secrets of the Temple*, 67.
20. Greider, *Secrets of the Temple*, 121.
21. Greider, *Secrets of the Temple*, 345.
22. Greider, *Secrets of the Temple*, 345.
23. Greider, *Secrets of the Temple*, 121.
24. Greider, *Secrets of the Temple*, 146.
25. See Greider's chap. 4, "The Liberal Apology," for a compelling account of the Democrats during this period; see also Thomas B. Edsall, *The New Politics of Inequality* (New York: W. W. Norton, 1984), for discussion of campaign contributions to the Democrats.
26. See the prologue to Bob Woodward, *Maestro: Greenspan's Fed and the American Boom* (New York: Simon and Schuster, 2000).
27. Woodward, *Maestro*, 36–48.
28. *Washington Post*, February 25, 1988, 1A.
29. Woodward, *Maestro*, 71.
30. Woodward, *Maestro*, 91.
31. "Bush Pins the Blame for '92 Election Loss on Alan Greenspan," *Wall Street Journal*, August 25, 1998, A16.
32. Woodward, *Maestro*, 102.
33. Woodward, *Maestro*, 126; for a slightly different account, see Bob Woodward, *The Agenda* (New York: Simon and Schuster, 1994), 84—Clinton there complains about being turned into an "Eisenhower Republican."
34. Woodward, *Maestro*, 100.
35. I am uncertain of the source of this quotation.
36. On Mexico, see Woodward, *Maestro*, 142. For a discussion of the Long-Term Capital hedge fund crisis, see James Arnt Aune, *Selling the Free Market* (New York: Guilford Press, 2001), 165–68.
37. See Rubin's account of these years in his engaging recent memoir (with Jacob Weisberg), *In an Uncertain World* (New York: Random House, 2003).
38. See Amos Kiewe and Davis Houck, *A Shining City on a Hill: Ronald Reagan's Economic Rhetoric, 1951–1989* (New York: Praeger, 1991); Davis Houck, *Rhetoric as Currency* (College Station: Texas A&M University Press, 2001); also Houck's *Argumentation and Advocacy* essay.
39. George C. Edwards III and Stephen J. Wayne, *Presidential Leadership*, 6th ed. (New York: St. Martin's, 2002); see chapter 13 on budgetary and economic policymaking. Lyn Ragsdale, *Presidential Politics* (Boston: Houghton Mifflin, 1993), 320. But see also Jeffrey E. Cohen and John A. Hamman, "The Polls: Can Presidential Rhetoric Affect the Public's Economic Perceptions?" *Presidential Studies Quarterly* 33, no. 2 (June 2003): 408–22 (contending that foreign policy presidential rhetoric appears to be more effective than economic rhetoric in influencing public perceptions of *the economy*).
40. Jeffrey Tulis, *The Rhetorical Presidency* (Princeton, N.J.: Princeton University Press, 1987).
41. Tulis, *Rhetorical Presidency*, 4.

42. Gabriel Kolko, *The Triumph of American Conservatism: A Reinterpretation of American History, 1900–1916* (Chicago: Quadrangle, 1963), chap. 9. For the most useful recent account, see James Livingston, *Origins of the Federal Reserve System: Money, Class, and Corporate Capitalism, 1890–1913* (Ithaca, N.Y.: Cornell University Press, 1986). See also Greider's populist discussion in part 2 of *Secrets of the Temple.*

43. James Forder, "Independence and the Founding of the Federal Reserve," *Scottish Journal of Political Economy,* 50, no. 3 (August 2003): 306. In the same issue see also Barbara Caporale, "The Influence of Economists on the Federal Reserve Act," 311–25.

44. See Greider, *Secrets of the Temple,* 51, and see the recent biography of Patman: Nancy Beck Young, *Wright Patman: Populism, Liberalism, and the American Dream* (Dallas, Tex.: Southern Methodist University Press, 2000).

45. Constantine J. Spiliotes, *Vicious Cycle: Presidential Decision Making in the American Political Economy* (College Station: Texas A&M University Press, 2002).

46. Robert J. Shiller, *The New Financial Order: Risk in the Twenty-First Century* (Princeton, N.J.: Princeton University Press, 2003), 202.

47. See the more extensive discussion in my *Selling the Free Market,* 132–35.

48. Pat Robertson, *The New World Order* (Dallas: Word, 1991).

49. Robertson, *New World Order,* 58.

50. See Michael Lind, "No Enemies to the Right: The Pat Robertson Scandal and What It Means," *Up from Conservatism* (New York: Free Press, 1996), 97–120.

51. See Robert Scheer, "Column Left," *Nation* online, January 12, 2004, at http://www.thenation.com/doc.mhtml?i=20040112&s=scheer0106.

52. Fredric Jameson, *Postmodernism, or The Cultural Logic of Late Capitalism* (Durham, N.C.: Duke University Press, 1991), ix.

53. Jürgen Habermas, *The Theory of Communicative Action,* vol. 2: *Lifeworld and System: A Critique of Functionalist Reason,* trans. Thomas McCarthy (Boston: Beacon Press, 1987), especially section 6.

CHAPTER 4

THE RETURN OF THE IMPERIAL PRESIDENCY

Marouf Hasian Jr., University of Utah

> *The last significant check on the imperial presidency was the electorate, and on November 2 it failed.*
>
> CHALMERS JOHNSON, 2004

When George W. Bush's administrative decision makers looked for judicial precedents that would help them deal with exigencies like 9/11, we now know that they had plenty of judicial cases from which to choose. On the one hand, our legal archives are filled with legal opinions that have jurists and treatise writers commenting on how the mere declaration of an emergency was enough to constitute a national exigency, how quick responses were needed in dangerous situations, and how wartime needs occasionally trumped civil liberties.[1] This would later be characterized as the *Ex parte Quirin*, or strong national security position.[2]

On the other hand, the spokespersons for the Bush Administration could have turned to those decision makers who have talked about inherited suspicions of standing armies, the primacy of legislative power, the importance of judicial review, and the need to have civilian oversight of military decisions.³ Since at least the time of Cromwell pundits have worried about the royal prerogatives, the rhetorical claims associated with the aggrandizement of power, and the importance of having legal constraints This second approach—what some scholars call the *Ex parte Milligan* line of argument (the Milligan case is discussed later)—would ask us to view emergencies as extraordinary events, when the concomitant discretionary powers of the executive would be relinquished with the end of temporary emergencies.⁴ In this chapter I argue that these two major frameworks for analyzing executive power are themselves the accretive remains of some older Anglo-American legal frameworks that take us back to the time of the Whigs and the Tories. It will be one of my contentions that both of these approaches make up a part of our complex modern discussions of the alleged "imperial" nature of Bush's presidency.⁵

During most of September 2001, American Democrats and Republicans rallied around the U.S. president, and there were few observers who doubted that the passage of the Patriot Act would be a matter of national security.⁶ There appeared to be a strong public consensus that communal necessities outweighed individual liberties—and these communal beliefs influenced our debates over airlines and racial profiling, deportation hearings, the surveillance of citizens, and the tracing of Al Qaeda funding.

The political landscape changed when President George W. Bush suddenly announced that part of his weaponry in the war against terrorists would include the "Military Order of November 13, 2001," which dealt with the "Detention, Treatment, and Trial of Certain Non-Citizens in the War against Terrorism."⁷ As George Will once observed, the potential use of these military tribunals, along with some of his other antiterrorist policies, was generating what Will called "imperial presidency anxiety."⁸ Both liberals and conservatives worried that perhaps the president's legal advisors were going too far too fast and taking us in directions that might hurt, rather than help, the war effort. One anonymous writer for the *Nation* would later aver that "the assumption of imperial powers" was reflected in Bush's unilateral activities and his supposed tendency to "mislead the public," but critics need to admit that there were many times when the president's views were very transparent.⁹ This was not the first time that the nation had an inkling that America's chief executive was thinking about taking this kind of action. On September 20, 2001, for example, President Bush told listeners that the country needed to "bring our enemies to justice or bring justice to our enemies." He also announced that he was going to give an executive order that allowed for the possibility that some of the "terrorists" would have to appear before military commissions. Josh Tyrangiel has noted that since that speech, "the sharpest legal minds in the White House and Department of Justice have been working to turn the President's poetic abstraction into specific judicial doctrine."[10] After hearing Bush talk about antiterrorism on national television, Michael Beschloss told listeners that "the imperial presidency is back. We just saw it."[11]

Other critics who lament the advent of Bush's "imperial presidency" focus on more macro, external activities that go beyond the study of single speeches or their reception. Robin Blackburn, for example, argues that the social construction of this particular manifestation of power is a much more complex affair:

> The most difficult thing for the strategists of empire to perceive, or explain to the American people, is that the best and perhaps most effective coalition against Al Qaeda and Islamic jihad would be one that they do not lead and do not control. The food drops in Afghanistan were accompanied by leaflets in English and Pushtu with the heading "The Partnership of Nations"—a hollow rubric which could not conceal that this was a U.S. and British action. . . . The secret of his [Bush's] strength—and his fatal flaw—may be the instinctive rapport he enjoys with those gripped by U.S. national messianism, the idea that only the U.S. can tackle the really big global threats and that whatever the U.S. does is *ipso facto* favorable to freedom. . . . The imperial role is justified on the grounds that the U.S. has a special destiny as world leader and champion of freedom.[12]

As I argue in what follows, if the American president was thinking about acting in imperial ways, then perhaps he was not alone.

For many observers of presidential politics, these were fighting words, because the very idea of having a new "imperial president" did not sit well with those who understood that this was a term loaded with ideological baggage. Thomas Cronin explains that although this idiomatic phrase "meant many things to many people," it "especially suggested the abuse and misuse of presidential powers."[13] Donald Wolfensberger, a former Republican congressional staff aide during the Vietnam and Watergate years, admitted that he was "startled by the buoyant tone of Beschloss's pronouncement. To me, 'imperial presidency' carries a pejorative connotation closely tied to those two nightmares. Indeed, *Webster's Unabridged Dictionary* bluntly defines imperial presidency as 'a U.S. presidency that is characterized by greater power than the Constitution allows.' Was Beschloss suggesting that President Bush was already operating outside the Constitution in prosecuting the war against terrorism, or did he have a more benign definition in mind? Apparently it was the latter."[14]

Defenders of Bush Administration policies attacked this type of labeling and yet defending the use of executive prerogatives as necessities in the war against terrorism.

Many scholars remember that it was Arthur Schlesinger Jr. who helped popularize the phrase "imperial presidency." In a 1973 book bearing that name, he argued that the historical study of American presidencies showed how various chief executives gravitated toward stylistic forms of governance, including revolutionary and constitutional types of presidencies.[15] As Richard Kirkendall once explained, the "imperial presidency" was believed to be one of these governmental styles, "largely a product of recent international crises," where leaders monopolized rather than shared power.[16] Since that time, commentators with a variety of political allegiances have used the phrase "imperial presidency" as a derisive term, signifying unlawfulness, unethical behavior, or impoverished political judgment.[17] An imperial president was someone who purportedly deviated from the traditional path of public service and honor, a social agent who upset the equipoise of the separation of powers that structurally or functionally existed within the American constitutional framework.

Critics of the usage of the phrase, such as Sam Tanenhaus, have argued that we should not confuse the mere use of presidential authority with the tyrannical abuse of power. As far as Tanenhaus was concerned, "every modern president has found power to be elusive, slippery, and at times treacherous," and we needed to realize that the idea of an imperial presidency was simply an "epithet" that was being "dredged up" any time a president combined "strength" with "imagination." Why not simply admit that strong leaders were not always imperial "at all"?[18]

Interestingly enough, many of the other observers who warn us about some of the dangers associated with imperial presidencies have also written about the periodic "end" of these imperial reigns.[19] When pundits watched or commented on the arrival of Watergate, or the passage of the War Powers Act of 1973, they hoped that this reassertion of "Congressional war powers into American foreign policymaking" would help end the "perceived imperialism of Nixon and President Lyndon B. Johnson during the Vietnam War."[20] Yet given the litany of relatively recent interventions and military actions with which many of us are familiar—Reagan in Grenada, Clinton in the former Yugoslavia, the Afghan and Sudan air strikes of the late 1990s against Bin Laden—is the idea of the "end" of the "imperial presidency" itself a convenient scholarly fiction, whistling in the dark alleys of international *realpolitik*?[21] If we do believe in the heuristic value of that term, and that the term *imperial presidency* does indeed describe the Bush Administration's actions, what valence will we now place on that label?

I would like to take up the question of whether we are actually seeing the "return" of the imperial presidency, and whether we can do anything about it. Although rhetoricians and other scholars may be interested in looking at a host of domestic and international actions that might provide us with some evidence of the growing power of the American presidency, I would like to focus on the costs and benefits of the United States' recent infatuation with the idea of unilateral usage of military tribunals. More specifically, I want to investigate how these debates about military tribunals contribute to our understanding of presidential politics, the constraints that can be placed on congressional and judicial power, and the influence that public popularity may have on twenty-first-century notions of constitutionalism.[22] Given the fact that we are empirically living in a post-9/11 world, are we witnessing a time when legislation such as the War Powers Act can no longer constrain the power of the American president? Have our perceptions about military necessities turned our Constitution into mere parchment? Have we given up the idea of the civilianization of the military? Moreover, have we permanently abandoned some of our Whig ideals that influenced everything from the addition of our Bill of Rights to the formation of international Nuremberg tribunals?[23] Are we now comfortable with the renascent Tory rhetorics that underscore our unilateral powers, our messianic sense of mission, or the collective ideas that link our military might to our exceptionalist nationalistic visions?

For some scholars and citizens, many of our current debates about the potential power of "imperial" presidents are inextricably tied to questions of plenary power, military struggles, and prior emergencies. Current and former members of the Bush Administration are now having to comb through the dustbins of history to find out how other wartime presidents had justified the use of their discretionary powers as commanders in chief of the armed forces.[24] This meant resurrecting the old debate between the *Ex parte Milligan* and *Ex parte Quirin* precedents, and tackling the issue of just how far the nation's systems of checks and balances could stand the strain of having an inordinately powerful executive leader. By January of 2006, writers for the *New York Times* were complaining that the Bush Administration's positions on detainee treatment at Guantánamo, the use of warrantless intelligence surveillance, the categorization of "enemy combatants," and military tribunal policies were all providing evidence that there were no limits "to his imperial presidency."[25]

These debates about the potential constitutionality of Bush's Military Order involve more than simply the search for the most accurate formalistic interpretations of legal codes and precedents. As Kenneth Anderson astutely observed, some audiences see trials as "theatre or as a spectacle of edification," where the "rhetoric" of a "trial's historic quality" exists in tension with "the rhetoric of law," which emphasizes "commonness."[26] Millions of individuals are impacted by the choice of rhetorics that we circulate about the "war" on terrorism, the military trial of enemy combatants, the detention of civilian suspects, or the search for "sleeper" cells in our midst. Globalization has altered forever the way that we think about the etched boundaries between police and military powers, national sovereignty, and individual liberties. How can we respect the rights of others, one might ask, when the battlefields of New York appear to resemble the latest rendition of the "Great Game" in Afghanistan? These are important questions, because there have been many detainees who have faced the very real prospect of being tried for their membership in Al Qaeda, and the list of potential candidates for trial before a military tribunal was constantly growing—from Jose Padilla to Saddam Hussein.[27] Yet in the early weeks that followed the collapse of the towers, there had been little public or elite commentary on the dangers or desirability of any military commissions.

This theoretically all changed when the Supreme Court decided the case of *Hamdan v. Rumsfeld* (2006).[28] In that particular case, the court issued a 5–3 decision holding that Salim Hamdan, a citizen of the Yemen and alleged driver for Osama bin Laden, could not be tried by the special military commission that was unilaterally established by President Bush. The court in this case did recognize that we were at war with terrorists, and it did buttress earlier decisions that had been made about the legality of detentions in general. What the members of this court were complaining about where the procedures that were set in place for the tribunals under Military Commission Order No. 1 (March 21, 2002). In an opinion that was authored by Justice Stevens, many members of the court indicated that they felt these special rules contravened both the Uniform Code of Military Justice and the Geneva Convention.

Some critics have argued that Supreme Court was saying "no to an imperial presidency."[29] But this may underestimate the rhetorical power of the Bush order and the arguments that have circulated in legal and public spheres focusing on the "unitary" power of the commander in chief. For some five years American publics have wanted an executive who emphasizes "security," and understand that all of us may have to give up some liberties, and clearly do not want any mollycoddling of dangerous aliens. President Bush understood these concerns, and from the very beginning of his administration, he continually indicated that he believed the alleged terrorists should not be treated as ordinary criminals who deserved the due process rights Americans were used to seeing. Moreover, he disagreed with his critics who characterized these captured terrorists as prisoners of war. In his January 2002 State of the Union Address, he told Congress that "thousands of dangerous killers, schooled in the methods of murder, often supported by outlaw regimes, are now spread throughout the world like ticking time bombs, set to go off without warning."[30] While American listeners could not always tell if he was implying that all of these individuals might be candidates for military tribunals, the tone of his address left no doubt that he was in no mollycoddling mood.

From a legal standpoint, President Bush's remarks raised as many questions as they answered. If these killers were all caught, would each be tried for war crimes or for crimes against humanity? Was the president talking about trying the leaders of the Al Qaeda forces, or was he also contemplating the trial of those who supported the leaders or gave them aid and comfort? What constitutional provisions, legislative statutes, precedents, or policies granted him the power to answer these questions?

On one thing we could be sure—the American public wanted to be guided by a strong president, who would deal swiftly with this emergency. If these exigent situations demanded that a commander in chief be granted unusual executive powers, then he would have the support of the ordinary U.S. citizen, who understood that sometimes extrajudicial situations called for exjudicial measures. If some measures had to be taken that appeared to be unconstitutional or legally suspect, then so be it—the nation's survival was at stake. Realism clashes with formalism during these turbulent times. In the immortal words of Justice Charles Evans Hughes, the U.S. Constitution is a "fighting Constitution."[31]

Some Congress critics, members of the press, or legal scholars might be concerned with the detention of enemy combatants or the rights of citizens who might be associated with Al Qaeda, but the American public was in no mood for legal hair splitting. After the passage of the Patriot Act, many Bush administrators turned their attention to the actual interpretations, implementations, and procedures that would be needed to carry out what they considered to be part of their public mandates. They publicly voiced their belief that perhaps the nation's civilian courts were not the best forums for trying enemy belligerents. Assistant Attorney General Michael Chertoff remarked that when nations are at war,

> military commissions are a traditional way of bringing justice to persons charged with offenses under armed conflict. The Supreme Court has upheld the use of such commissions. The use of such commissions is not only legally proper; there may be sound policy reasons to employ it in individual cases. Proceedings before military commissions may be needed to safeguard classified information at the trial of particular members of Al Qaida. Also, military commissions are equipped to deal with the significant security concerns that can arise from a trial of the terrorists. We are all aware that trying terrorists in our cities could place judges and juries—and, indeed, the cities themselves—at risk. Finally, bear in mind that the attacks of September 11 were launched by a foreign power and [and that they] killed thousands of innocent people. These are war crimes, in addition to domestic crimes. There is nothing inappropriate or unfair in trying war crimes as they often have been tried before military commissions.[32]

Put simply, the belief that an Anglo-American nation is at war changes the political calculus and the rhetorical frameworks that are used in the balancing of powers, interests, or rights.

Of course Chertoff was right that there had been times when individual nations had conducted their own "war crimes" proceedings—the *Eichmann* trial comes quickly to mind—but what about the Nuremberg Trial of the Major War Criminals, where the Four Powers led a coalition of dozens of Allied nations in the legal trial of Nazi aggression?[33] The exclusive focus on American military histories, and the brief commentary on constitutional precedents, glossed over a host of key questions: whether all of the various branches of government had been involved in the planning of these forums; whether the bombing of buildings constituted a national *military* emergency, and whether the use of military tribunals constituted a proportional response to that danger.

In cases like this, administrators can often come up with a series of popular arguments that they can use when they try to justify controversial decisions, and in this particular situation a plethora of possible rhetorical frameworks could be used in rationalizing the use of these new military commissions. Decision makers could argue that the Constitution confers emergency powers under Article I, or they could talk about inherent common-law prerogatives, or perhaps even point out that Congress had "repeatedly recognized and accepted" the existence of military tribunals.[34] Influential elites could also comment on how some executive action seemed to be aligned with popular, democratic sentiments. For example, William Barr, the former attorney general of the United States, perhaps expressed the dominant mood when he surmised that our "national goal in this instance is not the correction, deterrence and rehabilitation of an errant member of the body politic" but rather "the destruction of [a] foreign force that poses a risk to our national security."[35]

These types of justificatory remarks serve several rhetorical purposes. They help frame the discussion as one that focuses on military rather than criminal behavior, thus moving the violation outside the purview of civilian or police enforcement. This simultaneously magnifies the danger and invites audiences to think of stronger responses. In theory, the members of Al Qaeda or their supporters were no common criminals; they were foreigners, and they threatened the body politic. These terrorists could be configured as diseases that could not be reasoned with, infiltrators who could not be quarantined, or extraordinary criminals with almost mythic powers of resistance. Barr also assumes that the primary goal in this case is "destruction" and not trial of the enemy, turning any judicial proceedings into public spectacles and gratuitous acts that tell us more about the psychic needs of the nation than about the individual guilt of the defendant.

For a nation that prides itself on the importance of American liberties and the maintenance of the rule of law, this ideographic shift away from the primacy of individual rights and toward the paramount importance of alleged national "necessities" may also alter the ways that we think about imperial presidents.[36] How can we apply a phrase that touches on the *lack* of public accountability when the public is itself demanding the existence of empowered executives, who share Barr's views on the role of the chief executive? This certainly does not look like any Whig version of civilian-military relations, and it moved the discussion away from any idea that these activities were going to be treated as domestic matters of local policing. The majority of Americans seemed to accept the discursive militarization of the war on terror and appeared to be ratifying Bush's actions. Parts of this military framework also contained arguments about the infinite duration of this "war," and this in turn implied that the traditional warnings (which came from Whiggish assumptions about temporary emergencies) about executive abuse were now falling on deaf ears. The supposed global reach of Al Qaeda mandated that the reach of the president exceed the grasp of his predecessors, and the postcolonial power of the enemy (under the spell of the brainwashed Islamic "fundamentalists") required an equally resolute commander in chief—someone with preemptive powers and the will to use them.

During the early months of this war on terrorism, many of the president's supporters argued that since the attack on the World Trade Center resembled the Japanese attack on Pearl Harbor, decision makers needed to pay particular attention to the judicial decisions that had been handed down during World War II. Even this choice of punctuation of time did not automatically narrow the range of legal narratives or myths that could have been used in the discussion of the legitimacy of military tribunals, because this was a time when the air was filled with debates about the constitutionality of martial law, victor's justice, the need for collective "U.N." actions, the obedience of orders defense, and the importance of having the international rules of law replace summary execution in dealing with war criminals. For example, critics of military tribunals often wrote about the prejudices and miscarriages of justice associated with the American military trial of General Tomoyuki Yamashita, who was accused of having allowed the Japanese extermination of Filipino prisoners. In spite of the fact that the Allies had destroyed his communication infrastructure, he was found guilty of having allowed the cruel and inhumane treatment of both civilian detainees and prisoners of war.[37] Within some military and legal circles, the *Yamashita* case is viewed as a cautionary tale about the potential dangers of victor's justice, but this story would not become front-page news in the months following 9/11.

For a host of legal and political reasons, *Ex parte Quirin* was one of the key legal cases in the justificatory tales that were told by Bush administrators. This once obscure legal decision involved a secret 1942 military trial of some German saboteurs. In many legal circles, this decision is remembered as the case that upholds the principle that when a nation is at war, deference needs to be given to the nation's military authorities. As I have noted in a previous essay, some of the jurists involved in the *Quirin* case took pride in the fact that they had allowed for habeas corpus relief, but the dominant impressions that have been left of this case were that the American judiciary stood on the sidelines when war was declared.[38]

In theory, constitutional presidents are leaders who consult members of both the legislative and judicial branches, and this balancing of interests and powers is supposed to provide a democratic "check" on the power of would-be imperialist presidents. But what happens in situations where these congressional or judicial social agents share the beliefs of those who want an inordinately powerful chief executive? In this war on terrorism, for example, congressional leaders may have wanted someone else to take the lead in making determinations about the bombings in Afghanistan and Iraq, the decisions associated with the appropriation of monies during times of deficit spending, or the promotion of other Patriot Acts.[39] At the same time, the federal judiciary can constantly use talk of "jurisdiction" as a way of avoiding the messy procedural and substantive problems associated with the detention and trial of foreign and citizen "enemy combatants."[40]

It is my contention that the debates we have had about the desirability and legitimacy of military tribunals have served as representative anecdotes for larger debates about presidential power and American unilateral action. Moreover, I believe that many of the members of the legislative and judicial branches who have appeared as critics of the Bush Administration have knowingly or unknowingly expanded executive power, because they have accepted the major templates that channeled the arguments used in these discursive struggles. At the same time, these actions have raised the possibility that we are witnessing the return of a new type of imperial presidency, the aura of which comes from the combined imprimatur of the American public, Congress, and the judiciary. This novel imperial leader may wear new clothes, spun from cloth that would rival the majesty and mystery of the uniforms of those who almost guarded Nixon.[41] As Andrew Rudalevige noted during the fall of 2006, this was an administration willing to advance the argument that on the basis of "some evidence," detainees could be removed from the court system and held without charge or trial.[42] And if these prisoners were going to get any trial, they did not have to see all of the evidence that had been gathered together against them, and they had to stand idly by as coercive testimony was introduced into the military tribunal.[43]

Skeptics might contend that the attacks on some usages of presidential power are more than pseudo-events, that Congress does indeed hold the power of the purse strings, that the views of the French and other international communities should stay on the periphery of our discussion, and that this pragmatic president is cagey enough to know his constitutional limitations. Others may argue that even powerful presidents have to deal with some of the rhetorical constraints—perhaps imposed by public beliefs in Whiggish ideals, where talk of accountability, restraint, the sharing of power, and the ratification of emergency measures controls the grasp of imperial aspirants. Yet what is interesting to note here is that defenders of the president's unitary powers are claiming that the other branches are encroaching on his constitutional prerogatives. The vaunted Whig values can therefore be appropriated by neoconservatives and other defenders of the Bush Administration who complain about how *Hamdan* interferes with the president's Article II powers and how Congress is ignoring the military histories that have legitimized the use of special tribunals.

Yet if these Whig ideas are indeed that powerful, and if they do indeed act as rhetorical constraints on executive aggrandizement, then how do we explain the vociferous support of military tribunals, the acceptance of warrants that link our generation to the "Greatest generation," the often unquestioned necessity of actions that only tangentially related to real national securities, or the denigration of rights talk?[44] Yes, occasionally we do hear the voices of those who worry about the ascendancy of what I have called Tory discourse, but notice the assertions and the evidentiary leaps that have to be made about the significance of more Whiggish constraints. For example, Neal Katyal and Laurence Tribe—who are perhaps the most quoted of legal authorities on the question of the legality of the Bush Military Order—have recently averred that it is Congress that protects some of our most cherished legal rights:

> These constitutional principles, in conjunction with the provisions for a divided government, are our security, and to assert them here is to win at home the war we are waging so effectively abroad. Terrorists have attacked the Federal Building in Oklahoma and the Pentagon and have toppled the towers of the World Trade Center, massacring thousands of innocent civilians in the process. We must not allow them to tear down as well the structures of government, constituted by the separation of powers, that make our legal and political system—and the liberties it embodies and protects—unique.[45]

Notice the rhetorical gesturing of this particular fragment. It does not dispute the uniqueness of the American governmental structure—it simply shifts the locus or origins of that exceptionalism. It does not question the labeling of these acts of terrorism, thereby reinforcing the idea that military and not civilian solutions are warranted and justified. And perhaps most important for our discussion, it assumes that during times of "war" you have—or can have—"divided government." This divided government provides the mythic balance of power.

I share many of Katyal and Tribe's concerns about the importance of separation of powers, but I believe that they underestimate the executive power of this particular presidency. Moreover, I think that they overestimate the capabilities of this particular Congress—one that worried about public backlash and constantly deferred when military discussions appeared on the horizon. Neal

Katyal would later become one of the lead attorneys in the *Hamdan* case, and he was convinced that this court case was a "rejection of the administration's post 9/11 claims about inherent authority in all kinds of crisis."[46] Yet many congressional leaders and laypersons continue to believe that that inherent authority is needed by a strong executive who fights omnipotent and omnipresent powers. This particular imperial president has the backing of most members of the public and the other branches, and when we talk about military tribunals it is now a question of their shape and form, and not their very existence. By the fall of 2006, members of the Bush Administration were traveling up the Hill and asking Congress to pass legislation that would effectively overturn *Hamdan*.

This diatribe is obviously filled with contentious claims, and in order to back up my own positions I have divided the rest of the chapter into four major segments. The first part provides an overview of the notion of the imperial presidency, while the second section supplies a brief analysis of Bush's Military Order of November 13, 2001. The third section explores how Bush administrators responded to the attacks on the legitimacy of the military tribunals, and in the conclusion I comment on the evocative power of this new variant of the imperial presidency.

I begin my rhetorical journey with a cursory overview of some of the theoretical and political meanings associated with the idea of an imperial presidency.

THE SYMBOLIC IMPORTANCE OF THE IMPERIAL PRESIDENCY

George W. Bush is obviously not the first occupant of the White House who has been characterized as a leader of an imperial presidency. Not all of our chief executives have played the role of Cincinnatus, the humble and yet virtuous public servant who understood the importance of republican virtues. Wolfensberger explained in 2002:

> The growth of the imperial presidency was gradual. . . . The seeds of the imperial presidency were sown early. Schlesinger cites as examples Abraham Lincoln's 1861 imposition of martial law and his suspension of habeas corpus, and William McKinley's decision to send 5,000 American troops to China to help suppress the Boxer Rebellion of 1900. It is a measure of how much things have changed

that Theodore Roosevelt's 1907 decision to dispatch America's Great White Fleet on a tour around the world was controversial because he failed to seek congressional approval.[47] Then came Woodrow Wilson's forays into revolutionary Mexico, FDR's unilateral declaration of an "unlimited national emergency" six months after Pearl Harbor, and Harry Truman's commitment of U.S. troops to the Korean War in 1950, without congressional authorization, and his 1952 seizure of strike-threatened steel mills.[48]

For some purveyors of these ideas, the very existence of an imperial presidency is based on structural relationships, while others are more concerned with the devilish acts of a single social agent. Politicians of all different stripes have been caricatured as being imperial, and presidents as different as Ronald Reagan and William Clinton have occasionally been accused of being pretenders to the throne.[49]

If we go all the way back to the time of the Founders, we should not be too surprised when we find that they too were divided on questions involving the nature and scope of presidential authority. Elbridge Gerry, for example, once noted that he "never expected to hear in a republic a motion to empower the executive alone to declare war."[50] In 1789, Thomas Jefferson would note that "we have already given . . . one effective check to the Dog of war by transferring the power of letting him loose from the Executive to the Legislative body, from those who are to spend to those who are to pay."[51] Pragmatic writers, like James Madison in *The Federalist* 51, wanted to have "separate and distinct" powers of government that would each have the "necessary constitutional means and personal motives to resist" personal aggrandizement. Within this Newtonian world, human ambitions in each of the branches would "counteract" the ambitions of others.[52] After surveying these types of remarks, Beschloss concluded: "The founders never intended to have an imperial president. Always worried about tyranny, they drafted a Constitution that gives a president limited authority and forces him to use his political skills to fight for influence as he squeezes laws out of Congress and prods the American people to think in new ways."[53]

If this is the case, have we really inherited a constitutional system of government that is capable of controlling the aspirations of chief executives, especially during times of war? The same constitutional text that Beschloss was talking about also includes clauses that permit "unilateral presidential action to repel a sudden attack or to rescue Americans held abroad."[54] The polysemic and polyvalent nature of these constitutional clauses means that defenders of both constitutional presidents and imperial presidents have little trouble finding legal support for their positions.

Since the 1973 publication of Schlesinger's seminal work, interested parties have debated the descriptive accuracy of the term *imperial presidency* as a way of defining the political style of individual presidents, and they have interrogated the prescriptive standards associated with that phrase.[55] Following the passage of the War Powers Act and similar congressional measures, some observers in the 1980s and 1990s commented on the protean nature of "imperial presidency," while more optimistic critics pointed to the constraining aspects of growing congressional influence. Thomas Cronin would admit in 1980 that the ranks of "defenders of presidential government may have been temporarily thinned in 1973 and 1974"—but he was sure that there were plenty of other social agents ready to pick up the gauntlet: "As several analysts have observed, the Right worries about the imperial presidency at home and the Left worries about the imperial presidency abroad. What is not pointed out is that the Right doubtlessly wants a near-imperial Teddy Roosevelt kind of presidency abroad and the Left often wants something approaching an imperial, super-planning presidency at home . . . . Fears of another Watergate presidency seemed to disappear."[56] For critics who shared Cronin's views, it perhaps seemed as though some of the Founders may have been onto something when they structured a constitution around the idea of counterpoise, the balancing of human ambitions.

Yet if we believe in the heuristic value of the term *imperial presidency*, we need a more developed conceptual framework for our rhetorical analyses. As we survey the extant literature on the scholarly significance of the term, it seems as though we know we are in the presence of this imperial presidency when:

- the chief executive is said to be taking advantage of the demands of an emergency or the pretext of an emergency
- the American president, and not Congress, controls the *administrative* apportionment of monies and the powers of the purse
- the U.S. Supreme Court and other branches of the American judiciary are constantly deferring to the decisions of the president
- the press and the members of the public constantly recirculate many of the same public arguments and legal precedents that are used by the president and his supporters
- the alleged wrongdoing in cases like this involves either the "usurpation" or "abuse" of power; usurpation is when you temporarily use extensive power during wartime, while abuse is the systematic use of power during wartime and peacetime, often in situations where someone is "claiming a near absolute power" involving the "permanent prerogative of the presidency"[57]

- we witness congressional abdication of responsibility at the same time that we see a lack of presidential accountability

Are these apt descriptions of the way that we think about our commander in chief's constitutional powers in our post-9/11 world? In the next section I explore some of the implicit and explicit claims about executive discretionary power that appear in Bush's Military Order of November 13, 2001. I supplement this analysis with some examples of how other observers view this important text.

DECODING THE BUSH MILITARY ORDER

The Bush Military Order provides us with an example of what Vivian Grosswald Curran has called a "palimpsest," a layered parchment filled with evocative layers of meaning, complete with pasts that have "never been erased completely"—remaining "below the surface" and seeping up as new generations appropriate them for their own needs.[58] It begins by outlining the national exigency, where members of Al Qaeda, and other international terrorists, carried out attacks on the United States. The U.S. president is said to have responded by declaring a national emergency (September 14, 2001).[59]

The tenor of the document is defensive, and after touching on the massive deaths, injuries, and destruction of property. The authors of the order then proceed to explain just why military commissions are the appropriate forums for the trial of this type of enemy. This portion of the document provides a series of rationales that underscore the importance of having these tribunals:

(e) To Protect the United States and its citizens, and for the effective conduct of military operations and prevention of terrorist acts, it is necessary for individuals subject to this order pursuant to section 2 hereof to be detained, and, when tried, to be tried for violations of the laws of war and other applicable laws by military tribunals.

(f) Given the danger to the safety of the United States and the nature of international terrorism, and to the extent provided by and under this order, I find consistent with section 836 of title 10, United States Code, that it is not practicable to apply in military commissions under this order the principles of law and the rules of evidence generally recognized in the trial of criminal cases in the United States district courts.

(g) Having fully considered the magnitude of the potential deaths, injuries and property destruction that would result from potential acts of terrorism against the United States, and the probability that such acts will occur, I have determined that an extraordinary emergency exists for national defense purposes, that this emergency constitutes an urgent and compelling government interest, and that issuance of this order is necessary to meet the emergency.[60]

Robin Blackburn has noted that this type of artifact allows Bush to "decide who is the enemy," and that the "indefinite extension of his special powers" restores "an imperial potency to the presidency equal to—or even exceeding—that of the Reagan era."[61] Just days after the circulation of the order, the president told the American public that "I would remind those who don't understand the decision I made that Franklin Roosevelt made the same decision in World War II. Those were extraordinary times as well."[62] Alberto Gonzales, a leading presidential adviser, placed Bush in a long line of other presidents who used their executive powers in the trial of enemy "belligerents" who commit war crimes.[63] Any suspicious person who had ties to the terrorists could be detained and tried before one of these American military commissions.[64]

Katyal and Tribe articulated their belief that the order "installs the executive branch as lawgiver as well as law-enforcer, law-interpreter, and law-applier."[65] Defenders of the Bush Administration responded by noting that these "unlawful belligerents" had "pursued their deadly purpose in a training camp in Afghanistan or a flight school in Florida"—they had "cast their lot by waging war against the United States" and therefore "are properly judged by the laws of war."[66] Attorney General John Ashcroft followed the *Quirin* line of legal reasoning when he intoned: "Can you imagine the situations of apprehending or taking a soldier, terrorist, foreign prisoner in Afghanistan and having a circus atmosphere in a televised trial that might send signals to other terrorists around the world? The President should have a right to try alien war criminals in the military commission. It's something that's happened in previous settings, Franklin Roosevelt did it. This President has issued an order which makes it open, not secret, like the Roosevelt order."[67] If elite lawyers or politicians did not like these types of orders, then the "civil rights lobby" needed to remember that the majority of Americans had "no problem with bringing terrorists before military tribunals."[68]

When congressional witnesses and leaders reviewed the order, they expressed some mixed feelings about the legality of these particular tribunals. On the one hand, they acknowledged that "history" seemed to show that former presidents—including Democrats—had had no qualms about using military tribunals. They realized that there were many historic instances when Congress or the Supreme Court approved the use of these forums. Yet on the other hand, skeptical witnesses and congressional leaders were bothered by the evidentiary standards of the tribunals, the vagueness of the term *combatant*, and the attitude of the Bush administrators. Professor Philip Heymann lamented the fact that these tribunals could convict "without even the evidence that a jury of angry, patriotic Americans would demand."[69] Millions of citizens and noncitizens might lose the protections that were afforded by the Geneva Convention.

This was obviously not the position of President Bush or his supporters. In the next segment I look at how various defenders of these tribunals remembered (or forgot) about some rhetorics surrounding the *Ex parte Quirin* and *Ex parte Milligan* cases.

Defending the Bush Military Order and Remembering Key Tribunal Decisions

At the end of the Civil War, the Supreme Court was asked to try the case of one Lambdin P. Milligan, an Indiana citizen who had been tried before a Union military tribunal. Milligan was viewed as a dangerous southern sympathizer, a conspirator who did not deserve the privilege of having habeas corpus rights, but a majority of the U.S. Supreme Court ruled in Milligan's favor. The court reasoned that Congress had not authorized the military commissions in Indiana. Moreover, the local civilian courts were open and they had jurisdiction.[70] For those who want to take away formal legal principles from this case, military tribunals were supposed to be forums that would appear only in situations when martial law had been declared, when exigencies on the battlefield had spilled over and contributed to the closing of civilian courts.

Throughout the rest of the nineteenth century and the twentieth, critics of the 1866 *Milligan* decision argued that this was an idealistic and archaic decision, out of step with the realities of warfare and executive decision making. When defenders of the Bush Military Order looked back through the mists of time, they did want to material to support their decision, but Milligan was rarely in their sights. Instead, they focused attention on President Abraham Lincoln's words and deeds.[71]

Several observers have noted that the post–Civil War *Milligan* case might have been decided differently if the justices had been faced with wartime exigencies. For example, in 1998 Chief Justice Rehnquist opined that "*Quirin*, decided during the darkest days of World War II, actually cut down on some of the extravagant dicta favorable to civil liberty in *Milligan*."[72] Years later, military lawyers still find themselves in the middle of these debates about Bush's special tribunals, with some arguing that they need to resemble court-martial proceedings and others willing to defer to the powers of the command in chief. Jonathan Landay, Marisa Taylor, and Margaret Talev may be right when they argue that the Supreme Court has ruled that the administration "can't use ad-hoc military commissions to try suspected terrorists," but very few were willing to question the legitimacy of Bush's initial executive order.[73] Members of the Bush Administration are still writing proposed bills filled with defense of "special" tribunals with language that "seems to be trying to surgically remove from our compliance with Geneva the section of Common Article 3 that deals with humiliating and degrading treatment."[74]

THE IMPERIAL PRESIDENCY AND THE SYMBOLIC IMPORTANCE OF MILITARY TRIBUNALS

Dante Chinni has insightfully observed that the "bottom line is" that the "president is as imperial as the Congress, the press, and the public allows him to be," and I have posited that perhaps we have a new type of chief executive because we have asked for one.[75] The events of 9/11 may have transformed a relatively unknown son of a former president into an epic leader in his own right. Only time will tell whether scholars will remember him as a Cromwellian figure or a model of civic virtue who understood the importance of balancing civil liberties with national necessities. Is it not ironic that Michael Beschloss argued in 2000 that George W. Bush's inauguration spelled the "end" of the imperial presidency?[76]

In responding to those who believe that the notion of an imperial presidency is at an end, or that it is simply a "myth," I would suggest that vigilant critics and citizens need to focus on the full array of the new powers that have appeared on the horizon since 9/11. Bush administrators' defense of "unitary" executive powers have been used to justify the unilateral declaration of war, the invasions of Afghanistan and Iraq, the detention of suspected terrorists or their supporters, the warrantless surveillance of domestic and international communication, more stringent immigration regulation, the rendition of prisoners, the use of coercive interrogation, and the establishment of "special" tribunals.

In this chapter I have tried to tackle just one part of this spectrum of power, the debates surrounding the desirability and constitutionality of military tribunals. I have implied that in many ways the supposed 2001 "debate" over the legality of the Bush Military Order establishing military tribunals was a truncated one, because there were few participants who tried to alter the overarching framework that was used in these discussions. Bush administrators were able to maintain the dominance of a rhetorical edifice that highlighted the military nature of the events of 9/11, and they came with multiple rationalizations that explained why Congress needed to defer to the president on a number of matters, including the formation and composition of the military tribunals. We had little commentary on the potential problematics of military tribunals or the need for multinational, international solutions in dealing with the trial of belligerents. There were few detailed commentaries on prior criticisms of these tribunals, and many participants used labels that treated potential defendants as "terrorists" who had already had their day in court.

Sadly, even in those rare situations when congressional leaders did try to look at some of the legal histories behind the formation of some of these military tribunals (*Milligan, Yamashita, Quirin,* etc.), they often left us with transcripts filled with tiny summaries of some very complex legal cases. For example, when Senator Leahy tried to talk about J. Edgar Hoover's mistakes in the *Ex parte Quirin* case (the fact that much of the evidence in the case came from "two of the saboteurs" and the cover-up that was involved), he was cut off by colleagues who admonished him to remember that three hours had already passed.[77]

When decision makers and scholars are asked to choose between the *Ex parte Quirin* and *Ex parte Milligan* precedents—or Tory or Whig frameworks—they are receiving invitations that might lock them into some polarizing rhetorical frameworks that already assume the legitimacy of military solutions or the privileging of executive war powers. One no longer debates the question of whether we need military tribunals—by 2006 most of the issues focus on queries debating the relative merits of congressional plans for tribunals that look like courts-martial versus the most austere "special" tribunal proposals of the commander in chief. Instead of having any detailed analyses of the costs and benefits of particular executive orders, this binary framework hides the potential role of compromise and negotiation and prevents us from thinking about potential civilian solutions (domestic or international) to these detention and trial problems. If we are going to learn anything from our revisiting of cases like *Ex parte Milligan* or *Quirin*, it can only come from appreciating the broad range of selective arguments that were circulating by many communities within both the legal and public forums of the times. Instead of complaining about the misinterpretation of a particular

Supreme Court precedent (Whig or Tory), we need to focus our energies on assessing the costs and benefits of unilateral decision making, the nature and scope of twenty-first century rights during times of declared and undeclared wars, and the desirability of having an imperial president.

We need to be wary of rhetorics that are circulated in the name of symbolic "security," that provide leaders with unnecessary powers. Why should we support policies that are based on Bush's military tribunal order, that are used to create "special" trials that cover "war crimes" of defendants who cannot be treated as prisoners of war? Do we really want the institutionalization of a military system of justice where the president gets to decide who is deemed an enemy combatant, where the president gets to appoint the judges and jurors who set up the tribunal, where the president oversees the selection of the procedures, and where the president gets to review the verdict?[78] What adds to the tragedy of this situation is the realization that going through one of these military trials may at least give some respite to those detainees who have been held in indefinite detention for the length of a seemingly never-ending war.

Given the fact that the Supreme Court in *Hamdan* focused on the importance of respecting the Geneva Convention, one might wonder why we have so casually dismissed the idea of trying these detainees as war criminals in international tribunals. After all, if these "enemy combatants" have committed atrocities that are on par with the Pearl Harbor bombings, then why are we not willing to provide the type of evidence in a court of law that could be reviewed by audiences around the world? Are we really attached to the symbolic weight that comes from conducting American trials, with American rules, on American land (well, Guantánamo may be a stretch)? Diane F. Orentlicher and Robert Goldman have left us with these insightful comments:

> When active duty military officers assume the role of judges, they remain subordinate to their superiors in keeping with the established military hierarchy. The manner by which they fulfill their assigned task might well play a role in their future promotions, assignments, and professional rewards. It is because of this inherent dependence that these tribunals are not suited to try civilians. . . . Similar considerations have led the Inter-American Commission and Court of Human Rights, as well as the U.N. Human Rights Committee, to find that the use of military courts to try civilians in Guatemala, Peru, Chile, Uruguay, and elsewhere violated fundamental due process rights. Moreover, no human rights supervisory body has yet found the exigencies of a genuine emergency situation, such as that now

faced by the U.S., to justify suspending basic fair trial safeguards on a temporary basis.[79]

As Louis Fisher explains, we seem to be a nation that has lost our "constitutional moorings," a divided community that focuses on the importance of "American exceptionalism," a place that keeps drafting "muscular versions of foreign and military policy."[80]

As critics look back through the mists of time and the fog of an undeclared war, they may find ample justification for providing broad presidential powers and executive authority during necessitous times, but this does not mean that the simple declaration of war should translate into the closing off of civil jurisdiction in all cases. Does the existence of stock market dislocations, psychological fear of flying, or the existence of random terrorism mean that World War II provides the best legal precedents? Should we automatically accept some of the links that are being made between the dangers associated with September 11 and the need for military tribunals? Do we want legal edicts that confuse the "role of legislator, policeman [sic], prosecutor, judge, and court" of appeal?[81]

That being said, I do not want to give readers the impression that some of the public and legal debates that took place in the fall of 2001 reviewing Bush's Military Order did not accomplish some key public tasks, or that Bush's imperial presidency took away all social agency on the part of decision makers. While I am troubled by the easy passage of the Patriot Act, and the weak interrogation of the Bush Military Order, I do see some hopeful signs of modifications and negotiations that have transpired in the last several years. For example, let us at least give some of our media members and congressional leaders some credit for providing the forum for talking about the success or failure of the civil trials in cases like the 1993 World Trade Center attack or the 1998 embassy bombings trials. Moderate critics could remind Americans about the arguments that were made about open courts in *Ex parte Milligan*. Congressional leaders also encouraged us to think about the relative power of the executive, legislative, and judicial branches of government. While they still did a great deal of genuflection in the direction of broad executive powers, these types of debates also served as catalyzing moments that forced attention upon the rules that would govern any future use of military tribunals.

In the larger scheme of things, however, this is not enough. Some critics have argued that there are strategic reasons behind the recent congressional deference to the American president. Henrickson, for example, contends that for Congress "it is much easier to play a secondary role in war powers by waiting to judge the public's response to the use of force, rather than exercising the constitutional powers the founding fathers bestowed upon it."[82] This type of waiting game, based on an assessment of public will, does nothing but domesticate the power of our legislative branches. "To the extent that Congress does not push back and the public does not protest," argues Wolfensberger, "the armor of the imperial presidency is further fortified by precedent and popular support against future attacks."[83]

In the years ahead, how we remember the rhetoric surrounding these congressional debates—from many different sides—will tell us a great deal about how we ourselves are going to draw the line between state necessities and civil liberties. When we see the recirculation of the claims that were deployed during World War II, we can see how some familiar patterns of argumentation are being appropriated or domesticated to justify some extremely contentious claims. As critics and laypersons, we need to be aware of what is being said and left unsaid in the new tales that we are hearing about Bush's Military Order. In one of the most concise and moving commentaries on our present dilemma, Katyal noted:

> The issues raised by the Military Order concern not only today, but tomorrow. You can already hear how our treatment of the Nazi saboteurs in 1942 has become the guidepost for our treatment of individuals today. What will the present course of conduct mean for situations down the road? Once the President's power to set up military tribunals is untethered to the locality of war or explicit Congressional authorization, and given to the President by dint in the office he holds, there is nothing to stop future Presidents from using these tribunals in all sorts of ways. In this respect, it is important to underscore that the precedent the Bush administration seeks to revitalize, the Nazi saboteur case of *Ex parte Quirin*, 317 U.S. 1, 20, 37–38 (1942), explicitly goes so far as to permit military tribunals to be used against American citizens. We must be extraordinarily careful when revitalizing an old and troubling court decision, for doing so will set new precedent for future Presidents that can come back to haunt citizens and aliens alike.[84]

If Schlesinger is right when he argues that "history has shown the presidency to be the most effective instrumentality for justice and progress," then perhaps now is the time to ask that he give back some of his power.[85] Better yet, let us try to make sure that we have a constitutional and not imperial president in the first place.[86]

NOTES

1. For a summary of this expansive view of the military powers of the American chief executive, see the remarks of Neal K. Katyal and Laurence H. Tribe in "Waging War, Deciding Guilt: Trying the Military Tribunals," *Yale Law Journal* 111 (April 2002): 1290:

> Indeed, if the UCMJ were stretched to give the President the power to create tribunals purportedly authorized by this Order, then it would risk making the statute an unconstitutional delegation of power. Such an interpretation would leave the President free to define a "time of war," grant him the discretion to set up a military tribunal at will, bestow upon him the power to prosecute whomever he selects in a military tribunal, vest him with the authority to label something an offense and to try an offender for it, give him the power to try those cases before military judges that serve as part of the executive branch, and perhaps even empower him to dispense with habeas corpus review by an Article III court.

The chapter epigraph is from Chalmers Johnson, "Where Will America Stand in the World?" *In These Times,* December 13, 2004, paragraph 5, http://web.lexis-nexis.com/universe (January 8, 2005).

2. *Ex parte Quirin,* 317 U.S. 1 (1942). For an insightful discussion of how some presidents and military leaders have exercised their judicial powers, see Michal R. Belknap, "Alarm Bells from the Past: The Troubled History of American Military Commissions," *Journal of Supreme Court History* 28 (2003): 300–22.

3. This is the line that follows the *Milligan* precedent of having civilian oversight of military affairs. *Ex parte Milligan,* 71. U.S. 2 (1866).

4. For a modern echo of this ancient idea, see the words of Senator Abraham Ribicoff: "Reliance on emergency authority, intended for use in crisis situations would no longer be available in non-crisis situations. At a time when governments throughout the world are turning with increasing desperation to an all-power executive, this legislation is designed to insure that the United States travels a road marked by carefully constructed legal safeguards." Senator Abraham Ribicoff, quoted in Thomas E. Cronin, "A Resurgent Congress and the Imperial Presidency," *Political Science Quarterly* 95 (1980): 218.

5. For some recent examples of press commentaries that discuss the "imperial" nature of the Bush presidency, see Townsend Hoopes, "A Personal Tone in View of Our Dark Age," *Los Angeles Times,* September 10, 2004, http://web.lexis-nexis.com/universe (December 20, 2004); Michael D. Langan, "Assessing an 'Arrogant' Presidency," *Boston Globe,* September 5, 2004, http://web.lexis-nexis.com/universe (December 20, 2004).

6. The Patriot Act is properly called *United and Strengthening America by Providing Appropriate Tools Required to Intercept and Obstruct Terrorism* Act of 2001, Public Law, 107–56, 107th Cong., 1st sess. (October 2001).

7. *Military Order—Detention, Treatment, and Trial of Certain Non-Citizens in the War Against Terrorism,* 66 Fed. Reg. 57833 (November 16, 2001), Part IV. A copy of this also appears in *Weekly Compilation of Presidential Documents* 47 (November 13, 2001): 1665–68. Sara Fritz explains how "everyone except the most devoted civil libertarians" were "happy about Bush's actions until he decreed, without consulting Congress, that non-citizens suspected of terrorism would be tried by military tribunals, not in the federal courts." "Unchecked Power Can Be Dangerous," *St. Petersburg Times,* November 26, 2001, paragraph 9, http://proquest.umi.com.

8. George F. Will, "Devil's Island! Guillotines!" *Newsweek* 138 (December 10, 2001): 84. Note, for example, Craig Gilbert, "With Anxious Nation Facing a New Enemy," *Milwaukee Journal Sentinel,* October 21, 2001, A1.

9. Quotes are from "The Imperial Presidency," *Nation,* September 16, 2002, paragraph 5, http://web.lexis-nexis.com (December 4, 2004).

10. Josh Tyrangiel, "And Justice for All," *Time,* November 26, 2001, 66.

11. Michael Beschloss, quoted in Donald R. Wolfensberger, "The Return of the Imperial Presidency?" *Wilson Quarterly* 26 (2002): 36.

12. Robin Blackburn, "The Imperial Presidency, the War on Terrorism, and the Revolutions of Modernity," *Constellations* 9 (2002): 5–6.

13. Cronin, "A Resurgent," 209.

14. Wolfensberger, "The Return," paragraphs 2–3.

15. See Arthur M. Schlesinger, Jr., *The Imperial Presidency* (Boston: Houghton Mifflin, 1973). For some very general discussions of the political valences that are associated with the notion of an "imperial presidency," see Alan Theoharis and Athan G. Theoharis, *Truman Presidency: The Origins of the Imperial Presidency and the National Security State* (Stanfordville, N.Y.: Earl M. Coleman Enterprises, 1979); Vincent Davis, *The Post-Imperial Presidency* (New Brunswick, N.J.: Praeger, 1980); Christopher N. May, *Presidential Defiance of "Unconstitutional" Laws: Reviving the Royal Prerogative* (Westport, Conn.: Greenwood Press, 1998); Wesley T. Wooley, "Cold-War Afterthoughts: Morality, the Arms Race, and the Imperial Presidency," *Canadian Journal of History* 29 (1994): 550–60.

16. Richard S. Kirkendall, "Book Review: *The Imperial Presidency,*" *American Historical Review* 80 (1975): 529.

17. For Arthur Schlesinger's own commentaries on some of the actions of the Bush Administration, see Arthur S. Schlesinger Jr., "The Imperial Presidency Redux," *Washington Post,* June 28, 2003, A25.

18. Sam Tanenhaus, "The Myth of the Imperial Presidency," *Wall Street Journal,* European issue, December 27, 2002, paragraphs 2, 11, http:proquest.umi.com (December 4, 2004).

19. For an exception to this rule, see the work of Andrew Rudalevige, who understands the cyclical nature of some of these arguments. Andrew Rudalevige, "The Contemporary Presidency: The Decline and Resurgence and Decline (and Resurgence?) of Congress: Charting a New Imperial Presidency," *Presidential Studies Quarterly* 36 (2006): 506–23.

20. Quotes are from Ryan C. Henrickson, "American War Powers and Terrorists: The Case of Usama Bin Laden," *Studies in Conflict and Terrorism* 23 (2000): 161–74. It should be noted that even in section 2c of the War Powers Act, Congress allowed for the commander-in-chief to use force in "a national emergency created by attack upon the United States, its territories, or possessions, or its armed forces." *War Powers Act,* Public Law 93148 (November 7, 1973). For an insightful overview of presidential power in American politics, see Louis Fisher, *Presidential War Power* (Lawrence: University Press of Kansas, 1995).

For analyses of President Johnson's actions during the Vietnam years, see Richard A. Cherwitz, "Lyndon Johnson and the 'Crisis' of Tonkin Gulf: A President's Justification of War," *Western Journal of Speech Communication* 42 (1979): 93–104; Cal M. Logue and John H. Patton, "From Ambiguity to Dogma: The Rhetorical Symbols of Lyndon B. Johnson on Vietnam," *Southern Speech Communication Journal* 47 (1982): 310–29; John M. Murphy, "Crafting the Kennedy Legacy," *Rhetoric and Public Affairs* 3 (2000): 577–601.

21. On Grenada see Arthur M. Schlesinger, "The Imperial Temptation: Reagan Presidency Succumbs," *New Republic* 196 (March 16, 1987): 17. On the former Yugoslavia see William C. Banks and Jeffrey D. Straussman, "A New Imperial Presidency? Insights from U.S. Involvement in Bosnia," *Political Science Quarterly* 114 (1999): 195–217; Franz Schurmann, "Bill Clinton's Imperial Presidency," *San Francisco Examiner,* December 20, 1998, C19. For a very different take on the extent of Clinton's power, see Arthur Schlesinger Jr., "So Much for the Imperial Presidency," *New York Times,* August 3, 1998, A19. On air strikes—in late August, President Clinton authorized the launching of dozens of Tomahawk missiles on Bin Laden's positions in Afghanistan and the Sudan. These were viewed as retaliatory measures that were taken weeks after the bombing of embassies in Kenya and Tanzania. As Henrickson explains, these actions were very popular in America, where polls showed that more than 70 percent of the public approved of the strikes ("American War Powers," 169).

Arthur M. Schlesinger Jr. has also recently acknowledged that he may have underestimated the global reach of America's chief executive. In one of his recent books, he argues that the Bush Administration's contention that "enemy combatants" do not deserve habeas corpus rights is a modern illustration of the attitudes associated with an imperial presidency. Arthur M. Schlesinger Jr., *War and the American Presidency* (New York: Norton, 2004). Operating from within a related critical framework, see Robert C. Byrd, *Losing America: Confronting a Reckless and Arrogant Presidency* (New York: Norton, 2004).

22. One pollster told the *St. Petersburg Times* that "people just don't want terrorists to take advantage of a legal system that already bends over backwards too much for defendants." Andrew Kohut, quoted in Philip Gailey, "Perspective on Security vs. Liberties," *St. Petersburg Times,* December 16, 2001, paragraph 6, http://web.lexis-nexis.com/universe (December 4, 2004).

23. For an interesting interpretation of the symbolic impact of the Nuremberg trials, see Ann Tusa and John Tusa, *The Nuremberg Trial* (New York: Atheneum, 1986), 475–92. I develop in much more detail the idea that Anglo Americans have inherited both Whig and Tory legal ideologies as they debate about executive power in Marouf Hasian Jr., *In the Name of Necessity: Military Tribunals and the Loss of American Civil Liberties* (Tuscaloosa: University of Alabama Press, 2005).

24. See, for example, John Yoo, *The Powers of War and Peace: The Constitution and Foreign Affairs after 9/11* (Chicago: University of Chicago Press, 2005).

25. "The Imperial Presidency at Work," *New York Times,* January 15, 2006 paragraph 4, http://web.lexis.nexis.com (January 19, 2006).

26. Kenneth Anderson, "Nuremberg Sensibility: Telford Taylor's Memoir of the Nuremberg Trials," *Harvard Human Rights Journal* 7 (1994): 288.

27. "Winging It at Guantanamo" (editorial), *New York Times,* April 23, 2002, A22.

28. *Hamdan v. Rumsfeld,* 548 U.S. ___, 126 S. Ct. 2749 (2006).

29. Harvey Silvergate, "Court Says No to an Imperial Presidency," *Los Angeles Times,* June 30, 2006, http://web.lexis.com (July 15, 2006).

30. President Bush, "Text of President Bush's State of the Union Address to Congress," *New York Times,* January 30, 2002, A22, quoted in Katyal and Tribe, "Waging War," 1276.

31. Charles Evans Hughes, "War Powers under the Constitution," *American Bar Association Reports* 42 (1917): 238.

32. Michael Chertoff (Chertoff testimony), *Review of Military Terrorism Tribunals: Hearings before the Senate Judiciary Committee,* 107th Cong., 1st sess., November 28,

2001, paragraph 30, *Federal Document Clearing House,* http://web.lexis.nexis.com/congcom (July 9, 2004).

33. For an engaging defense of Israel's actions during the capture and trial of Eichmann, see Jacob Robinson, *And the Crooked Shall Be Made Straight: A New Look at the Eichmann Trial* (New York: Macmillan, 1965). For an excellent overview of the influence that the Nuremberg trials have had on modern war crimes tribunals, see Gary Jonathan Bass, *Stay the Hand of Vengeance: The Politics of War Crimes Tribunals* (Princeton: Princeton University Press, 2000).

34. Belknap, "Alarm Bells," 304.

35. William P. Barr (Barr testimony), *Review of Military Terrorism Tribunals: Hearings before the Senate Judiciary Committee,* 107th Cong., 1st sess., November 28, 2001, paragraph 1, Federal Document Clearing House, http://web.lexis.nexis.com/congcom (July 9, 2004). Like many other conservatives, Barr worried about how "artificial restrictions on our powers of self defense" were being created by those who were "gratuitously expanding constitutional guarantees beyond their intended office." Barr testimony, *Review,* paragraph 27. Here I should observe that the social act of designating true "liberties" or real "necessities" is itself a rhetorical enterprise. James Randall would note in 1945 that "one should treat military necessity not as an unanswerable formula but as having a degree of truth if properly interpreted while having a large degree of discredit if abused or wrongly interpreted." James G. Randall, "Civil and Military Relations under Lincoln," *Pennsylvania Magazine of History and Biography* 69 (July 1945): 200.

36. Here my discussion of ideographs is obviously building on the work of Michael Calvin McGee and some of his students. See, for example, Celeste M. Condit and John L. Lucaites, *Crafting Equality: America's Anglo-African Word* (Chicago: University of Chicago Press, 1993).

37. For more on the *Yamashita* case, see *In re Yamashita,* 327 U.S. 1 (1946); Bruce D. Landrum, "The Yamashita War Crimes Trial: Command Responsibility Then and Now," *Military Law Review* 149 (1995): 293–301; Adolf Frank Reel, *The Case of General Yamashita* (Chicago: University of Chicago Press, 1949); Belknap, "Alarm Bells," 304.

38. For a more detailed discussion of the *Quirin* precedent, see Marouf Hasian Jr., "Franklin D. Roosevelt, Wartime Anxieties, and the Saboteurs' Case," *Rhetoric and Public Affairs* 6 (2003): 233–60.

39. For an excellent discussion of congressional reluctance to take on some national responsibilities, see John Hart Ely, *War and Responsibility: Congressional Lessons of Vietnam and Its Aftermath* (Princeton, N.J.: Princeton University Press, 1993). Banks and Straussman contend that since the time of Truman's troop deployments to Korea, "Congress has demonstrated that it prefers not to take the risk of authorizing or forbidding risky national security ventures. If the president leads, Congress may remain silent and permit the president to act for the nation ("New Imperial Presidency," 199). For more on Truman's powers as president, see Richard S. Kirkendall, *Harry S. Truman, Korea, and the Imperial Presidency* (Saint Charles, Mo.: Forum Press, 1975).

40. See, for example, the time that was spent writing and talking about "jurisdiction" in the *Padilla* case. *Donald H. Rumsfeld v. Jose Padilla and Donna R. Newman, Oral Argument before the Supreme Court of the United States* (Washington, D.C.: Alderson Reporting, 2004).

41. George Will explains that "Emperor Nixon" was once "so roundly ridiculed for

dressing White House guards in Ruritanian uniforms that the uniforms quickly disappeared" ("Devil's Island," paragraph 5). I would like to thank Malcolm Sillars for this reminder of Nixon's imperial designs.

42. Rudalevige, "The Contemporary," 521.

43. "Military Tribunal Plan Fails U.S. Standards of Justice," *Chicago Sun Times*, September 11, 2006, http://web.lexis.nexis.com (September 24, 2006).

44. Some polls indicate that 53 percent of those questioned in December of 2001 about the use of secret military tribunals in place of regular courts of law felt that they would rather have suspected terrorists tried in military tribunals. See "If Suspected Terrorists Are Captured," *Public Opinion Online*, Roper Center at University of Connecticut, January 2002, http://web.lexis.com/universe (April 17, 2002).

45. Katyal and Tribe, "Waging War," 1310.

46. Neal Katyal, quoted in Jonathan S. Landay, Marisa Taylor, and Margaret Talev, "Ruling Rattles Bush Strategy," *Seattle Times*, July 1, 2006, paragraph 7, http://seattletimes.nwsource.com

47. For public commentary on Theodore Roosevelt's imperial presidency, see Tom Blackburn, "Our First Imperial Presidency," *Palm Beach Post*, January 12, 2003, http://web.lexis-nexis.com/universe (December 4, 2004).

48. Wolfensberger, "The Return," paragraph. 8.

49. For a much developed discussion of the history of presidents who have been accused of acting in imperial ways, see Andrew Rudalevige, *The New Presidency: Renewing Presidential Power after Watergate* (Ann Arbor: University of Michigan Press, 2006).

50. Elbridge Gerry from Massachusetts, quoted in James Madison, *Notes of Debates in the Federal Convention of 1787* (New York: Norton, 1987), 476; Henrickson, "American War Powers," 163.

51. Thomas Jefferson, quoted in P. Ford, ed., *The Writings of Thomas Jefferson* (New York: G. P. Putnam's Sons, 1895), 123; Banks and Straussman, "New Imperial Presidency," 196.

52. Madison, quoted in Wolfensberger, "The Return," paragraph 30.

53. Beschloss, "The End of the Imperial," paragraph 3.

54. Banks and Straussman, "New Imperial Presidency," 199.

55. For an example of this focus on presidential style, see the remarks of historian Warren Goldstein: "Americans are so devoted to what Arthur Schlesinger, Jr. once called 'the imperial presidency' that we find it hard to admire any other kind. But most of our strong' presidents have rewarded our trust with imperial swashbuckling (overt and covert) and media grandstanding. Distracted by their personalities, we have expended an inordinate effort analyzing the men instead of paying attention to their policies." Warren Goldstein, "A Strong Case for Weak Presidents," *Newsday*, February 12, 1999, paragraph 4, http://proquest.umi.com.

56. Cronin, "A Resurgent," 230.

57. Cronin, "A Resurgent," 211.

58. Vivian Grosswald Curran, "Competing Frameworks for Assessing Contemporary Holocaust Era Claims," *Fordham International Law Journal* 25 (2001): 110.

59. President George Bush, Proclamation 7463, *Declaration of National Emergency by Reason of Certain Terrorist Attacks*, September 14, 2001, http://www.whitehouse.gov/news/releases/2001/09/2001914-4.html (July 8, 2004).

60. *Detention, Treatment, and Trial of Certain Non-Citizens in the War against Terrorism,* Part IV, 66 Fed. Reg., 57833–34 (2001).

61. Blackburn, "The Imperial," 7.

62. Mike Allen, "Bush Defends Order for Military Tribunals, *Washington Post,* November 20, 2001, A14.

63. Alberto R. Gonzales, "Martial Justice, Full and Fair," *New York Times,* November 30, 2001, A27.

64. In theory this could impact the lives of millions of residents, but there were some officials who argued that the Military Order was really passed in order to prepare for the trial of only a few key people. See Barr testimony, *Review.*

65. Katyal and Tribe, "Waging War," 1265.

66. Barr testimony, *Review* paragraph 1.

67. John Ashcroft, quoted in "Leading the News," *Bulletin's Frontrunner,* November 20, 2001, http://web.lexis-neis.co/congcomp (July 8, 2004).

68. Gailey, "Perspective," D1.

69. Philip B. Heymann (Heymann testimony), *Review of Military Terrorism Tribunals: Hearings before the Senate Judiciary Committee,* 107th Cong., 1st sess., November 28, 2001, paragraph 6, *Federal Document Clearing House,* http://web.lexis.nexis.com/congcom (July 9, 2004).

70. Louise Fisher, *Nazi Saboteurs on Trial: A Military Tribunal and American Law* (Lawrence: University Press of Kansas, 2003), 44–45.

71. This attack on the *Milligan* decision was nothing new. For an overview of the relevance and irrelevance of the *Milligan* opinion for the Lincoln Administration, see Mark E. Neely Jr., *The Fate of Liberty: Abraham Lincoln and Civil Liberties* (New York: Oxford University Press, 1991). An analysis of public newspaper discussion of *Milligan* is ably presented in Joseph G. Gambone, "*Ex parte Milligan:* The Restoration of Judicial Prestige?" *Civil War History* 16 (September 1970): 246–59. By 1991, Adrian Cook could write that the once "sacred cow" of *Milligan* had been "unceremoniously butchered." Cook explained that the Civil War commissions, the Reconstruction incidents, the World War II cases, and the Red Scare all showed that "*Milligan* was only praised in times of peace: it could not withstand the fierce emotions generated by World War II and was swept away by *Korematsu v. United States* in 1944." Adrian Cook, "Book Review: The Fate of Liberty," *Journal of American History* 78 (December 1991): 1091–92.

72. William Rehnquist, *All the Laws But One: Civil Liberties in Wartime* (New York: Alfred A. Knopf, 1998), 221.

73. Landay, Taylor, and Talev, "Ruling Rattles," paragraph 1.

74. Peter Marguilies, quoted in Adam Liptak, "Supported by Bush, Opposed by Pentagon," *International Herald Tribune,* September 9, 2006, paragraph 14, http://proquest.umi.com (September 13, 2006).

75. Dante Chinni, "The Imperial Presidency Is Back–But Who's Watching?' *Christian Science Monitor,* March 11, 1993, paragraph 14, http:/web.EBSCOhost.

76. Michael Beschloss, "The End of the Imperial Presidency, *New York Times,* December 18, 2000, A27.

77. Patrick Leahy, *The Department of Justice and Terrorism: Hearings of the Senate Judiciary Committee,* December 6, 2001, *Federal News Service,* paragraphs 391–93, http://web.lexis-nexis.com/congcomp (July 9, 2004).

78. See Renee Montagne, Steve Inskeep, and Nina Totenberg, "High Court Hears Challenge to Military Tribunals," *National Public Radio,* March 28, 2006, http://web.lexis.com (September 9, 2004).

79. Diane F. Orentlicher and Robert Kogod Goldman, "When Justice Goes to War: Prosecuting Terrorists before Military Commissions," *Harvard Journal of Law and Public Policy* 25 (Spring 2002): 660.

80. Louis Fisher, "Lost Constitutional Moorings: Recovering the War Power," *Indiana Law Journal 81* (2005): 1247.

81. Katyal and Tribe, "Waging War," 1265.

82. Henrickson, "American War Powers," 171.

83. Wolfensberger, "The Return," paragraph 27.

84. Neal Katyal (Katyal testimony), *Review of Military Terrorism Tribunals: Hearings before the Senate Judiciary Committee,* 107th Cong., 1st sess., November 28, 2001, paragraph 7, *Federal Document Clearing House,* http://web.lexis.nexis.com/congcom (July 9, 2004). This seems to be partially based on Justice Jackson's warning in his *Korematsu* dissent:

Once a judicial opinion rationalizes such an order to show that it conforms to the Constitution . . . the Court for all time has validated the principle of racial discrimination in criminal procedure and of transplanting American citizens. The principle then lies about like a loaded weapon. . . . Every repetition embeds that principle more deeply in our law and thinking and expands it to new purposes. . . . A military commander may overstep the bounds of constitutionality, and it is an incident. But if we review and approve, that passing incident becomes the doctrine of the Constitution. There it has a generative power of its own, and all that it creates will be in its own image.

Korematsu v. United States, 323 U.S. 214, 245–246 (1944); quoted in Katyal, *Testimony,* paragraph 10, note 10.

85. Schlesinger, *Imperial Presidency,* 404.

86. One unnamed English writer has recently suggested that perhaps bipartisan politics and the memories of Vietnam may help "rein in" President "Bush's re-imperialised presidency." "The Imperial Presidency," *Economist,* November 3, 2001, paragraph 10, http://web.lexis-nexis.com (January 9, 2005). For a very different take on the actions of an "arrogant" and "imperial" presidency, see Michael D. Langdan, "Assessing an 'Arrogant' Presidency," *Boston Globe,* September 5, 2004, D9.

CHAPTER 5

TO PRODUCE A "JUDICIOUS CHOICE"

Presidential Responses to the Exercise of Advice and Consent by the U.S. Senate on Supreme Court Nominations

Trevor Parry-Giles, University of Maryland

On January 16, 2004, just three days before the annual commemoration of Martin Luther King Jr., President George W. Bush took a remarkable step in the ongoing struggle with the Senate over his judicial nominations. Bypassing the advice and consent provisions of the Constitution's Article II, the president issued a recess appointment for Mississippi's Charles Pickering, to the Fifth Circuit Court of Appeals. Pickering, according to his critics, is hostile to civil rights claims and has a past checkered by connections to Mississippi's infamous Sovereignty Commissions and defenses of anti-miscegenation laws. Pickering also was frequently reversed by higher courts, vigorously opposed reproductive rights for women, and actively promoted religion from the bench, his critics charged.[1] With this recess appointment, Bush assured Pickering a seat on the Fifth Circuit until January 2005. In December of 2004, Pickering announced that he was withdrawing his name from consideration by the Senate for confirmation and retired from the federal bench. Pickering published a book in 2006 detailing what he calls the "supreme chaos" of judicial confirmations.[2]

President Bush's statement appointing Pickering reveals many of the persistent themes that define this president's response to the exercise of advice and consent by the U.S. Senate. Bush's statement criticized a "minority of Democratic Senators" for using "unprecedented obstructionist tactics" that were "inconsistent with the Senate's constitutional responsibility." Bush was, his statement read, "proud to exercise my constitutional authority," and he called on the Senate to "stop playing politics with the American judicial system."³ As he confronts filibusters and other delaying tactics concerning his nominees to the federal bench, Bush routinely argues that the appointment process is too politicized and that the Senate is blocking his presidential prerogative.⁴ In this sense, Bush is the culmination of two hundred years of struggle between presidents and the Senate over executive appointments. I review that history in this chapter, paying particular attention to the various and shifting ways that U.S. presidents have responded to the Senate's advice and consent on Supreme Court nominations.⁵

For much of American history, Supreme Court nominations attracted little *public* attention, and much of the presidential commentary about such nominations was not aimed at a public audience. The rancorous public hearings that characterize some contemporary confirmation struggles were unheard of prior to the twentieth century.⁶ Because of a Senate procedure in place until 1929 that prohibited floor debates about nominations, there is little recorded public discussion in the Senate concerning Supreme Court nominees prior to the last century.⁷ Unsuccessful or rejected nominations to the Supreme Court in the early years of the republic were chiefly the result of partisan bickering, unpopular or lame-duck presidents, or the simple incompetence of the nominee.⁸

Even as much of the early discourse concerning Supreme Court nominations was outside the public realm, it nonetheless offers a telling symbolic archeology of the relational dynamics at work between the presidency and the U.S. Senate. Debates about Supreme Court nominees are significant instances of the ideological formation of American conceptions of law, justice, and democracy. Specifically, during the twentieth century the Supreme Court confirmation process rhetorically manifested and enacted the shift of the adherence to civil and human rights in American law while simultaneously personalizing American conceptions of "justice" with particular nominees to the high court.⁹ In addition, as presidents have responded to the exercise of advice and consent throughout the nation's history, they offer compelling commentary about the relationships between two different branches of the U.S. government and the very meaning of the constitutional principle of separation of powers. On several fronts, then, presidential discourse concerning the Senate's exercise of advice and consent, particularly as concerns Supreme Court nominations, is of considerable consequence.

Admittedly, such discourse rarely moves public opinion in meaningful ways. In a recent indictment of the public and rhetorical presidency, George Edwards maintains that "presidents typically do not succeed in their efforts to change public opinion," and that the "bully pulpit has proved ineffective not only for achieving majority support but also for increasing support from a smaller base."[10] The result, Edwards concludes, is that much presidential rhetoric falls "on deaf ears" and that presidents would be better off exploiting specific political opportunities presented to them and/or "staying private" in their attempts to govern.[11] With regard to Supreme Court nominations, Edwards might be correct—there are few if any examples where a president has been able to influence rhetorically the outcome of a nomination struggle in the U.S. Senate by marshaling public opinion.

Edwards's assault on the study of presidential rhetoric, however, relies too heavily on a narrow understanding of discursive influence. Putting aside Edwards's excessive dependence on public opinion polling as evidence for rhetorical effect, his overall indictment of presidential rhetoric is rooted in an overly myopic, indeed parochial, sense of rhetorical impact. As Martin J. Medhurst has suggested, Edwards "seems to want to treat rhetoric as nothing more than a causal factor in a chain of cause-and-effect reasoning."[12] There are, of course, different and better ways to examine the impact of presidential rhetoric.

Edwards relies on what might be called an instrumental sense of rhetorical effect. Instrumental impact is defined by James Jasinski as focused "on a relatively narrow sense of historical context, [which] usually encourages critics to assess textual influence on the immediate audience, and attempts to assess the advocate's attempt at solving a particular problem or exigence."[13] Edwards faults those who study presidential rhetoric for failing to find empirical evidence of the specific impact of such rhetoric—the best work on presidential rhetoric that he reviewed "virtually never offered proof, much less systematic evidence" of rhetorical effect.[14] Of course, this conclusion is hardly surprising. Finding such evidence of direct instrumental impact would be extremely difficult, if such evidence exists at all.

A more fruitful approach to assessing rhetorical impact attends to broader consequences of discourse, the constitutive power of rhetoric to specify "the way textual practices structure or establish conditions of possibility, enabling and constraining subsequent thought and action in ways similar to the operation of rules in a game."[15] Drawing on the work of James Boyd White, Maurice

Charland, Michael Calvin McGee, and others, Jasinski notes that a constitutive approach to rhetorical historiography "does not abandon the instrumental perspective but rather attempts to fold the instrumental moment of discursive action into the larger process of social and cultural (re)constitution."[16] Employing a constitutive approach allows the critic to escape the hegemonic empiricism of social science that seeks artificial correlations and unfounded causalities. This approach also permits the appreciation of rhetoric generally, and presidential rhetoric specifically, for its artistic and fluid impact, for its capacity to exert ideological rather than overt behavioral influence in the political lives of individual citizens and on the political culture as a whole. "A constitutive approach," Jasinski suggests, "explores the ways specific discursive strategies and textual dynamics shape and reshape the contours of political concepts and ideas."[17]

As presidents respond to the exercise of advice and consent by the U.S. Senate, they enact a constitutive articulation of key concepts in American law and politics. This chapter focuses on the ways that presidential rhetoric about advice and consent contributes to the understanding of separation of powers in the U.S. constitutional scheme. Ultimately, what presidents throughout U.S. history have done is adjust their reactions to senatorial advice and consent in ways that seek political and structural advantage for the executive in the appointments process. Early presidents answered setbacks in the appointments process with specifically political reactions, recognizing the relative equality of the two branches in making appointments to the Supreme Court, yet articulating a preeminent role for the executive in the initial disposition of appointments. As the presidency ascended to prominence in the twentieth century, presidential reactions shifted, articulating a presidential prerogative in Supreme Court nominations and defending a formalistic vision of judicial independence that sought to rob the confirmation process of its overtly political character. Finally, our most recent presidents have responded to the Senate's advice and consent power with proposals for reform, condemnations of the intrusion of politics into the process, and shifts in the nature of judicial appointments at the highest level. Following a brief discussion of the constitutional roots of the advice and consent provision of Article II, I review the evolving presidential responses to advice and consent. This review leads me to the conclusion that contemporary presidential rhetoric about advice and consent denigrates an important political process of government by depoliticizing it, to the detriment of important public discussions of legal questions, careful scrutiny of judicial nominees, and a sanitization of nominees in order to secure confirmation.

Article II, Advice and Consent, and Constitutional Separation of Powers

The origins of the confirmation process for Supreme Court justices are found in the constitutional provisions of Article II that require the president to nominate and, with the advice and consent of the Senate, to appoint judges of the Supreme Court. The precise meaning and historical derivation of that provision are matters of some dispute.[18] At bottom, most readings of constitutional history and the process of the Constitution's framing conclude, with Jack Rakove, that "on the matter of diplomatic and judicial appointments, the framers reached near consensus on the virtues of combining the 'responsibility' of executive nomination with the 'security' of senatorial advice and consent."[19] Importantly, the advice and consent powers of the Senate are found in Article II of the Constitution, the article that "lists powers that are *by nature* executive, even if shared in part with the Senate."[20] Nomination and appointments function, therefore, as an executive power that is shared with the legislative branch as a means of checking the control and dominance of the executive over this critical dimension of the government.

The Constitution was drafted in a symbolic and political environment dominated by the Articles of Confederation, a maligned and misunderstood foundation of the American constitutional experiment. Understanding the theoretical orientation of the Articles of Confederation "is useful, perhaps essential, to understanding better the full range of competing and interacting principles within American democracy," according to Robert Hoffert.[21] Indeed, much of the Constitution is simply an adaptation of provisions found in the Articles of Confederation. The supremacy, privileges and immunities, and full faith and credit clauses of the Constitution are all drawn directly from the Articles of Confederation, and "many of the additional textual powers granted to the new government [under the Constitution] were ones that the old government had been exercising in practice."[22]

While the articles provided for a loose federal government consisting primarily of a Congress, the Constitution constructs a governing structure that is sophisticated and delicately, almost precariously, balanced between branches with largely separate powers. Notably, however, while both documents construct governmental structures, only one, the Constitution, is significantly concerned with the individuals serving in that government. Only Articles V and IX of the Articles of Confederation address the staffing of the federal government, and the rhetoric of these Articles is decidedly different from the provisions of the Constitution framing similar concerns.

The Constitution's framers constructed a government in the first three articles of the document they drafted in 1787. Each article consists of two parts: first, a specification of who shall be allowed to hold public office and the conditions of their selection/election, and second, a designation of powers possessed by each of the three branches of government. Interestingly, the descriptions of election/selection procedures precede the specification of powers granted to the three branches. In so doing, the Constitution limits the exercise of power by first indicating *who* shall be allowed (and, by implication, not allowed) to exert power and authority with its governmental system.

Specifically, Article I specifies the age and residency requirements for members of Congress while also prescribing the methods of election and terms of office for representatives and senators. Section 5, clause 2 allows that "each house may determine the rules of its proceedings, punish its members for disorderly behaviour, and, with the concurrence of two-thirds, expel a member."[23] Before discussing the presidential role as commander in chief, or the specific executive powers of the presidency, the Constitution devotes a nine-clause section of Article II to the construction of an elaborate scheme for selecting and replacing the president of the United States. To ensure the fidelity of the executive, the framers commanded that the person elected president recite a public oath assuring a commitment to the Constitution and the president's willingness to "preserve, protect, and defend" it.[24] The president is also given the authority to nominate "and by and with the advice and consent of the Senate," to appoint ambassadors, judges of the Supreme Court, and "all other officers of the United States."[25] Article III establishes a judiciary, the officers of which are guaranteed steady compensation and an appointment for life and good behavior.[26] Impeachment of any officer of the United States Government is an arduous process, ensuring that the results of the election/selection procedures are respected.[27] And of the amendments ratified and added to the Constitution, seven deal directly with selection/election methods to public office (Amendments XII, XIV, XVII, XX, XXII, XXIII, and XXV)—well over one-fourth of the twenty-six amendments.

The theme that the Constitution's selection/election procedures protect popular liberty recurs regularly throughout *The Federalist Papers*—still "the single most authoritative source for understanding the character of our constitutional system," notes George Carey.[28] As specifically concerns Article II and the advice and consent clause, Hamilton concludes in Number 76 that this requirement will allow for the appointment of "judicious" individuals who will manifest the "character of its [the Union's] administration."[29] Finally, as to the structure of the judicial branch, Hamilton in Number 88 justifies its separation from the other branches by arguing that "liberty can have nothing to fear from the judiciary alone, [and] would have everything to fear from its union with either of the other departments." It is upon this basis that he advocates the system established by the Constitution allowing for judicial service during good behavior.[30]

As the foundation of the American civil religion, the Constitution is a multifaceted text that issues specific commands and forms the substance of the American republican system.[31] One primary motive of this text is its concern for the character of the individuals who occupy public office and who dominate public life. As it emerged from the Articles of Confederation, the Constitution sought to ensure that people of high caliber occupied its offices and that the selection procedures for those individuals protected and manifested that virtuous character. The system of government proposed by the Constitution depended upon that virtue for success, *The Federalist Papers* suggests, and the maintenance of that virtue allowed for the protection and expansion of republican liberty.[32] The political language of the American community, therefore, is often a language of character and personality such that the foundations of that language achieve their primary meaning through their embodiment with particular public characters. It is hardly surprising, thus, that the Senate's exercise of advice and consent has occasioned tension and conflict between various presidents and the United States Senate.

EARLY PRESIDENTIAL REACTIONS TO ADVICE AND CONSENT

In 1795, Chief Justice John Jay resigned from the Supreme Court to become the governor of New York. To replace Jay, President George Washington turned to John Rutledge of South Carolina—a former associate justice on the high court who was chief justice of the South Carolina Supreme Court at the time of his elevation. Though he served briefly as a result of a recess appointment, John Rutledge earns the distinction of being the first presidential Supreme Court nominee to be rejected by the U.S. Senate.

Rutledge was an eminent jurist, a well-regarded patriot with solid credentials and an established judicial temperament. He was rejected by the Federalist majority in the Senate for a straightforward, overtly political reason—he opposed the Jay Treaty. As reported in the *South Carolina State-Gazette* on July 17, 1795, Rutledge and other leaders from the state met in Charleston "to consider whether the impending treaty of amity, commerce, and navigation, between the United States and Great Britain, is not degrading to the national honour, dangerous to the political existence, and destructive of the agricultural, manufacturing, commercial, and shipping interests of the people of the United States." As reported by this newspaper and several others throughout the nation, Rutledge's opposition to the treaty was impassioned, as when he "declares he had rather, the President should die, dearly as he loves him, than he should sign that treaty." For Rutledge, the treaty "was an humble acknowledgement of our dependence upon his majesty; a surrender of our rights and privileges, for so much of his gracious favour as he should be pleased to grant."[33]

Among Federalists, Rutledge's speech was sacrilege, and because it was so widely reported, it caused a sensation in Philadelphia and New York. Edmund Randolph, for instance, wrote to President Washington on July 29 saying that "the conduct of the intended Chief Justice is so extraordinary, that Mr. Wolcott and Col. Pickering conceive it to be a proof of the imputation of insanity."[34] William Bradford also questioned Rutledge's sanity in a letter to Alexander Hamilton: "The crazy speech of Mr. Rutledge joined to certain information that he is daily sinking into debility of mind & body, will probably prevent him to receiving the appointment I mentioned to you."[35]

Upon Rutledge's rejection by the Senate on December 15, 1795, reactions poured forth in letters, all reacting to the decidedly political nature of the Senate's decision. Eight days after the Senate vote, President Washington wrote to Edward Carrington, expressing no surprise or particular displeasure at the exercise of advice and consent. "It had been expected that the Senate wou'd not confirm the appointment of Mr. R_," the president wrote, "and so it has happened."[36] While this is Washington's only surviving reaction to the Rutledge rejection, his immediate successors also commented on the Senate's move. John Adams, writing to Abigail Adams, noted the pain he felt for his friend John Rutledge but remarked that the negative vote could have positive consequences—"C. Justices must not go to illegal Meetings and become popular orators in favour of Sedition, nor inflame the popular discontents which are ill founded, nor propagate Disunion, Division, Contention, and delusion among the People."[37] Also appreciating the role of politics in the process, Thomas Jefferson wrote to William B. Giles at the end of the year that "the rejection of Mr. Rutledge by the Senate is a bold thing, because they cannot pretend any objection to him but his disapprobation of the treaty. It is of course a declaration that they will receive none but tories hereafter into any department of government."[38] None of these presidents expresses concern about the abuse of the Senate's power, a sense that the Senate passed its judgment on illegitimate grounds, or an argument for the president's preeminence in the appointments process. Instead, each of these founders articulates an understanding of advice and consent in all of its political meaning.

Few of the founders were more involved and more instrumental in forming and justifying the U.S. Constitution than James Madison, and his comments on the meaning of the advice and consent provision as the nation's fourth president are instructive of the early dynamics involving this constitutional power. In early 1811, Madison saw his nomination of Connecticut's Alexander Wolcott rejected by the Senate. Viewed as an extreme partisan by Federalists in the Senate, Wolcott was "an attorney of little distinction," who only received nine votes of the thirty-three cast.[39] At the time, Madison did not react, but two years later, in a message to the Senate, he responded to a request for meetings with Senators preliminary to his appointment of an ambassador to Sweden. In his reaction, Madison noted "the Executive and Senate, in the cases of appointments to office and of treaties, are to be considered as independent of and coordinate with each other. If they agree, the appointments or treaties are made; if the Senate disagree, they fail."[40] Madison defines the shared powers of Article II uniquely here, recognizing the consent dimension of the advice and consent clause as predominant and restricting the behavior of the Senate as concerns their advisory capacity. "The appointment of a committee of the Senate," Madison maintained, "to confer immediately with the Executive himself appears to lose sight of the coordinate relation between the Executive and the Senate which the Constitution has established, and which ought therefore to be maintained." For Madison, the president and the Senate shared power as a function of Article II, even as the advisory power of the Senate is limited. Interestingly, there is little sense in Madison's exposition of Article II here that envisions a presidential prerogative or primary right in the area of appointments and treaties.

Several presidents throughout the early nineteenth century reflected on the appointments power in Article II, usually arguing for the exclusive nomination power of the presidency. Facing a requested justification for the removal of a Tennessee surveyor from the Senate, Andrew Jackson refused to yield to what he saw as the "unconstitutional demands" of the Senate that were "an encroachment on the rights of the Executive."[41] For Jackson, removal of appointed officials from office is a presidential prerogative. The Senate also possessed a constitutional prerogative, in Jackson's view, and in a message to the Senate concerning appointments to the Bank of the United States he disclaimed all rights "on the part of the President officially to inquire into or call in question the reasons of the Senate for rejecting any nomination whatsoever." Even as he upheld the Senate's autonomy, though, Jackson also affirmed the president's independence: "As the President is not responsible to them [the Senate] for the reasons which induce him to make a nomination, so they are not responsible to him for the reasons which induce them to reject it."[42] From Jackson's presidency came a powerful expansion of the presidential prerogative in appointments and nominations, an expansion troubling to Jackson's opponents as the presidency became the preeminent site of federal appointment, patronage, and spoils.

One of Andrew Jackson's staunchest Whig opponents in the Senate was Virginia's John Tyler.[43] Upon his accidental elevation to the presidency with the death of William Henry Harrison in 1841, Tyler was forced to confront his views on advice and consent from a different perspective. At the outset of his term in office, as he sought to claim the presidency as his own, Tyler remained true to his Whig principles. In his Special Message to the Congress assembled in special session in June of 1841, Tyler vowed "with anxious solicitude to select the most trustworthy for official station," even as he acknowledged that "I can not be supposed to possess a personal knowledge of the qualifications for every applicant [and] I deem it, therefore, proper in this most public manner to invite on the part of the Senate a just scrutiny into the character and pretensions of every person I may bring to their notice in the regular form of a nomination for office."[44] Tyler further invited the Congress's involvement in presidential appointments, and promised that he would "also at the earliest proper occasion invite the attention of Congress to such measures as in my judgment will be best calculated to regulate and control the Executive power in reference to this vitally important subject."[45]

President Tyler soon discovered that Congress was more than willing to encroach upon his nomination prerogative, and his position regarding advice and consent shifted noticeably as he "broke with the Whig leaders in Congress and found himself a President without a party."[46] The relationship between Tyler and Congress deteriorated fairly quickly, and by March of 1842, the president was rebutting the attempt by the House of Representatives to submit background information about presidential appointees and the appointment process. In reply to the House, Tyler articulated an almost Jacksonian vision of presidential prerogative: "The appointing power, so far as it is bestowed on the President by the Constitution, is conferred without reserve or qualification. The reason for the appointment and the responsibility of the appointment rest with him alone."[47] For the rest of his term, particularly as concerned his Supreme Court nominations, Tyler learned quickly of the Senate's ability to "paralyze the constitutional functions of one or both of the other branches of the government," as it stalled, refused to act, or rejected outright several of Tyler's nominations to the high court.[48] But from his relatively untenable position as the first vice president to succeed to the presidency, Tyler argued for a primacy in the executive's role over appointments, advancing further the constitutive understanding of advice and consent and separation of powers.

Justice Henry Baldwin's death in 1844 offered John Tyler another chance to fill a Supreme Court seat, though he was unable to secure assent to his choices—Tyler holds the distinction of having had the most nominees to the Supreme Court rejected by the Senate.[49] The Baldwin seat remained open for many months, and the appointment of George Woodward to the seat by James K. Polk is another revealing instance in the history of advice and consent. Polk's primary consideration in making the Woodward appointment was party loyalty and geographical representation on the court—he first offered the seat to his secretary of state, James Buchanan.[50] Buchanan rejected the offer, and some months later, Polk turned to Woodward. Woodward was a nativist who incurred disfavor from Democrats and Whigs alike, including the powerful Pennsylvania senator, Simon Cameron, and was rejected by the Senate on a vote of 20 to 29 in January of 1846.

The most interesting aspect of the Woodward case was Polk's struggles with Buchanan over influence and advice in filling Baldwin's seat. The president's diary is a fascinating document for what it reveals about Buchanan's persistence. On Christmas Eve, 1845, Buchanan visited the White House to lobby Polk on behalf of John M. Read, a Federalist from Philadelphia. Polk was reluctant to nominate a Federalist: "I have never known an instance of a Federalist who had after arriving at the age of thirty," the President wrote, "professed to change his opinions, who was to be relied on in his constitutional opinions." Polk further noted his resolve "to appoint no man who was not an original Democrat and strict constructionist."[51] The next day, Christmas, Polk reported no visitors except Buchanan, who claimed to have spent "two sleepless nights" worrying about the Woodward appointment. Polk reports that his secretary of state complained that the president should only have made the Woodward appointment upon consultation with his cabinet. "I promptly answered," Polk reported, "that as President of the United States I was responsible for my appointments, and that I had a perfect right to make them without consulting my Cabinet, unless I desired their advice."[52] It is an interesting moment, Polk reacting not to the exercise of advice and consent by the Senate but to an assertion of advisory prerogative by a member of his cabinet. Reacting to rumors that Buchanan would leave the cabinet in January 1845, Polk recorded in his diary that Buchanan's "greatest weakness is great sensitiveness about appointments to office. He has repeatedly seemed to be troubled, and taken it greatly to heart when I have differed with him about appointments and made my own selections."[53] Indeed, throughout his diary accounts of the nomination and rejection of George Woodward, Polk never complains about the Senate's action, except to note the hypocrisy of a senator who feigned fidelity to Polk after voting against Woodward. Instead, Polk confronted a claim of advisory power by a member of his cabinet, and he upheld presidential authority in the process. Curiously, Buchanan faced his own conflict with the Senate when he sought to appoint Jeremiah S. Black in early 1861, just a few months before the end of his term. Black's nomination failed by one vote.[54]

For the remainder of the nineteenth century, presidents faced several contested and rejected nominees for the Supreme Court as the Senate exerted its advice and consent powers. During the Grant Administration, the Senate rejected the nomination of Ebenezer Hoar, and opposition in the Senate forced Grant to withdraw the nomination of George Williams to be chief justice. In all of the writing about the Hoar nomination, Grant never records a reaction at all, and other correspondents simply express disappointment at the result.[55] In the case of Williams, numerous allegations of impropriety were raised in the Senate about the nominee. Williams wrote to Grant in January of 1874 to lament that "my abilities have been disparaged, and my integrity brought in question, and it seems to me that a public opinion adverse to my appointment has been created which might hereafter embarrass your Administration, and, perhaps, impair my usefulness upon the bench."[56] The next day, Grant withdrew the nomination. Again, we have no reaction from Grant and no argument concerning the Senate's proper role or the propriety of their action against Supreme Court nominees.

Twenty years following the withdrawal of the Williams nomination, President Grover Cleveland faced the rejection of two nominees to the Supreme Court in one year. Justice Samuel Blatchford died in 1893. Cleveland nominated William Hornblower to replace Blatchford, only to have that nomination stopped by New York Senator David Hill. Hill was part of the anti-Cleveland faction in New York and "Cleveland made no secret of his determination not to conciliate his party enemies."[57] After the Senate rejected Hornblower, Cleveland put forth Wheeler H. Peckham, only to have Hill block that nomination as well. Cleveland's reaction to the rejection was muted. He defended Hornblower's nomination, writing to Don Dickinson that "a man should not be rejected for the place simply because corporations are among his clients, and I hope you will agree with me that in these days of wildness, conservatism and steadiness should not be at a discount."[58] Again, a president thwarted by the politics of the confirmation process, seeing his will rejected by the Senate, withholds comment as to the propriety of the Senate's action or their legitimacy in the advice and consent process.

A century passed from the Senate's rejection of John Rutledge in 1795 to its dismissal of Grover Cleveland's nominees in 1894, and presidential reactions to advice and consent changed little over that period. Presidents from James Madison on sought to preserve presidential independence in the appointments process, rebutting congressional attempts to encroach upon their power in the form of requests for consultation or justification. But missing from the presidential reactions of the eighteenth and nineteenth centuries were complaints about the politicization of the confirmation process or calls for a presidential prerogative in the appointment of justices or government officials. Eighteenth- and nineteenth-century presidents accepted the vagaries of a political confirmation process and in so doing confirmed the dual, coordinate nature of appointments as demarcated in the U.S. Constitution.

CONTEMPORARY PRESIDENTIAL REACTIONS TO ADVICE AND CONSENT

When the name Louis D. Brandeis was announced on the Senate floor as President Woodrow Wilson's newest nominee for the United States Supreme Court, observers report that the gathered senators "simply gasped."[59] So notorious was Brandeis, so complete and well known his reputation for progressivism that the possibility of his ascending to the highest court in the land sent shivers throughout the political worlds of Boston and Washington. His nomination became a signature moment in the early twentieth century and it demarcated the parameters of Supreme Court confirmations for much of the century, forever altering this critical constitutional ritual in American political life.[60] Wilson's response to the intensity of reaction to the Brandeis nomination is also revealing for its contribution to constituting the advice and consent relationship between the executive and the Senate.

The Brandeis confirmation hearings tell an ideological tale of American culture and U.S. legal politics in the Progressive era. As the Senate assessed the character of Louis D. Brandeis and his fitness for the Supreme Court, it also publicly scrutinized the progressivism and reformism that the nominee embodied. Ultimately, on June 1, 1916, the Senate confirmed Louis D. Brandeis by a vote of 47 to 22, with twenty-seven senators not voting.[61] With their vote, the United States Senate reached its verdict about the suitability of placing Louis Brandeis on the Supreme Court. In so doing, it ended what one historical commentator called "the bitterest nomination controversy in the history of the Court."[62]

A key moment in the Brandeis confirmation occurred when Woodrow Wilson engaged the controversy directly in a letter to Senator Charles Culberson, chair of the Judiciary Committee, in May 1916. Wilson wholeheartedly supported his nominee, arguing that of all the individuals he knew at the bar in the United States, Brandeis was "exceptionally qualified," because of his "impartial, impersonal, orderly, and constructive mind."[63] The president's letter also referred to the importance of the Constitution's nomination powers: "There is probably no more important duty imposed upon the President in connection with the general administration of the Government than that of naming members of the Supreme Court; and I need hardly tell you that I named Mr. Brandeis as a member of that great tribunal only because I knew him to be singularly qualified by learning, by gifts, and by character for the position."[64]

Wilson's letter reflects a clear understanding of the political struggle under way in the Brandeis confirmation, and his comments engage the politics directly. Indeed, one explanation for Brandeis's eventual confirmation is direct persuasion of key senators by Wilson and Brandeis. Brandeis met personally with Senators Hoke Smith of Georgia and James Reed of Missouri, both critical members of the Judiciary Committee, and both men were favorably persuaded by their meetings with the nominee.[65] President Wilson made a stop in the hometown of North Carolina's Senator Lee Overman and lavishly praised the senator in a speech. Soon thereafter, Overman became an ardent Brandeis champion.[66] Wilson's appreciation of the political nature of the appointments process is reinforced in his theories of constitutional government. "A series of bad appointments might easily make them [the federal courts] inferior to every other branch of government," Wilson worried, "[and this] is an argument for electing the right men to the presidency and to the Senate [and] not an argument for changing our constitutional arrangements."[67]

Few nominations in the twentieth century matched the intensity and fervor of the Brandeis nomination. For much of the century, presidents remained relatively distant from the confirmation of their nominees for the Supreme Court. For instance, there was little overt involvement by Herbert Hoover over his controversial nominations of Charles Evans Hughes and John J. Parker in 1930.[68] Even in his memoirs, Hoover devotes little attention to these nominations, noting only that the Parker nomination was made solely on the basis of qualification and not as a part of a larger southern strategy to break Democratic dominance in the South.[69] Franklin Roosevelt, aside from his ill-advised attempt to pack the Supreme Court in

1937, remained significantly silent regarding his Supreme Court nominees, probably because most of his selections were confirmed with relative ease by a Senate dominated by Democrats. Even when Lyndon Johnson made the remarkable nomination of Thurgood Marshall, he reserved comment on the process except to remark at the Rose Garden introduction of Marshall: "I believe it is the right thing to do, the right time to do it, the right man and the right place. I trust that his nomination will be promptly considered by the Senate."[70]

Even with the absence of public presidential involvement, intense, highly political contests over Supreme Court nominees were not unusual by the time Richard Nixon came to the presidency in 1969. The clashes between the executive and the Senate that characterized Supreme Court nominations in the nineteenth century continued, albeit with less frequency, in the twentieth century. What was unusual was Nixon's response to the controversy his nominees generated. Nixon used the Warren Court and its "permissive" rulings as a powerful campaign tool in 1968. The Republican candidate held the Supreme Court responsible for much of the social upheaval of the 1960s.[71] Nixon even reflected on this view in his memoirs: "I felt that some Supreme Court Justices were too often using their interpretation of the law to remake American society to their own social, political, and ideological precepts."[72] Along with his pledge to bring an "honorable end to the war in Vietnam," Nixon promised to restore "law and order" to an America rife with crime and turmoil. In a not-so-veiled indictment of the Warren Court, Nixon told the delegates at the 1968 Republican Convention in Miami to "recognize that some of our courts in their decisions have gone too far in weakening the peace forces as against the criminal forces in this country."

Nixon promised throughout the campaign to appoint judges and Supreme Court justices who would be "strict constructionists"; who would interpret the laws rather than make the laws.[73] Nixon's rhetorical antipathy toward the Warren Court had meaningful political consequences, particularly as his attacks worked to advance his southern electoral strategy. Harry Dent, Nixon's advisor on southern political tactics, remarked that the GOP candidate's 1968 pledge to appoint more conservatives to the Supreme Court was one of his "most appealing points."[74] There was a "deep-seated resentment in the land, especially in the South, against decisions for civil rights and civil liberties by the Supreme Court," and Nixon capitalized on that resentment.[75] Indeed, as Nixon said in an unguarded moment in the 1968 campaign, praising a campaign commercial: "It's all about law and order and the damn Negro–Puerto Rican groups out there."[76]

When two of his nominees faced difficult confirmations, President Nixon responded angrily, asserting a presidential prerogative over Supreme Court nominations unprecedented in U.S. history. To replace Justice Abe Fortas, Nixon tapped Clement F. Haynsworth, a South Carolina jurist who soon faced confirmation difficulties over ethical and ideological concerns. Correctly sensing that his nomination of Haynsworth was in trouble, President Nixon convened an "informal meeting" with members of the news media to answer the charges made against the judge. Calling the ethical attacks against Haynsworth "a vicious character assassination," Nixon proceeded to rebut the specific ethics charges against Haynsworth individually.[77] The president then claimed it was improper to reject a nominee because of that nominee's philosophical outlook. Nixon cited the remarks of some senators during the Marshall hearings that rejected judicial philosophy as a confirmation criterion, declaring that "if Judge Haynsworth's philosophy leans to the conservative side, in my view that recommends him to me."[78] Citing the Parker and Brandeis nominations as precedent, President Nixon concluded that "it is not proper to turn down a man because he is a southerner, because he is a Jew, because he is a Negro, or because of his philosophy."[79] Nixon sought, in these remarks, to direct and shape the nature of the confirmation process. As other presidents had argued before, a nominee's qualifications should dominate the confirmation process, but Nixon worked to limit the role of "philosophy" in that process.

Nixon's comments, of course, were unsuccessful. Just before the floor vote on the nomination, Senator Roman Hruska pleaded with his colleagues: "Where do we go from here, if there is a rejection of the nominee? It will amount to a rejection of the President's plan to make appointments to the Supreme Court which will restore balance. . . . There is every reason why we should confirm the nomination."[80] Despite such lamentations, the Senate rejected the Haynsworth nomination 45–55, with many Republicans deserting their newly inaugurated president and voting to reject. Senator Mark Hatfield, an Oregon Republican who voted nay on the nomination, expressed his frustration immediately following the vote: "This nomination will not reestablish the trust and respect that is needed so gravely today for our Nation's Highest Court. For the sake of the Court, I opposed it."[81]

Nixon, predictably, was upset by the Senate's rejection of Haynsworth, especially since he had every reason to expect a "halo" effect for his nominee so soon after the 1968 elections and his inauguration in January.[82] Maintaining that Haynsworth's "integrity is unimpeachable, his ability unquestioned," the president promised to nominate another individual using the same criteria he had employed with the Haynsworth choice. Nixon also suggested that the "majority of people in the Nation regret" the Senate's rejection.[83]

Following the rejection of Clement Haynsworth, Richard Nixon committed a serious miscalculation—he nominated G. Harrold Carswell to the Supreme Court. Dubbed as "one of the most ill-advised public acts of the early Nixon Presidency," the Carswell nomination was hurried to the Senate and probably resulted from several converging factors.[84] Nixon wanted another southerner but needed a nominee who lacked any financial or ethical entanglements, and Carswell qualified on these criteria. The president received assurances that a nominee without ethical problems would be confirmed. And because of his pique about Haynsworth, Nixon's other motives for nominating Carswell might have included insulting both the Supreme Court and the Senate by putting forth such a blatantly unqualified individual.[85] Furthermore, the fact that the White House was caught unprepared by confirmation revelations about Carswell—regarding judicial incompetence and white supremacy—and by opposition to this nomination indicates its hastiness.[86]

As the Carswell nomination progressed, the Nixon Administration worked both to defend the nominee and to distance the president from him.[87] Just a week before the full Senate vote on Carswell, President Nixon publicly exchanged letters with Senator William Saxbe of Ohio. After a standard defense of Carswell, Nixon remarked: "What is centrally at issue in this nomination is the constitutional responsibility of the President to appoint members of the Court." Nixon concluded: "If the Senate attempts to substitute its judgment as to who should be appointed, the traditional constitutional balance is in jeopardy and the duty of the President under the Constitution impaired."[88] In part, this rhetorical shifting occurred because the administration realized it had made "a blunder of mammoth proportions" in nominating Carswell.[89] The reason for this conclusion was fairly simple Carswell was clearly not qualified for the Supreme Court.

But Nixon's letter to Saxbe is more significant than simply a defense of Carswell and an attempt to create distance from the failing nomination. What Nixon does in this letter is make an explicit claim for an overt presidential prerogative—a prerogative that is almost absolute. Should the Senate try to fulfill its constitutional responsibility, Nixon suggested, they would violate the Constitution's sense of balance and threaten the integrity of the presidency. A dramatic charge and an aggressive, even bold, attempt to grab power, Nixon's letter is a meaningful moment in the development of the advice and consent provision. Indeed, Nixon's rhetorical themes emerge in subsequent presidential responses to advice and consent, from Ronald Reagan to Bill Clinton to George W. Bush.

With his nominations of Judges Haynsworth and Carswell, Richard Nixon asked the U.S. community to affirm or deny his vision of a strict constructionist, conservative Supreme Court. When the U.S. Senate rejected these men, they likewise rejected Nixon's judicial vision. At the same time, the Senate rejected Nixon's threats about upsetting the Constitution's balance and rebutted the president's exertions of presidential prerogative. But the legacy of Nixon's claims about the nature of advice and consent and presidential appointments powers lingers still as confirmation debates have intensified and the controversy they generate becomes ever more partisan.

Each time a Supreme Court seat opened during the Reagan presidency, speculation centered on the administration's likely nomination of Robert Bork. Reagan had placed Bork on the D.C. Federal Circuit Court and the judge was widely seen as one of the intellectual and judicial leaders of the conservative "original intention" movement.[90] Thus, when Reagan nominated O'Connor in 1981, then elevated Rehnquist and nominated Scalia in 1986, most observers were surprised, and Bork himself was reportedly "crushed" at being passed over.[91] By 1987, the time had come. When Justice Lewis F. Powell announced his resignation from the court on June 26, the Reagan Administration turned to Robert H. Bork. In announcing Bork's nomination on July 1, the president said: "Judge Bork, widely regarded as the most prominent and intellectually powerful advocate of judicial restraint, shares my view that judges' personal preferences and values should not be part of their constitutional interpretations."[92] Reagan's reaction to the Bork confirmation controversy was to argue that his nominee was well qualified and that "special interests" had hijacked the confirmation process.

The confirmation debate over Robert Bork enacted an escalation in arguments about Supreme Court nominees, away from nominal concerns about the nominee as potential jurist and toward a focus on the dramatic, sometimes exaggerated, consequences of the nominee for U.S. law. The threat that Bork was said to pose to civil rights and privacy rights. and the power of the discourse that personified Bork as such a threat, speak to the role of this Supreme Court confirmation struggle to enact the nature of American jurisprudence for the larger polity. In addition, the stark rhetoric used to define Bork reflected the increasing intensity and expanding importance of the Supreme Court confirmation process in American politics. Thus, despite the best efforts of the Reagan Administration and Bork's supporters, the construction of the nominee as a representative of extremist approaches to the law and the evolution of the debate into a political spectacle overwhelmed any attempts to paint him as a moderate and reasonable jurist.

By September and October of 1987, the pressure to reject Bork's nomination was intense, and the prospects of confirmation were dim. At the White House, the administration scripted a series of calls for the president to undecided senators. Reagan's scripts highlight the administration's focus on what they saw as the distortion of Bork's record. For instance, in his call to Mississippi Democrat John Stennis, Reagan was supposed to say: "What really disturbs me is that some of these interest groups are blatantly distorting the facts with regard to Judge Bork's record and literally turning this into a political campaign." The same argument was made to Senators Ford, Evans, and D'Amato and other senators.[93] Ultimately, there was anger from the White House, frustration from Senate Republicans, and satisfaction from the hundreds of individuals and groups who opposed the nomination. And there was defiance from Robert Bork, who insisted on a vote by the full U.S. Senate. That vote would not matter—the result was a foregone conclusion. In the end, fifty-eight senators voted against Robert Bork, and his margin of defeat was the largest of any Supreme Court nominee in history. In explaining this defeat, Ronald Reagan and his administration advanced the argument that the process of advice and consent was broken, too politicized, and dominated by special interests and illegitimate voices. Reagan's discourse again reconstitutes the meaning of advice and consent, adding to Nixon's assertion of presidential prerogative by promoting a formalistic vision of judicial independence and a depoliticized confirmation process.

Conclusions

When it comes to judicial nominations, most contemporary presidents sound pretty much alike. Republicans and Democrats both complain from the White House of Senate intransigence, partisan politics, and the impending danger to the federal judiciary as a result of congressional unwillingness to approve nominees. Zealous in defense of their prerogative to shape the judiciary as they see fit, contemporary U.S. presidents rail against the inconvenience of having to secure the Senate's consent to their nominations as they tell a tale of a politicized confirmation process with dire consequences for the republic. In 1997, Bill Clinton lamented that "the Senate's failure to act on my nominations, or even to give many of my nominees a hearing, represents the worst of partisan politics. Under the pretense of preventing so-called judicial activism, they've taken aim at the very independence our Founders sought to protect."[94] Six years later, a different president from a different party, George W. Bush, fretted that "we face a vacancy crisis in the federal courts, made worse by senators who block votes on qualified nominees. These delays endanger American justice. Vacant federal benches lead to crowded court dockets, overworked judges and longer waits for Americans who want their cases heard."[95]

Usually, presidential arguments about advice and consent degenerate quickly, from practical concerns about the lack of staffing in the federal courts to *ad hominems* and hyperbolic charges of partisanship and inequity. The Senate is not much better. Nominees are denied hearings or votes and nominations are filibustered by senators opposed to the president. While a large percentage of presidential nominations are confirmed with relative ease, the high profile nature of controversial nominations means that the vitriol coming from both Capitol Hill and the White House is intense.[96] These constant complaints about the politicized confirmation process, offered so frequently by presidents and senators, ignore the complicity of both the White House and the Senate in creating and politicizing the process in the first place.

While these ongoing conflicts over judicial nominations are often inane and overblown, over the last two administrations the tensions regarding judicial nominations have intensified. A Republican Senate stalled or delayed dozens of President Bill Clinton's nominees, while a Democratic Senate did the same to President George W. Bush's appointments.[97] So concerned was George W. Bush about the process and its consequences for his nominees that he announced a plan in October 2002 to ensure "timely consideration of judicial nominees" by the Senate. Among other provisions, the plan called for advanced notice of judicial retirements and an up-or-down vote on judicial nominees by the full Senate 180 days after their announcement.[98]

Several themes, then, emerge from presidential reactions to the Senate's exercise of advice and consent. Our early presidents sought to limit the encroachment of the Congress in the area of appointments even as they recognized the legitimacy of the Senate's political exercise of advice and consent. These presidents saw numerous nominees rejected on the basis of the basest politics—personal antipathy, opposition to stated political positions, intraparty conflict, etc. Never did an eighteenth- or nineteenth-century president attempt to depoliticize the process or argue that such reasons for rejection by the Senate were illegitimate.

Presidential reaction shifted in the twentieth century as presidents from Wilson through George W. Bush defended the qualifications of their nominees even as they reflected on the nature of the appointments process. Two basic themes emerge from these responses. First, lurking beneath many presidential responses was the argument that Richard Nixon made explicit—that presidents are vested with primary power in the case of judicial appointments. Nixon and other presidents rejected the coordinancy of Madison's vision of advice and consent to achieve an advantage in confirmation controversies. Many of the reform proposals to change the process of judicial appointments, from FDR's court-packing plan to George W. Bush's reform efforts, seek to limit Senate power and preserve presidential prerogative in the appointments process. These efforts typically fail.

The second theme was that the Supreme Court confirmation process is too political, that somehow politics should be removed from this important constitutional process. As such, following the Bork and Thomas nominations in particular, numerous proposals emerged to make the process less political, and President Bush's recent reform outline continues this movement.[99] As I have tried to demonstrate here, this view is historically myopic. Virtually every thorough account of the history of the advice and consent provisions in the Constitution and the Supreme Court nominations of the eighteenth and nineteenth centuries reveals a highly political process.[100] At some point, curiously, a rhetoric took hold that divorced law from politics and articulated the mythology that judicial confirmations should be apolitical. Undoubtedly rooted in a commitment to legal formalism, this rhetoric was useful for presidents who disliked the Senate's interference in the nomination process. It worked to truncate arguments and questions about the judicial philosophy and political viewpoints of nominees and it upheld another mythology—the independent, apolitical judiciary.

This rhetoric of a depoliticized confirmation process must be resisted for a series of compelling reasons. First, politicized confirmations affirm our constitutional and historical heritage, carrying out the constitutional commandment of advice and consent and subjecting the appointment of Supreme Court justices to the checks and balances established by the Constitution.

Second, the U.S. political culture is stronger for the politicized discussions occasioned by the various confirmation controversies of the twentieth century. Debates about the meanings of social justice, human rights, civil rights, and privacy rights are debates a free and democratic society should be having, and the advice and consent process provides a useful enactment for those debates. Moreover, the process of ideological embodiment articulated in those debates gives citizens a concrete, material manifestation of ideological meaning. Louis Brandeis represented social justice; Thurgood Marshall embodied civil rights—and the larger culture achieved a clearer, more specific understanding of what these commitments mean and how they function in collective life. In this way, confirmation debates are democratizing as they materialize the remote, distant ideologies that are the basis of social knowledge and collective life in the U.S. polity.

Finally, depoliticized confirmations bankrupt an important democratic process, sanitizing its power to contribute meaningfully to national debate about vital ideological matters. In the wake of the Bork hearings, regrettably, the pressures for confirmability resulted in nominations that were either "stealth," celebritized, or safe. A stealth nominee, as in the case of David Souter, is an individual who lacks a significant public "paper trail" and who will thus face less questioning by the Senate. The nominations of Clarence Thomas and Ruth Bader Ginsburg represented another strategy responsive to confirmability pressures—the marketing of nominees on the basis of their celebrity, their emotional, personal narrative. Simply put, Thomas and Ginsburg were celebritized, and the rhetorical strategies of the Bush and Clinton administrations, supporters of the nominations, the nominees, and the news media prompted an affective and epideictic response to the nominations.[101] Another approach is to nominate an individual who is well known to senators and who has generated, for whatever reason, a wealth of goodwill in the Senate. This approach worked well for President Clinton when he named Judge Stephen Breyer to the Supreme Court in 1994 to replace Justice Harry Blackmun.

In short, the debate about the propriety and prudence of a given nomination has been subsumed by other, ancillary concerns. This tendency must be withstood. In the absence of rigorous scrutiny of political positions and judicial philosophy, the process becomes simply an assessment of qualifications and the vague quality of "judicial temperament." More politics, not less, makes the confirmation process of Supreme Court justices a meaningful enactment of the rhetorical, legal, and political culture in the United States. As Keith Whittington maintains, "The constitutional division of powers contributes to a unique and unpredictable dynamic that can feed government action, encourage institutional development, and foster political and constitutional deliberation."[102] Such enactments should tell us much, in this ongoing democratic experiment that we call the United States, about the mainstream of U.S. law, the nature of rights and duties in the constitutional system, and the power of legal ideologies in political life.

Notes

1. See Report of People for the American Way Opposing the Confirmation of Charles W. Pickering Sr., to the U.S. Court of Appeals for the Fifth Circuit, January 24, 2002, available at http://www.pfaw.org. Other groups actively opposing the Pickering nomination include the National Organization for Women, the Alliance for Justice, Planned Parenthood, and a group of eighty southern and African-American historians that includes John Hope Franklin, Julian Bond, Roger Wilkins, and Sheldon Hackney.

2. Charles W. Pickering, *Supreme Chaos: The Politics of Judicial Confirmations and the Culture War* (Macon, Ga.: Stroud and Hall, 2006).

3. "Statement by the President," January 16, 2004, available at http://www.whitehouse.gov/news/releases/2004/01.

4. For a discussion of the alleged breakdown of the appointments process, see the collection of essays in G. Calvin Mackenzie, ed., *Innocent Until Nominated: The Breakdown of the Presidential Appointment Process* (Washington, D.C.: Brookings Institution Press, 2001).

5. Some of the material in this chapter also appears in Trevor Parry-Giles, *The Character of Justice: Rhetoric, Politics, and Law in the Supreme Court Confirmation Process* (East Lansing: Michigan State University Press, 2006).

6. The change in the publicity surrounding the nomination of individuals to the Supreme Court is discussed fully in John Anthony Maltese, *The Selling of Supreme Court Nominees* (Baltimore: Johns Hopkins University Press, 1995); and Richard Davis, "Supreme Court Nominations and the News Media," *Albany Law Review* 57 (1994): 1061–79.

7. The most comprehensive history of Supreme Court nominations is offered in Henry J. Abraham, *Justices, Presidents, and Senators: A History of the U.S. Supreme Court Appointments from Washington to Clinton*, rev. ed. (Lanham, Md.: Rowman and Littlefield, 1999). Other historical surveys include John P. Frank, "The Appointment of Supreme Court Justices: Prestige, Principles and Politics," *Wisconsin Law Review* 1941 (1941): 172–210, 343–79, 461–512; Paul A. Freund, "Appointment of Justices: Some Historical Perspectives," *Harvard Law Review* 101 (1988): 1146–63; Maltese, *The Selling of Supreme Court Nominees*; Paul Simon, *Advice and Consent: Clarence Thomas, Robert Bork and the Intriguing History of the Supreme Court's Nomination Battles* (Washington, D.C.: National Press Books, 1992); and Laurence H. Tribe, *God Save This Honorable Court: How the Choices of Supreme Court Justices Shapes Our History* (New York: Random House, 1985).

8. See Simon, *Advice and Consent*; Abraham, *Justices, Presidents, and Senators*. The early history of such nominations is a story of political intrigue and personal vilification resulting in the rejection or withdrawal of eleven nominees by the turn of the twentieth century. By contrast, the Senate only rejected outright four nominees to the Supreme Court in the twentieth century (John J. Parker, Clement Haynsworth, G. Harrold Carswell, and Robert Bork). See Tribe, *God Save This Honorable Court*, 142–47. This figure does not count the nominations that were declined or postponed or those where no action was taken by the Senate.

9. See Trevor Parry-Giles, "Character, the Constitution, and the Ideological Embodiment of 'Civil Rights' in the 1967 Nomination of Thurgood Marshall to the Supreme Court." *Quarterly Journal of Speech* 82 (1996): 364–82; and Parry-Giles, *The Character of Justice*.

10. George C. Edwards III, *On Deaf Ears: The Limits of the Bully Pulpit* (New Haven, Conn.: Yale University Press, 2003), 241.

11. Edwards, *On Deaf Ears*, 248–54.

12. Martin J. Medhurst, "Afterword: The Ways of Rhetoric," in *Beyond the Rhetorical Presidency*, edited by Martin J. Medhurst (College Station: Texas A&M University Press, 1996), 224–25.

13. James Jasinski, "A Constitutive Framework for Rhetorical Historiography: Toward an Understanding of the Discursive (Re)constitution of 'Constitution' in *The Federalist Papers*," in *Doing Rhetorical History: Concepts and Cases*, ed. Kathleen Turner (Tuscaloosa: University of Alabama Press, 1998), 73.

14. Edwards, *On Deaf Ears*, x.

15. Jasinski, "A Constitutive Framework," 75.

16. Jasinski, "A Constitutive Framework," 91.

17. Jasinski, "A Constitutive Framework," 74.

18. See Arthur Bestor, "'Advice' from the Very Beginning, 'Consent' When the End Is Achieved," *American Journal of International Law* 83 (1989): 718–27; Joseph R. Biden Jr., "The Constitution, the Senate, and the Court," *Wake Forest Law Review* 24 (1989): 951–58; Robert H. Bork, *The Tempting of America: The Political Seduction of the Law* (New York: Free Press, 1990); Robert A. Friedlander, "Judicial Selection and the Constitution: What Did the Framers Originally Intend?" *Saint Louis University Public Law Review* 8 (1989): 1–11; Michael J. Gerhardt, *The Federal Appointments Process: A Constitutional and Historical Analysis* (Durham, N.C.: Duke University Press, 2000); Joseph P. Harris, *The Advice and Consent of the Senate: A Study of the Confirmation of Appointments by the United States Senate* (Berkeley: University of California Press, 1953); Orrin G. Hatch, "More Marbury Myths," *Cincinnati Law Review* 57 (1989): 891–901; Nathaniel R. Jones, "Whither Goest Judicial Nominations, *Brown* or *Plessy?*—Advice and Consent Revisited," *SMU Law Review* 46 (1992): 735–49; Joseph S. Larisa Jr., "Popular Mythology: The Framers' Intent, the Constitution, and Ideological Review of Supreme Court Nominees," *Boston College Law Review* 30 (1989): 969–86; Charles H. Percy, "Advice and Consent: A Reevaluation," *Southern Illinois University Law Journal* 1978 (1978): 31–43; Tribe, *God Save This Honorable Court*; Norman Vieira and Leonard E. Gross, "The Appointments Clause: Judge Bork and the Role of Ideology in Judicial Confirmations," *Journal of Legal History* 11 (1990): 311–52; and Christopher Wolfe, "The Senate's Power to Give 'Advice and Consent' in Judicial Appointments," *Marquette Law Review* 82 (1999): 355–79.

19. Jack N. Rakove, *Original Meanings: Politics and Ideas in the Making of the Constitution* (New York: Knopf, 1997), 266.

20. Joseph M. Bessette and Gary J. Schmitt, "Executive Power and the American Founding," in *Separation of Powers and Good Government*, ed. Bradford P. Wilson and Peter W. Schramm (Lanham, Md.: Rowman and Littlefield, 1994), 49 (emphasis in original). Additional discussions of the historical roots of separation of powers are found in W. B. Gwyn, *The Meaning of the Separation of Powers* (New Orleans: Tulane University Press, 1965); Arthur T. Vanderbilt, *The Doctrine of Separation of Powers and Its Present-Day Significance* (Lincoln: University of Nebraska Press, 1953); and M. J. C. Vile, *Constitutionalism and the Separation of Powers* (Oxford: Clarendon Press, 1967).

21. Robert W. Hoffert, *A Politics of Tension: The Articles of Confederation and American Political Ideas* (Niwot: University Press of Colorado, 1992), xiii.

22. Eric M. Freedman, "Why Constitutional Lawyers and Historians Should Take a Fresh Look at the Emergence of the Constitution from the Confederation Period: The Case

of the Drafting of the Articles of Confederation," *Tennessee Law Review* 60 (1993): 784. See also Arthur R. Landever, "Those Indispensable Articles of Confederation—Stage in Constitutionalism, Passage for the Framers, and Clue to the Nature of the Constitution," *Arizona Law Review* 31 (1989): 79–125; and Donald S. Lutz, "The Articles of Confederation as the Background to the Federal Republic," *Publius* 20 (1990): 55–70.

23. *U.S. Constitution,* Art. I, sec. 5, cl. 2.
24. *U.S. Constitution,* Art. II, sec. 1, cl. 9.
25. *U.S. Constitution,* Art. II, sec. 2, cl. 2.
26. *U.S. Constitution,* Art. III, sec. 1, cl. 1.
27. See Richard A. Posner, *An Affair of State: The Investigation, Impeachment, and Trial of President Clinton* (Cambridge, Mass.: Harvard University Press, 1999), 97–98.
28. George Carey, *The Federalist: Design for a Constitutional Republic* (Urbana: University of Illinois Press, 1994), xi. See also David F. Epstein, *The Political Theory of The Federalist* (Chicago: University of Chicago Press, 1984); Robert Ferguson, "Ideology and the Framing of the Constitution," *Early American Literature* 22 (1987): 157–65; Albert Furtwangler, *The Authority of Publius: A Reading of The Federalist Papers* (Ithaca, N.Y.: Cornell University Press, 1984); and Edward Millican, *One United People: The Federalist Papers and the National Idea* (Lexington: University Press of Kentucky, 1990).
29. James Madison, Alexander Hamilton, and John Jay, *The Federalist Papers,* ed. Issac Krammick (Middlesex, U.K.: Penguin, 1987), 428.
30. Madison, Hamilton, and Jay, *The Federalist Papers,* 437–38.
31. Sanford Levinson, "'The Constitution' in American Civil Religion," in *The Supreme Court Review 1979,* ed. Philip B. Kurland and Gerhard Casper (Chicago: University of Chicago Press, 1979), 123–51.
32. An economically driven reading of the Constitution would view such rhetoric as a ruse designed solely to assure that like-minded elites were selected to office via procedures that limited the franchise and restricted popular access to government. I do not deny this reading, though I believe it is reductionistic to assert that such a reading is the *only* way to interpret the complex text of the Constitution and its accompanying rhetorical justifications. Forrest McDonald maintains, for instance, that a clearer understanding of republican virtue emerges from the personality of George Washington, a man "ever concerned, almost obsessively, with creating and then living up to what he called his 'character'—what in the twentieth century would be called his reputation or public image." See Forrest McDonald, *Novus Ordo Seclorum: The Intellectual Origins of the Constitution* (Lawrence: University Press of Kansas, 1985), 193.
33. "South Carolina State-Gazette, July 17, 1795, Charleston, South Carolina," in *The Documentary History of the Supreme Court of the United States, 1789–1800,* vol. 1, part 2: *Commentaries on Appointments and Proceedings,* ed. by Maeva Marcus and James R. Perry (New York: Columbia University Press, 1985), 765–67 (hereafter DHSC).
34. "Edmund Randolph to George Washington, July 29, 1795, Philadelphia, Pennsylvania," DHSC, 773.
35. "William Bradford, Jr., to Alexander Hamilton, August 4, 1795, Philadelphia, Pennsylvania," DHSC, 775.
36. "George Washington to Edward Carrington, December 23, 1795, Philadelphia, Pennsylvania," DHSC, 817. In early January, Washington would write to Henry Lee about his concern that the bench be filled by the time they were scheduled by law to reconvene. See

"George Washington to Henry Lee, January 11, 1796, Philadelphia, Pennsylvania," DHSC, 829.

37. "John Adams to Abigail Adams, December 17, 1795, Philadelphia, Pennsylvania," DHSC, 813.

38. "Thomas Jefferson to William B. Giles, December 31, 1795, Monticello, Albemarle County, Virginia," DHSC, 821.

39. Abraham, *Justices, Presidents, and Senators*, 66.

40. James Madison, "To the Senate of the United States, July 6, 1813," in *A Compilation of the Messages and Papers of the Presidents, 1789–1897*, vol. 1, edited by James D. Richardson (Washington, D.C.: Government Printing Office, 1897), 531.

41. Andrew Jackson, "To the Senate of the United States, February 10, 1835," in *A Compilation of the Messages and Papers of the Presidents, 1789–1897*, vol. 3, ed. James D. Richardson (Washington, D.C.: Government Printing Office, 1897), 133. For more on Jackson's struggles over advice and consent, see Harris, *The Advice and Consent of the Senate*, chap. 4.

42. Andrew Jackson, "To the Senate, March 11, 1834," in *A Compilation of the Messages and Papers of the Presidents, 1789–1897*, vol. 3, 42.

43. Tyler's opposition to Jackson's spoils system is discussed in Dan Monroe, *The Republican Vision of John Tyler* (College Station: Texas A&M University Press, 2003), 150–53.

44. John Tyler, "Special Session Message, June 1, 1841," in *A Compilation of the Messages and Papers of the Presidents, 1789–1897*, vol. 4, ed. James D. Richardson (Washington, D.C.: Government Printing Office, 1897), 50.

45. Tyler, "Special Session Message," 50.

46. Harris, *The Advice and Consent of the Senate*, 66. See also William F. Swindler, "John Tyler's Nominations: 'Robin Hood,' Congress, and the Court," *Yearbook of the Supreme Court Historical Society* (1977): 39–43.

47. John Tyler, "To the House of Representatives of the United States, March 23, 1842," in *A Compilation of the Messages and Papers of the Presidents, 1789–1897*, vol. 4, 106.

48. Robert J. Morgan, *A Whig Embattled: The Presidency under John Tyler* (Lincoln: University of Nebraska Press, 1954), 87. See also Oscar Doane Lambert, *Presidential Politics in the United States, 1841–1844* (Durham, N.C.: Duke University Press, 1936); and Monroe, *The Republican Vision of John Tyler*.

49. For a discussion of Tyler's attempt to fill Baldwin's seat, see Henry A. Wise, *Seven Decades of Union* (Philadelphia: J. B. Lippincott, 1881).

50. Abraham, *Justices, Presidents, and Senators*, 80–81. For a discussion of the role of geography in Supreme Court appointments, see William J. Daniels, "The Geographic Factor in Appointments to the United States Supreme Court: 1789–1976," *Western Political Quarterly* 31 (1978): 226–37.

51. James K. Polk, *The Diary of a President, 1845–1849*, ed. Allan Nevins (London: Longmans, Green, 1929), 37.

52. Polk, *The Diary of a President*, 39.

53. Polk, *The Diary of a President*, 45.

54. Abraham, *Justices, Presidents, and Senators*, 85–86. There is no mention of the appointment or the Senate's rejection in the authorized biography of Black. See Mary Black Clayton, *Reminiscences of Jeremiah Sullivan Black* (St. Louis, Mo.: Christian Publishing, 1887). Buchanan commented on the president's power of appointments in a response dated

January 15, 1861, to the Senate, who requested information concerning a temporary appointment. Buchanan upheld the president's autonomy: "I take it for granted that the Senate did not mean to call for the reasons upon which I acted in performing an Executive duty nor to demand an account of the motives which governed me in an act which the law and the Constitution left to my own discretion." See James Buchanan, "To the Senate of the United States, January 15, 1861," in *A Compilation of the Messages and Papers of the Presidents, 1789–1897,* vol. 5, ed. James D. Richardson (Washington, D.C.: Government Printing Office, 1897), 661.

55. See *The Papers of Ulysses S. Grant,* vol. 20, ed. John Y. Simon (Carbondale: Southern Illinois University Press, 1995), 54–57, 92, 405. Importantly, Hoar was Grant's attorney general and had generated considerable hostility in the Senate. Upon his rejection, Senator Cameron was reported to have said: "What could you expect for a man who had snubbed seventy senators?" See Moorfield Storey and Edward W. Emerson, *Ebenezer Rockwood Hoar: A Memoir* (Boston: Houghton Mifflin, 1911), 197.

56. "George Williams to USG," in *The Papers of Ulysses S. Grant,* vol. 24, ed. John Y. Simon (Carbondale: Southern Illinois University Press, 1995), 287.

57. Richard E. Welch Jr., *The Presidencies of Grover Cleveland* (Lawrence: University Press of Kansas, 1988), 207.

58. *Letters of Grover Cleveland, 1850–1908,* selected and edited by Allan Nevins (Boston: Houghton Mifflin, 1933), 332.

59. Alpheus Thomas Mason, *Brandeis: A Free Man's Life* (New York: Viking Press, 1946), 466.

60. For more on the Brandeis nomination, see Trevor Parry-Giles, "For the Soul of the Supreme Court: Progressivism, Ethics, and 'Social Justice' in the 1916 'Trial' of Louis D. Brandeis." *Rhetoric and Public Affairs* 2 (1999): 83–106; A. L. Todd, *Justice on Trial: The Case of Louis D. Brandeis* (Chicago: University of Chicago Press, 1964).

61. *Congressional Record,* 64th Cong., 1st sess., 1916, 53, pt. 9: 9032. As was the custom at the time, debate concerning the nomination was held in executive session, and thus was not recorded in the *Congressional Record.* In late April, 1916, there was a discussion on the Senate floor regarding the conduct of the hearings and their openness and decorum. See *Congressional Record,* 64th Cong., 1st sess., 1916, 53, pt. 7: 6970–73. President Wilson's letter was entered into the *Record* on May 9, 1916. See *Congressional Record,* 64th Cong., 1st sess., 1916, 53, pt. 8: 7627–28.

62. Richard D. Friedman, "Tribal Myths: Ideology and the Confirmation of Supreme Court Nominations," *Yale Law Journal* 95 (1986): 1310.

63. Arthur S. Link, ed., *The Papers of Woodrow Wilson,* vol. 36 (Princeton, N.J.: Princeton University Press, 1981), 611. The letter is also found reprinted in the majority report from the Judiciary Committee considering the Brandeis nomination in 1916. See Senate Committee on the Judiciary, *Nomination of Louis D. Brandeis: Report,* 64th Cong., 1st sess., June 1, 1916, Ex. Rept. No. 2, Part 1, 240.

64. Link, ed., *The Papers of Woodrow Wilson,* 610. Interestingly, a former president, William Howard Taft, also participated in the debate over the Brandeis nomination, joining a group of past ABA presidents to petition the Senate: "The undersigned feel under the painful duty to say to you that, in their opinion, taking into view the reputation, character and professional career of Mr. Louis D. Brandeis, he is not a fit person to be a member of the Supreme Court of the United States." See Senate Committee on the Judiciary, *Nomination of Louis D. Brandeis,* 298.

65. See Alfred Lief, *Brandeis: The Personal History of an American Ideal* (New York: Stackpole Sons, 1936), 391; Dewey W. Grantham Jr., *Hoke Smith and the Politics of the New South* (Baton Rouge: Louisiana State University Press, 1958), 298. Richard Rovere offers a slightly different interpretation of the confirmation. He credits the unflagging work of Walter Lippmann and Felix Frankfurter who "in letters, articles, and conversations . . . worked tirelessly for Brandeis." Rovere labels the confirmation "Lippmann's greatest triumph." See Richard Rovere, "Walter Lippmann," *American Scholar* 44 (1975): 589.

66. See Todd, *Justice on Trial*, 232–34; and "Remarks from a Rear Platform at Salisbury, North Carolina," in *The Papers of Woodrow Wilson*, vol. 37, ed. Arthur S. Link (Princeton, N.J.: Princeton University Press, 1981), 78–79. Southern support for the nomination was tenuous at best, and great effort was expended to assure party loyalty in the vote for confirmation by the Judiciary Committee. Only Florida Senator Duncan Fletcher, a member of the subcommittee investigating the nomination, was unreservedly for Brandeis among southern senators. See Wayne Flynt, *Duncan Upshaw Fletcher: Dixie's Reluctant Progressive* (Tallahassee: Florida State University Press, 1971), 73.

67. Woodrow Wilson, *Constitutional Government in the United States* (New York: Columbia University Press, 1908), 165.

68. For discussions of the Hoover nominations, see Peter G. Fish, "*Red Jacket* Revisited: The Case That Unraveled John J. Parker's Supreme Court Appointment," *Law and History Review* 5 (1987): 51–104; Kenneth W. Goings, *"The NAACP Comes of Age": The Defeat of Judge John J. Parker* (Bloomington: Indiana University Press, 1990); Darlene Clark Hine, "The NAACP and the Supreme Court: Walter F. White and the Defeat of Judge John J. Parker," *Negro History Bulletin* 40 (1977): 753–57; Hugh David Jones, "The Confirmation of Charles Evans Hughes as Chief Justice of the Supreme Court of the United States," M.A. thesis, Duke University, 1962; Francis Wilson O'Brien, "Bicentennial Reflections on Herbert Hoover and the Supreme Court," *Iowa Law Review* 61 (1975): 397–417; Trevor Parry-Giles, "Property Rights, Human Rights, and American Jurisprudence: The Rejection of John J. Parker's Nomination to the Supreme Court," *Southern Communication Journal* 60 (1994): 57–67; Merlo J. Pusey, *Charles Evans Hughes*, 2 vols. (New York: Columbia University Press, 1963); and Richard L. Watson Jr., "The Defeat of Judge Parker: A Study in Pressure Groups and Politics," *Mississippi Valley Historical Review* 50 (1963): 213–34.

69. See Herbert C. Hoover, *The Memoirs of Herbert Hoover: The Cabinet and the Presidency, 1920–1933* (New York: Macmillan, 1952). Historian Donald Lisio argues for the Hoover southern strategy, highlighting in particular the Parker appointment. See Donald J. Lisio, *Hoover, Blacks, and Lily-Whites: A Study of Southern Strategies* (Chapel Hill: University of North Carolina Press, 1985).

70. Lyndon B. Johnson, "Remarks to the Press Announcing the Nomination of Thurgood Marshall as Associate Justice of the Supreme Court," *Public Papers of the Presidents of the United States: Lyndon B. Johnson, 1967* (Washington, D.C.: Government Printing Office, 1968), 611. The last sentence was undoubtedly referring to the fact that President Kennedy's nomination of Marshall to the Second Circuit Court of Appeals in New York in 1961 was stalled in the Senate for almost a year by opposing southern senators, notably Strom Thurmond of South Carolina. See Carl T. Rowan, *Dream Makers, Dream Breakers: The World of Justice Thurgood Marshall* (Boston: Little, Brown, 1993), 279. These remarks appear to be the thoughts and feelings of LBJ, and not the product of a speechwriter or aide. The substance of the speech is found in handwritten notes prepared by LBJ prior to

the introduction of Marshall. See Notes, "June 1967 (3 of 3)," Handwriting File, box 23, LBJ Library. For more on the Marshall nomination, see Parry-Giles, "Character, the Constitution."

71. See John Robert Greene, *The Limits of Power: The Nixon and Ford Administrations* (Bloomington: Indiana University Press, 1992), 36–37.

72. Richard Nixon, *RN: The Memoirs of Richard Nixon*, vol. 1 (New York: Warner Books, 1978), 517. See also Stephen E. Ambrose, *Nixon: Volume 2, The Triumph of a Politician, 1962–1972* (New York: Simon and Schuster, 1989).

73. This refrain becomes a rather persistent theme in Republican politics for the next thirty years. Even Governor George W. Bush pledges to appoint "strict constructionists" to the court, often using the exact same language as Nixon, Reagan, and Bush, the father, before him.

74. Harry S. Dent, *The Prodigal South Returns to Power* (New York: John Wiley and Sons, 1978), 207.

75. Rowland Evans Jr. and Robert D. Novak, *Nixon in the White House: The Frustration of Power* (New York: Random House, 1971), 160.

76. Quoted in Dan T. Carter, *George Wallace, Richard Nixon, and the Transformation of American Politics* (Waco, Tex.: Markham Press Fund, 1992), 21. See also Kenneth O'Reilly, *Nixon's Piano: Presidents and Racial Politics from Washington to Clinton* (New York: Free Press, 1995).

Nixon's southern strategy was of such importance to him and his campaign that he convened a meeting of southern Republicans in May of 1968. Present at the meeting, held in Atlanta, were Senators Strom Thurmond of South Carolina and John Tower of Texas, among others. Nixon expressed his concern for the increased pace of desegregation efforts by the federal government as well as his feeling that liberal judges had taken over the judiciary. He pledged that he would regularly consult with southern GOP leaders and that he would seek to appoint "strict-constructionists" to the federal bench. As Theodore White concludes in his account of this meeting, when it was over, Nixon's "nomination was secure." See Theodore E. White, *The Making of the President, 1968* (New York: Atheneum, 1969), 138. See also Nadine Cohodas, *Strom Thurmond and the Politics of Southern Change* (New York: Simon and Schuster, 1993); and Bruce H. Kalk, "Wormley's Hotel Revisited: Richard Nixon's Southern Strategy and the End of the Second Reconstruction," *North Carolina Historical Review* 71 (1994): 85–105. The apparent connection between Nixon and southern Republicans would fuel speculation that the Haynsworth appointment was the result of a deal struck at this and other meetings. See John P. Frank, *Clement Haynsworth, the Senate, and the Supreme Court* (Charlottesville: University Press of Virginia, 1991), 66.

77. "Remarks at an Informal Meeting with Members of the White House Press Corps on Judge Haynsworth's Nomination to the Supreme Court. October 20, 1969," *Public Papers of the Presidents of the United States: Richard Nixon, 1969* (Washington, D.C.: Government Printing Office, 1971), 815.

78. "Remarks at an Informal Meeting," *Public Papers of the Presidents*, 818.

79. "Remarks at an Informal Meeting," *Public Papers of the Presidents*, 819. The comparison between Haynsworth and Parker is common in the historical accounts of the Haynsworth episode. See most notably Joel B. Grossman and Stephen Wasby, "Haynsworth and Parker: History Does Live Again," *South Carolina Law Review* 23 (1971): 345–59; and Stephen L. Wasby and Joel B. Grossman, "Judge Clement F. Haynsworth, Jr.: New Perspective on his Nomination to the Supreme Court," *Duke Law Journal* 1990 (1990): 74–80. Judge Haynsworth even noted the comparison in his letter to President Nixon following his

rejection. Haynsworth wrote that "I am beginning to think that the travail of the last few months and the action of the Senate, instead of impairing my usefulness on the Court of Appeals may have conditioned me for even better service. Judge Parker made it that way and I believe I can do it, too." See "Letter to Richard Nixon, November 25, 1969," Haynsworth, Clement: White House Special Files, Staff Member and Office Files: President's Personal File, box 9, Richard M. Nixon Materials Project, National Archives.

80. *Congressional Record*, 91st Cong., 1st sess., 1969, 115, pt. 26: 35395.

81. *Congressional Record*, 91st Cong., 1st sess., 1969, 115, pt. 26: 35398.

82. Joel B. Grossman and Stephen L. Wasby, "The Senate and Supreme Court Nominations: Some Reflections," *Duke Law Journal* 1972 (1972): 580. The mismanagement of the nomination by the White House is noted in Dean J. Kotlowski, "Trial by Error: Nixon, the Senate, and the Haynsworth Nomination," *Presidential Studies Quarterly* 26 (1996): 72. This view was reflected in the comments by Democratic Senator Russell Long on *Face the Nation* when he faulted President Nixon for failing to lobby personally on behalf of Haynsworth's nomination. See CBS News, *Face the Nation, 1969* (New York: Holt Information Systems, 1972), 298.

83. "Statement Following the Senate Vote on the Nomination of Judge Clement F. Haynsworth, Jr., as Associate Justice of the Supreme Court. November 21, 1969," *Public Papers of the Presidents of the United States: Richard Nixon, 1969* (Washington, D.C.: Government Printing Office, 1971), 957. See also Dent, *The Prodigal South*, 210–12. Dent also records how popular the Haynsworth nomination was in the South, and how the rejection of the judge, and Nixon's outrage, were particularly effective in that region of the country. Dent's view is confirmed by Michael A. Genovese, *The Nixon Presidency: Power and Politics in Turbulent Times* (New York: Greenwood Press, 1990) 43.

84. William Safire, *Before the Fall: An Inside View of the Pre-Watergate White House* (New York: Ballantine Books, 1977), 342.

85. Ambrose, *Nixon,* 330. Nixon's antipathy toward Congress is also discussed in Keith Whittington, *Constitutional Construction: Divided Powers and Constitutional Meaning* (Cambridge, Mass.: Harvard University Press, 1999), 159–67.

86. Grossman and Wasby, "The Senate and Supreme Court Nominations," 579.

87. As John Ehrlichman records in his memoirs, "Nixon knew instinctively that he should keep some distance between the Carswell debacle and the White House, but he couldn't let the fight alone." See John Ehrlichman, *Witness to Power: The Nixon Years* (New York: Pocket Books, 1982) 106.

88. "Exchange of Letters with Senator William B. Saxbe on the Nomination of Judge G. Harrold Carswell to the Supreme Court. April 1, 1970," *Public Papers of the Presidents 1970,* 332. This exchange of letters prompted responses from senators upset with President Nixon's characterization of his prerogative on Supreme Court nominations. See, for example, *Congressional Record*, 91st Cong., 2nd sess., 1970, 116, pt. 8: 10158–92.

89. Greene, *The Limits of Power,* 40.

90. For a discussion of Robert Bork's view of constitutional interpretation and its failure to recognize the linguistic dimensions of judicial analysis, see Henry L. Ewbank, "The Constitution: Burkeian, Brandesian and Borkian Perspectives," *Southern Communication Journal* 61 (1996): 220–32.

91. Ethan Bronner, *Battle for Justice: How the Bork Nomination Shook America* (New York: W. W. Norton, 1989), 27.

92. *The Public Papers of the Presidents of the United States: Ronald Reagan, 1987,* book 1 (Washington, D.C.: Government Printing Office, 1989), 736.

93. "Recommended Telephone Calls for the President," September 30, 1987, October 5, 1987, WHORM—Subject File, Ronald Reagan Presidential Library.

94. "The President's Radio Address, September 27, 1997," *The Public Papers of the Presidents of the United States, William J. Clinton,* book 2 (Washington, D.C.: Government Printing Office, 1999), 1253.

95. "President's Weekly Radio Address, February 22, 2003," available at http://www.whitehouse.gov/news/releases/2003/02/20030222-1.html

96. Typical of this escalating tension is the 2002–2003 conflict over the Bush Administration's appointment of Miguel Estrada to the D.C. Circuit Court of Appeals. Frustrated by the administration's unwillingness to release memoranda from the nominee's tenure in the solicitor general's office, Democratic senators filibustered the nomination. The president called the Senate's actions "a disgrace." See "President Bush Says Senate Filibuster Decision a 'Disgrace,'" March 6, 2003, available at http://www.whitehouse.gov/news/releases/2003/03/20030306.html. For an analysis of Republican complicity in the shifting confirmation process, see Stephan O. Kline, "The Topsy-Turvy World of Judicial Confirmations in the Era of Hatch and Lott," *Dickinson Law Review* 103 (1999): 247–342.

97. In stark contrast to the fights over district and circuit court appointments, the last two nominees to the Supreme Court were confirmed with relative ease. Utah Republican Senator Orrin Hatch attributes these easy confirmations to President Clinton's willingness to seek advice before asking for the Senate's consent. See Orrin Hatch, *Square Peg: Confessions of a Citizen Senator* (New York: Basic Books, 2002), 179–80.

98. "President Announces Plan for Timely Consideration of Judicial Nominees, October 30, 2002," available at http://www.whitehouse.gov/news/releases/2002/10/print/20021030."

99. See, for example, Stephen L. Carter, *The Confirmation Mess: Cleaning up the Federal Appointments Process* (New York: Basic Books, 1994); Mark Silverstein, *Judicious Choices: The New Politics of Supreme Court Confirmations* (New York: W. W. Norton, 1994); and Twentieth Century Fund, *Judicial Roulette: Report of the Twentieth Century Fund Task Force on Judicial Selection* (New York: Priority, 1988).

100. See Abraham, *Justices, Presidents, and Senators;* Maltese, *The Selling of Supreme Court Nominees;* and Jeffrey K. Tulis, "Constitutional Abdication: The Senate, the President, and Appointments to the Supreme Court," *Case Western Reserve Law Review* 47 (1997): 1331–57.

101. I have developed this argument more fully in Trevor Parry-Giles, "Celebritized Justice, Civil Rights, and the Clarence Thomas Nomination," in *The White House and Civil Rights Policy,* ed. James Arnt Aune and Enrique Rigsby (College Station: Texas A&M University Press, 2005), 268–300.

102. Whittington, *Constitutional Construction,* 19.

CHAPTER 6

THE RHETORICAL PRESIDENCY AND THE MYTH OF THE AMERICAN DREAM

Leroy Dorsey, Texas A&M University

The. American. Dream. Three words, arguably, that identify one of the most powerful yet complex ideas in human existence. James Adams's 1931 groundbreaking work *The Epic of America* gave name to this idea when he summarized centuries of experience on the North American continent. He defined America as "that dream of a land in which life should be better and richer and fuller for every man, with opportunity for each according to his ability or achievement." For Adams, the American Dream did not solely prescribe material success. Instead, it represented a multifaceted vision of opportunity and success for an interconnected community of individuals. According to him, it invoked a "social order in which each man and each woman shall be able to attain to the fullest stature of which they are innately capable, and be recognized by others for what they are, regardless of the fortuitous circumstances of birth or position."[1]

The belief in the Dream—that America is a land of equal opportunity for all—is perhaps undeniable. For instance, the Dream has always called to outsiders. The number of legal immigrants increased by 20 percent over the last few years (topping a million new citizens), with the number of illegal immigrants increasing from an estimated 7 million to nearly 12 million.[2] The Dream has omnipresence in novels, television shows, sermons, movies, speeches, and plays. It reflects a multitude of manifestations that revolve around the core concept of equal opportunity, including but not limited to owning a home, having children, providing service to others, getting rich, attaining an education, succeeding in business, enjoying good health, and having a satisfying job.[3] The American Dream manifests the ideology of the national experience. Martin Luther King Jr.'s "I Have a Dream" speech, considered to be one of the greatest speeches—if not the greatest speech—of all time, testifies to that fact, in that the essence of this country is "deeply rooted in the American Dream" and the belief that "all men are created equal."[4]

The American Dream represents the ultimate reward, yet it is not without its risks. Specifically, there exists a tension between the opportunity for the individual to achieve whatever he or she can achieve and the effect that individualism could have on the overarching sense of community. In other words, can the individual choose self-actualization at the expense of the group? Can the community survive if an individual uses the Dream to become "more equal" than someone else?

While long-lived, the American Dream is not necessarily the definitive answer to creating an indestructible sense of national community. The Dream is not a "kind of miracle glue." In the "twenty-first century, the American Dream remains a major element of our national identity," Jim Cullen remarks, "and yet national identity is itself marked by a sense of uncertainty that may well be greater than ever before." The Dream might lead to social chaos as more people come to believe that it is a "hypocritical sham." Jennifer Hochschild notes that the American Dream is an "impressive ideology" that has "lured people to America and moved them around within it" while keeping some "striving in horrible conditions against impossible odds." It can be "used to club the poor into accepting their lot," she observed, "but it can also be used to make the rich squirm about their luxuries. It encourages people not even to see those aspects of society that make the dream impossible to fulfill for all Americans."[5] The illusion created by the Dream is not foolproof. Hochschild concludes that even those who lived the American Dream, such as Malcolm X, whose life she believed was the "classic stuff of the ideology of the American Dream," still refused to embrace it. Malcolm X declared his disdain for the Dream in his "The Ballot or the Bullet" speech, less than a year after King's celebratory articulation of the Dream: "I'm one of the 22 million black people who are the victims of . . . democracy, nothing but disguised hypocrisy. . . . I'm speaking as a victim of this American system. And I see America through the eyes of the victim. I don't see any American dream; I see an American nightmare."⁶

Whether it is a blessing or a bromide, the power—and fragility—of the American Dream merits rhetorical examination. While parts of this epic story are scattered across countless media, perhaps one of the most important means to synthesize it in a coherent and substantive way rests with the office of the president.

As the rhetorical leader of the nation, the president seeks to lead through words. Not simply an administrator, the president seeks to influence the moral imagination of the country and to inspire its citizenry. As James Ceaser, Glen Thurow, Jeffrey Tulis, and Joseph Bessette note, the rhetorical president engages in a discourse that "soars above the realm" of mundane debate to invoke a loftier discussion of "common purpose and a spirit of idealism."⁷ In many ways, the president acts as the conscience of the nation, reminding us of our responsibilities to achieve an almost magical destiny far grander than any mundane, self-absorbed pursuits we might regularly undertake. Rhetorical presidents can take the disparate elements of individualism and community and shape them into a coherent vision. They can craft an American Dream not only to preserve the integrity of the individual but also to safeguard the sanctity of the community.

But how can they succeed at this feat of rhetorical alchemy? Or, as Robert Bellah wonders, "if the entire social world is made up of individuals, each endowed with the right to be free of others' demands, it becomes hard to . . . cooperate with other people, since such bonds would imply obligations that necessarily impinge on one's freedom."⁸ In fact, what makes the Dream more than the unimaginative state of simply attaining as much as possible as easily as possible? Cullen provides a clue: "The American Dream would have no drama if it were self-evident falsehood or a scientifically demonstrable principle." Rather, the "mystique" of the American Dream derives from the "mythic power" it is able to generate.⁹

Presidents cannot simply perpetuate the various mythic elements of the Dream haphazardly. They must ensure its fidelity as a story that promotes a wondrous and life-affirming vision. This mythic vision, then, has the potential to raise the consciousness of the individual, as well as of the community, regarding their respective responsibilities to each other. Presidents need to connect the fundamental elements of individualism and community in the American Dream. They must provide a coherent, mythological framework that interconnects those key elements while preserving their integrity as discrete concepts.

Time does not allow for an exhaustive examination of each president's expression of the American Dream. I can only begin to illuminate the possibilities open to those in the Oval Office to articulate a myth of the American Dream that promotes individual initiative as a means to unite the community. To that end, I will concentrate initially on two chief executives: Theodore Roosevelt and Ronald Reagan. Both men are recognized as accomplished rhetorical presidents of the modern era. Both were presidents beset by what they considered crises of spirit, realized in overwhelming pursuits of greed. As a result, Roosevelt and Reagan constructed the American Dream as a coherent myth that attempted to transcend any pedestrian expression of it. Their myths projected the future of a sacred community maintained by heroic individuals. And both, for their time, epitomized a common conception of the American Dream: that no matter your origins or beliefs—whether you are a volatile cowboy or a second-rate actor—with hard work, you could be anything, even the president of the United States.

For the most part, Roosevelt focused on the individual hero in the Dream. For him, these individuals resembled the Puritans, willing to work hard for themselves as individuals as well as for the community. However, unlike his typical portrait of mythic heroes who distinguished themselves with their martial abilities, Roosevelt recontextualized heroism. Within the myth of the American Dream, he distinguished heroes as simply those men and women who exhibited the Puritan work ethic in striving to establish a healthy home life. For him, the very act of working toward a positive home life, regardless of the outcome, constituted the American Dream.

Like Roosevelt, Reagan emphasized the mythic hero as well. However, here Reagan deviated from his predecessor. For Reagan, the heroes of the American Dream were the business adventurers, those people who resembled the ancient frontiersmen in their ability to civilize a world, in this case an entrepreneurial world. Furthermore, Reagan articulated a vision of an idyllic universe that existed through cooperation and that had to be preserved as part of America's destiny.

Finally, using Roosevelt and Reagan as benchmarks, I briefly visit George W. Bush's articulation of the American Dream. Like his predecessors, Bush also faced a crisis in the economic spirit of the nation. Moreover, with the supposed fracturing of the American Dream in the twenty-first century, how Bush engaged the Dream deserves attention. For the most part, he stripped his heroes of the grandeur of working for some larger, godly purpose. Instead, the protagonists of Bush's Dream sought a more direct, materialistic existence than their analogues in the Rooseveltian and Reaganesque mythology.

MYTHOLOGIZING AMERICAN HISTORY

Scholarly works that examine the American Dream trace its roots to the Puritans and their odyssey to North America. The Puritans appeared as simple men and women who forged a place where religious freedom could flourish and who constructed a free and democratic government to oversee their new lives.[10] Aboard the flagship *Arbella*—one of four ships escaping to the New World from the strictures of the Church of England—lawyer John Winthrop outlined the beginnings of the Dream. According to Winthrop, God had charged them to work together for a greater good. "We must delight in each other," Winthrop proclaimed, "make others' conditions our own, rejoice together, mourn together, labor and suffer together, always having before our eyes our commission and community."[11] Paradoxically, Puritanism also contained a strong element of individualism. Cullen notes: "So much of their [Puritan] faith was premised on the fate of the solitary soul" that the sense of community invoked by Winthrop provided a "compensating dimension."[12]

Puritans may not actually have used the term *American Dream*, Cullen claims, "but they would have understood the idea: after all, they lived it as people who imagined a certain destiny for themselves."[13] While religious freedom was a motivating factor for the Puritans' escape from the Old World, their destiny involved something much simpler: success. Whatever the endeavor, those settlers pursued worldly success as a sign of otherworldly blessedness. Material success was "given religious sanction by the Puritan doctrine of the secular 'calling' with its assumption that God expected His servants to succeed in some worldly occupation," rewarding such "virtue with wealth."[14] For Puritans, the individual motivations for material success needed to work in tandem with, and not counter to, the success of the group. Writ large, the Puritans sought happiness on earth as a sign of future benefits in God's Paradise. Writ small, a person's contentment sprang from the freedom of opportunity that he or she had to find happiness through material success.

America's Founding Fathers captured this sentiment in a document that is considered a blueprint for the American Dream.[15] The Declaration of Independence formally bestows "these truths to be self-evident, that all men are created equal, that they are endowed by their Creator with certain unalienable Rights, that among these are Life, Liberty and the pursuit of Happiness."[16] However, this document did not guarantee success. What it guaranteed was an opportunity at success. As Hochschild notes, the American Dream promises "that all Americans have a reasonable chance to achieve success as they define it . . . through their own efforts, and to attain virtue and fulfillment through success."[17] The Declaration of Independence provides an open-ended framework for Americans to live their life, tying success to individual initiative, an initiative unhindered by the group. In other words, America's founding document not only tells us what rights irrevocably belong to each of us, but it actually structures "the minutiae of everyday existence: where we go to school, who we marry, [and] what we buy,"[18] since these and many other human activities mark success, happiness, and godly blessing.

As rhetorical leaders for the country, presidents have reaffirmed these Dreams of America throughout the nation's history. At times that discourse promoted success in the here and now as a symbol of otherworldly benefits, earmarked individual will as a means to that success, and assured that the Dream was available to all regardless of their station in life. George Washington's "Farewell Address" noted the separate strengths of the East, West, North, and South and paid homage to their ability to work together to increase their commercial success. Thomas Jefferson's "First Inaugural Address" called for individuals to remember the "overruling Providence" that provided many blessings for the "happiness of man here and his greater happiness hereafter."[19] Abraham Lincoln's Emancipation Proclamation took steps to extend the Dream farther than it had previously reached. The decades following Lincoln's death were a "struggle to realize Lincoln's vision of an entrepreneurial society whose citizens are unencumbered by parentage or origin."[20] Chief executives of the early twentieth century, such as Warren Harding, Calvin Coolidge, and Herbert Hoover, trumpeted a "gospel of success," linking individual business achievement with the public good.[21] Franklin Roosevelt invoked the Dream for every American with his "Four Freedoms."[22] Lyndon Johnson's promotion of a "Great Society," where he declared "unconditional war on poverty," attempted to realize that Puritan vision of American destiny.[23] And so on. This abbreviated history of the American Dream highlights an important notion. It reveals the Dream as mythic in nature.

Myths are culturally meaningful stories that provide human beings with an understanding of their place in the universe. According to Joseph Campbell, that place is next to the gods. "Now the peoples of all the great civilizations everywhere," Campbell notes, "have been prone to . . . regard themselves as favored in a special way, in direct contact with the Absolute."[24] Myths are stories that infuse human behavior with a certain mystical quality, making what we do seem a part of the cosmic functioning of the universe. To that end, Richard Slotkin argues that myths abstract history—making it more sacred in the process—and reduce history "to a set of powerfully evocative and resonant 'icons'" such as the Pilgrims' landing, the Pantheon of Founding Fathers, the self-made man, the Alamo, and the overarching term for them all, the American Dream. Ironically, given their roots in historical accounts, Slotkin concludes that myths are more meaningful than history because "they appear to be repetitions of ageless and transcendent traditions and principles, [stories] that have lost 'the memory that once they were made.' They have transformed 'history into nature,' temporal contingency into divine law."[25] As Ivan Strenski warns, myths are stories that constitute a "bag of tricks we play upon the dead."[26]

This chimerical tendency of myth—to promote a sort of memory loss about history yet create sacred knowledge from that same history—demonstrates its power. Myths act as repositories of eternal truths, making "reality" obvious yet obfuscating. Discussions of the American Dream perpetuate the myth. Advocates choose moments from history to define the Dream, moments that exemplify a way of life—an origin—that supposedly gives a person an individual and a group identity. Even when the inequities in the American Dream are revealed, they unknowingly fuel its hold on the imagination by simultaneously acknowledging the historical precedents that supposedly give the Dream its mythic foundation. For example, while the Puritans left the Old World to experience religious freedom, they were not willing to extend that freedom, or many others, to anyone else.[27] Puritans were like anybody else, Sacvan Bercovitch claims: "They were as eager as any other group of emigrants for land and gain. The difference was that they managed more effectively to explain away their greed."[28] The mythic aspects of the American Dream, however, obscure such pedestrian truths and elevate participants, such as the Puritans, to a revered and iconic status. As Roland Barthes observes, myth is "a pure ideographic system" that "can reach everything" and can "corrupt everything," even in the "very act of refusing oneself to it."[29]

However, the power of myth comes not simply from its ability to leave out the harsher aspects of human interaction. Its rhetorical power rests in its ability to present what it leaves *in* in a compelling way. As a result, myths do not hide the truth as much as reducing it to its simplest form. "Myth does not deny things," Barthes wrote, it simply "purifies" things. . . . It abolishes the complexity of human acts [and] organizes a world which is without contradictions because it is without depth, a world wide open and wallowing in the evident, it establishes a blissful clarity: things appear to mean something by themselves."[30] Myths transform the complexity of human behavior, submerging the foibles and fanaticism of the Puritans, for example, to provide a quintessential truth that identifies a group of people as transcendent in their existence. According to William Dowling, myths deny the "intolerable contradictions" of life and build upon "the very ground cleared by such denial a substitute truth" that makes life bearable.[31] Whether they hide, distort, or deny human action, myths provide the framework for an individual's and a community's existence.

America could be trapped in a mythic construct of its own making; that point is arguable. But the fact that the Dream is powerful is undeniable; it acts as a necessary component to individual and national progress. The Puritans knew this, constructing what Bercovitch describes as a "set of metaphysically (as well as naturally) self-evident truths; a moral framework within which a certain complex of attitudes, assumptions, and belief can be taken for granted as being not only proper but right." In other words, the Puritans needed a Dream of America, one that endorsed individualism, linked private and public concerns, and absolved them of any wrongdoing in the process.[32] In his collection of "stories from the heart of our nation," Dan Rather's book *The American Dream* illustrates the promise and the peril of the constellation of ideas surrounding the Dream. According to Rather, the Dream initially promised freedom for all while leaving "African-Americans in chains and women without franchise." It brought hope to countless immigrants while bringing a "blind spot" to the "massacre and scattering of the Native American nations." For both individuals and the community, the American Dream makes anything possible.[33]

To create a world with endless possibilities, the myth of the American Dream emphasizes two interrelated elements.[34] First, it provides listeners with an avatar in a story. This avatar—the hero—represents a metaphor "for our personal and collective progress through life and history."[35] It embodies a figure walking in the footsteps of our revered ancestors, aspiring to a state of existence with which contemporary listeners can identify. Second, the myth of the American Dream provides audiences with a universe simultaneously like their own, yet grander. Those avatars face incredible challenges in this wondrous universe, a place where heroes discover who they are and what they belong to within the plans of a higher power. The universal scene represents a state where the hero discovers the sublime knowledge of his or her existence.[36] And in many stories, that existence involves safeguarding the community. Thus, successful rhetors construct a myth of the American Dream that reflects the integration of the individual and the community within a wondrous scene that then provides audiences with grand lessons of self-identity.

As the nation's rhetorical visionaries and storytellers, Theodore Roosevelt and Ronald Reagan attempted to mythologize the American Dream. To varying degrees, both men regaled audiences with avatars facing the challenges of a mythic universe, with the destiny of the community at stake.

THE ROOSEVELTIAN DREAM

Although the term *American Dream* had not yet come into common usage, Theodore Roosevelt's presidential discourse invoked a defining element of it. As he remarked in 1904, "We can keep this Republic true to the principle of those who founded it . . . [by] treating each man on his worth as a man; neither holding it for nor against him that he occupies any particular station in life."[37] This interpretation of the Dream rested upon the democratic ideal that each person deserved an opportunity to succeed. For Roosevelt, the American Dream meant an "equality of opportunity" and an "equality of conditions" so that "each man [can] show the stuff that is in him."[38] In short, each person deserved the chance to seize his or her destiny. Roosevelt argued this point metaphorically in his famous "Square Deal" speech in 1905. At a banquet in Dallas, Texas, the president admitted that it was not possible to "give every man the best hand," nor would every man be able to succeed with the cards dealt to him. However, what was essential, he declared, was that there would be no "crookedness in the dealing."[39] As long as there was a level playing field for all participants, the nation would embody the Founders' conception of what would become known as the American Dream.

Roosevelt undoubtedly found his interpretation of the Dream under fire, given the circumstances of the time. In particular, the playing field appeared less than even due to the rise of corporate America, and the resulting public backlash accompanying that rise. Industrial production in America grew markedly during the late 1800s and early 1900s. Because of the country's abundant resources, waves of immigrant labor, and breakthroughs in technology, America became the world's leading exporter by 1900. Coinciding with these revolutionary changes in production and distribution was a control mechanism far different than people had known before: the corporation. Corporations dominated many important industries, thus controlling nearly all aspects of purchasing, production, distribution, and wholesaling. Corporations, with their watchwords of management, efficiency, and profit, soon became "central to the economic growth and well-being of the nation." In the process these industrial powerhouses fashioned themselves to overcome any problem, including those they perceived emanating from the government and the public itself.[40]

Roosevelt understood the necessity of material success for the nation's well-being, but he also warned the public in 1902 that "evils are real and some of them are menacing, but they are the outgrowth, not of misery or decadence, but of prosperity—of the progress of our gigantic industrial development."[41] His concern of corporate power outpacing that of the government caused him to admit in his autobiography that the question was not which method could be used to control corporations. "The absolutely vital question," he wrote, "was whether the Government had power to control them at all."[42] With government's multiple levels of bureaucracy, complex policies of operation, and ability to transform legally a group of people into a fictive "single entity" that was seemingly unaccountable for the sins of the group, corporations "grew increasingly arcane and mysterious."[43]

As the number of corporations increased at the turn of the twentieth century, distrust and envy of them increased as well, particularly when journalists trumpeted the questionable practices of corporations in newspapers and magazines. Termed *muckrakers* by Roosevelt in 1906, these reporters catalogued a host of corporate abuses. These abuses by corporate owners ranged from the somewhat benign to the reprehensible, such as protecting assets in holding companies for family dynasties, controlling prices of consumer goods, declaring violent war on unions, and disregarding the public's well-being by selling unsafe products.[44] Corporations made the playing field of opportunity uneven for individuals and smaller companies, corrupting the American Dream in the process, and in turn creating resentment in the public at large.

For Roosevelt, not only did corporate power seem beyond the law; it also created a greater problem. He worried that muckraking exposés would exacerbate the public's bitterness and cause people to lash out destructively at the trusts, thus jeopardizing the financial stability of the nation. In his autobiography, he concluded: "Sweeping attacks upon all . . . men of means . . . would sound the death-knell of the Republic; and such attacks become inevitable" if the corrupt practices of corporate America are left "unchecked and unhindered."[45]

However, Roosevelt realized that neither laws nor Progressive remedies alone were the sole answers. Rather, as is evident in much of his discourse, the moral uplift of the nation became paramount when dealing with the Dream in America. "In the last analysis," he declared, "the vital factor in each man's effort to achieve success in life must be his own character."[46] To that end, he used the "bully pulpit" in an attempt to minimize the twin evils of selfishness and anger that seemed to infect the nation's spirit. He reminded everyone—corporate owners and individual citizens alike—of the meaning of responsibility, opportunity, and success in American life. In other words, President Roosevelt sought to reenergize the tenets of the American Dream.

Through much of his public advocacy, Roosevelt invoked mythic themes as a means to influence audiences, particularly for the avatar in the story.[47] These mythic heroes represent the epitome of the human spirit—a spirit that reaches beyond its limitations to achieve incredible feats.[48] As Roosevelt suspected, such stories and their heroic protagonists contained those lessons of history that people must learn as a means to manage their own world.[49] Using the Puritan as a legendary hero, Roosevelt called for modern audiences to embrace that example. "The Puritan's task was to conquer a continent," the president asserted on one occasion," and the Puritan accomplished that by his "iron sense of duty, his unbending, unflinching will to do the right as it was given him to see the right."[50] The president's invocation of the Puritans' spirit taught the frontier lesson of "rugged individualism" to his listeners. However, in highlighting the mythic lesson of individual character, Roosevelt used it as a prerequisite to experiencing the American Dream. As a result, not everyone could experience the Dream—only those heroes who could show the "right stuff" were eligible.[51] With this prerequisite, the president defined the essential elements of the Dream—opportunity and success—in a way that also addressed the twin evils of greed and envy.

Regarding the president's interpretation of the American Dream, the individual's character proved vital to this myth. According to Roosevelt, individuals had the responsibility to help themselves rather than look for an external savior. As such, Roosevelt invoked the theme of rugged individualism: the hero's ability to be independent as he or she asserted control over a harsh environment.[52] For his audience, this became the first qualification for access to the American Dream. "The first requisite of a good citizen in this Republic," he stated at a Chamber of Commerce banquet in 1902, "is that he shall be able and willing to pull his weight."[53] In a variety of forums, listeners repeatedly heard this mythic theme of self-reliance as a definition of what it meant to embrace the Dream. In fact, Roosevelt routinely assessed individuals by their ability to seize opportunities.[54] He noted that the "highest standard" of citizenship involved standing up "manfully" for your rights.[55] At the Alamo in 1905, he declared, "Every man of us at times needs a helping hand. . . . But if [your] brother lies down, you can do mighty little in carrying him. You can help him up; but once up he has got to walk himself."[56] Embracing a quasi-Darwinian rationale, Roosevelt believed that if you could not help yourself, you proved unworthy of citizenship and thus of the Dream itself.

Like any heroic avatar, the president demanded that the individual be not only willing but capable of taking hold of an opportunity and gaining success with it. While the term *opportunity* invokes a myriad of possible avenues for an individual, Roosevelt ensured that his audiences understood the limits of that term. For him, the as-yet-to-be-named American Dream that promised an equality of opportunity simply meant a person had the opportunity to work hard. For Roosevelt, this is what the universe provided. "The best prize that life offers," he announced at the New York State Fair in 1903, "is a prize open to every man," and that involved the "chance to work hard at work worth doing."[57] This Rooseveltian philosophy of the "strenuous life"—the "life of toil and effort, of labor and strife"—elevated the notion of the Puritan work ethic as the goal in and of itself. He attempted to replace any notions that people had that opportunities requiring little effort were worthwhile.[58] Hard work itself was the embodiment of opportunity, Roosevelt urged, because there was "no room in our healthy American life for the mere idler."[59] He emphasized the democratic nature of this point to a group of firefighters in 1902: "Your work is hard. Do you suppose I mention that because I pity you? No; not a bit. I don't pity any man who does hard work worth doing. I admire him. I pity the creature who doesn't work.... The work is what counts, and if a man does his work well and it is worth doing, then it matters but little in which line that work is done."[60] Rather than be envious of wealthy executives, Roosevelt stressed to audiences that they needed to be appreciative of their own hard work in and of itself, even if it was mundane labor. He created a contemporary universe that resembled the scene Puritans discovered on the frontier: a sometimes harsh realm where strenuous effort was necessary to survive and grow.

Roosevelt's message also aimed at corporate owners, whose greed had been creating luxury and ease for themselves and their descendants; according to Roosevelt, they had not attained the real Dream. Opportunity simply meant hard work, whether a person was rich or poor. Invoking the mythos of the Puritan's drive for individual accomplishment, Roosevelt reminded a 1907 audience that the "life of mere pleasure, of mere effortless ease, is as ignoble for a nation as for an individual."[61] The opportunity for hard work could help a person now—just as it had the Puritans—to become the type of citizen that could realize the American Dream.

Opportunity was not the only component that Roosevelt defined narrowly. Again limiting the expanse of the Dream, Roosevelt linked success primarily to raising an upright family. He stated it bluntly during his second term: "No piled up wealth," he warned, "no splendor of material growth . . . will permanently avail any people unless its home life is healthy."[62] For him, a "healthy" home life placed men and women in their traditional roles. According to him, "No man . . . can deserve the respect of his fellows, unless first of all he is a good man in his own family, unless he does his duty faithfully by his wife and children."[63] Likening him to the mythic avatar of the frontier, Roosevelt said the modern husband demonstrated courage, common sense, and a willingness to work hard and to fight hard in service to his family. Roosevelt also charged women with an equal burden to be successful. In short, the good wife managed the home and procreated. "There are certain old truths," he announced to the National Congress of Mothers in 1905, that the woman "is to be the helpmeet, the housewife, and mother." As such, they undertook the "first and greatest duty of womanhood" by having and raising healthy children "so that the race shall increase." The president measured individual success metaphorically, in military terms: "The man or woman who deliberately forgoes [having children]" is a "creature" that "merits contempt as hearty as any visited upon the soldier who runs away in battle."[64]

Roosevelt undoubtedly recognized the potential backlash from emphasizing the individual; emphasis on individual needs had, for him, given way to rampant greed, and consequently, unchecked envy in modern America. To counter this, Roosevelt added one more facet to the mythic hero's role in the American Dream. The Puritan owed his success, Roosevelt admitted, "to the fact that he combined in a very remarkable degree both the power of individual initiative . . . and the power of acting in combination with his fellows."[65] The hard work and successful family life of the individual, as he described, were the building blocks for the larger community. The president observed in his "First Annual Message" that without individual citizens embracing this notion, the nation itself would suffer: "The fundamental rule in our national life . . . is that, on the whole, and in the long run, we shall go up or down together."[66]

Roosevelt narrowed the definitions of opportunity and success in the American Dream. Nevertheless, in the process, he also provided an epic and eloquent vision of it in 1905:

> See what the things are that you are proudest of as you look back, and you will in almost every case find that those memories of pride are associated not with days of ease but with days of effort, with the day when you had to do all that was in you for some worthy end, and the worthiest of all worthy ends is to make those that are closest and nearest to you . . . happy and not sorry that you are alive; and after that has been done to be able so to handle yourself that you can feel[,] when the end comes[,] that on the whole[,] your country . . . [is] a little better off and not a little worse off because you have lived. This kind of success is open to every one of us.[67]

While not denying the need for material success of some sort, Roosevelt focused on the individual and prescribed a limited interpretation of the American Dream. He sought to replace the selfishness and greed that had been the watchwords of the nation with his homely definitions of opportunity and success.

Under the Rooseveltian model, establishing a morally strong home became the benchmark of individual and public success.

Like Roosevelt, Ronald Reagan mythologized an American hero in his stories. However, Reagan also focused on the godly nature of the universe created by such heroes.

Dreaming in Reagan's America

Ronald Reagan's association with the American Dream has been established. Kurt Ritter and David Henry observe that Reagan invoked the concept from his earliest days on the stump throughout his presidency, moving the nation to a distinctively Reaganesque worldview of communism and government bureaucracy. Cullen also remarks that Reagan inspired audiences through repeated retellings of John Winthrop's "city upon a hill." For G. Thomas Goodnight, Reagan's vision of the American Dream resonated not just at home but abroad as well, promoting a form of "American exceptionalism—a language of special purpose, divine providence, and epochal destiny."[68]

For Reagan, the American Dream meant freedom, and in particular, it symbolized a nation "that enshrines liberty, democratic rights, and dignity for every individual." As he stated in his 1984 State of the Union Address, the Dream "isn't one of making government bigger; it's keeping faith with the mighty spirit of free people under God." Freedom's success, he maintained repeatedly, could only come with the country's economic success.[69] Upon entering the White House, however, Reagan faced a set of challenges that had the potential to impede the nation's willing acceptance of what he considered the American Dream.

For Reagan, the economy inherited from his predecessor, Jimmy Carter, was problematic. In his 1981 Inaugural speech, Reagan began by thanking Carter for his "gracious cooperation in the transition process" but then quickly blasted the former president for his mishandling of the economy. "These United States are confronted with an economic affliction of great proportions," Reagan declared, "We suffer from the longest and one of the worst sustained inflations in our national history. It distorts our economic decisions, penalizes thrift, and crushes the struggling young and the fixed-income elderly alike."[70] The culprit for this was the "excessive growth of government," whose "intervention and intrusion" in the nation's life had stifled its economic development. These words undoubtedly resonated with audiences who were currently living with a double-digit inflation rate, plunging corporate profits, and an increasing unemployment rate.⁷¹ Thus, as Erwin Hargrove notes, Carter's inconsistent energy and tax policies, and his lack of rhetorical leadership at home and abroad, paved the way for a "Republican president who promised to act boldly to overcome the contradictions" of the previous presidency.⁷²

Reagan touched on the myriad forms of freedom and the American Dream in his first Inaugural Address. For example, regarding freedom from oppression, he announced that Americans were a "united people pledged to maintaining a political system which guarantees individual liberty to a greater degree than any other." On the issue of freedom from want, Reagan assured listeners that they were "ready to do what must be done to ensure happiness" for themselves and their children. Ensuring equality for all, he maintained, "with no barriers born of bigotry or discrimination," was also essential.⁷³ Reagan took these manifestations of freedom—happiness, equality, and liberty—and placed them within two seemingly contradictory frames. On the one hand, he contextualized national life by linking it to the drive for economic prosperity. On the other hand, Reagan also declared that the nation would be unbounded by mundane concerns such as economic matters. Reagan brought these contradictory elements together seamlessly in his myth of the American Dream.

While Roosevelt generally downplayed material prosperity as the means and the consequence of the American Dream, Reagan focused substantially on economic issues. According to Reagan, the nation realized the American Dream by achieving a robust economy. In an address to the nation less than three weeks after his first Inaugural, Reagan gave voice to what many contemporary Americans have come to consider the essence of the Dream. Early in the address, Reagan asked a simple, yet provocative question: "What's happened to that American dream of owning a home?" According to him, a decade earlier virtually any family could afford to buy a home, while currently, "fewer than 1 out of 11 families" could afford one. Reagan alleged that this Dream had suffered due to an organizational entity that had become uncontrolled and reckless with its spending. "Since 1960 our government has spent $5.1 trillion," Reagan revealed, "our debt has grown by 648 billion. Prices have exploded by 178 percent. How much better off are we for all that? Well, we all know we're very much worse off."⁷⁴

Reagan placed the blame squarely on government during his first speech to Congress in February, 1981. Reminiscent of Roosevelt's condemnation of corporate institutions that punished individuals, Reagan chastised the government repeatedly for subverting the individual Dream of Americans. According to Reagan, overregulation by government agencies had caused small business owners to delay plans for growth, stifle new job creation, and lower national productivity. Furthermore, the government's penchant for borrowing money at "excessive" interest rates to provide low-interest loans penalized the taxpayer with higher interest rates overall, and mismanagement involving tax dollars—including outright fraud—constituted a "national scandal" that demoralized the nation.[75]

Even abroad, Reagan carried a similar message about economic freedom. The president promoted the American Dream overseas, again calling particular attention to those governments that interfered with the people's right to attain economic freedom in their lives. Speaking at the Brandenburg Gate in West Berlin in 1987, where he uttered the famous line, "Mr. Gorbachev, tear down this wall," Reagan identified the "most fundamental distinction of all between East and West"—a totalitarian government that produced "backwardness because it does such violence to the spirit" that it cripples the "human impulse to create." The remedy, according to the president, involved linking economic prosperity to freedom and in turn realizing the American Dream: "Prosperity can come about only when the farmer and businessman enjoy economic freedom. . . . And freedom itself is transforming the globe. In the Philippines, in South and Central America, democracy has been given a rebirth. Throughout the Pacific, free markets are working miracle after miracle of economic growth." Reagan put it bluntly when he presciently warned: "The Soviet Union faces a choice: it must make fundamental changes, or it will become obsolete."[76] Implicit in his condemnation of the Soviet government preventing economic freedom was a criticism of America's government for engaging in similar practices.

Reagan had created a harsh reality of economic distress at home caused by the federal government, a large, organizational entity that, like the corporations in Roosevelt's era, had stifled the fulfillment of the American Dream. Such a portrait of a governmental machine out of control could perhaps prepare Reagan's listeners to embrace his mythic, individual-driven version of the American Dream. While curtailing the excesses of government was a necessary step in economic recovery, Reagan looked to individual Americans as the true avatars of change. "We can restore our economic strength and build opportunities like none we've ever had before," the president declared in his first public speech following an attempt on his life, and "all we need to begin with is a dream that we can do better than before." This mystical quality of dreaming marked Americans as different, Reagan believed: "We've always reached for a new spirit and aimed at a higher goal," having always demonstrated courage and bold determination.[77] To that end, he charged individual listeners with the responsibility of restoring the American Dream for themselves and the nation.

Like Roosevelt, Reagan provided his audience with mythic heroes who exemplified the American Dream. These heroes, in the classic sense however, Reagan largely eschewed. Rather, the Great Communicator merged the traditional hero who engaged in fantastic feats of derring-do with a more entrepreneurial form of heroics.

Reagan frequently used anecdotes of "real" heroes to teach lessons about citizenship. Such larger-than-life protagonists simultaneously stand apart from ordinary people and act as models for them.[78] In his State of the Union addresses, the president promoted the notion of individual heroism. His anecdotes in the 1982 State of the Union, for example, glorified the martial strength and courage reminiscent of traditional heroes. "We don't have to turn to our history books for heroes," Reagan said of Jeremiah Denton, former Vietnam POW and now U.S. Senator, who was in attendance during the speech. Reagan lauded him as epitomizing heroism.[79] Reagan identified the "common" people who exhibited the traits of mythic heroes. Two weeks before that 1982 address, a passenger plane taking off during a snowstorm from a Washington, D.C., airport crashed into the Potomac River. Reagan lauded the heroes of that hour: "We saw again the spirit of American heroism at its finest—the heroism of dedicated rescue workers saving crash victims from icy waters. We saw the heroism of one of our young government employees, Lenny Skutnik, who, when he saw a woman lose her grip on the helicopter line, dived into the water and dragged her to safety."[80] These anecdotes reflected the mantle of traditional heroism worn by everyday people, acting as a touchstone for America's heroes of yesteryear. However, these were not the ultimate heroes of the president's story about the American Dream.

For Reagan, the true heroes of the American Dream did not emerge during the sensational moments of traditional heroism. Rather, true heroic individuals engaged in the quieter pursuits that pushed the nation along the path of economic prominence. These were the "quiet everyday heroes of American life," Reagan observed in his 1982 State of the Union address. These heroes were the "parents who sacrifice long and hard so their children will know a better life than they have known . . . unsung heroes who may not have realized their dreams themselves but who then reinvest those dreams in their children."[81] This theme of everyday heroes who advanced the economic viability of the nation, and thus the American Dream of freedom, appeared frequently. In his 1984 State of the Union, Reagan again lauded the economic champions of American myth. Reminiscent of Roosevelt's requirement of the "right stuff" to gain access to the American Dream, Reagan called for people to be "risktakers" who not only had the vision to "create tomorrow's opportunities," but the diligence to make those visions a reality. Reagan identified the "heroes for the eighties" as "people like Barbara Proctor, who rose from a ghetto to build a multimillion-dollar advertising agency in Chicago," and avatars such as "Carlos Perez, a Cuban refugee, who turned $27 and a dream into a successful importing business." For the president, these people constituted heroes because they and others like them had "helped 4 million Americans find jobs."[82] Although focused on acquiring financial stability for themselves, these people also worked for the nation's good.

Strategically, Reagan's economic heroes resembled the time-lost heroes of American culture who challenged the unknown and brought back wonders to those they left behind, transforming the universe in which they lived. "The American Dream is a song of hope that rings through the night winter air," Reagan observed in 1986, creating an urge:

> to venture a daring enterprise; to unearth new beauty in music, literature, and art, to discover a new universe inside a tiny silicon chip or a single human cell. We see the dream coming true in the spirit of discovery of Richard Cavoli—all his life he's been enthralled by the mysteries of medicine [and does] work that could reduce the harmful effects of X rays on patients. . . . And we see the dream born again in the joyful compassion of a thirteen year-old, Trevor Ferrell. . . . Trevor left his suburban Philadelphia home to bring blankets and food to the helpless and homeless. And now, 250 people help him fulfill his nightly vigil.[83]

These heroes, like the business entrepreneurs, demonstrated that "big government" was an unnecessary prop for an individual's economic viability. America's new heroes, and their quiet yet ambitious pursuits unhampered by government interference, bolstered the Dream of an economic freedom to be enjoyed by everyone in the nation.

Reagan's direct coupling of economic prominence to the fulfillment of the American Dream undoubtedly helped to lead pundits to identify the 1980s as the "Greed Decade."[84] Whether Reagan understood the potential of his stories to afflict the citizenry with the so-called sin of greed is unknown. Yet, his messages revealed a safeguard—a means of absolution. Despite his heroes' individual drives for economic prosperity, they also worked to create a reality in which others would share in that prosperity. Reagan articulated a wondrous universe that sprang from the actions of heroic individuals.

The universe that President Reagan created in his public speeches resembled the mystical and fantastic worlds typical of grand myths.[85] His heroes worked toward transforming the nation into an idyllic bastion of liberty. Invoking crucial moments in America's search for freedom, including the American Revolution and the events of the Alamo, Reagan asked that we "hear again the echoes of our past.... It is the American sound. It is hopeful, big-hearted, idealistic, daring, decent, and fair. That's our heritage, that's our song.... And may [God] continue to hold us close as we fill the world with our sound—in unity, affection, and love—one people under God, dedicated to the dream of freedom that He has placed in the human heart."[86] Just as the discoveries by early explorers of the North American continent helped to transform the civilization that they left behind, so had Reagan's heroes signaled the possibilities for the nation. Through their hard work and their sacrifices for economic viability, the national universe would be empowered by the American Dream and become akin to a mystical oasis of freedom, blessed by the hand of God. Invoking the Puritans on the *Arbella* as progenitors of his audience, Reagan declared that "divine providence" had brought and continued to bring a "special kind of people from every corner of the world, who had a special love for freedom" to America's shores. "We're bound together," he declared, "because, like them, we too dare to hope—hope that our children will always find here the land of liberty in a land that is free." Thus, it was imperative that everyone understand that their work "can never be truly done until every man, woman, and child shares in our gift, in our hope, and stands with us in the light of liberty." Such a light symbolized "faith with a dream of long ago and [guided] millions still to a future of peace and freedom."[87]

Perhaps Reagan's most eloquent characterization of the universe in which his heroes lived came during his farewell address. On that occasion, he articulated the overarching framework of America's destiny. "I wasn't a great communicator," he admitted, "but I communicated great things" that "came from the heart of a great nation—from our experience, our wisdom, and our belief in the principles that have guided us for two centuries." That wisdom, Reagan declared, involved the realization of America's sacred place in the cosmos:

> I've spoken of the shining city all my political life, but I don't know if I ever quite communicated what I saw when I said it. But in my mind it was a tall, proud city built on rocks stronger than oceans, windswept, God-blessed, and teeming with people of all kinds living in harmony and peace.... And how stands the city on this winter night ...? After 200 years, two centuries, she still stands strong and true

on the granite ridge, and her glow has held steady no matter what storm. And she's still a beacon, still a magnet for all who must have freedom, for all the pilgrims from all the lost places who are hurtling through the darkness, toward home.[88]

Given the American Dream's multifaceted nature, it is no wonder that Roosevelt and Reagan differed as much they did on the particulars in the myth. Reagan allowed virtually anyone access to the Dream, but Roosevelt guarded it more closely. Reagan focused his heroes on proving their mettle in both the economic and social arenas; Roosevelt believed his avatars needed to find success at a more homely level. Ultimately, though, their visions promoted the fundamental substance of the Dream—the heroic individual in service to a morally uplifted community. Now, how fared George W. Bush?

BUSH AND THE AMERICAN DREAM

Almost from the start of his presidency, George W. Bush faced an onslaught of national and international problems and catastrophes. One of the first involved the near miss of Bush actually becoming president. Given the problems in the 2000 election, including voter disenfranchisement through miscounted ballots, lawsuits brought by the candidates to the U.S. Supreme Court, and the high court's "political" decision to decide the case in Bush's favor, many Americans questioned the integrity of the democratic process. As a result, *Newsweek* declared that Bush rode to Washington "weaker than Superman in a Suburban full of kryptonite—all name and no mandate."[89] Next, by all accounts, the terrorist attack at the World Trade Center on September 11, 2001, forever changed America. No longer would the citizenry feel safe in the comfort of its freedoms with terrorists enjoying those same freedoms to plot against the nation.[90] America's subsequent "wars on terror," in Afghanistan and Iraq, have led to growing discontent at home. Soldiers and their families have questioned extended stays overseas, critics have wondered about the validity of information regarding Iraqi weapons of mass destruction, and many citizens have decried the Patriot Act's abridgment of several constitutional freedoms.[91] In terms of the economy, like Roosevelt, Bush faced seemingly out-of-control corporate greed in the forms of Enron, WorldCom, and Arthur Anderson. Like Reagan, Bush found himself confronted with a sagging economy and a high—though not double-digit—jobless rate. Particularly, the "war on terror" had exacerbated the economic problems in the nation, as many people saw the 87-billion-dollar price tag for the war in 2003 as straining an already overtaxed America.[92]

As President Bush settled into the White House, the validity of the American Dream seemed in doubt. Entering the twenty-first century, the nation has found near simultaneous challenges to its ideals involving equality, happiness, freedom, and material success. As one Time/CNN/Harris poll indicated in early 2003, 50 percent of Americans agree that the "American dream has become impossible for most people to achieve."[93] Even Bush admitted that "some people aren't sure that dream extends to them."[94] In fact, he explained in early 2001 that one of the reasons he ran for president was due to his concern "that the American Dream, the idea that you can . . . have a dream and work hard to achieve it . . . is bright for everybody in America."[95] For Bush's success as a rhetorical leader, reaffirming the mythic Dream becomes even more critical for the nation's sense of self and progress.

Although he did not use the term *American Dream* in his 2001 Inaugural Address, Bush invoked it when he articulated that the rights of the individual must balance with the needs of the community. Coming off the events of the 2000 post-election phase when many voters felt disenfranchised, Bush reminded Americans of their shared story of equality. According to him, America's story was a "story of a new world that became a friend and liberator of the old, [and] a story of a slave-holding society that became a servant of freedom." Like Reagan, Bush offered the Dream to everyone. America embodied a land of ideals and, for Bush, the "grandest of these ideals is an unfolding American promise that everyone belongs, that everyone deserves a chance, that no insignificant person was ever born." Bush also ensured that individuals understood their responsibility to a larger good. "I ask you to seek a common good beyond your comfort," he declared, "to serve your nation, beginning with your neighbor. I ask you to be citizens: citizens, not spectators; citizens, not subjects; responsible citizens, building communities of service and a nation of character."[96]

In terms of the economic impulses of the American Dream, Bush followed Reagan's lead and tied the Dream directly to economic matters. In front of the New Jersey Chamber of Commerce in 2001, Bush identified one goal of the Dream. "It seems like, to me the harder you work, the more money you ought to put in your pocket."[97] From this point, however, Bush deviated from Roosevelt and Reagan. The avatars in Bush's Dream achieved their heroic status by engaging primarily in economic feats such as owning a business or by owning a home. Gone, essentially, were the achievements of classic heroes, as told by Roosevelt and Reagan—protagonists who worked to pull themselves up materially, while helping to pull up those around them. Bush's American

Dream revolved extensively around the individual avatar and not the relationship between the individual and the community.

One set of Bush's avatars attained their heroic status as business owners. Particularly, the president heralded minority ownership of business as representing the American Dream. "One of the most hopeful statistics I heard was in the great State of California," Bush announced to the National Conference of State Legislators in March, 2001, "where there are over 700,000 Latino-owned small businesses in that State." For Bush, that represented a "fantastic statistic about the American Dream and the American experience and the whole concept of owning something."[98] Three weeks later, while visiting Bajan Industries, a minority-owned packaging company in Missouri, the president remarked that the owner's immigrant roots, as well as the owner's wish to provide for his children, earmarked the company as a symbol of the American Dream. "If part of the American experience is realizing a dream and building up your own asset base, an equally important part of that is passing your asset base on to your kin. . . . It's part of the American Dream."[99] Bush's observation contradicted Roosevelt's interpretation of this aspect of the Dream. For Roosevelt, families who simply passed their wealth to their offspring served not the community but their own selfish natures.

Bush's other protagonists in the Dream were the homeowners. According to him, "owning a home lies at the heart of the American Dream" and represented a "foundation for families." During one of his Radio Addresses in 2002, the president revealed his worry about that aspect of the American Dream. "While nearly three-quarters of all white Americans own their homes," he observed, "less than half of all African Americans and Hispanic Americans are homeowners." Like Roosevelt, Bush called for leveling the playing field to provide equal opportunities for all. To close the gap of home ownership between different groups of people, Bush proposed the American Dream Downpayment fund. This legislation would provide about forty thousand low-income families with grants to help them with down payments and closing costs. Because of the fund, home ownership would be available for more citizens and would thus empower "people to help themselves and to help one another."[100]

Bush's merger of individual and community concerns mirrored Reagan's position, but his depiction of the American universe differed substantially from that of the former president. Reagan described a wondrous scene that already existed because individuals and communities shared the American Dream. Bush delayed providing such a comforting vision by observing that the existing universe would have to change before the Dream could be realized. At a church in Georgia in 2002, Bush articulated the road Americans must follow to realize the Dream:

> I understand . . . there are too many people who say . . . "My eyes are shut to the American Dream. I don't see the Dream." And we'd better make sure, for the good of the country, that the dream is vibrant and alive. It starts with having great education systems. . . . It means that we unleash the faith-based programs to help change people's hearts. . . . In order to change America and to make sure the great American Dream shines in every community—every community—we must unleash the compassion and kindness of the greatest nation on the face of the earth.[101]

For Bush, the American Dream would be open to anyone but would not exist until enough individuals could achieve material success through largely entrepreneurial heroics. With the mythic universe not in existence, Americans might see the delay of the Dream as its denial.

CONCLUSION

Immigrants flock to this country for it. Native-born citizens jealously guard its access. Foreign powers seek to destroy us because of it. Individuals attempt to see whatever they need to see in it. It can mean everything and, consequently, nothing. "The American dream is a term used in so many different contexts," Joseph Daleiden observes, "that today it is probably devoid of a common understanding."[102] Some form of "common understanding," however, must exist. In some manner, the appeal of individual success must be balanced (enough) for the community itself to attain success.

To create that balance, presidents Roosevelt, Reagan, and Bush engaged the myth of the American Dream. Myths represent transcendent stories that sanctify not only a group's origin but its destiny as well. Within such narratives, the storyteller invokes heroic avatars that exist within a wondrous place, acting as archetypes for the audiences. To varying degrees, Roosevelt, Reagan, and Bush accomplished this.

To combat a malaise of spirit that he believed had gripped the nation, Roosevelt attempted to energize his mythic version of the American Dream. To that end, he focused on the individual citizen-as-hero to achieve the Dream, an opportunity open only to those willing to work for it, and in which success served not just the individual but the community as well.

The key for Roosevelt was the larger-than-life hero worthy of emulation. Moreover, Roosevelt's universe subtly echoed the Puritan's world-scene in which unyielding determination and homely character were needed to prosper materially and spiritually.

Reagan addressed the exigencies of the nation's economic crisis by introducing new avatars for his age. For him, the true heroes of the American Dream represented those individuals who, like their mythic predecessors, challenged the entrepreneurial frontiers to discover new ways of creating financial viability. This viability, however, proved not just for economic satisfaction; Reagan's heroes epitomized those legendary champions whose determination and ingenuity earmarked them as archetypes of good character. The new avenues these protagonists discovered provided opportunities for others to realize their Dream. For Reagan, this drama took place in a numinous setting, one that not only indicated the blessing of some Cosmic Authority but placed Americans particularly as the chosen people of God.

Bush, like Roosevelt, concentrated more on the individual in the Dream. However, unlike Roosevelt, Bush limited the Dream largely to material success. In the process, he may have lessened the importance of the other areas of the Dream that could provide comfort to an individual waiting for the opportunity to achieve success in the financial arena. Furthermore, Roosevelt's avatars and their resemblance to the Puritan's connected modern listeners to a legendary past universe and bespoke of an idyllic present; and Reagan provided a mystical setting for the realization of the Dream. Bush's scene—with no distinct, historical analogue or sense of wonder—limited the epic sense of scene in the myth. Bush's invocation of the American Dream appeared counter to both the Rooseveltian expression of homely virtues and the Reaganesque mythology of heroic charity and community development.

Despite all the warm feelings that we as a nation have because the Dream distinguishes us as special, there exists a guttural, almost a distasteful aura to it. At perhaps its most common conception, as Bush articulated, the Dream simply means attaining financial stability as easily as possible. For Roosevelt, such a conception of the Dream would signal the end of American culture. Or as Paul Krugman observed, combining the research that shows social mobility "has declined considerably over the past few decades" with "other research that shows a drastic increase in income and wealth inequality, you reach an uncomfortable conclusion: America looks more and more like a class-ridden society. . . . Goodbye, Horatio Alger. And goodbye, American Dream."[103]

However, the Dream cannot remain at that most common of individualistic levels; it becomes too severe and exclusionary, leading, quite possibly, to a fracturing of American identity and sense of community.[104] As the nation's leader—perhaps more appropriately as its conscience—the rhetorical president must attempt to reconcile the dichotomy inherent in the Dream between the advancement of the individual and the progress of the nation. The president must engage the Dream, giving it a mythic coherence that affirms the better nature of its heroes and the community. To be sure, the president must realize that the nation is only as strong as the myth that he tells about it.

NOTES

1. James T. Adams, *The Epic of America* (1931; Boston: Little, Brown, and Company, 1946), 415.

2. For the immigration numbers, see U.S. Dept. of Justice, Immigration and Naturalization Service, "Annual Report: Legal Immigration, Fiscal Year 2001," August 2002, at http://www.bcis.gov/graphics/shared/aboutus/statistics/IMM2001.pdf; U.S. Dept. of Justice, Immigration and Naturalization Service, "Executive Summary: Estimates of the Unauthorized Immigrant Population Residing in the United States, 1990–2000," January 31, 2003, at http://www.bcis.gov/graphics/shared/aboutus/statistics/2000ExecSumm.pdf; CNN, "Estimated Number of Illegal Immigrants in U.S.," May 11, 2006, http://www.cnn.com.

3. James T. Adams, *The American: The Making of a New Man* (New York: Charles Scribner's Sons, 1943), 364; Jim Cullen, *The American Dream: A Short History of an Idea That Shaped a Nation* (Oxford: Oxford University Press, 2003), 5; Dan Rather, *The American Dream: Stories from the Heart of Our Nation* (New York: Perennial, 2001).

4. For King's speech, see Ronald F. Reid, *American Rhetorical Discourse*, 2nd ed. (Prospect Heights, Ill.: Waveland Press, 1995), 777–83. For the top hundred speeches by rank, see http://www.americanrhetoric.com/top100speechesall.html.

5. Cullen, *The American Dream*, 189; Jennifer Hochschild, *Facing Up to the American Dream: Race, Class, and the Soul of the Nation* (Princeton: Princeton University Press, 1995), 25, 250.

6. Hochschild, *Facing Up to the American Dream*, 169; Malcolm X, "The Ballot or the Bullet, April 3, 1964" at http://www.americanrhetoric.com/speeches/malcolmxballot.htm.

7. James W. Ceaser and others, "The Rise of the Rhetorical Presidency," *Presidential Studies Quarterly* 11 (1981): 163.

8. Robert N. Bellah and others, *Habits of the Heart: Individualism and Commitment in American Life* (Berkeley: University of California Press, 1985), 23.

9. Cullen, *The American Dream*, 7; Walter R. Fisher, "Reaffirmation and Subversion of the American Dream," *Quarterly Journal of Speech* 59 (1973): 160–67.

10. Adams, *The American*, 62; Andrew Delbanco, *The Real American Dream: A Meditation on Hope* (Cambridge: Harvard University Press, 1999), 15–20; Charles R. Hearn, *The American Dream in the Great Depression*, Contributions in American Studies no. 28 (Westport, Conn.: Greenwood Press, 1977), 5.

11. John Winthrop, "Christian Charity," in Reid, *American Rhetorical Discourse*, 24, 34.

12. Cullen, *The American Dream*, 5.

13. Cullen, *The American Dream*, 5, 22.

14. Hearn, *The American Dream in the Great Depression*, 5–6.

15. Cullen, *The American Dream*, 59.

16. "The Declaration of Independence, July 4, 1776," in *Great Issues in American History: From Settlement to Revolution, 1584–1776*, ed. Clarence L. Ver Steeg and Richard Hofstadter (New York: Vintage Books, 1969), 469.

17. Hochschild, *Facing Up to the American Dream*, xi.

18. Cullen, *The American Dream*, 38.

19. George Washington, "Farewell Address," in Reid, *American Rhetorical Discourse*, 213; Thomas Jefferson, "First Inaugural Address," in Reid, *American Rhetorical Discourse*, 227.

20. Delbanco, *The Real American Dream*, 87.

21. Hearn, *The American Dream in the Great Depression*, 25–26.

22. Cullen, *The American Dream*, 57.

23. David Zarefsky, *President Johnson's War on Poverty* (Tuscaloosa: University of Alabama Press, 1986), ix.

24. Joseph Campbell, *Myths to Live By* (New York: Penguin Books, 1972), 10.

25. Richard Slotkin, *The Fatal Environment: The Myth of the Frontier in the Age of Industrialization, 1800–1890* (New York: HarperCollins, 1985), 16, 24.

26. Ivan Strenski, *Four Theories of Myth in Twentieth-Century History: Cassirer, Eliade, Levi-Strauss and Malinowski* (Iowa City: University of Iowa Press, 1987), 3.

27. Cullen, *The American Dream*, 11–13.

28. Sacvan Bercovitch, *The Rights of Assent: Transformations in the Symbolic Construction of America* (New York: Routledge, 1993), 32.

29. Roland Barthes, *Mythologies*, trans. Annette Lavers (New York: Noonday Press, 1957), 127, 132.

30. Barthes, *Mythologies*, 143.

31. William C. Dowling, *Jameson, Althusser, Marx: An Introduction to the Political Unconscious* (Ithaca: Cornell University Press, 1984), 54.

32. Bellah et al., *Habits of the Heart*, 33, 41.

33. Rather, *The American Dream*, xvi, xxi.

34. Richard Slotkin lists three elements—hero, universe, and narrative—but I subsume the narrative within the other elements. See Slotkin's *Regeneration through Violence: The Mythology of the American Frontier, 1600–1860* (Middletown, Conn.: Wesleyan University Press, 1973), 8.

35. David Leeming, *Myth: A Biography of Belief* (Oxford: Oxford University Press, 2002), 7–8.

36. Joseph Campbell, *The Hero with a Thousand Faces* (Princeton: Princeton University Press, 1973), 97–192.

37. Theodore Roosevelt, "Remarks Introducing Rev. Charles Wagner, at the Lafayette Opera House, Washington, D.C., Nov. 22, 1904," in *Presidential Addresses and State Papers of Theodore Roosevelt*, 4 vols. (New York: Kraus Reprint Company, 1970), 3:113–14.

38. Theodore Roosevelt, "Industrial Democracy, October 3, 1907," in *The Roosevelt Policy: Speeches, Letters and State Papers, relating to Corporate Wealth and Closely Allied Topics*, 3 vols., ed. William Griffith (New York: Krause Reprint Company, 1971), 2:611.

39. Theodore Roosevelt, "The Square Deal, April 5, 1905," in *The Roosevelt Policy*, 1:252.

40. Sean D. Cashman, *America in the Age of the Titans: The Progressive Era and World War I* (New York: New York University Press, 1988), 10, 12, 38–39, 44.

41. Theodore Roosevelt, "Highest Level of Prosperity Ever Attained, December 2, 1902," in *The Roosevelt Policy*, 1:179.

42. Theodore Roosevelt, *An Autobiography* (New York: Charles Scribner's Sons, 1926), 426.

43. Alan Trachtenberg, *The Incorporation of America: Culture and Society in the Gilded Age* (New York: Hill and Wang, 1982), 84.

44. Theodore Roosevelt, "The Man with the Muck Rake," in Reid, *American Rhetorical Discourse*, 673–81; Trachtenberg, *The Incorporation of America*, 86; George E. Mowry, *The Era of Theodore Roosevelt and the Birth of Modern America, 1900–1912* (New York: Harper and Row, 1958), 10; Arthur S. Link, *American Epoch: A History of the United States since the 1890s*, 2nd ed. (New York: Alfred A. Knopf, 1966), 61–62; Cashman, *America in the Age of the Titans*, 80.

45. See Roosevelt, "The Man with the Muck Rake," in Reid, *American Rhetorical Discourse*, 673–81; Roosevelt, *An Autobiography*, 459.

46. Theodore Roosevelt, "Enforcement of Law and the Railways, October 4, 1907," in *The Roosevelt Policy*, 2:632.

47. Leroy G. Dorsey, "The Frontier Myth in Presidential Rhetoric: Theodore Roosevelt's Campaign for Conservation," *Western Journal of Communication* 59 (1995): 1–19; Leroy G. Dorsey and Rachel M. Harlow, "'We Want Americans Pure and Simple': Theodore Roosevelt and the Myth of Americanism," *Rhetoric and Public Affairs* 6 (2003): 55–78.

48. Campbell, *The Hero with a Thousand Faces*, 37–38.

49. Slotkin, *The Fatal Environment*, 16.

50. Theodore Roosevelt, "The Puritan Spirit and the Regulation of Corporations, August 20, 1907," in *The Works of Theodore Roosevelt: American Problems*, National ed., 20 vols. (New York: Charles Scribner's Sons, 1926), 16:77.

51. Theodore Roosevelt, "Demands of Labor Organizations, March 21, 1906," in *The Roosevelt Policy*, 2:361.

52. Janice H. Rushing, "Mythic Evolution of 'The New Frontier' in Mass Mediated Rhetoric," *Critical Studies in Mass Communication* 3 (1986): 265–96; Janice H. Rushing, "The Rhetoric of the American Western Myth," *Communication Monographs* 50 (1983): 14–32.

53. Theodore Roosevelt, "Industrial Peace, November 11, 1902," in *The Roosevelt Policy*, 1:101.

54. Harold Zyskind, "A Case Study in Philosophic Rhetoric: Theodore Roosevelt," *Philosophy and Rhetoric* 1 (1968): 242.

55. Theodore Roosevelt, "Temperance and the Wage Earner, August 10, 1905," in *The Roosevelt Policy*, 1:288.

56. Theodore Roosevelt, "Fair Treatment of the Rich Man, April 7, 1905," in *The Roosevelt Policy*, 1: 259.

57. Theodore Roosevelt, "National Unity versus Class Cleavage, September 7, 1903," in *The Works of Theodore Roosevelt: American Problems*, 16:57.

58. Theodore Roosevelt, "The Strenuous Life, April 10, 1899," in *The Works of Theodore Roosevelt: American Ideals/The Strenuous Life/Realizable Ideals,* National ed. (New York: Charles Scribner's Sons, 1926), 13:319.

59. Roosevelt, "National Unity versus Class Cleavage," in *American Problems,* 16:57.

60. Theodore Roosevelt, "Labor and Brotherhood, September 8, 1902," in *American Problems,* 16:153.

61. Theodore Roosevelt, "The Puritan Spirit and the Regulation of Corporations, August 20, 1907," in *American Problems,* 16:78.

62. Theodore Roosevelt, "The Woman and the Home, March 13, 1905," in *American Problems,* 16:165.

63. Theodore Roosevelt, "At Wilkesbarre, PA., August 10, 1905," in *Presidential Addresses and State Papers of Theodore Roosevelt,* 4:438.

64. Theodore Roosevelt, "The Woman and the Home, March 13, 1905," in *American Problems,* 16:165, 168.

65. Theodore Roosevelt, "At the Laying of the Corner-Stone of the Pilgrim Memorial Monument, Provincetown, Mass., August 20, 1907," in *Presidential Addresses and State Papers,* Homeward Bound ed., 7 vols. (New York: Review of Reviews Company, 1910), 6:1347.

66. Theodore Roosevelt, "First Annual Message, December 3, 1901," in *The Works of Theodore Roosevelt: State Papers as Governor and President, 1899–1909,* 15:89.

67. Theodore Roosevelt, "Address at the Hungarian Club Dinner, New York City, Feb. 14, 1905," in *Presidential Addresses and State Papers,* 6:240.

68. Kurt Ritter and David Henry, *Ronald Reagan: The Great Communicator* (New York: Greenwood Press, 1992), 15; Cullen, *The American Dream,* 24; G. Thomas Goodnight, "Ronald Reagan and the American Dream: A Study in Rhetoric Out of Time," in *The Presidency and Rhetorical Leadership,* ed. Leroy G. Dorsey (College Station, TX: Texas A&M University Press, 2002), 216.

69. Ronald Reagan, "Ronald Reagan Addressing a Joint Session of Congress, 1984," at http://www.presidentreagan.info/speeches/reagan_sotu_1982.cfm, 1–2; Ronald Reagan, "Ronald Reagan Addressing a Joint Session of Congress, 1985," at http://www.presidentreagan.info/speeches/reagan_sotu_1985.cfm, 8.

70. Ronald Reagan, "Inaugural Address, January 20, 1981," at http://www.reagan.utexas.edu/resource/speeches/1981/12081a.htm, 1.

71. Alberto Alesina and Geoffrey Carliner, "Introduction," in *Politics and Economics in the Eighties,* ed. Alberto Alesina and Geoffrey Carliner (Chicago: University of Chicago Press, 1991), 1–2; Burton I. Kaufman, *The Presidency of James Earl Carter, Jr.* (Lawrence: University Press of Kansas, 1993), 183.

72. Erwin C. Hargrove, *Jimmy Carter as President: Leadership and the Politics of the Public Good* (Baton Rouge: Louisiana State University Press, 1988), 78, 192.

73. Ronald Reagan, "Inaugural Address, January 20, 1981," at http://www.reagan.utexas.edu/resource/speeches/1981/12081a.htm, 1–2.

74. Ronald Reagan, "Address to the Nation on the Economy, February 5, 1981," at http://www.reagan.utexas.edu/resource/speeches/1981/20581c.htm, 1, 5.

75. Ronald Reagan, "Address Before a Joint Session of the Congress on the Program for Economic Recovery, February 18, 1981," at http://www.reagan.utexas.edu/resource/speeches/1981/21881a.htm, 1, 3, 5.

76. Ronald Reagan, "President Reagan's Words at the Brandenburg Gate, June 12, 1987," at http://www.presidentreagan.info/speeches/brandenburg_gate.cfm, 5–6.

77. Ronald Reagan, "Economic Recovery Program, April 28, 1981," in Ritter and Henry, *Ronald Reagan: The Great Communicator,* 165.

78. James O. Robertson, *American Myth, American Reality* (New York: Hill and Wang, 1980), 6–7.

79. Ronald Reagan, "Ronald Reagan Addressing a Joint Session of Congress, 1982," at http://www.presidentreagan.info/speeches/reagan_sotu_1982.cfm, 10–11.

80. Ronald Reagan, "Ronald Reagan Addressing a Joint Session of Congress, 1982," at http://www.presidentreagan.info/speeches/reagan_sotu_1982.cfm, 10–11.

81. Reagan, "Ronald Reagan Addressing a Joint Session of Congress, 1982," at http://www.presidentreagan.info/speeches/reagan_sotu_1982.cfm, 11.

82. Ronald Reagan, "Ronald Reagan Addressing a Joint Session of Congress, 1984," at http://www.presidentreagan.info/speeches/reagan_sotu_1984.cfm, 2.

83. Ronald Reagan, "Ronald Reagan Addressing a Joint Session of Congress, 1986," at http://www.presidentreagan.info/speeches/reagan_sotu_1986.cfm, 7.

84. Stuart Elliott, "The Media Business," *New York Times,* December 28, 1992, 7; Michael Schrage, "How to Make Even More out of Lawsuits," *Washington Post,* August 16, 1991, B9.

85. Henry N. Smith, *Virgin Land: The American West as Symbol and Myth* (Cambridge: Harvard University Press, 1950); David A. Leeming, *The World of Myth* (Oxford: Oxford University Press, 1990).

86. Ronald Reagan, "Inaugural Address, January 21, 1985," at http://www.reagan.utexas.edu/resource/speeches/1985/12185a.htm, 4–5.

87. Ronald Reagan, "Remarks at the Opening Ceremonies of the Statue of Liberty Centennial Celebration in New York, New York, July 3, 1986," in *Public Papers of the Presidents of the United States: Ronald Reagan, 1981–1989* (Washington, D. C.: Government Printing Office, 1982–91), 919.

88. Ronald Reagan, "President Reagan's Farewell Speech," at http://www.presidentreagan.info/speeches/farewell.cfm, 2, 6.

89. Howard Fineman and Martha Brant, "The Test of His Life," *Newsweek,* December 25, 2000, 33; Howard Fineman, "Disorder in the Courts," *Newsweek,* December 18, 2000, 31.

90. Daniel Klaidman and others, "The Enemy Within," *Newsweek,* June 23, 2003, 40–46.

91. Christian Parenti, "Stretched Thin, Lied to and Mistreated," *Nation,* October 6, 2003, 11–14; CNN, "Bush Defends Iraq War after Weapons Report," CNN.com, October 3, 2003, at http://www.cnn.com/2003/ALLPOLITICS/10/03/sprj.irq.kay/index.html; Kevin Bohn, "ACLU Files Lawsuit against Patriot Act," CNN, July 30, 2003, at http://www.cnn.com/2003/LAW/07/30/patriot.act/index.html.

92. Terry Frieden, "Ashcroft Vows Tough Stand on Combating Corporate Crime," CNN, September 27, 2002, at http://www.cnn.com/2002/LAW/09/27/ashcroft.corporate.crime/index.html; CNN, "U.S. Jobless Soars," CNN.com, July 3, 2003, at http://www.cnn.com/2003/BUSINESS/07/03/us.jobless/index.html; Dana Bash, "Bush: $87 Billion 'Worth It' for Security," CNN, September 10, 2003, at http://www.cnn.com/2003/ALLPOLITICS/09/10/sprj.irq.bush.request/index.html.

93. Roper Center at University of Connecticut, sponsored by Time/CNN/Harris Interactive Poll, January 17, 2003 Release of Source Document, February 12, 2003 Load-Date, Accession Number: 0419984, at http://web.lexis-nexis.com/universe/document?_m=ef2fa02f=9162b7787ff8c352dc91d60.

94. George W. Bush, "Remarks on National Homeownership Month, June 18, 2002," in *Public Papers of the Presidents: George W. Bush—2002* (Washington, D.C.: Government Printing Office Online, 2002), 1031.

95. George W. Bush, "Question-and-Answer Session at Lakewood Elementary School in North Little Rock, Arkansas, March 1, 2001," in *Public Papers of the Presidents: George W. Bush—2001*, 164–65.

96. George W. Bush, "President George W. Bush's Inaugural Address, January 20, 2001," at http://www.whitehouse.gov/news/inaugural-address.html.

97. George W. Bush, "Remarks to the New Jersey Chamber of Commerce in East Brunswick, New Jersey, March 14, 2001," in *Public Papers of the Presidents: George W. Bush—2001*, 241.

98. George W. Bush, "Remarks to the National Conference of State Legislatures, March 2, 2001," in *Public Papers of the Presidents: George W. Bush—2001*, 178.

99. George W. Bush, "Remarks to Employees of Bajan Industries in Kansas City, March 26, 2001," in *Public Papers of the Presidents: George W. Bush—2001*, 302.

100. George W. Bush, "The President's Radio Address, June 15, 2002," in *Public Papers of the Presidents: George W. Bush—2002*, 1025.

101. George W. Bush, "Remarks at St. Paul AME Church in Atlanta, Georgia, June 17, 2002," in *Public Papers of the Presidents: George W. Bush—2002*, 1030.

102. Joseph L. Daleiden, *The American Dream: Can It Survive the 21st Century?* (Amherst, N.Y.: Prometheus Books, 1999), 11.

103. Paul Krugman, "The Death of Horatio Alger," *Nation*, January 5, 2004, 16–17.

104. Hochschild, *Facing Up to the American Dream*, 258–60.

CHAPTER 7

OF ALLIES AND ENEMIES

Old Wine in New Bottles or New Wine in an Old Jug?

Marilyn J. Young, Florida State University

The advice given by George Washington in his Farewell Address, "to steer clear of permanent alliances with any portion of the foreign world," was taken to heart by subsequent administrations for nearly 150 years and still seems to inform much of our interaction with foreign governments.[1] When Winston Churchill spoke to the nation from Fulton, Missouri, in 1945, his address was remarked (then) not by the words that became the metaphor for a world gone mad—"From Stettin in the Baltic to Trieste in the Adriatic, an iron curtain has descended across the Continent"—but by the proposal he made for a military alliance of English-speaking peoples.[2] Even after engaging in a successful alliance to rid the world of the Nazi horror, most Americans, while treating Churchill as a hero, rejected his suggestion for a permanent relationship with Great Britain.[3]

Newspapers of the time chronicled the reaction of officials and ordinary citizens alike. Virtually every story focused on the proposed alliance; none noticed that Churchill had named the line the Soviet Union had drawn across Europe. Nevertheless, Churchill laid the rhetorical groundwork for American foreign policy throughout the rest of the century—and beyond. The stark image of the iron curtain gained currency when juxtaposed against the events of the postwar period—the fall of China, atomic spies, the Truman doctrine, the Berlin blockade—and became an organizing principle for Cold War rhetoric. By drawing a rhetorical barricade, Churchill and his ideological equivalents in the United States divided the world into black and white, friend and foe. In *Visions of Order* Richard Weaver writes about the power of the tyrannizing image; surely, communism (and its counterpart, anticommunism) became the tyrannizing image of the latter half of the twentieth century in America.[4] The notion also fortified the growing sense of American exceptionalism that had been reinforced in the first half of the century by victories in World Wars I and II.

Looking back over the rather brief history of American alliances, it seems George Washington's dictum also captured the essence of relationships that formed after World War II, providing the template for Cold War coalitions and post–Cold War collaborations. In light of this, in the remainder of this chapter, I examine the nature of alliances and allies, the evolution of alliances since World War II, and prospects for the future.

Allies and Enemies

Alliances and foreign policy are inextricably bound together, such that the history of American foreign policy is necessarily a story of allies and enemies. Alliances—or allies—are a vehicle for expressing foreign policy, and a country's relationship with its allies can be a measure of its foreign policy values and principles. Further, the rhetorical net used to capture allies, alliances, and enemies reveals a nation's estimation of itself and those friends, partners, or enemies. For many, the rhetoric used during the Cold War to describe the Soviet Union revealed as much about the fears of our own country and its citizens as it did about the USSR.

Alliances exist to serve a number of foreign policy goals. Military alliances, for example, are designed to prevent or deflect conflict. Obviously, the United States joined a military alliance with England, France, and others to defeat Hitler's Germany. After World War II, the United States hoped to stave off anticipated Soviet aggression in Europe by presenting a unified front through NATO. However, alliances can also be a source of conflict; had the NATO presence not worked, the United States would have been obligated to enter into any war that resulted from Soviet aggression. Of course, this pledge derived its power from U.S. nuclear capability, which ultimately backed any deterrent effect of the alliance. In contrast, by not being involved in military alliances, the United States was able to defer entering either World War I or World War II until directly threatened.[5]

Trade relations are another form of alliance that is both a tool of foreign policy and a source of friction at home and abroad. Like most allies, trading partners come to our attention only when there is a problem; such relations are currently strained because of the movement of jobs abroad and the flood of cheaper goods into the American market, to the disadvantage of domestic workers and products. But Republican and Democratic administrations alike have favored freer trade, in part because they believed it would help American business in the long run and in part because it suited their foreign policy objectives. Cold War constructions argued that economic deprivation favored the growth of communist sympathies; in recent months similar statements have been made about the conditions that foster terrorism, opening up the potential for expanded aid and trade agreements.[6]

Trading partners are not necessarily allies, although trade with enemies presents some interesting rhetorical—and policy—dilemmas. U.S. farmers had become so dependent on grain sales to the Soviet Union that they protested vigorously when those sales were embargoed after the USSR invaded Afghanistan in 1979. The embargo ended up costing the Carter and Reagan administrations billions of dollars in increased farm price supports and farm assistance.

Allies seem to fall into two categories: "natural" allies and (for lack of a better term) "convenient" allies. Natural allies are those countries to whom we are tied by heritage and tradition: France supported the colonists in the Revolutionary War and, recent recriminations notwithstanding, was the first ally of the United States; Britain is our closest friend. Other natural allies might include countries in close proximity, especially our contiguous neighbors, Canada and Mexico. Yet, while we obviously have a vested interested in protecting our allies militarily, we have not always treated them well economically—particularly the Latin American countries.

Indeed, it is interesting to examine the nature of U.S. foreign policy toward different geographic regions. Despite the suspicions of our forefathers, over the long term most U.S. foreign policy relationships have been maintained with European countries. As dependence on foreign oil grew, the United States became increasingly involved in the Middle East—a relationship that has been marked by fierce rivalries and glaring inconsistencies, culminating in the U.S. invasion of Iraq in March 2003. Toward Latin America, the United States has primarily served as hegemon, though not always successfully.[7] This posture dates at least to the Monroe Doctrine, which was intended to secure the isolation of the Western Hemisphere.[8] Africa, except during specific crises, has been largely ignored. Asia has been the testing ground of American foreign policy, a test the United States has too often failed. When one thinks of foreign policy toward Asia, one thinks of China, Korea, or Vietnam. Then there is Israel, one of the most complex arrangements the United States has ever had.

Some of these historical relationships appear to be shifting. George W. Bush took office proclaiming a sea change in the focus of U.S. foreign policy; his emphasis would be to the south, on Latin America, that region so often taken for granted by previous administrations. Accordingly, Bush's first state visit was to Mexico. The attacks of September 11 changed the focus and, once again, Latin America has dropped off the radar. Trade agreements, which Bush proclaimed had the power to transform and unite the hemisphere, are being hammered out in hard-nosed bargaining that many feel overlook Latin American interests.[9] For their part, many Latin American countries are now dividing their trade among the United States, Europe, and Asia; the Group of 20, led by Brazil, has emerged to challenge Washington "on issues from free trade to patents."[10] Most recently, Hugo Chavez of Venezuela has assumed a leadership role in South American efforts to curb U.S. influence in developing countries, forming an alliance with Iran. When Chavez visited Tehran in July 2005, the leaders of these two countries "agreed to produce jointly nearly a dozen products, including crude oil and medicines." Iran is rapidly becoming Venezuela's closest ally outside Latin America, and Venezuela has become "the most vociferous defender of Iran's nuclear program at a time when Iran feels increasingly isolated."[11] From Tehran Chavez journeyed to Damascus, Syria, where he proclaimed that the two countries would "build a new world" free of domination by the United States and vowed to "dig the grave of U.S. imperialism."[12] Despite all this, Venezuela maintains close economic ties with the United States; nevertheless, Chavez again challenged American hegemony in his speech to the United Nations, where, in a colorful flourish reminiscent of past UN oratory, he called President George W. Bush "a devil who had left a telltale scent of sulfur on the speaker's podium."[13]

The Middle East, which became the focus of U.S. foreign policy after 9/11, will likely remain so for the foreseeable future, regardless of the outcome of the situation in Iraq. America's relationship with Israel continues to complicate relationships with Arab countries, but the general feeling was perhaps summed up by Nabil Fahmy, Egypt's ambassador to the United States, in a speech at the American University in Cairo, when he remarked that "we cannot afford, as Egypt, to pursue any of our national interests and expect to succeed, unless we engage America. Neither side has the option in the near term, nor in the medium term, of ignoring the other."[14] Even if the United States were able to end its dependence on Middle Eastern oil, the resurgence of Hamas and Hezbollah as military and political actors will force continued engagement until a peace accord is forged between the Arab states and Israel. Indeed, the recent emergence of China as a prime consumer of Middle Eastern oil has compromised the leverage U.S. oil consumption has provided Washington in its efforts to broker an accord.

Asia continues to be the testing ground for foreign policy. Trade relations with China have spurred economic development there, while continued U.S. support for Taiwan remains a thorn. Complicating this relationship is the amount of U.S. debt held by China—an amount that is increasing with the mounting costs of the war in Iraq—and our reliance on China as an intermediary with North Korea. When North Korea tested a nuclear device in early October 2006, China's role became even more critical.

Europe, meanwhile, is looking at a diminished relationship with the United States. Strained relations over the war in Iraq and the weakened dollar have contributed to a sense that, as Bernard-Henri Lévy put it, "the center of gravity in the United States has completely shifted west, to Asia rather than Europe. It's not because of American mischief. The map of the world has a different shape."[15]

What, then, is an ally? What is an alliance? Possible synonyms for *ally* include *friend, helper, supporter, assistant, partner,* and *collaborator. Webster's New Universal Unabridged Dictionary* defines *alliance* as "the union between nations, contracted by compact, treaty, or league; the treaty, league, or compact which is the instrument of confederacy between states or provinces." One has the sense that there is a subtle difference between the notion of "ally" and that of "alliance," with the former implying a closer relationship, the latter a more utilitarian arrangement, much like the difference between the U.S. bond with Great Britain and its alliance with the USSR in World War II. Nevertheless, these are broad terms that encompass a wide range of associations, from traditional friends and trading partners to coalitions based on expediency or exigence. In the period following World War II, U.S. allies have primarily been defined by where we saw enemies; as a result, over the past sixty years, U.S. foreign policy has been characterized by the twin themes of containment of communism and American exceptionalism. As we appear to be shifting more and more to expedient alliance rather than relying on traditional allies, those themes have been intensified.[16]

CONTAINMENT AND EXCEPTIONALISM

Seymour Martin Lipset writes in *American Exceptionalism: A Double-Edged Sword*: "The American creed can be described in five terms: liberty, egalitarianism, individualism, populism, and laissez-faire."[17] American exceptionalism is the idea that the United States was envisaged by the Founding Fathers as a nation with a mission to propagate a special form of political morality. Humanity was visualized in terms of its "rights"—life, liberty, and the pursuit of happiness; the Enlightenment rationalism that prevailed at the time concluded that a form of government had to be devised to protect those rights. The result was perceived as something unique and superior to political experience in the Old World. This was a society committed in principle to justice and freedom for all. It was an ambitious, moral enterprise, and "American values" were cast in universal language, which referred to all humanity, not just Americans.[18]

Historians and political scientists generally agree that the Second World War demonstrated to the United States that it could not remain aloof from the rest of the world, much as it might want to do so. If doubt remained, it was quickly dispelled by the rift that formed between the Soviet Union and the United States shortly after the end of the war. Thus, America, which to this point in its history had articulated its sense of exceptionalism in terms of isolation from the power politics of the Old World, had to reframe those values in terms of a larger stage.

When President Truman announced a program of aid to Greece and Turkey in March, 1946, he effectively proclaimed that the United States would not retreat from the global arena but would move toward internationalism, engaging threats when and where they occurred. The significance of this policy initiative is underscored by the fact that the announcement was made in a special address to a joint session of Congress, which necessarily engaged the public as well. Truman's directive was the first move toward containing the perceived communist threat—a strategy that was institutionalized following the long telegram sent by George Kennan in February 1946 outlining the expansionist tendencies of the Soviet government.[19] Our primary ally in this endeavor was Great Britain, predicated on Churchill's dire warnings; yet, the aid to Greece and Turkey was necessitated by England's announcement that it could no longer provide assistance to those embattled regimes.

Once the Kennan assessment was accepted, the United States began a series of moves designed to contain the spread of communism. That policy was given credibility and urgency by the "fall" of China to communism in 1949—an event that scarred the psyche of American foreign policy for years—and the atomic bomb test conducted by the USSR that same year. Even the Marshall Plan and the rebuilding of the European economy after WWII incorporated an element of anticommunism, as analysts felt that weak economies would be fertile ground for communist sympathies to develop. (Without question, the anticommunist argument eased the way for acceptance of the Marshall Plan and continued involvement in the affairs of Europe.) Similarly, the Japanese economy was restored in an effort to provide the United States with an economic and military outpost in Southeast Asia. Thus the United States was placed in the ironic position of rebuilding economies—especially those of former enemies Germany and Japan—that would later become serious economic rivals.

Whether offering economic or military assistance, successive administrations have framed the action in the language of universal values—those held by the United States, yet general enough to resonate with the rest of the international community. As McMahon notes, "American statesmen have consistently downplayed any exclusively national interests undergirding U.S. actions. They have instead highlighted the selflessness of American motives and the universality of U.S. objectives."[20] Nevertheless, the public justification for these moves was the interest and security of the United States itself, as president after president linked the defense of America to the defense of peace and freedom abroad. In a departure from this trend, George W. Bush initially evoked the security of the United States in his decision to invade Iraq; yet, when no weapons of mass destruction were found by U.S. troops in Iraq, the justification for that war shifted to more universal concerns: liberty, freedom from oppression, and democratic statehood for Iraqi citizens.

Interestingly, the U.S. attitude toward the Cold War communist threat was something of a paradox: the sense of American exceptionalism tempered by fears of subversion that manifested themselves in the security excesses of the 1950s and '60s, what Robert Ivie has labeled "distempered *demos*."[21] This fear of communism forced the United States into an Old Europe mindset, as a former ally (the USSR) became the enemy and former enemies (Germany and Japan) became allies.[22]

It is not possible to discuss the rhetorical evolution of containment policy without taking into account the impact of another administration policy directive, one that became known simply as NSC-68. Conceived by Paul Nitze, Kennan's successor with the Policy Planning Staff, NSC-68 crystallized the rhetorical trajectory of the Cold War. Reiterating the expansionist nature of the Soviet Union, the resolution affirmed the peril threatening the free world; its bold stroke was in identifying the United States as the leader of the resistance against the "red menace." "The novelty of NSC-68 lay in its global reach, its military emphasis, and its harsh tone."[23] The language of NSC-68 echoed the bifurcated world of old-line Puritanism—he who is not with us is against us—a concept that was used against those who tried to remain neutral in the escalating tension between the United States and the USSR. Dubbed "National Insecurity" by Robert Newman, NSC-68 laid the rhetorical foundation for the apocalyptic rhetoric of the radical right in the 1960s.[24] Thus, after nearly two centuries of disdaining foreign entanglements, especially with Old Europe, the United States found itself intimately involved in creating alliances designed to confine the communist threat. This desire to contain communism informed the foreign policy of every administration from Truman through George H. W. Bush, as U.S. foreign policy took on an increasingly "realist" view of the world.[25]

As Beer and Harriman argue, the realist *narratio* "sets the scene" for the arguments that are entailed in its taut vision of world politics:

> In the discourse of realism, nation-states are the primary actors in world politics. Since these states necessarily inhabit a condition of anarchy, they learn to conduct their foreign policies on the basis of national interest defined in terms of power. Consequently, they calculate and compare benefits and costs of alternative policies and rank each other according to their power, which is measured primarily in terms of material and especially military capabilities. Thus, national foreign policy decision makers use whatever means are most appropriate, including direct violence, to achieve the ends of national interest defined in terms of power.[26]

In this worldview, international competition is grounded in human nature, which makes it not only ubiquitous but also permanent and ultimately self-sealing, for it requires that we "see things as they are, not as we would wish them to be." This simple phrase allows the proponents of policy to dismiss alternative explanations and ideas as "fuzzy thinking" or, worse, ingenuous distortions of reality.[27]

Both the policy of containment and the realist explanation dovetailed nicely with the notion of American exceptionalism in the conduct of foreign policy. Communism represented the ultimate evil and America's role—and gift to the world—was to contain it in order to provide fertile space for democracy. The realist calculation could guarantee that freedom and democracy would prevail only if the United States were powerful enough militarily—through its own armament and that of its allies—to persuade freedom's enemies that encroachment was not in their best interest. In the realist view, only the United States, with its nuclear umbrella and its ability to arm and defend its friends, had the material and moral character to assume such a role. It was a small step to viewing democratic forms of government, military might, containment, and America's special mission as bound up together. This complex view probably achieved its apotheosis in the late 1950s, in the period known as "Mutually Assured Destruction" or MAD, as both the United States and the Soviet Union amassed enough nuclear warheads to obliterate each other several times over; at that time, this "balance of power" was credited with maintaining peace and stability in the world and was publicly justified on that basis.[28]

Inevitably, the requirements of realism-containment-exceptionalism also influenced America's choice of allies, as the nation employed all the weapons in its considerable arsenal: military action, foreign aid, and espionage. The policy of containment, conceived by Kennan as a flexible, utilitarian response system, became instead a rigid policy; this, in turn, forced the United States into alliances and aid packages that all too often propped up governments and leaders who belied the American commitment to democratic rule, free market economies, and human rights. Autocratic rulers and vicious terrorist organizations were grouped into two camps—"ours" and "theirs." This anomaly produced considerable rhetorical contortion and excess, epitomized by Ronald Reagan calling the Nicaraguan Contras "freedom fighters."

The result has been mixed, to say the least. In some respects, the pursuit of a single goal—protecting national security by containing the spread of communism—embodied the advice given by George Washington: to steer clear of permanent alliances. But the effects have been strange indeed and sometimes border on the macabre. Thus, weapons provided to a government such as in Afghanistan to aid their fight against the USSR are used against U.S. troops when a different regime comes to power and that nation harbors the new enemy. Repressive governments installed to protect U.S. interests after engineering the overthrow of a previous regime are themselves replaced with rulers hostile to America and its values. Over the years since Truman's 1946 announcement, the United States has befriended cruel dictators and ignored incipient democracies; it has encouraged revolutions in places like Iran, tried to crush them in places like Cuba, and turned its back on them in Hungary and Czechoslovakia.[29] After more than fifty years, a period that saw the demise of America's dominant enemy and the end of the Cold War, it is safe to say that the world is no more secure for American interests than it was in 1946. Indeed, it may well be less so. Ironically, the United States, which provides more humanitarian and economic aid than almost any other nation, finds itself despised by many of the recipients of that assistance.

Complicating this picture is the pervasive belief, both among U.S. citizens and within their government, in that American exceptionalism first conceived at the dawning of the republic. From the beginning, the Founding Fathers felt that the United States was embarking on a better way. By guaranteeing the rights of citizens and making them the source of government legitimacy, the United States saw itself as substantively and materially different than other nations, particularly those of Old Europe. Indeed, it was the European powers, with their court intrigues and machinations, that Washington warned against. That sense of not wanting to be drawn into the ancient rivalries of Old Europe is one factor that slowed America's entry into both World War I and World War II. Following World War II, the United States either encouraged or imposed the development of democratic forms of government in both its allies and the powers it had defeated. The success of these endeavors almost certainly influenced subsequent U.S. policy, which frequently made the appearance of democracy a condition for U.S. assistance.[30]

Some of these nations grew into staunch allies of the United States (e.g., Great Britain, Japan), while others ultimately chafed under the moral debt, despite the fact that the Marshall Plan was more self-serving than selfless: remember that a major impetus behind approval of reconstruction assistance was the fear that a Europe weakened economically and militarily would be vulnerable to Soviet subversion as well as aggression.[31]

It was the policy of containment, along with a substantial amount of hubris, that led us into Vietnam. John Kane, writing in *Presidential Studies Quarterly*, agrees with Henry Kissinger that the Vietnam War broke the myth of American exceptionalism—"American power was defeated, delivering a blow to American pride; American virtue was assailed, causing a loss of faith in American innocence." The chief casualty, according to Kane, was the sense of optimism that had for so long been a hallmark of the American character.[32] That war was quickly followed by the oil embargo, which in turn was followed by the hostage crisis—both humbling experiences for a superpower. Certainly, as Dobson and Marsh point out, the Vietnam experience stimulated a reassessment of U.S. foreign policy vis-à-vis the Soviet Union. Prior to the growth of antiwar sentiment in the late '60s, the Eisenhower, Kennedy, and Johnson administrations were able to exploit the rhetorical force of NSC-68 to confront communism wherever it arose. Vietnam had taught the United States that it could not afford to police the globe—not economically, nor in terms of allies, and certainly not in terms of human capital. Rather than concern itself with ideological containment, the Nixon Administration introduced a new calculus based primarily on geopolitical interests and began the process of détente with the Soviet Union. Kennan's original ideas were resurrected: flexible response based on a clear sense of U.S. interests. Not every battle need be won—or even fought. The American colossus had proved to have feet of clay and a limited reach.

President Carter attempted to leverage détente to move U.S. foreign policy away from the rhetorical (and practical) burdens imposed by traditional notions of exceptionalism. Carter felt that the world had become too complicated for standard Cold War frames of reference. He believed that American values were too often seen as self-serving cultural imperialism. Kane has written that "America, by adopting the human rights doctrine as central to its foreign policy, would no longer hypocritically and systematically betray its own ideals by supporting unfree regimes for the sake of their anti-communism."[33] In this way, by subsuming American values—which tend to focus on individual and political rights—to universal concepts of human rights, Carter hoped to realize the rhetorical tradition of American exceptionalism more fully.[34]

Carter's presidency was ill fated, however, culminating in the disastrous hostage crisis in Iran and ending in electoral defeat. The idea of placing the human rights doctrine at the cornerstone of U.S. foreign policy did not survive his presidency. "By the time the Soviets [invaded] Afghanistan, Carter's concern for human rights had become his Achilles' heel and the President was in full retreat from *détente* and swinging violently to a new hard-line. High technology sales were halted, feed grain shipments were embargoed, and America boycotted the 1980 Olympics. While this failed to save either Carter or the SALT II treaty, . . . it laid the platform for Ronald Reagan's 'Second Cold War.'"[35]

The rhetorical situation that confronted the country during the 1980 campaign and as Reagan took office in January, 1981, proved to be an exigence to which he could respond. The notion that the United States had an obligation to export democracy and democratic values such as free speech, free press, and the rule of law reached its apotheosis during the Reagan Administration, when Reagan's mythic "shining city on the hill" became the mantra of a more aggressive foreign policy. Ideological containment was revived, even as defense spending was given new life. "Reagan re-emphasized ideology and placed moral crusade at the forefront of containment policy." His solution to the "malaise" that Carter had identified was threefold: recover military supremacy; renew messianic purpose; and return to free enterprise.[36] Many, both in and out of the academy, credit Reagan's policies, coupled with his more aggressive rhetoric ("evil empire" comes to mind), with hastening the demise of the Soviet Union by forcing that country to spend beyond its means. These arguments overlook two factors: the sorry state of the Soviet economy even before Reagan came to office and the so-called "Reagan paradox": his inflammatory language choices on the one hand and practical peacemaking on the other. In general, however, relations with the Soviet Union, while not always happy, were well managed during the Reagan years.[37]

Nevertheless, Reagan's policy exposed many of the contradictions inherent in U.S. Cold War strategy and in its selection of allies. By resurrecting the notion of ideological containment, Reagan returned the United States to a contorted principle that "virtuous [U.S.] power" had to be protected by ensuring anticommunist regimes, particularly in the Western Hemisphere, regardless of the cost to the democratic process. "We had to destroy the village in order to save it."

From the end of the Cold War to the devastation of 9/11, American foreign policy had been in some disarray, lacking the clear focus demanded by a dominant enemy. The United States began the post–Cold War period by angering some of the potential allies who were spinning off the carcass of the dying Soviet Union. Much as it had in 1956 and in 1968, the United States held back as first Lithuania, then Ukraine demanded independence. In an irony of history, at the moment of achieving its greatest foreign policy desire, the United States hesitated, losing the momentum that had been generated by the dramatic events of 1989. Similarly, the United States squandered much of its opportunity in Russia after 1991 by linking democratization too closely with market reform. In all likelihood, Russia would never have become a dependable ally in the manner of Great Britain, but better management of the post–Cold War period could surely have lessened tensions that have arisen in more recent years. It is likely, moreover, that most, if not all, of the nations of Eastern Europe might have allied themselves more closely with the United States.

Instead, the first Bush Administration chose a cautious course, opting merely to support Gorbachev and the reforms he was trying to make rather than to reach for the bigger prize and risk chaos. In fairness, it is hard to know what the best course is when the world seems to be spinning out of control, and there were many voices in the administration arguing against greater engagement for fear the reforms were a ruse.[38] Nevertheless, it cannot have been lost on Lithuania, Ukraine, and the governments of Eastern Europe that, at the end of the Cold War, the doctrine of containment, which had been used to bottle up communist expansion, was turned on its head and used to prop up the Soviet state, containing instead Soviet weakness, forgoing the victory the United States had sought for over forty years.

On the other hand, there was little doubt that the United States would remain actively involved in the Middle East after the Cold War—the country was too dependent on oil to walk away from the region simply because the rivalry with the USSR no longer existed. In addition, there was the special relationship with Israel, which was still a target of enmity in the area, and a growing concern about the rise of Islamic fundamentalism—not to mention the increase in terrorism.[39] Indeed, the collapse of communism initially benefited the United States in the Middle East because anti-American forces there lost their primary benefactor; this, in turn, enabled the United States to develop new relationships with countries such as Syria. As a result, Israel lost some of its geopolitical importance, which enabled Washington to put additional pressure on Israel to advance the peace process.[40]

In the "First Gulf War" in 1990, U.S. troops, leading an international coalition under the auspices of the United Nations, expelled Iraqi forces from Kuwait. The aftermath of that effort has demonstrated the difficulties of maintaining international collaboration; in 1996, when the United States responded to Iraqi recalcitrance regarding weapons inspections, there was a conspicuous lack of international support—a portent of things to come.

Absent the Cold War, but confronted initially with a budget deficit and a recession, Bill Clinton emphasized economic alliances during his two terms as president. Economic policy, free enterprise, and the promotion of American business abroad had always been a major factor in foreign policy decisions. However, without a Cold War policy to maintain, economic issues came to the fore, with organizations such as the WTO and the G-7 (then 8) grabbing the headlines. Clinton was well liked in Europe, but without the need to contain communism, European allies were less inclined to accept American leadership in either military or economic matters. This trend became more pointed as the Cold War faded into the past and Europe concentrated on bringing the newly independent nations of Eastern Europe into the economic fold, thus filling the void in leadership left by the United States.

As the Cold War receded, the Middle East, one of the prime "battlegrounds" of containment policy, began to resurface as an area of concern in U.S. foreign policy. More than anywhere else in the world, the Middle East has confounded presidential administrations and pushed the limits of presidential rhetoric. It brings together in one place the major forces driving most policy: geopolitical and geoeconomic, combined with domestic pressures. Brokering peace in the Middle East has become the Holy Grail of modern presidencies, as the governments of that oil-rich region, fraught with deep and ancient political and cultural divisions, continue to find their own voice in the new world order.

George W. Bush came to office in 2001 disdaining the notion of traditional allies, vowing to reform American foreign policy to emphasize hemispheric neighbors. He had little patience for the ancient capitals of Europe or the niceties of diplomacy. He had campaigned on a platform of a return to America's exceptionalist roots, using the slogan "Strength and Humility," an amalgamation of American power and virtuosity.[41] Even before the terrorist attacks of September 11, 2001, however, Bush had begun to learn that without its old friends the United States could not function effectively in the new world order.

New Wine in Old Jugs

The terrorist attacks are said to have introduced a new era, to have turned the world upside down. In terms of America's understanding of itself and its place in the world, that may well be true. However, the attacks also provided the justification the Bush Administration needed to "go it alone," without regard for the opinions of allies or enemies—or the United Nations. At the same time, the exigence of the attacks created rhetorical space for the reversion of policy to familiar ground.

Despite the uniqueness of an attack on American soil, the loss of the twin towers and the damage to the Pentagon provided a stable frame for viewing the terrorist threat, much as communism provided an organizing principle for foreign policy rhetoric and a lens through which to view the world. One of the problems of dealing with terrorism as long as it was confined to foreign soil was the absence of a state actor; the terrorist era is characterized by the rise of the nonstate actor, the terrorist who moves freely through several countries. September 11 provided a rhetorical solution to that problem: those who are not with us are our enemies, those who harbor terrorists are our targets.

For fifty years, the United States had viewed the world as "bipolar," dominated by the two superpowers. The bipolar world of the Cold War period was a unique American construction—if you are not with us, you are against us, you are the enemy, or (if you are an American) you are a traitor, you are unpatriotic. As Wander and others have noted, this "prophetic dualism" was fueled by the exceptionalist notion that the United States was powerful because it deserved to be, and it therefore had a responsibility to the rest of the world.[42] Foreign leaders who tried to steer a course of nonalignment between the superpowers did so at their peril, as in the case of India and Nasser of Egypt, among many others. In the words of John Foster Dulles, "Neutrality has increasingly become an obsolete [idea] and except under very exceptional circumstances, it is an immoral and shortsighted conception."[43] However, in the 1990s this view had no real world analog. September 11, 2001, changed all that. It effectively restored the rhetorical justification for a bipolar view of the world—allies and enemies. George W. Bush wasted no time in making this clear by drawing a sharp rhetorical line in the sand of the Middle East. The stark polarization of NSC-68 found new life in the words of George W. Bush in 2001: "Every nation, in every region, now has a decision to make. Either you are with us, or you are with the terrorists."[44]

In his 1960 Inaugural Address, John F. Kennedy promised that America would "pay any price and bear any burden" to extend the blessings of liberty around the world. Thus, the burden of exceptionalism merged with the policy of containment, modified by the militarism implicit in NSC-68, and ultimately led us into Vietnam. Though Kennedy's rhetoric was aggressive, his reasoning was defensive. Only by ridding the world of despotic communism, taking liberty to every corner of the globe, could the United States secure its own safety.

> Let the word go forth . . . that the torch has been passed to a new generation of Americans, born in this century, tempered by war, disciplined by a hard and bitter peace . . . and unwilling to witness or permit the slow undoing of those human rights to which this nation has always been committed. . . . Let every nation know, whether it wishes us well or ill, that we shall pay any price, bear any burden, meet any hardship, support any friend, oppose any foe to assure the survival and the success of liberty.[45]

Forty years later, threatened by terrorism, George W. Bush declared that the United States would never ask permission to defend itself and led us into Iraq. Again, the message was one of liberating oppressed peoples—and of securing the safety of the United States through aggressive action. An overwhelming preemptive strike was cast as a defensive action—a pretty neat rhetorical trick.[46]

In the run-up to the invasion of Iraq, Bush's rhetoric took on an apocalyptic tone echoing that of the radical Right of the 1960s as they described the horrors of communism—("it's 5 minutes to midnight . . ."). In the period between the terrorist attacks and the invasion of Iraq, much of the rhetorical burden was borne by Bush's surrogates: Rice, Rumsfeld, Powell, and Cheney. But it was the president who put the issue in its harshest terms.

It is difficult to recall today that the initial justification for the invasion of Iraq was the administration's belief that Saddam Hussein harbored not only terrorists but weapons of mass destruction:

> The stark reality of 2001 is that America is now a battlefield, that the war has come home. And therefore, this Nation must also confront

not only shadowy terrorist networks but the gravest danger in the war on terror: outlaw regimes arming to threaten the peace with weapons of mass destruction.[47]

Now you're called to defend our freedom and to defend the security of America against a new kind of enemy. This enemy reaches across oceans. It targets the innocent. There are no rules of war for these cold-blooded killers. They seek biological and chemical and nuclear weapons to commit murder on a massive scale. This enemy will not be restrained by mercy or by conscience. . . . Today, the gravest danger in the war on terror, the gravest danger facing America and the world, is outlaw regimes that seek and possess nuclear, chemical, and biological weapons. These regimes could use such weapons for blackmail, terror, mass murder. They could also give or sell those weapons to terrorist allies who would use them without the least bit of hesitation. That's the reality of the world we live in, and that's what we're going to use every ounce of our power to defeat.[48]

Today, the gravest danger in the war on terror, the gravest danger facing America and the world, is outlaw regimes that seek and possess nuclear, chemical, and biological weapons. These regimes could use such weapons for blackmail, terror, and mass murder. They could also give or sell those weapons to terrorist allies, who would use them without the least hesitation. This threat is new; America's duty is familiar. Throughout the 20th century, small groups of men seized control of great nations, built armies and arsenals, and set out to dominate the weak and intimidate the world. In each case, their ambitions of cruelty and murder had no limit. In each case, the ambitions of Hitlerism, militarism, and communism were defeated by the will of free peoples, by the strength of great alliances, and by the might of the United States of America.

Now, in this century, the ideology of power and domination has appeared again, and seeks to gain the ultimate weapons of terror. Once again, this nation and all our friends are all that stand between a world at peace, and a world of chaos and constant alarm. Once again, we are called to defend the safety of our people, and the hopes of all mankind. And we accept this responsibility.[49]

Bush's post-9/11 rhetoric seemed to provide a new frame for a new situation— the doctrine of the defensive preemptive strike. This move, which appeared to fly in the face of American values and virtue, was not to be seen for what it was: after all, America had been attacked. Thus, in the current rhetorical climate, to attack others in order to prevent further attacks against the United States is constructed as a defensive strategy.

But what is most remarkable about the passages quoted is the way in which the words echo those of administrations past: America's special mission in the world, the universality of its values, the need to secure liberty abroad in order to ensure safety at home. By labeling the government of Iraq an "ideology of power and domination," Bush reaches through time to more familiar enemies. "Once again," he says, the United States is all that stands between darkness and light, placing this conflict in sequence with those that have gone before.

There are other ghosts of enemies past, most notably the weakening of civil liberties in the name of national security: the felt need on the part of the Bush Administration to limit democratic values at home in order to promote them abroad—the obverse of the argument that U.S. security can be increased by imposing democracy elsewhere.[50]

Looking at the totality of the rhetoric coming out of the Bush Administration, it is clear that we have replaced the Soviet Union as the archenemy of freedom and have reenergized the concept of containment. Prior to 9/11, the United States was perfectly content to confine its concern over terrorist acts abroad to humanitarian aid and murmurs of sympathy. Similarly, as the justification for the invasion of Iraq moved from finding weapons of mass destruction to the need to liberate the Iraqi people, we hear distinct echoes of the rhetoric of American exceptionalism—"to secure the blessings of liberty" at home and abroad.

Undoubtedly, this reversion to type reached its apotheosis in George W. Bush's second Inaugural Address, on January 20, 2005. This speech finished the transformation of U.S. involvement in Iraq from a preemptive defensive strike to a mission to liberate the Iraqi people. The war on terror has morphed into a war against tyranny as an explanation for U.S. action. Remarkably, whole portions of the speech might have been lifted from the exceptionalist bible:

> There is only one force of history that can break the reign of hatred and resentment and expose the pretensions of tyrants, . . . and that is the force of human freedom.
>
> The survival of liberty in our land increasingly depends on the success of liberty in other lands.
>
> From the day of our Founding, we have proclaimed that every man and woman on this earth has rights, and dignity . . . because

they bear the image of the Maker of heaven and earth. . . . Advancing these ideals is the mission that created our nation. . . . Now it is the urgent requirement of our nation's security. . . .

So it is the policy of the United States to seek and support the growth of democratic movements and institutions in every nation and culture, with the ultimate goal of ending tyranny in our world.

We will persistently clarify the choice before every ruler and every nation: The moral choice between oppression, which is always wrong, and freedom, which is eternally right.[51]

We have come full circle. When you ask someone: "Why study history?" the inevitable answer is: "So we won't repeat it." If one thinks about this response, it is clear that it generally refers to foreign policy *faux pas*. With much the same idea in mind, Ted Windt once made the point that rhetoric is a series of historical analogies. And that is, of course, the fear: Chamberlain returned from Munich to proclaim "Peace in our time," and the world learned to fear appeasement. The Munich analogy held until it was replaced by Vietnam. As we prepared for the first Gulf War, the cry was heard, "no more Vietnams!" (although even then, George Bush could not resist the older comparison, referring to Saddam Hussein as a modern-day Hitler who could not be appeased). The Munich analogy proved powerful again in the run-up to the U.S. invasion of Iraq in 2003. It seems the two Gulf wars have given us a new tyrannizing image. We have replaced the international communist conspiracy with the international terrorist conspiracy, rearming and refurbishing the rhetorical arsenal of containment and exceptionalism.

Neustadt and May, in *Thinking in Time: The Uses of History for Decision Makers*, describe what they believe is the way history ought to be used for decision-making purposes. In explicating their formula, Neustadt and May discuss a number of situations where history was well used and still more where it was not. Interestingly, the assumption usually is that we study history so that we can avoid repeating it; the lesson is a negative one. Seldom, it seems, does history provide a model that bears repeating.

In Robert Ludlum's last book, *The Altman Code,* his fictional president of the United States is faced with a foreign policy crisis involving current enemy Iraq and burgeoning ally China.[52] A Chinese freighter loaded with biochemical weapons is headed for Iraq. Ludlum's fictional president knows about the secret cargo but does not have the evidence to board the ship in international waters. On the eve of signing a historical human rights treaty, the last barrier to free trade with China, the president must decide whether the potential threat of a biochemical attack from Iraq is greater than the economic and national security benefits of an alliance with China. Prior to making his decision, Ludlum's president comments to his chief of staff, "Wouldn't it be great to be able to return to the good old days, when only two behemoth nations stalked each other with metaphorical clubs?"

NOTES

I would especially like to thank Dan Maguire, my research assistant at Florida State University, for his assistance with the original version of this essay. Prof. Maguire is currently Assistant Professor of Speech Communication at Ithaca College.

1. George Washington, "Farewell Address," in *Three Centuries of American Rhetorical Discourse,* ed. Ronald F. Reid (Prospect Heights, Ill.: Waveland Press, 1988), 199.

2. Winston Churchill, "The Sinews of Peace," Fulton, Mo., March 5, 1946, in *Churchill Speaks, 1897–1963,* ed. Robert Rhodes James (New York: Barnes and Noble Books, 1998), 881. This was not the first time Churchill had used the phrase "iron curtain"; he used it the preceding August in a speech to the House of Commons, but it did not attract the attention it received after the speech in Fulton, Missouri.

3. Marilyn J. Young, "The Rhetorical Origins of American Anti-Communism," unpublished paper, University of Pittsburgh, 1969. For an extended discussion of Churchill's speech, see Lynn Boyd Hinds and Theodore Otto Windt, *The Cold War as Rhetoric* (New York: Praeger, 1992).

4. Richard M. Weaver, *Visions of Order: The Cultural Crisis of Our Time* (Baton Rouge: Louisiana State University Press, 1964), 12.

5. There have always been questions about the legitimacy of the act that brought the U.S. into World War I [generally thought to be the sinking of the *Lusitania*], and some have even questioned the role of President Roosevelt in provoking and/or abetting the attack on Pearl Harbor that brought this country into the Second World War. And it was certainly true that in both instances the United States had been providing assistance to England and its allies well in advance of formally entering the war.

6. Were such agreements to materialize, one would have to ask how these arrangements square with the policy of isolating those nations that harbor terrorists. In any event, there is evidence to suggest that terrorists, at least, may not be the fruit of economic deprivation, as many who join terrorist ranks are educated and materially well-off. See, for example, Alan B. Krueger, "Cash Rewards and Poverty Alone Do Not Explain Terrorism," http://www.irs.princeton.edu/krueger/05292003a.pdf. See also R. Borum, "Understanding the Terrorist Mindset," *FBI Law Enforcement Bulletin,* 2003.

7. Alan P. Dobson and Steve Marsh, *U.S. Foreign Policy since 1945* (London: Routledge, 2001).

8. J. D. Richardson, ed., *Compilation of the Messages and Papers of the Presidents*, vol. 2 (Washington, D.C.: GPO, 1987), 287. In Monroe's message to Congress on December 2, 1823, he delivered what we have always called the Monroe Doctrine, although in truth it should have been called the Adams Doctrine. Essentially, the United States was informing the powers of the Old World that the American continents were no longer open to European colonization, and that any effort to extend European political influence into the New World would be considered by the United States "as dangerous to our peace and safety." The United States would not interfere in European wars or internal affairs, Monroe declared, and Europe was cautioned to stay out of American affairs.

Although it would take decades to coalesce into an identifiable policy, John Quincy Adams did raise a standard of an independent American foreign policy so strongly that future administrations could not ignore it. One should note, however, that the policy succeeded because it addressed British as well as American interests and for the next hundred years was secured by the backing of the British fleet. Accessed at http://usinfo.state.gov/usa/infousa/facts/democrac/50.htm.

9. See Larry Rohter, "The World Wants the World from America; Latin America—Hey, Remember Us, Right Next Door?" *New York Times*, January 16, 2005.

10. Rohter, "The World Wants the World."

11. Simon Romero, "Venezuela, Tired of U.S. Influence, Strengthens Its Relationships in the Middle East," *New York Times*, August 21, 2006. Accessed at http://select.nytimes.com.

12. "Venezuelan Seeks Another Anti-U.S. Ally in Syria," *New York Times*, August 31, 2006. Accessed at http://select.nytimes.com.

13. Warren Hoge, "The World; A Speech That Khrushchev or Arafat or Che Would Admire," *New York Times*, September 24, 2006. Accessed at http://select.nytimes.com. For a copy of Chavez's UN speech, see www.informationclearinghouse.info/article10315.htm.

14. Neil MacFarquhar, "The World Wants the World from America; The Arab World—Can't Live With; Can't Live Without," *New York Times*, January 16, 2005.

15. Mark Landler, "The World Wants the World from America; Europe—Breaking Up Is Hard to Do," *New York Times*, January 16, 2005. See also Tomas Valasek, "Listening to Europe, Pushing for Rapprochement," *CDI Defense Monitor* 33, no. 6 (November–December 2004), 3–4.

16. In what is perhaps an ironic twist of fate, our most loyal ally in the Iraq war is our old friend, Great Britain.

17. Seymour Martin Lipset, *American Exceptionalism: A Double-Edged Sword* (New York: W. W. Norton, 1996), 19.

18. See Dobson and Marsh, *U.S. Foreign Policy since 1945*, 2. When Jimmy Carter tried to operationalize these concepts in foreign relations, however, it quickly became clear that individual rights were the "human rights" most valued by Americans.

19. To view the long telegram in its entirety, see http://www2.gwu.edu/~nsarchiv/cold-war/documents/episode-1/kennan.htm. Kennan also published the essence of his views under the pseudonym "X" in *Foreign Affairs* in 1947 as "The Sources of Soviet Conduct." See the essay at http://www.historyguide.org/europe/kennan.html.

20. Robert J. McMahon, "By Helping Others, We Help Ourselves: The Cold War Rhetoric of American Foreign Policy," in *Critical Reflections on the Cold War*, ed. Martin J. Medhurst and H. W. Brands (College Station: Texas A&M University Press, 2000), 324.

21. See Robert L. Ivie, *Democracy and America's War on Terror* (Tuscaloosa: University of Alabama Press, 2005).

22. Of course, the Soviet Union was an ally of convenience to begin with: almost no one outside a few socialists and communists thought of the USSR as a natural—or even desirable—ally of the United States. Thrown together in the Herculean quest to defeat Hitler, the two nations soon parted ways once World War II ended. Thus, WWII itself had forced America into an Old World mode; the perceived threat of communism made it difficult to set that lens aside.

23. Dobson and Marsh, *U.S. Foreign Policy since 1945*, 23.

24. Robert P. Newman, "NSC (National Insecurity) 68: Nitze's Second Hallucination," in *Critical Reflections on the Cold War*, ed. Martin Medhurst and H. W. Brands (College Station: Texas A&M University Press, 2000), 55–94.

25. Obviously, it influenced some domestic policy as well, since the line between domestic and foreign policy became increasingly blurred with the growth of internationalism and because the fear of communism included fear of domestic subversion. However, the focus of this chapter is foreign policy. See Francis A. Beer and Robert Harriman, *Post Realism: The Rhetorical Turn in International Relations* (East Lansing: Michigan State University Press, 1996).

26. Beer and Harriman, *Post Realism*, 3.

27. During the McCarthy period, such thinking was dubbed "pink." At the height of Vietnam, those seeking an alternate route for that benighted conflict were said to be giving "aid and comfort to the enemy." Echoes of this last charge have been heard in the discourse surrounding the current Bush Administration's policy in Iraq.

28. It is generally thought that it was the relative strength of American nuclear capability that forced Nikita Khrushchev to turn back Soviet ships carrying nuclear weapons to Cuba during the standoff between the United States and the USSR in October 1962.

29. Some have argued that the USSR took advantage of the American focus on the Suez Canal crisis in timing its put-down of the Hungarian freedom movement.

30. The exceptions, of course, were those dictators whose help was thought to be needed in the fight against communism.

31. See Dobson and Marsh, *U.S. Foreign Policy since 1945*, 56–60.

32. John Kane, "American Values or Human Rights? U.S. Foreign Policy and the Fractured Myth of Virtuous Power," *Presidential Studies Quarterly* 33, no. 4 (December 2003), 774.

33. Kane, "American Values," 784.

34. Of course, a human rights standard works both ways, and President Carter was embarrassed when Andrew Young, then UN ambassador, labeled continuing poverty in America a violation of human rights. See Kane, "American Values," 785.

35. Dobson and Marsh, *U.S. Foreign Policy since 1945*, 37.

36. Dobson and Marsh, *U.S. Foreign Policy since 1945*, 38 ff.

37. See John Lewis Gaddis, *The United States and the End of the Cold War: Implications, Reconsiderations, Provocations* (New York: Oxford University Press, 1992), 123 ff. See also Jack F. Matlock Jr., *Gorbachev and Reagan: How the Cold War Ended* (New York: Random House, 2004).

38. Some of these voices could still be heard at late as the mid-90s, arguing that the collapse of the USSR and its communist government was a hoax.

39. There are many accounts of the U.S.-Israeli relationship, but one of the most recent is Robert P. Newman, "Hypocrisy and Hatred," *Controversia* 2, no. 1 (Spring 2003): 12–39.

40. Dobson and Marsh, *U.S. Foreign Policy since 1945*, 116.

41. Kane, "American Values," 772.

42. Philip Wander, "The Rhetoric of American Foreign Policy," *Quarterly Journal of Speech* 70, no. 4 (November 1984): 342.

43. John Foster Dulles, June 9, 1955, at Iowa State College, quoted in the May 25, 1959, obituary in the *New York Times,* accessed at www.arlingtoncemetery.com/jfdulles.htm.

44. George W. Bush, "Address to the Nation," September 20, 2001. Accessed at www.americanrhetoric.com.

45. John F. Kennedy, "Inaugural Address, 1961," in *American Rhetoric from Roosevelt to Reagan,* 2nd edition, ed. Halford Ross Ryan (Prospect Heights, Ill: Waveland Press, 1987), 156. Fortunately, the closest we came to an all-out war during Kennedy's time in office was the Cuban Missile Crisis.

46. During the Cold War period known as "Mutually Assured Destruction" or MAD, having the weaponry to destroy a target's ability to respond (second strike capability) was known as first strike capability. Given the overwhelming force used to decimate the Iraqi military, it would be difficult to describe the U.S. invasion as anything other than a first strike. While the U.S. always possessed first strike capability, it was generally accepted that America would never strike first—hence the emphasis on protecting missile sites.

47. George W. Bush, Remarks at Carl Harrison High School in Kennesaw, Georgia, February 20, 2003. Weekly Compilation of Presidential Documents, from the 2003 Presidential Documents Online via GPO Access, frwais.access.gpo.gov.

48. George W. Bush, Remarks at Mayport Naval Station, Jacksonville, February 13, 2003. Weekly Compilation of Presidential Documents, from the 2003 Presidential Documents Online via GPO Access, frwais.access.gpo.gov.

49. George W. Bush, State of the Union, January 28, 2003. Accessed at http://www.presidentialrhetoric.com/speeches/01.28.03.html.

50. For a detailed analysis see Robert L. Ivie, *Democracy and America's War on Terror.*

51. George W. Bush, Inaugural Address, January 20, 2005. Accessed at www.whitehouse.gov/news/releases/2005.

52. Newer books "by" Altman can be found, but all are co-"authored" by someone writing in Altman's stead. Robert Ludlum, *The Altman Code,* paperback ed. (New York: St. Martin's Press, 2003); Richard E. Neustadt and Ernest R. May, *Thinking in Time: The Uses of History for Decision Makers* (New York: Macmillan, 1996).

CHAPTER 8

REVISING THE COLD WAR NARRATIVE TO ENCOMPASS TERRORIST THREATS

Vietnam and Beyond

Carol Winkler, Georga State University

In September of 2006, the Bush Administration released its *National Strategy for Combating Terrorism*. The document portrayed the current war on terror as different from previous conflicts, with a key distinguishing feature being the nature of the threat. As the *National Strategy* surmised, "Our understanding of the enemy has evolved as well. Today, the principal terrorist enemy confronting the United States is a transnational movement of extremist organizations, networks, and individuals—and their state and non-state supporters—which have in common that they exploit Islam and use terrorism for ideological ends."[1]

Presidential depictions of terrorists as transnational actors with ideological objectives, however, are not new. The nation's leaders named Nazi terrorists and communist terrorists during the twentieth century as global movements in conflict with democratic models of governance. John F. Kennedy introduced communism and terrorism as a linguistic merger reminiscent of the "Nazi terrorist" label employed during World War II. In an open letter written to President Diem of South Vietnam in 1961, Kennedy applauded the people of South Vietnam for their refusal to submit to "Communist terror."[2] The Johnson and Nixon administrations echoed Kennedy's approach with their own repeated references to communist terrorists in their Cold War narratives.[3]

This chapter explains how presidents have retrofitted the Cold War narrative, complete with its ideological underpinnings, to construct terrorism in the post–Cold War period. The Vietnam War functions as a critical starting point, given the decision by presidents elected from both parties to rely on the Cold War strategy to discuss terrorism publicly. As I indicate, the subsequent executive branch statements of Republican administrations have continued to utilize elements of the Cold War narrative to frame their public responses to terrorism. Democratic administrations are omitted from this analysis due to their decisions to adopt crime (not war) narratives to explain the threat from terrorism.[4]

To illustrate the progressions of terrorism's merger with the Cold War narrative, I examine three conventional elements of the narrative: the scene, the enemy character, and the hero character. Internal memoranda, polling results, and drafts of public reports provide insight into the motivations that lay behind the administration's public communication strategies. The analysis demonstrates that while the Cold War narrative has been resilient in terrorism discourse, it has undergone subtle shifts that influence public knowledge of American foreign policy information.

Scene

Conventional Cold War discourse locates the scene of its narrative in the newly free nations around the globe. The defeat of fascism left many nations on the precipice of enhanced freedom and liberty, uncertain of whether they could nurture their newly acquired freedoms into full-fledged democratic regimes.[5] Cold War narratives always depict newfound freedoms around the globe to be precarious. Robert Ivie focuses on the dominance of such a theme in his metaphorical analysis: "Cold War rhetors talk variously of the beacon of liberty as a flickering flame, freedom as a frail body threatened by the cancer of Communism, as a defenseless quarry set upon by relentless predators, and so on."[6] Cold War scenes are fragile, requiring a strong commitment by both the United States and the emerging democratic nation to bring the promise of self-determination to fruition.

In presidential terrorism discourse during the Vietnam War, South Vietnam functioned as the emerging democracy that required assistance to ensure its own freedom. The various administrations depicted South Vietnam as having no realistic hope of defending itself from forces outside its own border without U.S. military assistance. Johnson reasoned: "Most of the non-Communist nations of Asia cannot, by themselves and alone, resist the growing might and the grasping ambition of Asian communism."[7] Nixon pointedly blamed the Johnson Administration for the ongoing fragility of the scene, arguing: "The policy of the previous administration . . . did not adequately stress the goal of strengthening the South Vietnamese so that they could defend themselves when we left."[8] Even when Nixon touted his policy of Vietnamization, he portrayed South Vietnam as incapable of mounting an effective indigenous defense.

As the Vietnam War entered its second decade, the Nixon Administration expanded the scope of the narrative's fragile scene beyond South Vietnam. Advocating the domino theory, Nixon maintained that other fledgling democracies would be at risk should South Vietnam fall to the communists. He warned that "abandoning our commitment in Vietnam here and now would mean turning 17 million South Vietnamese over to Communist tyranny and terror. . . . An American defeat in Vietnam would encourage this kind of aggression all over the world, aggression in which smaller nations armed by their major allies could be tempted to attack neighboring nations at will in the Mideast, in Europe, and other areas. World peace would be in grave jeopardy."[9] By recognizing vulnerable democracies beyond Southeast Asia, the administration's narrative heightened the need to attend urgently to the scene.

The next president who depicted the scene of his terrorist narrative in accordance with the Cold War discourse was Ronald Reagan. Reagan identified two areas of the world particularly vulnerable to outside forces. The first was Central America. Reagan maintained: "In Honduras, democratic institutions are taking root. In El Salvador, democracy is beginning to work even in the face of externally supported terrorism and guerrilla warfare."[10] The other vulnerable region was Lebanon. Reagan depicted Lebanon as "a small country" and a "troubled land" but insisted it had "made important steps toward stability and order."[11] The administration's narrative insisted democracy would flourish if it were simply permitted to grow.

Public acceptance of Reagan's recall of the conventional Cold War narrative was waning by the start of his second term. The American public no longer limited their interpretations of the fragile setting to the new and emerging democracies worldwide. Reagan's Task Force on Combatting [sic] Terrorism indicated that Americans themselves felt threatened. Young and Rubicam, the firm hired by the task force to gauge the viewpoint of the public, concluded that terrorism reduced "America's status to being seen as a pawn: powerless, easily manipulated, and at the mercy of those who attack us because we cannot fight back."[12] Reagan's analysts concluded that the public was frustrated with the ability of terrorists to expose the limits of America's power.

Within the specific context of Central America, public reaction was no better. By 1985, internal administration polls recorded that 66 percent of the public responded positively to the statement: "There is little point to our condemning a state of terrorism against American interests in the Middle East if we support our own terrorists in Central America."[13] The administration responded by committing its spokespersons to a sharp, public distinction between terrorism and insurgency.[14] Behind the scenes Reagan's national security advisors warned that despite the coordinated implementation of the rhetorical strategy, the "distinction [between terrorism and insurgency was] *not* clear."[15] Administration analysts concluded that even Reagan himself could not soften the growing public mindset against their Central American campaign.[16]

Perhaps the strongest motivation for the administration's retooling of the conventional Cold War narrative involved events in Lebanon. Reagan's aides were still stinging from the humiliation of having to withdraw U.S. troops from Lebanon in 1983 after the terrorists' successful assault on the military barracks and the U.S. embassy in Beirut. Current retrospectives with the administration's central players reveal the depth of the reaction to the forced retreat. Vincent Cannistraro, Reagan's director of National Security Council Intelligence, summed up the reigning sentiment at the time: "Hezbollah won a victory. That war was over. We lost that war. I don't know if it was recognized at the time, but the withdrawal of the U.S. represented a victory for Hezbollah."[17] The U.S. State Department coordinator for counterterrorism, Robert Oakley, likewise remembered: "It was a huge shock . . . it caused us to reevaluate a lot of things."[18] Convinced they had lost a war, the Reagan Administration committed to making a change.

Recasting the scene consistent with the administration's prior rehearsals of the narrative, however, was problematic. Many of the targets of terrorism by the mid-1980s (i.e., United States citizens abroad and European nations) were no longer fragile democracies or new nations in search of their right to self-determination. They had established governments, they had stable economies, and they belonged to the world's preeminent security alliance. To argue that such democracies were fragile risked a loss of credibility, if not ridicule, at home and abroad.

To resolve the problem, the scene of the new narrative shifted the emphasis away from the fragility of any particular foreign nation to the vulnerability of democracy as a whole to terrorism. Reagan reasoned: "Terrorism is the antithesis of democracy. By brutal acts against innocent persons, terrorists seek to exaggerate their strength and undermine confidence in responsible government, publicize their cause, intimidate the populace, and pressure national leaders to accede to demands conceived in violence. Where democracy seeks to consult the common man on the governance of his nation, terrorism makes war on the common man, repudiating in bloody terms the concept of government by the people."[19] Reagan insisted that the openness of democratic societies made them uniquely exposed to the horrors of terrorism. His new approach reconstituted terrorism to be an inevitable outcome of a healthy democracy, not a sign of national fragility or governmental weakness.

As Reagan publicly expanded the scene of his narrative from a single emerging democracy to democracy as a whole, his aides had reached a different conclusion. The task force report, touted by the administration as its most comprehensive examination of international and domestic terrorism, concluded that attacks on democracies were not the sole or the primary cause of terrorism. Approved by the National Security Council, the Department of Defense, the Central Intelligence Agency, the Joint Chiefs of Staff, the Federal Bureau of Investigation, and the White House, among others, the report noted: "Because acts of terrorism vary so much in time, location, jurisdiction, and motivation, consistent response is virtually impossible."[20] The report further acknowledged that rather than oppose democracies, terrorists' actual motivations included the ability of such violence to serve as a strong-arm, low-budget foreign policy or as a means to further national insurgency movements. It went on to mention that Middle Eastern nations (i.e., those without democratic forms of government) were frequently the intended targets of terrorism.[21] Reagan's depiction of terrorism as a juxtaposed enemy of democracy was simply not as nuanced as the administration's available intelligence at the time.

The first Bush Administration, having been inaugurated in the post–Cold War era, faced a similarly difficult rhetorical challenge in casting the 1990 Persian Gulf crisis within the Cold War narrative framework. Bush's Persian Gulf Working Group reviewed a report that compared two previous Cold War conflicts with the situation in Kuwait. The analysis concluded that the scenes of the varied conflicts were not comparable. It noted: "The present situation in the Persian Gulf does not feature the same compelling cold war motivations as earlier conflicts. The need to destroy Iraq's nuclear and chemical capabilities, the need to protect U.S. hostages, and the removal of Saddam Hussein from power are all factors that may be able to fill the gap left by the absence of cold war labels, but not one of these justifications is as deeply rooted in American culture as the cold war psychology was in early conflicts."[22]

In the end Bush chose, in part, to follow the lead of his predecessor. Like Reagan, Bush borrowed the theme of a fragile scene from the Cold War narrative. The Kuwaiti monarchy, however, functioned neither as an emerging democracy (the conventional backdrop of Cold War discourse) nor as a preexisting democracy vulnerable due to its open form of government (Reagan's reconstituted scene). The Bush Administration resolved the problem by ascribing the characteristic of fragility to the New World Order. Bush explained: "Today that new world is struggling to be born, a world quite different from the one we've known. A world where the rule of law supplants the rule of the jungle. A world in which nations recognize the shared responsibility for freedom and justice. A world where the strong respect the rights of the weak."[23] For Bush, the New World Order constituted a frail international context that held the promise to yield a more peaceful, a more just, and a more free world.

The Bush Administration further recalled the conventional Cold War narrative by expanding the scope of the scene beyond the nation under direct attack. The Bush narrative claimed that emerging democracies all around the globe were vulnerable to Hussein's actions. While Iraq had not yet invaded a democratic nation, Bush maintained that the emerging democracies nevertheless shouldered the bulk of the economic consequences of its conflict with Kuwait. He explained: "The fledgling democracies in Eastern Europe are being severely damaged by the economic effects of Saddam's actions. The developing countries in Africa and in our hemisphere are being victimized by this dictator's rape of his neighbor Kuwait."[24] Privately, the Bush Administration was also concerned about the economic impact of the Iraqi move on the United States. Early in the Iraq-Kuwaiti conflict, aides confided in Bush their fears of a future recession, a potential $300 billion deficit, and even worse long-term economic problems.[25] When the New World Order became the label for the fragile scene in the reconstituted Cold War narrative, it encompassed both old and new democracies worldwide as well as their allies.

The current Bush Administration further revised the scene of the Cold War narrative. George W. Bush consistently maintained that the events of 9/11 had demonstrated to the entire international community that all nations were at risk from terrorism, free or not, democratic or other. Fragility remained a theme, enhanced by the recognition that oceans could no longer protect nations from terrorist violence. Bush repeatedly underscored the precarious state of the entire globe in statements like the one he made before the Australian parliament:

"No country can live peacefully in a world that the terrorists would make for us. And no people are immune from the sudden violence that can come to an office building or an airplane or a nightclub or a city bus."[26] Any nation could become a front in the new war on terrorism because all were potentially vulnerable to the twenty-first- century threat.

Viewed over the course of history since the Vietnam War, the presidents have gradually expanded the scene in their reconstituted Cold War narratives. The theme of a fragile environment has remained constant, but presidents have enlarged its application from emerging democracies to democracy as a whole, to an ordered world, to any nation on earth. The justification for U.S. intervention concurrently expanded to anywhere on the globe.

Enemy Character

Conventional Cold Warriors name communists as the characters who harbor destructive motivations against the fragile scenes of emerging peace and freedom. Likened to Hitler's fascists, communists seek to impose totalitarian rule on the objects of their triumphs.[27] Cold War narratives depict control as a necessary first step toward the enemy's ultimate goal of worldwide conquest. Communists are willing to rely on ruthless and barbaric means to achieve their expansive, destructive objectives.[28] The savagery of communism offers a sharp contrast with the behavior of the rest of the civilized world.

In the Vietnam narrative, it was the Vietcong, supported by the North Vietnamese and the communist Chinese, who sought to destroy the noncommunist government of South Vietnam. The Kennedy Administration insisted that North Vietnam, a nation fearful of unfavorable comparisons between the growing economy of South Vietnam and its own languishing economy under a communist dictatorship, used terror to reverse South Vietnam's economic and educational advances. Kennedy explained to the citizens of South Vietnam: "The Communist response to the growing strength and prosperity of your people was to send terror into your villages, to burn your new schools and to make ambushes of your new roads."[29] Within Kennedy's public perspective, the communists worked to dupe fragile democracies into changing their political allegiance by undermining societal advances.

Presidents in the Vietnam era insisted that besides halting community progress, the communist alliance sought to enslave the South Vietnamese citizenry. Administration accounts emphasized the communists' intention to deny the South Vietnamese their rights of self-determination. The statements of various spokespersons paired *communism* with terms of domination such as *aggression, Communist slavery, Communist masters, dictatorial control, tyranny, totalitarianism,* and *dictatorship.* The narrative posited that the citizenry of South Vietnam had no hope of determining their destiny under communist rule.

According to administration accounts, the communists' thirst for domination was not limited to South Vietnam. Roger Hilsman, assistant secretary for Far Eastern affairs, introduced the theme of world conquest to the 1963 Conference on Cold War Education, when he stated: "The aim of the Chinese Communist is to gain predominant control in Asia and eventually to secure the establishment of Communist regimes throughout the world."[30] Public officials in the Johnson Administration argued that the Chinese would use a communist victory in Vietnam to demonstrate to the Soviet Union that wars of liberation could be fought and won around the globe.[31]

As the process of achieving such far-reaching goals unfolded, U.S. leaders maintained that North Vietnam and its communist allies were barbaric. Johnson argued that North Vietnam planned to engage in a "war of unparalleled brutality," because it could not defeat the combined forces fighting for South Vietnam in a traditional military confrontation.[32] Administration officials catalogued assassinations, kidnappings, strangulations, harassment, and destruction of civilian property as the commonplace and unconventional tactics of the Vietcong. The targets of Vietcong terrorism underscored the image of communist barbarity. Victims included schoolteachers, local chiefs, and medical personnel. The enemy's barbarity both vilified the Communist Party and became the administration's public rationale for why U.S. troops from time to time had to resort to unconventional methods themselves.

During Ronald Reagan's first term in office, the administration relied on conventional Cold War enemies to characterize global terrorism. A number of internal memoranda provide various rationales for doing so. A primary impetus was Reagan's own political future. As early as 1983, Republican House Minority Whip Newt Gingrich wrote to Ken Duberstein, Reagan's chief of staff, to express his concerns about Reagan's political future. He worried the American public and media were shocked by all the violence around the world, including outbreaks in Lebanon, Grenada, Nicaragua, El Salvador, and the nuclear missile demonstrations in Europe.[33] He stressed the urgency of the administration adopting a single explanation for why so much global violence was occurring. He warned Reagan: "It will begin to sink in to many Americans that if they are separate incidents, then maybe we ought to get a less violence-prone President. After all, if he has found four different areas of tension simultaneously, maybe he really is a troublemaker."[34] Having won a recent presidential election where his opponent characterized him as irresponsible in the foreign policy arena, Reagan could ill afford to compound the problem.

The solution, according to Gingrich, was to blame the Soviet Union for international violence whenever and wherever it occurred. He predicted that such a rhetorical framing would have considerable political advantages for Reagan. As he explained, "If in fact we are faced with Soviet trained, financed and guided terrorists, guerilla and military coups, then it is Andropov rather than Reagan who is the real cause of the all the problems. Then the American people can focus their anger on Andropov, the KGB, and the Soviet Union."[35] The approach, Gingrich predicted, would result in a lasting political alliance between the friends of Israel, those who cared about access to oil fields, and those who wanted freedom in the Caribbean.

Members of Reagan's State Department advocated a similar public communication approach but did so for policy reasons. The State Department was struggling with a lack of public support for its Central American policy and a Congress steadily withdrawing its financial support from the Contras. An analysis of two years of polls on Nicaragua led departmental analysts to conclude that "conflicts in Central America have aroused *less concern* among the public than such other foreign policy issues as relations with the Soviet Union, arms control negotiations, trying to deal with terrorism, and reducing the U.S. trade imbalance."[36] In response to the problem, Presidential Assistant Robert Smalley recommended a reframing of the threat posed by the Sandinistas. He maintained that a shift in focus to Soviet terrorism would attract needed public support for the administration's policy in Nicaragua. He told the secretary of state: "Perception of threat to the U.S. would be enhanced to the extent the Sandinista regime could be credibly pictured as a surrogate of Cuba or the USSR, as repressive at home, or as subversive among its neighbors."[37] In agreement, the minority whip of the House and the State Department worked in tandem to persuade Reagan to blame all international terrorism on the Soviet Union.

One difficulty with the plan at the time was that Reagan's CIA analysts did not believe that the Soviets were involved in organizing the bulk of international terrorism. A December 1981 report of the National Foreign Assessment Center of the CIA noted: "The actions of some terrorist groups may influence future behavior of other groups, but we see no evidence of a central coordinating authority.... The U.S. is facing terrorist threats from several quarters which, although unconnected, will challenge the U.S. ability to react to widely dispersed and potentially serious international terrorist attacks."[38] Reagan's intelligence at the time was unequivocal: the Soviet Union was simply not responsible for all acts of terrorism around the globe.

In a recent interview, Vincent Cannistraro remembered how the administration resolved the discrepancy between the recommended public strategy and the extant realities of terrorism. He recalled: "[CIA Director] Bill Casey had already been trying to cook the analytical books on terrorism, particularly by the pressure he had placed on the analysts to come up with an analysis that said the Soviet Union was behind these acts of terrorism."[39] Despite such drawbacks, the proposed strategy gathered momentum as the preferred administration approach.

In the Reagan narrative, the Soviet Union and its client states became the public enemy attempting to capitalize on the fragile nature of the emerging democracies. Reagan maintained the general rise of state-sponsored terrorism could be traced back to "increased Soviet support for terrorism, insurgency, and aggression coupled with the perception of weakening U.S. power and resolve" in the 1970s.[40] In Central America Reagan warned of a "Soviet-Cuban-Nicaraguan plan to destroy the fragile flower of democracy . . . a plan that could, for the first time, bring tyranny to our own borders, carrying the same specter of economic chaos, the same threat of political terrorism, the same floodtides of refugees we've seen follow every Communist takeover from Eastern Europe to Afghanistan, Laos, Vietnam, Cambodia, Ethiopia, and, now, Central America."[41] In Lebanon, he maintained that Syria, backed by the Soviet Union, was using terrorism in hopes of acquiring portions of Lebanon to create greater Syria.[42] The goal in each global region, according to Reagan, was the same: "to bring about a one-world Communist state."[43]

Like portrayals of communists in previous presidential rhetoric, Reagan's terrorists relied on savage acts of barbarism to instill fear in civilian populations. He told Congress that terrorists relied on "indiscriminate threatening, intimidation, detention, or murder of innocent people."[44] He labeled their methods "uncivilized," "crude," "cowardly," and "evil to its core and contemptible in all its forms."[45] Reagan's communist terrorists embodied both the motives and the means to threaten the globe.

By the beginning of Reagan's second term, the American public was no longer accepting that the Soviet Union was behind all acts of international terrorism. Internal administration polling related to the 1985 hijacking of TWA Flight 847 revealed that the public blamed Iran for the hijacking, not the Soviet Union or Syria.[46] By the mid-1980s, the case demonstrated that the public was assigning responsibility for terrorist acts on a case-by-case basis, not in accordance with the Cold War narrative.

Reagan introduced a new approach to enemy character development in a speech he delivered before the American Bar Association in May of 1985.[47]

The Soviet Union was no longer the sole source of evil and terrorism around the globe; instead, five foreign states that sponsored terrorism became the focus. The offending nations included Iran, Libya, North Korea, Cuba, and Nicaragua. Like their Soviet counterparts before them, Reagan cast each of these state sponsors of terrorism as willing to use savage, barbaric means to achieve political objectives.

More difficult was making a credible case that the five individual states were not separate threats that might again risk Reagan's political future. In a 1985 interview with *Time* magazine, CIA Director William Casey admitted: "There is no one person, there is no one capital in the world that controls terrorism. . . . This is a war without clear borders, without clear enemies."[48] Kent Oots's 1986 study of transnational terrorism agreed, adding that coalitions among such groups were infrequent, ad hoc, and short in duration.[49] Martha Crenshaw's three-year study of international terrorism between 1985 and 1987 reached a similar conclusion: "in reality there is no monolithic terrorist entity. Instead, terrorism appears highly eclectic and pluralistic."[50] At the time the administration shifted to its new narrative, a globally networked group of state-sponsored terrorists simply did not exist.

Nevertheless, the administration's revised narrative held to the notion that state sponsors of terrorism were an internationally orchestrated syndicate of criminals. Reagan insisted: "Most of the terrorists who are kidnapping and murdering American citizens and attacking American installations are being trained, financed and directly or indirectly controlled by a core group of radical and totalitarian governments—a new, international version of Murder, Incorporated."[51] By drawing the explicit analogy between organized crime and terrorism, the administration framed individual acts by any of the named nations as part of a larger, coordinated assault.

To comply with the Cold War narrative, the administration also needed to establish that the state sponsors of terrorism harbored a goal of world conquest. Reagan's task force report belied the expansive goal when it pronounced, "The motivations of those who engage in terrorism are many and varied."[52] Spokespersons for the Reagan administration undercut the contention that terrorists even placed American society at risk. James Holloway, the executive director of the task force, told reporters on March 6, 1986, "While terrorism poses no serious challenge to the national will or national survival, it remains a complex, dangerous threat for which there is no quick or easy solution."[53] Considering the totality of public positions taken by the full range of executive branch speakers, terrorists did not rise to the same level of global threat as that achieved previously by their communist counterparts.

Nevertheless, Reagan did hold publicly to the position that his new group of terrorism state sponsors harbored a shared goal of global conquest. Reagan insisted: "Government-sponsored terrorism, in particular, cannot continue without gravely threatening the social fabric of all free societies."[54] He maintained that the consequences of the new alliance were particularly lethal for American interests. He noted that "all of these states are united by one simple criminal phenomenon—their fanatical hatred of the United States, our people, our way of life, our international stature."[55] Reagan's transference of communist means and methods to state sponsors of global terrorism projected the characterizations of the conventional Cold War narrative.

In the first Bush Administration's public strategy, Iraq assumed many of the negative characteristics common to the communists in the Cold War narrative. Iraq, like the communist menace before it, harbored the goals of worldwide conquest. Only this time the purpose of the expansion was control of the world's economic resources, rather than the spread of an ideological perspective. Bush held that Saddam Hussein was "bent on regional domination," and wanted to establish "a chokehold on the world's economic lifeline."[56] Bush insisted the reason Hussein sought dominance over Kuwaiti oil supplies was because of his "desires to control one of the world's key resources."[57] In the Bush narrative, greed and economic power replaced ideological dominance as the primary motivations behind Hussein's thirst for conquest.

Credibly presenting Saddam Hussein as a worldwide economic threat, however, posed a rhetorical challenge for the administration. Bush himself had been involved in a number of executive branch decisions that presumed Iraq to be an ally, not a dangerous enemy, of the United States. A few of the more significant indicators of the positive alliance included the decision by then Vice President Bush readily to resume friendly relations with Iraq after it had fired missiles on the *U.S.S. Stark*, the decision by the Bush Administration to omit Iraq from the list of state sponsors of terror despite evidence of ongoing sponsorship activities, the Bush Administration decision to adopt an official policy of cooperative engagement between the United States and Iraq, and the failure of the Bush Administration to anticipate and prevent the Iraqi invasion into Kuwait. In light of the administration's strategy of working with Iraq to encourage its moderation, transforming Saddam Hussein into an evil menace bent on control over a key world resource would not come easily.

The administration returned to the enemy characterizations of the Cold War narrative to vilify the Iraqi leader in the Persian Gulf conflict. In the months preceding the decision for the United States to go to war, Bush presented the actions of Saddam Hussein and his troops as barbaric. The most horrifying and vivid story of barbarity involved Iraqi soldiers throwing premature babies out of incubators before stealing the machines to take home to Iraq. Eventually, the truth of the incubator incident became suspect. Amnesty International retracted its confirmation of the story after its fact-finding team found "no reliable evidence that Iraqi forces have caused the deaths of babies by removing them or ordering their removal from incubators."[58] Some supposed witnesses to the incident recanted particular details of the story, while others discounted it altogether. Revelations that the main witness to tell the incubator story before the Congressional Human Rights Caucus was the daughter of the Kuwaiti ambassador to the United States and that she had been coached for her testimony by the public relations firm of Hill and Knowlton further undermined the claim's credibility.

To dramatize the barbaric nature of the Iraqi enemy, the administration emphasized the plight of Americans held hostage in Kuwait and Iraq. By late October of 1990, James Baker expounded on the unacceptable conditions the hostages faced in captivity. He announced: "Americans are being forced to sleep on vermin-ridden concrete floors. They are kept in the dark during the day and moved only at night. They have had their meals cut to two a day. And many are becoming sick as they endure a terrible ordeal."[59] On November 1, 1990, the administration highlighted the conditions of the hostages' confinement in its briefing to fifteen congressional leaders on the status of the Persian Gulf conflict. Bush began the meeting by explaining that the United States was receiving more reports of maltreatment of American and British hostages. Unlike in the case of the incubator story, the members of the delegation were skeptical this time. They questioned whether any escalation of maltreatment had occurred. They suggested the administration might simply be using the plight of the hostages to justify going to war. Senator William Cohen, vice chair off the Senate Intelligence Committee, offered that the Central Intelligence Agency and Defense Intelligence Agency, when testifying before his committee the preceding week, had indicated there was no new evidence of mistreatment.[60]

Finally, the Bush Administration reinforced Iraqi barbarity by recalling the Iraqi leadership's prior bad acts with chemical weapons. Bush ostracized Hussein as not belonging to the civilized international community by denouncing his callous use of weapons of mass destruction against "innocent villagers, his own people."[61] The statement made reference to an earlier incident in 1988 when Hussein had used chemical weapons to kill more than eight thousand Kurdish civilians living in Iraq. Ironically, the Bush Administration had worked previously to downplay that incident and weaken a bill in Congress to impose economic sanctions in response to the atrocity.[62] They had done so aware that the United States had supplied Iraq with six strains of botulinum toxin, three strains of anthrax, three strains of gas gangrene bacteria, West Nile fever virus, and Dengue fever virus since 1983.[63] Despite the shift in its public stance, the Bush Administration adopted a reiterative posture of presenting Iraq as an enemy that shared the characteristic barbarity of the communist threat.

The second Bush Administration continued the characterization of terrorists consistent with the expectations of the enemy character in the Cold War narrative. Encompassing all individuals or groups who had committed acts of terrorists violence into a single, homogeneous collective, George W. Bush insisted: "Terrorists . . . [do] have a common ideology, and that is, they hate freedom and they hate freedom-loving people. And they particularly hate America at this moment."[64] At various points, Bush labeled terrorists "people who hate freedom," as "a threat to established governments," and as "an enemy of all law, all liberty, all morality, all religion."[65] Ignoring Bin Laden's and Saddam Hussein's public disagreements with U.S. foreign policy goals and methods, the Bush Administration insisted that both men constituted ideological threats to the foundational principles of American society.

Making the case that terrorists had ambitions of global conquest was more challenging. Al Qaeda cells had not warranted Bush's priority attention during the first months of his administration.[66] The Bush narrative elevated the global nature of the threat by reiterating the international reach of such terrorists, their current presence in more than sixty countries nationwide, and their lack of a stable homeland. Bush insisted that the terrorists had "no borders" and had "no geography."[67] Terrorists' ability to cross borders quickly and effectively take over foreign governments had ominous implications for their global ambitions. In Afghanistan, where the Taliban appeared to have stable residency, administration officials announced that the government came "for one single purpose; to invade that country, be a foreign presence, a hostile presence in Afghanistan so they could conduct terrorist activities around the world."[68] In Iraq, where Saddam Hussein had ruled for decades, the administration compared the Iraqi regime to the "small groups of men [in the twentieth century that had] seized control of great nations."[69] Repeated reference to multiple instances of Iraqi aggression throughout the Middle East underscored Saddam Hussein's lack of respect for existing national boundaries. Terrorists not only had the capacity to reach and base from any nation around the globe; they also had the ability to usurp the governing authority of existing states.

Within the George W. Bush narrative, terrorists employed violent tactics consistent with conventional Cold War enemies. Bush called the terrorists who committed the 9/11 attacks "evil-doers" and "barbaric people."[70] He labeled the Taliban in Afghanistan "one of the most repressive regimes in the history of mankind."[71] Bush displayed the barbarity of Saddam Hussein by pronouncing that "on Saddam Hussein's orders, opponents have been decapitated, wives and mothers of political opponents have been systematically raped as a method of intimidation, and political prisoners have been forced to watch their own children being tortured."[72] For Bush, terrorists were comparable to the uncivilized nemesis of past Cold War narratives.

The Bush narrative underscored the barbarity of terrorists by focusing on weapons of mass destruction. Public spokespersons stressed how terrorists were now using airplanes as a weapon of mass destruction. Abandoned Al Qaeda laboratories capable of producing chemical and biological agents prompted frequent mention and increased concern. In the campaign against Saddam Hussein, Bush called the Iraqi leader a "homicidal dictator . . . addicted to weapons of mass destruction."[73] Memories of the World Trade Center and Pentagon attacks removed most doubts about the destructive potential of America's worst nightmare.

Taken together, characterizations of the terrorist enemy by Republican presidents since the Vietnam War have borrowed much from the Cold War narrative. While the specific identity of the enemy has shifted from communists to terrorists, the drive to treat opposing forces as members of a dangerous, homogeneous collective continues. Motivations of control and world domination abound, as do the barbaric tactics that distinguish the enemy from the civilized members of the international community. The impetus to maintain a publicly consistent narrative over several decades, however, has trumped available U.S. intelligence that reveals clear differences between the identities, motivations, and means of communists and terrorists. The conventions of enemy characterization in the Cold War narrative, as a result, become crucial points for investigating exaggerated or manipulated claims by the nation's leadership.

Hero Character

For conventional Cold Warriors, a strong United States is essential for an effective response to the communist threat. America, as the narrative's hero, adopts the persona of a missionary for freedom.[74] Cold War discourse is steeped in religious references, presenting America as righteous and committed to the sacred cause of freedom.[75] Wander dubs the approach "prophetic dualism," and explains it as, "One side acts in accord with all that is good, decent, and at one with God's will. The other acts in direct opposition. Conflict between them is resolved only through the total victory of one side over the other."[76] As missionary for the divine, the United States acts not only to assist those countries too weak to defend themselves but to liberate itself. America becomes the hero who can "barely tolerate and no longer endure a world that was half free and half slave."[77] For good to triumph over evil in accordance with God's will, the U.S. government cannot act alone; the public must also have faith in the American cause.[78]

Consistent with Cold War expectations, the United States assumed the role of missionary for freedom in the Vietnam War narrative. Politically, the United States sought elections free from terror that would permit the South Vietnamese people to exercise their rights of self-determination. Johnson announced: "We insist and we will always insist that the people of South Viet-Nam shall have the right of choice, the right to shape their own destiny in free elections in the South and throughout all Viet-Nam under international supervision, and they shall not have any government imposed upon them by force and terror as long as we can prevent it."[79] Committed to freedom and the right of self-determination, the narrative positioned the United States as a strong counterpart to the communist menace.

In the economic arena, the narrative presented the United States as committed to increasing the prosperity for the people of Vietnam. Goals of progress, human welfare, economic growth, rural development, and education were recurrent themes throughout administration discourse. Following a 1966 meeting of the highest level officials of both South Vietnam and the United States in Honolulu, Johnson called for a revolutionary transformation in the Vietnam economy that could not "wait until the guns grow silent and until the terrorism stops."[80] Within the rhetorical vision, the United States was committed to rebuilding the South Vietnamese economy, even as opposing forces tried to dismantle it.

The narrative depicted the final goal of the United States to be the restoration of peace in South Vietnam. By coming to the aid of small countries unable to defend their own freedom, the United States ensured global security. Evoking the words of his predecessor, Harry Truman, Johnson declared: "We shall not realize our objectives unless we are willing to help free peoples to maintain their free institutions and their national integrity against aggressive movements that seek to impose upon them totalitarian regimes."[81] By emphasizing the mutual interests of protecting South Vietnamese security, the United States underscored the depth of its commitment to its ally's defense.

Reagan's hero character likewise borrowed heavily from conventional Cold War discourse. As in the case of the Vietnam War narrative, the United States emerged as a missionary for peace and freedom in the global arena. Reagan described the moral nature of his quest in a toast to Queen Elizabeth II: "The greatest glory of a free-born people is to transmit that freedom to their children. That is a responsibility our people share. Together, and eager for peace, we must face an unstable world where violence and terrorism, aggression and tyranny constantly encroach on human rights. Together, committed to preservation of freedom and our way of life, we must strengthen a weakening international order and restore the world's faith in peace and the rule of law."[82] For Reagan, the mission of the United States was a religious one. Speaking to Christian evangelists in Florida, he described the confrontation between the United States and the Soviet Union as a struggle between good and evil. He labeled the Soviet Union the "evil empire," thus elevating the mission of the United States into a religious calling. He declared, "There is sin and evil in the world, and we're enjoined by Scripture and the Lord Jesus to oppose it with all our might."[83] Placing his argument within the context of the divine, Reagan argued that the public should accept the responsibility for spreading peace and freedom on faith.

Reminiscent of American policy toward Vietnam, the United States adopted a multifaceted model of political, economic, and security assistance for rooting out terrorism. A briefing paper for Ambassador Kirkpatrick's visit to Central and South America demonstrated the three-pronged strategy of promoting democratization, economic revitalization, and security support.[84] As the Cold War narrative portended, the constructive approach of the United States promised to guard effectively against the evil forces operating around the globe.

By the start of Reagan's second term, concerns about the ineffectiveness of the administration's terrorism approach underscored the need to change public strategies. The administration was having difficulty making a credible case that its strategy in Central America was actually bolstering democratic governments, economic recovery, or national security.[85] In the Middle East, the peace process had stalled. Terrorism against Americans was on the rise and administration officials anticipated further escalations of violence in response to U.S. covert activities against terrorism.[86]

The public was also losing patience with Reagan's approach to terrorism. The administration's internal polls showed that by 1985 almost half of the public reporting said they disapproved "of the way Ronald Reagan is handling terrorism."[87] A *Newsweek* poll appearing in a widely circulated internal memorandum provided the explanation that "54% believe that Reagan's actions have not been tough enough."[88] After conducting focus group interviews and reviewing polling about terrorism, Reagan's Task Force on Combatting

[sic] Terrorism maintained that Americans felt that the government should do something to fight terrorism. The report concluded: "Americans will welcome actions against terrorists that are swift, forceful and even aggressive. They would endorse these actions even if inadvertent casualties result."[89]

The administration's revised second-term narrative continued the theme that the United States was critical for an effective response to the global threat of terrorism. The characterization of the U.S. motivations remained the same: restoring peace, freedom, and civilized values around the globe. The stated mission also preserved its religious quality. Reagan told the International Forum of the Chamber of Commerce, "I'll remind our allies of the truth of what Edmund Burke said long ago: 'When bad men combine, the good must associate; else they will fall, one by one.' Well, together the free people of this world will ensure that liberty not only survives but triumphs and that our sons and daughters, too, will know the blessings of the winds of freedom."[90] By again placing his appeal to unity within the context of the divine, Reagan underscored the Cold War theme of needing all members of the community to have faith for the mission to succeed.

While the goal of secure, free nations around the globe remained constant, the means of the hero character shifted from defensive measures to offensive ones. On April 3, 1984, Ronald Reagan signed NSDD 138, which authorized the use of "active defense measures" in response to state-sponsored terrorism. Reagan's active defense measures included preemptive military strikes against groups or individuals planning strikes against U.S. interests "when the host country [was] unable or unwilling to take effective action."[91] The directive, which generally remains classified, authorized sabotage, killing of suspected guerillas and lower-level state officials, preemptory and retaliatory raids, deception, and expanded intelligence against suspected radicals and people regarded as their sympathizers. The countries initially impacted by implementation of the directive included Iran, Libya, Syria, Cuba, Nicaragua, North Korea, and the USSR.[92]

The public defense of the preemptive approach began in 1985. The Reagan task force publicly empowered the Interdepartmental Group on Terrorism to "prepare and submit to the NSC for approval policy criteria for deciding when, if and how to use force to preempt, react and retaliate" to terrorism.[93] The administration publicly touted that its improved preemptive intelligence had helped abort 126 terrorist incidents in 1985 alone.[94] The administration's talking points related to its Libyan bombing included the "on-going plans for violence against U.S. citizens and facilities in Europe, the Middle East, Africa and Latin America."[95] Careful to discuss a traditional, Article 51 defensive posture through discussion of intercepts involving the Libyan Bureau in East Berlin, the Reagan Administration expanded their public justification by defending preemptive intelligence as a further rationale for the aerial bombardment of Libya.

The first Bush Administration preserved the prior persona of the Cold War hero character in its terrorist narrative. Bush grounded the nation's motivations in those rehearsed many times for his domestic audience. He laid out his administration's goals as, "You know how America remains the hope of 'liberty-loving people everywhere.'"[96] On a mission to bring freedom and self-determination to all members of the international community, the United States retained its earlier objective. Bush, however, framed the crisis as one facing the entire civilized international community: "We're not in this alone. . . . It is the United Nations against Saddam Hussein. It is not Iraq against the United States."[97] He touted the rewards of global cooperation for ultimate success in the conflict when he stated: "Together, we can successfully oppose tyranny and help those nations who look to us for leadership and vision."[98] While the United States still played a vital role in the narrative's battle against terrorism, it no longer assumed sole responsibility for defeating the threat.

In an effort to avoid the Reagan Administration's experience with invoking the Cold War and having the public view their quest in Central America as another Vietnam, the Bush Administration took specific care to distinguish the means of the United States from previous Cold War heroes. The Bush camp, claiming to have learned the lessons of the Vietnam War, reiterated that it would not repeat those mistakes. By late November, 1990, the public diplomacy themes of the administration stressed five key differences that all official spokespersons should emphasize between the two conflicts: "U.S. interests/stakes critical and clear in Gulf; U.S. has support of almost entire international community; U.S. position has strong UN backing; unlike North Vietnam, Iraq is not receiving massive outside assistance; and if we must use force, it will be decisive from the outset. We are here to succeed."[99] In the Bush Administration's narrative, the Persian Gulf conflict and the Vietnam War were not the same; this time, the United States would prevail.

After the public communication strategy was implemented, Bush's State Department polling analysts concluded that the majority of the public were drawing distinctions between the Vietnam War and the Persian Gulf conflict. On February 1, 1991, they reported: "At present, most Americans believe the war against Iraq will be won in a matter of 'months' (62%) and the cost of lives of fewer than 5,000 U.S. troops (55%). Of those holding these views, about two-thirds support the war."[100] Only a minority (26%) believed the war would cost more than 5,000 lives, the key benchmark where support for the war dropped to less than half of the public.[101] Optimism that the United States would prevail in the conflict was high as the nation prepared to begin its ground offensive.

The current Bush Administration also retained conventional Cold War hero motivations for the United States. Bush defined his war on terrorism by saying, "This is a fight for freedom."[102] He evoked the long-standing role of America for encouraging and preserving liberty globally, calling the United States the "defender of liberty all over the world."[103] Religious sanction for the administration's approach was also evident in Bush's words: "The course of this conflict is not known, yet its outcome certain. Freedom and fear, justice and cruelty, have always been at war, and we know that God is not neutral between them."[104] The American mission required the public's faith and commitment if it were to yield its intended results.

In many ways, the George W. Bush Administration recalled the Cold War hero's conventional means of handling the enemy's assault on freedom. In both Afghanistan and Iraq, Bush echoed the promises made in Vietnam that the United States could be trusted to provide assistance in the areas of garnering political freedom, economic assistance, and effective security apparatus for the people in those countries who did not participate in terrorism. In essence, Bush articulated the domino theory of the Vietnam era in reverse. Now, having a flourishing democracy in Iraq would portend added pressures for continued growth in democracies throughout the Middle East.

Like his Republican predecessors, George W. Bush continued to expand the means available for stopping the terrorist enemy from achieving global conquest. Examples abound, such as indefinite detention of suspects, altered due process rights of those accused of terrorism, and expanded use of secret courts. Preemptive warfare again emerged as a strategic necessity. Rumsfeld explained the rationale for taking such a perspective: "The reality is that a terrorist can attack at any time in any place using any technique, and it is physically impossible for a free people to defend in every place at every time against every technique. Now what does that mean? It means . . . that we have to take this battle, this war to the terrorists, where they are. And the best defense is an effective offense in this case, and that means they have to be rooted out."[105] As the first dramatic public example of the new doctrine, the war with Iraq prompted serious and continuing questions about the accuracy and use of preemptive war intelligence.

The assumption of the right to change foreign sovereigns was an equal, if not more compelling, change in the means that could be employed to fight terrorism.

Bush insisted that his administration would "make no distinction between the terrorists who committed these acts and those who harbor them."[106] As the administration's public campaign developed, the administration broadened the parameters of the enemy to include those who harbored, housed, supported, facilitated, financed, tolerated, provided haven, and provided succor to terrorists. Individuals, entities, organizations, and states could all qualify for inclusion.[107] Nations affiliated with terrorists became equated with terrorists, rendering their sovereign rights moot if they became "a front" in the U.S. war on terror. The administration presented regime change in Afghanistan and Iraq as the only fitting response. With Al Qaeda cells alone in more than sixty nations around the globe, the possible applications of regime change could be far-reaching.

Taken as a whole, the hero character in presidential terrorism narratives has been consistent both in identity and in motivation with the Cold War hero. Whether alone or leading other members of the international community, the United States remains committed to the divine mission of defending freedom around the globe. The methods incorporated by the hero, however, have changed sharply. While political, economic, and security assistance have functioned as retained components, an expansive list of other prerogatives has emerged. With the scene of the Cold War narrative expanded, with the character traits of the enemy intact, and with the motivations of the United States consistent and clear, the nation's leadership has created a rhetorical environment conducive to a wide expansion of their own powers.

As this chapter has demonstrated, the Cold War narrative takes on increased importance in the post–Cold War era. America's leadership not only understands the psychological import of the narrative but has, at times, manipulated public depictions of terrorism threats to fit within the Cold War's rhetorical expectations. In the process, it has justified expanded executive branch powers that erode foundational principles of American society.

Notes

1. The White House, *National Strategy for Combating Terrorism*, September 2006, at http://www.state.gov/s/ct/rls/wh/71803.html.

2. John F. Kennedy, "Letter to President Ngo Dinh Diem on the Sixth Anniversary of the Republic of Viet-Nam," *Public Papers of the Presidents: John F. Kennedy, 1961* (Washington, D.C.: Government Printing Office [hereafter GPO], 1962).

3. See, for example, Lyndon B. Johnson, "White House Statement on the Situation in South Viet-Nam," *Public Papers of the Presidents: Lyndon B. Johnson, 1963–1964*

(Washington, D.C.: GPO, 1965), 388; and Henry Cabot Lodge, "15th Plenary Session of Viet-Nam Held at Paris," *Department of State Bulletin* 60 (May 19, 1969): 419.

4. Jimmy Carter described terrorism as a crime against humanity in his use of the tragic drama narrative, while Bill Clinton proffered crimes against God in his prophetic narrative. For a more detailed description of the presidents' usage of these alternative public communication strategies, see Carol Winkler, *In the Name of Terrorism: Presidents on Political Violence in the Post–World War II Era* (Albany: SUNY Press, 2006).

5. Martin J. Medhurst, "Rhetoric and Cold War: A Strategic Approach," in *Cold War Rhetoric: Strategy, Metaphor, and Ideology*, ed. Martin J. Medhurst, Robert L. Ivie, Philip Wander, and Robert L. Scott (New York: Greenwood Press, 1990), 19–27; and Robert L. Scott, "Cold War and Rhetoric: Conceptually and Critically," in *Cold War Rhetoric*, 1–16.

6. Robert L. Ivie, "Cold War Motives and the Rhetorical Metaphor: A Framework of Criticism," *Cold War Rhetoric*, 75.

7. Lyndon Johnson, "The President's News Conference of 7/28/65," *Public Papers of the Presidents: Lyndon B. Johnson, 1965* (Washington, D.C.: GPO, 1966), 794.

8. Richard Nixon, "Address to the Nation on the War in Vietnam," *Public Papers of the Presidents: Richard Nixon, 1969* (Washington, D.C.: GPO, 1971), 906.

9. Richard Nixon, "Address to the Nation on the Situation in Southeast Asia," *Papers of the Presidents: Richard Nixon, 1969* (Washington, D.C.: GPO, 1971), 584.

10. Ronald Reagan, "Remarks at the Annual Convention of the American Legion in Seattle, Washington," *Public Papers of the Presidents: Ronald Reagan, 1983* (Washington, D.C.: GPO, 1985), 1192.

11. Ronald Reagan, "Address to the Nation on Events in Lebanon and Grenada," *Public Papers of the Presidents: Ronald Reagan, 1983* (Washington, D.C.: GPO, 1985), 1517, 1518.

12. Memo, Young and Rubicam, Inc. and Populus, Inc., Terrorism: Viewpoint of the American People, Nov. 1985, folder "Terrorism [4 of 9]," OA/ID 19849, Bush Vice Presidential Records, National Security Affairs, George Bush Presidential Library.

13. Folder, "Libya, July, 1985 [2 of 3]," box 90753, Donald Fortier Files, Ronald Reagan Library.

14. Memo, Robert M. Kimmitt to Robert Sims, June 3, 1984, folder "Nicaragua Vol. III 11/1/83–7/31/84 [2 of 5]," box 91368, Executive Secretariat, National Security Council, Country File, Ronald Reagan Library.

15. See, for example, Memo, Doug Menarchik to Don Gregg, June 10, 1985, folder, "Terrorism II [3 of 3]," OA/ID 19849, Bush Vice Presidential Records, National Security Affairs, George Bush Presidential Library.

16. Memo, Menarchik to Gregg.

17. "Frontline: Target America: Interviews: Vincent Cannistraro," at wysiwyg://30/http://www.pbs.org /wgbh/pa . . . hows/target/interviews/cannistraro.html, October 16, 2001, 10:06 A.M.

18. "Frontline: Target America: Interviews: Robert Oakley," at wysiwyg://39/http://www.pbs.org/wgbh/pa . . . ine/shows/target/interviews/Oakley.html, October 16, 2001, 10:14 A.M.

19. Ronald Reagan, "Letter to President Jose Napoleon Duarte of El Salvador on the Investigation of the Murder of United States Citizens in San Salvador," *Public Papers of the Presidents: Ronald Reagan, 1985* (Washington, D.C.: GPO, 1988), 1019.

20. J. L. Holloway III to V Adm. John Poindexter, et al., February 10, 1986, WHORM Subject File, FG 258, 381703, Ronald Reagan Library.

21. Public Report of the Vice President's Task Force on Combatting [sic] Terrorism, Feb. 1986, "Terrorism," OA/ID 14923 Press Office, Bush Vice Presidential Records, George Bush Presidential Library.

22. Historical Overview of Public Support for Korea and Vietnam, with Notes on the Current Persian Gulf Situation, no date, folder "Persian Gulf Working Group: Handouts/Articles," OA/ID 03195, Paul McNeill, Office of Communications, Bush Presidential Records, George Bush Presidential Library.

23. George Bush, "Address before a Joint Session of Congress on the Persian Gulf Crisis and the Federal Budget Deficit," *Public Papers of the Presidents, 1990* (Washington, D.C.: GPO, 1991), 1219.

24. George Bush, "The President's News Conference of 11/30/90," *Public Papers of the Presidents: George Bush, 1990* (Washington, D.C.: GPO, 1991), 1719.

25. For Discussion, August 20, 1990, folder "Persian Gulf War 1991," OA/ID CF00472 [6 of 11], Chief of Staff, John Sununu Files, Bush Presidential Records, George Bush Presidential Library.

26. George W. Bush, "Remarks to the Australian Parliament in Canberra," October 27, 2003. *Federal Document Clearing House Political Transcripts*, 2003, Lexis-Nexis.

27. John F. Cragan, "The Origins and Nature of the Cold War Rhetorical Vision 1946–1972: A Partial History," in *Applied Communication Research: A Dramatistic Approach*. ed. John F. Cragan and Donald C. Shields (Prospect Heights, Ill.: Waveland Press, 1981).

28. David Campbell, *Writing Security: United States Foreign Policy and the Politics of Identity* (Minneapolis: University of Minnesota Press, 1992).

29. John F. Kennedy, "Letter to President Ngo Dinh Diem," 680.

30. Roger W. Hilsman, "The Challenge to Freedom in Asia," *Department of State Bulletin* 49 (8 July 1963): 44.

31. For an example of this line of argument, see Robert S. McNamara, "United States Policy in Viet-Nam," *Department of State Bulletin* 50 (April 13, 1964): 562–70.

32. Lyndon Johnson, "Address at Johns Hopkins University: 'Peace without Conquest,'" *Public Papers of the Presidents: Lyndon Johnson, 1965* (Washington, D.C.: GPO, 1966), 394.

33. Memo, Newt Gingrich to Ken Duberstein, October 25, 1983, ID # 188583/4, SP818, WHORM: Subject File, Ronald Reagan Library.

34. Memo, Gingrich to Duberstein.

35. Memo, Gingrich to Duberstein.

36. Memo, Robert M. Smalley to Secretary of State, May 16, 1885, ID #323840, PR015, WHORM: Subject File, Ronald Reagan Library.

37. Memo, Smalley to Secretary of State.

38. Memo, Growing Terrorist Danger in America: Report of the CIA National Foreign Assessment Center, 12/23/81, folder, "Terrorism 1/20/81–12/31/83, Vol. I [2 of 5]," box 91393. Executive Secretariat, NSC: Records (Subject File), Ronald Reagan Library.

39. Cannistraro interview, 2001.

40. Ronald Reagan, "Remarks at the National Leadership Forum of the Center for International and Strategic Studies of Georgetown University," *Public Papers of the Presidents: Ronald Reagan, 1984* (Washington, D.C.: GPO, 1986), 480.

41. Ronald Reagan, "Radio Address to the Nation on the Situation in Central America," *Public Papers of the Presidents: Ronald Reagan, 1985* (Washington, D.C.: GPO, 1988), 370.

42. See, for example, Ronald Reagan, "Interview with Garry Clifford and Patricia Ryan of People Magazine," *Public Papers of the Presidents: Ronald Reagan, 1983* (Washington, D.C.: GPO, 1985).

43. Reagan interview with Clifford and Ryan, 1714.

44. Ronald Reagan, "Message to the Congress Transmitting Proposed Legislation to Combat International Terrorism," *Public Papers of the Presidents: Ronald Reagan, 1984* (Washington, D.C.: GPO, 1986), 576.

45. See, for example, Ronald Reagan, "Interview with Jung-suk Lee of the Korean Broadcasting System on the President's Trip to the Republic of Korea," *Public Papers of the Presidents: Ronald Reagan, 1983 (*Washington, D.C.: GPO, 1985), 1556 ; Ronald Reagan, "Address before a Joint Session of the Irish National Parliament," *Public Papers of the Presidents: Ronald Reagan, 1984* (Washington, D.C.: GPO, 1986), 806.

46. Memo, Robert M. Smalley to Secretary of State, June 20, 1985, folder, "TWA 847 [6]," SRB 378, Box 93267, President's Special Review Board (Tower Board): Records. Ronald Reagan Library.

47. Ronald Reagan, "Remarks at the Annual Convention of the American Bar Association," *Public Papers of the Presidents: Ronald Reagan, 1985* (Washington, D.C.: GPO, 1988).

48. "An Interview with William Casey," *Time,* October 28, 1985, 34.

49. Kent Layne Oots, *A Political Organization Approach to Transnational Terrorism* (New York: Greenwood Press, 1986).

50. Martha Crenshaw, *Terrorism and International Cooperation.* (New York: Westview Press, 1989), 10–11.

51. Reagan, "Remarks at the Annual Convention of the American Bar Association," 897.

52. Public Report of the Vice President's Task Force on Combatting [sic] Terrorism (see endnote 21).

53. Draft Statement by James L. Holloway III, Executive Director, Vice President's Task Force on Combatting [sic] Terrorism, New Briefing, White House Press Room, March 6, 1986. Casefile 400506, CFOA 871, Office of the President: Presidential Briefing Papers: Records, Ronald Reagan Presidential Library.

54. Ronald Reagan, "Remarks to the International Forum of the Chamber of Commerce of the United States," *Public Papers of the Presidents: Ronald Reagan, 1986* (Washington, D.C.: GPO, 1988), 512.

55. Reagan, "Remarks to the International Forum," 512.

56. George Bush, "The President's News Conference of 11/8/90," *Public Papers of the Presidents: George Bush, 1990* (Washington, D.C.: GPO, 1991), 1580.

57. Bush, "The President's News Conference of 11/30/90," 1719.

58. Letter, Response to a Letter by Edward M. Koch, no date, ID# 235124, C0072—Countries, WHORM: Subject File—General Scanned Records, Bush Presidential Records, George Bush Presidential Library.

59. Secretary Baker, "Why America Is in the Gulf," *US Department of State Dispatch* 1.10 (1990): 237.

60. Bob Woodward, *The Commanders* (New York: Simon and Schuster, 1991).

61. George Bush, "Radio Address to the Nation on the Persian Gulf Crisis, 1/5/91," *Public Papers of the Presidents: George Bush, 1991* (Washington, D.C.: GPO, 1992), 11.

62. For a more extensive discussion of U.S. conciliatory policy, see Larry Berman and Bruce W. Jentleson, "Bush and the Post–Cold War World: New Challenges for American Leadership," in *The Bush Presidency: First Appraisals,* ed. Colin Campbell and Bert A. Rockman (Chatham, N.J.: Chatham House, 1991), 93–128; and Barry Rubin, "The United States and Iraq: From Appeasement to War," in *Iraq's Road to War,* ed. Amatzia Baram and Barry Rubin (New York: St. Martin's Press, 1993), 255–72.

63. As reported in Michael I. Niman, "What Bush Didn't Want You to Know about Iraq," *Humanist* (March–April 2003): 20–22.

64. George W. Bush, "George W. Bush Meets with Indonesian President Megawati Soekarnoputri," September 19, 2001. *Federal Document Clearing House Political Transcripts,* 2001, Lexis-Nexis, December 6, 2001.

65. Quoted text is from George W. Bush, "President George W. Bush Holds News Media Availability," September 17, 2001, *Federal Document Clearing House Political Transcripts,* 2001, Lexis-Nexis, December 6, 2001; George W. Bush, "Remarks by President George W. Bush and President Kim Dae-Jung of the Republic of Korea in a Photo Opportunity," October 19, 2001, *Federal News Service,* 2001, Lexis-Nexis, December 6, 2001; George W. Bush, "George W. Bush delivers Keynote Address at Memorial Service for Victims of the September 11th Attacks on the Pentagon," October 11, 2001, *Federal Document Clearing House Political Transcripts,* 2001, Lexis-Nexis, December 7, 2001.

66. Richard Clark, *Against All Enemies: Inside America's War on Terror* (New York: Free Press, 2004); and Bob Woodward, *Bush at War: Inside the Bush White House* (New York: Simon and Schuster, 2003).

67. Bush, "President George W. Bush Holds News Media Availability," September 17, 2001; Colin Powell, "Secretary of State Colin Powell Holds Media Availability with Turkish Foreign Minister Ismail Cem," September 27, 2001, *Federal Document Clearing House Political Transcripts,* 2001, Lexis-Nexis, November 27, 2001.

68. Colin Powell, "Colin Powell Delivers Remarks to Business Leaders," October 18, 2001. *Federal Document Clearing House Political Transcripts,* 2001, Lexis-Nexis, November 27, 2001.

69. George W. Bush, "President Delivers 'State of the Union,'" January 28, 2003, at http://www.whitehousee.gov/news/releases/2003/01/print/20030128–19.html.

70. All references cited here appear in George W. Bush, "President George W. Bush Holds News Media Availability," September 17, 2001.

71. George W. Bush, "News Conference with George W. Bush and Vladimir Putin," November 13, 2001. *Federal News Service,* 2001, Lexis-Nexis, December 6, 2001.

72. George W. Bush, "President Bush Outlines Iraqi Threat," October 7, 2002, at http://www.whitehouse.gov/news/releases/2002/10/print/20021007–8.html.

73. Bush, "President Bush Outlines Iraqi Threat," October 7, 2002.

74. Philip Wander, "The Rhetoric of American Foreign Policy," in *Cold War Rhetoric,* 153–83.

75. Cragan, "Origins and Nature of the Cold War Rhetorical Vision" (see endnote 27).

76. Wander, "Rhetoric of American Foreign Policy," 157.

77. Cragan, "Origins and Nature of the Cold War Rhetorical Vision," 62.

78. Cragan, "Origins and Nature of the Cold War Rhetorical Vision."

79. Lyndon Johnson, "The President's News Conference of 7/28/65," *Public Papers of the Presidents: Lyndon Johnson, 1965* (Washington, D.C.: GPO, 1966), 796–97.

80. Lyndon Johnson, "Remarks at the Los Angeles International Airport following the President's Return from Honolulu," *Public Papers of the Presidents: Lyndon Johnson, 1966* (Washington, D.C.: GPO, 1967), 156.

81. Lyndon Johnson, "Message to King Constantine of Greece on the 20th Anniversary of the Truman Doctrine," *Public Papers of the Presidents: Lyndon Johnson, 1967* (Washington, D.C.: GPO, 1968), 317–18.

82. Ronald Reagan, "Toasts of the President and Queen Elizabeth II at a Dinner Honoring the President at Windsor Castle in England," *Public Papers of the Presidents: Ronald Reagan, 1982* (Washington, D.C.: GPO, 1983), 752.

83. Ronald Reagan, "Remarks at the Annual Convention of the National Association of Evangelicals in Orlando, Florida," *Public Papers of the Presidents: Ronald Reagan, 1983* (Washington, D.C.: GPO, 1984), 362, 364.

84. See Memo, Department of State Briefing Paper, Central America, folder "Briefing Book, Amb. Kirkpatrick Visit to Central and South America, Feb 3–12, 1983 [1 of 3]," box 90500, Jacqueline Tillman files, Ronald Reagan Library.

85. For a more extensive assessment of how the Cold War frame failed to produce results in American foreign policy in Reagan's first term, see Robert Dallek, *Ronald Reagan: The Politics of Symbolism* (Cambridge, Mass.: Harvard University Press, 1984).

86. Memo, Robert C. McFarlane to Edwin Meese III, August 15, 1984, folder "Terrorism Vol. II 1/1/84–8/31/84 (8404913)," box 91400, Subject File, Executive Secretariat, National Security Council, Records, Ronald Reagan Library.

87. Memo, Decision Making Information, Flash Results, August 7–10, 1985, #3262-01, folder, "PR 015, Public relations: Public Opinion Polls (318001–318860)," WHORM: Subject File, Ronald Reagan Library.

88. Memo, Rodney B. McDaniel to Robert C. McFarlane, June 27, 1985, folder "TWA 847 (6)," SRB 378, box 93207, President's Special Review Board (Tower): Records, Ronald Reagan Library.

89. "Terrorism-II [3 of 3]," OA/ID 19849, National Security Affairs, Bush Vice Presidential Records, George Bush Presidential Library.

90. "Terrorism-II [3 of 3]."

91. Memo, Charles Hill to Robert C. McFarlane, June 19, 1984, folder "Terrorism (8404913)," box 90761, files of D. Fortier, Ronald Reagan Library.

92. Christopher Simpson, *National Security Directives of the Reagan and Bush Administrations: The Declassified History of U.S. Political and Military Policy, 1981–1991* (Boulder, Colo.: Westview Press, 1995).

93. Public Report of the Vice President's Task Force on Combatting [sic] Terrorism.

94. Ronald Reagan, "The President's News Conference, 1/7/86," *Public Papers of the Presidents: Ronald Reagan, 1986* (Washington, D.C.: GPO, 1988), 20.

95. White House Talking Points, U.S. Action against Libyan Terrorists, April 16, 1986. "Terrorism [1 of 4]," OA/ID 14880, Speechwriter Files, Press Office, Bush VP records, George Bush Presidential Library.

96. George Bush, "Remarks at the Annual Conference of the Veterans of Foreign Wars in Baltimore, Maryland," *Public Papers of the Presidents: George Bush, 1990* (Washington, D.C.: GPO, 1991), 1148.

97. George Bush, "Remarks to United States Army Troops Near Dhahran, Saudi Arabia," *Public Papers of the Presidents, 1990* (Washington, D.C.: GPO, 1991), 1669.

98. Bush, "Remarks to United States Army Troops," 1669.

99. Memo, Richard Haass to John Sununu, Brent Scowcroft, Bob Gates, Andy Card, David Demarest, and Deb Amend, November 28, 1990, folder, "Persian Gulf Working Group," OA/ID CF 00472, John Sununu, Chief of Staff Files, Bush Presidential Records, George Bush Presidential Library.

100. PA/Opinion Analysis, U.S. Department of State, Bureau of Public Affairs, Opinion Analysis Staff, February 1, 1991, folder, "Persian Gulf Working Group: Notebooks of David Demarest [7]," OA/ID 03195, Paul McNeill, Office of Communications, Bush Presidential Records, George Bush Presidential Library.

101. PA/Opinion Analysis, U.S. Department of State.

102. George W. Bush, "President George W. Bush Holds News Media Availability," September 17, 2001.

103. George W. Bush, "Press Availability with President George W. Bush and Italian Prime Minister Silvio Berlusconi," October 15, 2001. *Federal New Service*, 2001, Lexis-Nexis, December 6, 2001.

104. George W. Bush, "George W. Bush Addresses a Joint Session of Congress," September 20, 2001. *Federal Document Clearing House Political Transcripts*, 2001, Lexis-Nexis, December 6, 2001.

105. Donald Rumsfeld, "Donald Rumsfeld Holds Department of Defense News Briefing," September 16, 2001. *Federal Document Clearing House Political Transcripts*, 2001, Lexis-Nexis, December 7, 2001.

106. George W. Bush, "George W. Bush Addresses the Nation," September 11, 2001. *Federal Document Clearing House Political Transcripts*, 2001, Lexis-Nexis, November 27, 2001.

107. This summary is taken from the public statements of George W. Bush, Dick Cheney, Donald Rumsfeld, John Ashcroft, Tom Ridge, and Colin Powell available from Lexis-Nexis from September 11 through December 31, 2001.

CHAPTER 9

GEORGE W. BUSH, PUBLIC FAITH, AND THE CULTURE WAR OVER SAME-SEX MARRIAGE

Martin J. Medhurst, Baylor University

No one knows when the culture wars started. It is entirely possible that there have always been culture wars in America—over slavery, women's rights, temperance, the rights of labor, pacifism in time of war, and on and on. Clearly such issues divided the electorate, revolved around values, and resulted in significant changes in public policy. On most of these issues, the American presidency eventually weighed in on one side or the other. But the contemporary culture wars seem of a somewhat different order—narrower, more personal, more grounded in religious sentiments, more connected to the debate about individual rights as against community consensus, and perhaps more intractable. The issues are familiar: school prayer, displays of religious symbols on public property, the content of educational curricula, abortion, gay rights, faith-based social services, school vouchers, and the list goes on.

For purposes of this chapter, I want to focus on the contemporary debate over the culture wars, with special reference to the controversy over same-sex marriage. I begin by reviewing the sociological theory of culture wars set forth by James Davison Hunter in his 1991 work *Culture Wars: The Struggle to*

Define America and his subsequent elaborations on that theory. I then use the ongoing debate about same-sex marriage both to test that theory and to apply it to the rhetoric of President George W. Bush on that subject.

My argument has three parts: (1) to understand how George W. Bush has responded rhetorically to the debate over same-sex marriage, one must first understand Bush's Christian worldview, for it is his worldview, not primarily political calculation, that guides his rhetoric; (2) that commitment to this worldview impels Bush to speak in a different idiom about even so controversial a topic as same-sex marriage; his rhetoric is substantially different than that of the Religious Right or other hard-right conservatives inasmuch as it always pairs a message of respect and tolerance for gay Americans with principled opposition to same-sex marriage; and (3) that this different rhetorical approach is the closest instantiation that we have seen to date of Hunter's call for a middle way through the culture wars. I now turn to the theory of noted sociologist James Davison Hunter.

HUNTER'S THESIS

Hunter minces no words. From the very outset of his 416-page book, he claims that what is at stake in the culture wars is *"how we as Americans will order our lives together."*[1] Such ordering revolves around competing notions of moral authority. As he notes:

> Because this is a culture war, the nub of political disagreement today on the range of issues debated—whether abortion, child care, funding for the arts, affirmative action and quotas, gay rights, values in public education, or multiculturalism—can be traced ultimately and finally to the matter of moral authority. By moral authority I mean the basis by which people determine whether something is good or bad, right or wrong, acceptable or unacceptable, and so on. Of course, people often have very different ideas about what criteria to use in making moral judgments, but this is just the point. It is the commitment to different and opposing bases of moral authority and the world views that derive from them that create the deep cleavages between antagonists in the contemporary culture war.[2]

Based on extensive survey research, Hunter finds that the primary dividing lines in American culture today are not so much political (Republican vs.

Democrat vs. Independent) or traditionally religious (Protestant vs. Catholic vs. Jew vs. Muslim) but rather ideological, a divide he labels Progressive vs. Orthodox. In the world of the ideologically orthodox, "moral authority arises from a common commitment to transcendence . . . to an external, definable, and transcendent source of authority."[3] Such an authority may be a sacred scripture (the Bible), or an authoritative person (the Pope), or a body of tradition (Torah), or a group of authoritative teachers (Magisterium, the Ayatollahs). Thus orthodox adherents of any religion—Christianity, Judaism, or Islam—have more in common with one another than do the proponents of progressivism within those same religions. Hence, evangelical Protestants often find themselves in league with conservative Catholics and orthodox Jews on questions of abortion, rather than with other Protestants of a more progressive ideology. It is the bounds and commitments of orthodoxy that form one axis on the dividing line of the culture war.

The other axis is the progressive worldview, which commences with a rejection of orthodoxy. As Hunter notes:

> Such a rejection varies in degree and intensity, as one might imagine, but all progressivists maintain to a certain degree that the language and programmatic thrust of traditional faith—at least as appropriated by their orthodox counterparts—is no longer relevant for modern times. Traditional faith must be reworked to conform to new circumstances and traditions; it must respond to new challenges and needs. What compels this rejection of orthodoxy is the conviction that moral and spiritual truth is not a static and unchanging collection of scriptural facts and theological propositions, but a growing and incremental reality.[4]

Such progressivists reject the idea of revealed truth, whether that revelation comes from scripture, an authority figure, or a historical tradition. There is no such thing as absolute Truth, or if there is, it is unknowable. "Thus," as Hunter observes, "moral and spiritual truth can only be conditional and relative."[5] The progressivist ideology "implies a moral pragmatism centered around the individual's perception of his or her own emotional needs or psychological disposition. In this situation, reason linked with a keen awareness of subjective orientation provides the ultimate crucible for determining what is right and wrong, legitimate and illegitimate—and ultimately what is good and evil."[6]

These two ideologies, the orthodox and the progressive, form the fulcrum upon which the various battles of the contemporary culture wars turn. The weapons in this battle are, for the most part, symbols. They are words, gestures, icons, direct mail propaganda, television spots, films, lecture tours, marches, parades, debates, books, articles, websites, congressional resolutions, presidential proclamations and, on occasion, legislative remedies or court decisions. Hunter is quite clear that these symbols represent ultimate reality for each side in the culture wars—"deeply rooted and fundamentally different understandings of being and purpose."[7] Hence "any mutually agreeable resolution of policy, much less cultural consensus, is almost unimaginable."[8]

It was, in fact, two court decisions during 2003—one by the U.S. Supreme Court (*Lawrence* v. *Texas*) and the other by the Supreme Judicial Court of Massachusetts (*Hillary Goodridge et al. v. Department of Public Health*)—that set the stage for same-sex marriage to become a central issue in the 2004 presidential campaign. To understand these decisions, the rhetorical fallout that arose from them, and how both the decisions and the fallout have affected the rhetoric of President George W. Bush, I set forth the cultural warfare contexts within which the decisions are embedded, examine both the pre-presidential and presidential rhetoric of George W. Bush on the subject of gay marriage, and analyze the ways in which Bush's discourse conforms to the patterns of orthodoxy identified by Hunter.

THE RHETORICAL CONTEXT

The legal context for the court's decision in *Lawrence v. Texas* was the 1986 decision in *Bowers v. Hardwick,* in which the Supreme Court, in a 5–4 decision, ruled that there was no constitutional right to engage in homosexual sodomy. And while that legal precedent remained in place until the *Lawrence* decision, it was really the cultural wars of the 1990s in general, and Bill Clinton's open embrace of the gay rights movement and its various issues—during the 1992 campaign and throughout his eight years in office—that set the stage for the current battle.

Clinton was the first candidate of either major party actively to pursue and openly to embrace the political agenda of the gay rights movement. While earlier candidates on both the Left and the Right may have welcomed gay support, it was Clinton who first melded gay activists into his presidential campaign, featured them at the Democratic National Convention in 1992, and appointed them to high-level positions within his administration. In return for this support, Clinton promised, among other things, to remove the prohibition against gays serving openly in the military. His failure to deliver on this promise resulted, instead, in the "don't ask, don't tell" policy that Clinton ultimately signed into law. The whole episode cost Clinton dearly—with military brass who opposed allowing homosexuals to serve openly, with the ideologically orthodox who found homosexuality to be morally wrong, and, ultimately, with the gay community itself, which accused the president of backing away from his promise and bowing to political pressures. As Torie Osborn, executive director of the National Gay and Lesbian Task Force (NGLTF), put it: "We must recognize that the President sparked a very important debate that helped move the country out of the monumental state of denial that surrounded gays and lesbians in the military. But it says something about his character that he sparked the debate and then ran."[9]

Other cultural indicators followed in quick secession—Colorado voters passed Amendment 2, which overturned the state's gay rights law and prohibited the state from passing legislation that protected only one group; the massive March on Washington in 1993 for gay rights; the founding in 1995 of the NGLTF's Policy Institute, which took as its first order of business the production of a "Marriage Organizing Kit"; and the passage of the federal Defense of Marriage Act (DOMA) in 1996, an act that holds: "No State, territory, or possession of the United States, or Indian tribe, shall be required to give effect to any public act, record, or judicial proceeding of any other State, territory, possession, or tribe respecting a relationship between persons of the same sex that is treated as a marriage under the laws of such other State, territory, possession, or tribe, or a right or claim arising from such a relationship." The DOMA then went on to provide the first federally sanctioned definition of marriage: "In determining the meaning of any Act of Congress, or of any ruling, regulation, or interpretation of the various administrative bureaus and agencies of the United States, the word "marriage" means only a legal union between one man and one woman as husband and wife, and the word 'spouse' refers only to a person of the opposite sex who is a husband or a wife."[10]

In that same year, 1996, the U.S. Supreme Court struck down Colorado's Amendment 2 in the case of *Romer v. Evans*. Justice Anthony Kennedy, writing for the majority in the 6–3 decision, said: "We find nothing special in the protections Amendment 2 withholds. These protections . . . constitute ordinary civil life in a free society."[11] In 1997, the NGLTF's Policy Institute issued its "Blueprint for the Second Clinton Administration Regarding GLBT Issues." In 1998, Matthew Shepherd was murdered in Wyoming, igniting a new thrust to add sexual orientation to the nation's list of hate crimes. In 1999, the Policy Institute issued "Courting the Vote: 2000 Presidential Candidates Positions on GLBT Issues." With the subsequent election of George W. Bush, NGLTF

Executive Director Elizabeth Toledo proclaimed: "George W. Bush is heading to Washington, and now is the time for lesbian, gay, bisexual and transgender activists—arm in arm with all social justice activists—to be visible and vocal."[12]

THE PRE-PRESIDENTIAL BUSH RECORD

George Bush's record on issues of interest to gay activists was rather slim going into the 2000 presidential election. According to former U.S. Representative Steve Gunderson, an openly gay Republican: "He's a guy who was raised in Midland, Texas. He just didn't have that much exposure to the gay community. . . . I think his heart is in the right place. I don't know what that means in terms of politics and policy."[13] As governor of Texas, Bush refused to back the addition of sexual orientation to a state hate crime bill, opposed gay adoption, and vocally supported the state's anti-sodomy law. Even so, he made it clear that he intended "to treat every person with respect and dignity," and called for an end to "name calling" against gays. That was the extent of the Bush record heading into the 2000 campaign.

Gay rights was not a major campaign issue, but Bush did address the same-sex marriage question twice, once during the primaries and again during the general election. Appearing on the *Larry King Show* on February 15, 2000, Bush had this exchange:

> Q: So if you have gays working for you, that's fine and you don't have a problem—you'd appoint gays in the cabinet and so forth.
> A: Well, I'm not going to ask what their sexual orientation is. I'm going to put conservative people in the cabinet. It's none of my business what somebody's [orientation is]. Now, when somebody makes it my business, like on gay marriage, I'm going to stand up and say I don't support gay marriage. I support marriage between men and women.[14]

Later, during the presidential debate at Wake Forest University on October 19, 2000, Bush once again responded to a question about gay marriage:

> Q: What is your position on gay marriage?
> Bush: I'm not for gay marriage. I think marriage is a sacred institution between a man and a woman. . . . I will be a tolerant person. I've been a tolerant person all my life. I just happen to believe strongly

that marriage is between a man and a woman. I don't really think it's any of my concern how you conduct your sex life. That's a private matter. I support equal rights but not special rights for people.[15]

Precisely what Bush's position was on the appointment of gay Republicans to his administration remained murky throughout the campaign. In June of 2000 Patrick Buchanan, presidential candidate of the Reform Party, predicted that "the Republican Party . . . will try to avoid antagonizing the gay rights movement because it feels that it can pick up some votes by not doing so without losing votes by embracing gay rights. So they'll probably try to find a happy medium between the gay rights movement and the cultural and social conservatives."[16] *Time* magazine, on the other hand, reported in October 2000 that Bush was "on record as being adamantly opposed to hiring an openly gay person in his Administration," even though Bush had repeatedly said that sexual orientation was not the main issue for him—qualifications, party loyalty, and agreement with George W. Bush's agenda topped his list of what he wanted in an appointee.[17]

BUSH AS PRESIDENT

During the first year of the Bush Administration several high-level appointments went to openly gay Republicans. These included Stephen E. Herbits as special consultant to the secretary of defense, Scott H. Evertz as head of the White House Office of National AIDS Policy, Donald A. Capoccia as a member of the U.S. Commission on Fine Arts, and most notably, Michael Guest as U.S. ambassador to Romania. In addition, Bush appointed numerous pro–gay rights Republicans to high office, including former Massachusetts governor Paul Cellucci as U.S. ambassador to Canada, Marc Racicot as chair of the Republican National Committee, and Mary Matalin as senior advisor in the White House. Bush even gave implicit approval to a new group calling itself the Republican Unity Coalition, a group of current and former Republican officeholders who sought to form a "gay straight alliance" within the party.

Naturally such actions were not without controversy. As early as May 2001, the Concerned Women for America's Culture and Family Institute accused the Bush Administration of "pursuing a gay Republican agenda."[18] Institute director Robert Knight pointed both to the appointments made by Bush and to the fact that Bush had not "rolled back any of the Clinton homosexual activism." Knight said: "It all adds up to us as a move to either make the Republican Party silent on this very pressing social issue or to join the other side, to actually promote homosexuality as something good and normal and decent and up there with ethnicity and skin color as a civil rights category. We think that's wrong. We think laws that add sexual orientation actually have the effect of putting people with traditional values outside the law."[19] Ken Connor, president of the Family Research Council, agreed: "The president's actions, tantamount to an endorsement, are imparting legitimacy to the homosexual political cause."[20]

The Log Cabin Republicans, a long-time advocacy group for gay causes within the party, praised Bush in their January 2002 newsletter: "President Bush has not only confounded his many gay detractors but has also enraged the far right, stood down their criticism, and moved ahead with his inclusive agenda."[21] Other gay activists were not so sure. Lorri L. Jean, executive director of NGLTF, observed: "The President's gay appointments are on the positive side of the balance sheet. But they may be the only significant positive things he's done, unless you decide to list the fact that he didn't do something bad as a positive."[22] Even so, gay activists were somewhat surprised by the lack of animus in the Bush Administration's approach to the gay community. Summarizing the first year of the administration, Lou Chibbaro Jr., writing in the *Washington Blade*, noted:

> Bush has left in place two key executive orders issued by President Clinton. One prohibits job discrimination against gay federal workers and the other bans government agencies from denying security clearances to an individual based solely on sexual orientation. Bush has ignored repeated requests by anti-gay groups that he repeal the two orders.
>
> The administration has also continued to allow gay federal workers' groups to meet in government buildings and has continued a Clinton policy of allowing these groups to use government meeting facilities to hold events commemorating Gay Pride week.[23]

Even some scholars of the presidency perceived a change in the new Republican administration. Larry Sabato, for example, noted: "They know they have a lot of contradictory elements within their big tent. They want to please both sides if they can. But the President has already tipped his hand. He wants it to be known that he has no desire to be prejudiced against gays or Arab Americans, or a whole host of other groups."[24] Not everyone, however, shared Sabato's view. Chad Johnson, executive director of the National Stonewall Democrats, put it like this: "They talk and do different things. They talk about being compassionate conservatives and try to put on a nice face. But when it comes to issues of interest to our community, they are as far right as the religious right."[25]

With the advent of September 11, the ensuing war on terror, and the subsequent invasion of Iraq, most domestic issues, including gay rights, receded into the background. Earlier the state of Vermont had adopted the first "civil union" law, which was signed on April 26, 2000, by then little-known governor Howard Dean, thus propelling him to the front of the pack of potential Democratic nominees for president and reigniting, if only for a moment, the debate over gay marriage. While Dean was riding this debate to frontrunner status, few seemed to notice that the public backlash over the new law had swept sixteen Vermont lawmakers out of office and turned the Vermont House of Representatives back to the Republican Party for the first time in more than a decade. Dean himself barely survived his reelection bid, winning only 50.5 percent of the vote. The politics of gay marriage, even if under the label of "civil unions," were already in motion.

But neither Dean nor Bush seemed to anticipate the cultural earthquake unleashed by the rulings in *Lawrence v. Texas* on June 26, 2003, and *Hillary Goodridge et al. v. Department of Public Health* on November 18, 2003. Together these court rulings put the entire question of same-sex marriage front and center for the 2004 presidential campaign. Now everyone would have to declare where they stood—and why. To understand the "why" behind Bush's stance, we must return to Hunter's thesis about the ideologically orthodox.

BUSH AS "ORTHODOX" REPRESENTATIVE

Clearly, George W. Bush ought to be classified as theologically orthodox, even evangelical in his faith commitments. Although he does not apply the terms *orthodox* or *evangelical* to himself, other long-time observers of religion and the presidency have ascribed those terms to him. What do we know about the religious commitments of George W. Bush? In point of fact, we know quite a lot. We know that unlike most presidents, Bush came to faith as a forty-year-old adult. We know that his faith commitment was directly linked to his desire to quit drinking. We know, by his own testimony, that Billy Graham planted a seed of faith in him during a walk along Walker's Point in Kennebunkport in 1985 and that what Graham had planted came to fruition primarily through Bush's attendance at a local Community Bible Study in Midland, Texas.[26]

Writing in his campaign autobiography, *A Charge to Keep,* Bush explained: "Reverend Graham planted a mustard seed in my soul, a seed that grew over the next year. I had always been a religious person, had regularly attended church, even taught Sunday school and served as an altar boy. But that weekend my faith took on new meaning. It was the beginning of a new walk where I would recommit my heart to Jesus Christ. I was humbled to learn that God sent his Son to die for a sinner like me."[27] Bush's conversion was not an immediate, miraculous turnaround. He did not stop drinking immediately, nor were many of his bad habits—among them swearing like a sailor and spitting tobacco juice—immediately transformed. But a process had begun that would lead, over the course of the next several years, to Bush self-identifying as a born-again Christian. He began to read the Bible regularly, to pray, and to participate more fully in the life of his church. This chronology is important, because it is very clear that George Bush was a practicing Christian long before he decided to seek the governorship of Texas, much less the presidency of the United States. Faith came first; politics followed. As he told his commencement audience at Yale University in May 2001: "When I left here, I didn't have much in the way of a life plan. I knew some people who thought they did. But it turned out that we were all in for ups and downs, most of them unexpected. Life takes its own turns, makes its own demands, writes its own story. And along the way, we start to realize we are not the author."[28]

Much of Bush's belief system seems to track Hunter's description of the ideologically orthodox. Bush believes in a transcendent God who orders the universe, One who is the Author of our days. He believes that the primary bases for moral authority are the teachings of the biblical prophets, found in both Old and New Testaments, along with the moral teachings of Jesus and the early Church. He clearly derives his worldview from these beliefs and uses that worldview to formulate policy positions on a wide range of issues, including, as I argue, same-sex marriage. Let us look at each of these elements before turning to the debate over same-sex marriage.

First, Bush believes in a transcendent God. He has told us so since before the 2000 election. In his speech accepting the 2000 Republican presidential nomination, Bush said: "I believe in a God who calls us not to judge our neighbors but to love them. I believe in grace because I've seen it, and peace because I've felt it, and forgiveness because I've needed it."[29] He followed this with his Inaugural Address, in which he proclaimed: "We are not this story's Author, who fills time and eternity with His purpose. Yet, His purpose is achieved in our duty. And our duty is fulfilled in service to one another. . . . This work continues, the story goes on, and an angel still rides in the whirlwind and directs this storm."[30] And in the 2003 State of the Union address, Bush observed: "We Americans have faith in ourselves, but not in ourselves alone. We do not claim to know the ways of Providence, yet we can trust in them, placing our confidence in the loving God behind all of life, and all of history."[31]

Second, Bush grounds moral authority in biblical teachings which are timeless, not relative. During the 2000 campaign, he identified Christ as the philosopher who had most influenced his life, explaining: "When you accept Christ as your savior, it changes your heart, it changes your life."[32] Not surprisingly, then, it is the teachings of Jesus that form the backbone of Bush's sense of moral authority. Speaking at a Hispanic prayer breakfast in 2002, Bush said: "I often tell people that if you want to respond to what has happened to our country you can do so with prayer, but, as importantly, you can do so by loving your neighbor like you'd like to be loved yourself."[33] That teaching is found in Matthew 22:39. On the subject of same-sex marriage, Bush advised: "I am mindful that we're all sinners, and I caution those who may try to take a speck out of the neighbor's eye when they got a log in their own."[34] That teaching is found in Matthew 7:3–5 and Luke 6:41–42. Over and over, either through quotation or allusion, Bush references biblical teachings as the source for his moral vision.

Third, this belief in a transcendent God and the words of scripture as moral authority lead Bush to a worldview that is distinctively orthodox in Hunter's terms. Bush clearly believes that there is a moral order to the universe and that the universe, including all of what we call history, is under the control of God.[35] While serving as governor of Texas, Bush remarked: "I could not be governor if I did not believe in a divine plan that supersedes all human plans."[36] In Bush's world there is no such thing as chance or random occurrence. God is active in history, even if we cannot completely fathom His ways. During Bush's September 20, 2001, speech following the terrorist attacks on New York and Washington, he allowed that "freedom and fear, justice and cruelty, have always been at war, and we know that God is not neutral between them."[37] How does he know? Because his worldview has been shaped by reading the Bible and coming to believe, as he told the American Jewish Committee, that "the Lord God of Israel neither slumbers nor sleeps."[38] Even his election as president of the United States was somehow part of a Divine plan, not because Bush was unique but because for evangelical Christians all of life, whether one is a president or a plumber, is ordained by God. He has willed it to be so.

Gregg Easterbrook sums up the case for considering Bush as ideologically orthodox when he writes: "I suspect Bush takes the view (which may prove right) that the ultimate argument will be between people who believe in something larger than themselves, and people who believe that it's all an accident of chemistry."[39] While that may be a reductionist portrait of some progressives, particularly religious progressives, it does set forth in very clear terms the two extremes identified by Hunter when he writes: "Each side operates from within its own constellation of values, interests, and assumptions. At the center of each are two distinct conceptions of moral authority—two different ways of apprehending reality, of ordering experience, of making moral judgments."[40]

On no subject are these "distinct conceptions of moral authority" more starkly drawn than homosexuality, in general, and gay marriage, in particular. Hunter notes: "For the orthodox communities, homosexuality is 'the zenith of human indecency—a sin 'so grievous, so abominable in the sight of God that he destroyed Sodom and Gomorrah because of [it].' For most progressivists, homosexuality is 'not unscriptural' but simply an alternative sexual lifestyle; one other way in which loving relationships can be expressed."[41] While the cultural battle over gay rights has been ongoing since at least 1969, it was the June 2003 Supreme Court decision in *Lawrence v. Texas* that set the stage for the current conflict over same-sex marriage and created a rhetorical exigence that George Bush could not avoid.

BUSH ON SAME-SEX MARRIAGE

As I have noted, Bush was on record as being opposed to gay marriage even before his election to the presidency. His standard refrain in the 2000 campaign was simply that "marriage is a sacred institution between a man and a woman." The phrase contains three separate but equally important ideas. First, it identifies marriage as "sacred." This immediately places the debate in the realm of the transcendent. It also functions to displace the domain of the debate from that of the civil realm to that of the sacred, by which Bush appears to mean holy or set apart. Second, it claims that marriage is an *institution*, a term that can be read in at least two different ways. It can mean that marriage is a social institution rather like the military, schools, churches, or other organized branches of civilization. Or it can be read as *institution* in the sense of traditional, longstanding, established—a foundational and defining element of the society that has become an institution by virtue of its continuity through time. Third, marriage is "between a man and a woman." While the phrase may seem to need no elaboration, in point of fact it expresses a central tenet of the Judeo-Christian worldview. It is a condensation of Genesis 2:24, which Jesus himself reaffirms in Matthew 19:4–6: "Have you not read, that He which made them at the beginning, made them male and female, and said, 'For this cause shall a man leave father and mother and be joined to his wife, and the two shall become one flesh'? So they are no longer two but one. What therefore God has joined together, let no one put asunder."[42] To state that marriage is "between a man and a woman" is simply a shorthand way of affirming the teachings of Jesus.

When the Supreme Court announced its decision in *Lawrence v. Texas* on June 26, 2003, the immediate reaction from the Bush White House was silence, perhaps stunned silence. Not only did the court overturn the Texas sodomy statute; it went even further and reversed its own findings in *Bowers v. Hardwick,* thus invalidating all sodomy statutes nationwide and placing homosexual relations on an equal footing with heterosexual relations. In his sweeping majority opinion, Justice Kennedy wrote: "When sexuality finds overt expression in intimate conduct with another person, the conduct can be but one element in a personal bond that is more enduring. The liberty protected by the Constitution allows homosexual persons the right to make this choice."[43] Thus did Kennedy and cohorts find in the Constitution the very right to homosexual conduct which Justice White claimed to be nonexistent in 1986.

Equally alarming to the Bush White House was the stinging dissent from Justice Scalia, who wrote:

> Today's opinion dismantles the structure of constitutional law that has permitted a distinction to be made between heterosexual and homosexual unions, insofar as formal recognition in marriage is concerned. If moral disapprobation of homosexual conduct is "no legitimate state interest" for purposes of proscribing that conduct, *ante*, at 18; and if, as the Court coos (casting aside all pretense of neutrality), "[w]hen sexuality finds overt expression in intimate conduct with another person, the conduct can be but one element in a personal bond that is more enduring," *ante*, at 6; what justification could there possibly be for denying the benefits of marriage to homosexual couples exercising "[t]he liberty protected by the Constitution," *ibid.*?[44]

Bush waited almost a week before making any direct comment on the court decision. When he did finally break his silence on July 2, he merely reiterated his standard position that marriage is between a man and a woman. When asked if he would support a constitutional amendment to enshrine that definition, Bush said: "I don't know if it's necessary yet. Let's let the lawyers look at the full ramifications of the recent Supreme Court hearing."[45] Thus Bush refused immediately to endorse the idea of a constitutional amendment, even though such an amendment had been urged on him by leaders of the

Religious Right and had, in fact, already been endorsed by Republican Senate leader Bill Frist.

The Religious Right reacted immediately to Bush's seeming reticence to enter the fray. "I think there's probably going to be a war at the 2004 [Republican] convention," said Genevieve Wood of the Family Research Council.[46] "Bush officials apparently think homosexual activists make better leaders than the conservative activists who delivered millions of votes," complained Robert Knight of the Culture and Family Institute.[47] Even some in the journalistic community wondered about Bush's tepid response. Writing in his column on Beliefnet.com, Steven Waldman asked: "Why was Bush more vague? Is it because the White House has thrown in the towel on civil unions? Is that now viewed as the moderate middle ground?"[48] As if in answer to Waldman's query, Colin Stewart of the Family Research Council warned: "We cannot mount a true defense of marriage if we are willing to give away all its privileges to counterfeit legal arrangements bearing another name. As the president heads into the campaign season he will surely be asked to defend what he today called 'the sanctity of marriage.' Pro-family voters are counting on him to do just that."[49]

It would be four more weeks before Bush would even touch on the subject again. But at his July 30 news conference, responding to a question about his own views on homosexuality, Bush said:

> Yes. I am mindful that we're all sinners, and I caution those who may try to take a speck out of their neighbor's eye when they got a log in their own. I think it's very important for our society to respect each individual, to welcome those with good hearts, to be a welcoming country. On the other hand, that does not mean that somebody like me needs to compromise on an issue such as marriage. And that's really where the issue is headed here in Washington, and that is the definition of marriage.[50]

Bush then repeated his standard lines about the "sanctity" of marriage and his belief that marriage is "between a man and a woman" but with one difference. He went on to add: "And I think we ought to codify that one way or the other. And we've got lawyers looking at the best way to do that."[51]

While some gay rights activists attacked the president for allegedly calling them "sinners," a closer reading of the statement reveals something quite different. The first part of the statement, with its reference to Matthew 7:3–5, appears to be a warning to members of the Religious Right about the possibility of having a log in their own eyes as they pass judgment on homosexuals. It is, after all, they who claim to take the Bible seriously. It is they who condemn the sin of homosexuality. And it is the Right that is pushing Bush to endorse a constitutional amendment, something he is not yet ready to do. Bush follows this admonition to the Right immediately with a statement about "respect" for "each individual," a message of tolerance intended to convey his goodwill to everyone but especially to gay Americans. He will respect their rights as individuals but not as a group that seeks to redefine marriage. Thus, he observes, "that does not mean that someone like me needs to compromise on an issue such as marriage." The reference to "someone like me" is a clear signal to his base to remember who he is and what he believes. He will not "compromise," because one cannot compromise on something that is definitional, such as the meaning of marriage. For Bush, marriage between one man and one woman is foundational, grounded in the worldview by which he orders his life. Hence, it must be "codified" in civil law, just as it is already codified in sacred scriptures.

Many of Bush's progressive opponents understood exactly what he was saying. John Sonego of the Gay and Lesbian Alliance against Defamation (GLAAD) noted: "It is equally important that the media carefully scrutinize and hold up for debate President Bush's invocation of religion as the fundamental rationale for his policy of excluding same-sex couples and families from the protections of marriage. By saying he has charged government attorneys to explore ways to 'codify' the 'sanctity of marriage,' and through numerous biblical references in his discussion about this issue, the president is clearly signaling his conviction that his personal religious beliefs should be the basis for governing law."[52] Throughout the months of August and September Bush was relatively quiet. On August 28, 2003, he issued a presidential proclamation, making September 22 "Family Day" and promising to push a $300 million-dollar initiative to "find the most effective programs to strengthen marriage."[53] Then, on October 3, Bush proclaimed the week of October 12 through 18 as "Marriage Protection Week." His proclamation read, in part: "We must support the institution of marriage and help parents build stronger families. And we must continue our work to create a compassionate, welcoming society, where all people are treated with dignity and respect."[54] One of the distinctive features of every Bush message on the topic of same-sex marriage or related subjects is the pairing of a message of respect and tolerance with every statement of traditional belief about marriage and family. It is as if Bush is trying to say, "I will not compromise on my beliefs about marriage, but this is no reason to ostracize or abuse gay Americans. They, too, are our brothers and sisters." There is every indication that something very much like this formulation is what Bush actually believes, and both his private communications with gay people and his appointments during his first two years in office would seem to support this view.[55]

It is precisely because of Bush's Christian worldview that such a reminder is necessary—because we are all God's children, we are all "fallen" in one way or another, and we are all in need of forgiveness. Throughout the debate Bush has never attacked or even questioned the gay rights movement, the various progressivists who have repeatedly attacked him, or any leader of the campaign for same-sex marriage. What he has done is call on all Americans to respect the dignity and worth of each individual without regard to sexual orientation.

When the Supreme Judicial Court of Massachusetts ruled in a 4–3 decision in favor of Hillary Goodridge and her same-sex partner on November 18, 2003, Bush was at a conference in London. He issued a two-sentence response that merely reiterated his belief that marriage was "sacred" and repeated his intention of working with "congressional leaders and others" to "defend the sanctity of marriage."[56] Others were more outspoken. Evan Wolfson, executive director of Freedom to Marry, hailed the decision, saying that most people "will embrace this just as we have embraced other civil rights strides in American history." Pointing to such earlier battles as interracial marriage, contraception, and gender equality, Wolfson noted that "now we will soon have the reality of married gay couples in Massachusetts. Once people get a chance to see the sky doesn't fall, they will support it."[57]

But for orthodox opponents of same-sex marriage, the sky *was* falling. As Dr. D. James Kennedy, noted evangelical pastor of the Coral Ridge Presbyterian Church, wrote: "Whatever four members of the Supreme Judicial Court of Massachusetts may say, the intimate coupling of two men or two women is not marriage. It is a pale and misshapen counterfeit that will only serve to empty marriage of its meaning and destroy the institution that is the keystone in the arch of civilization."[58]

On the very same day that the Massachusetts court rendered its decision, the Pew Research Center for the People and the Press released its in-depth survey of beliefs and attitudes about homosexuality. Based on a survey of 1,515 adults, conducted from October 15 to 19, 2003, the Pew Center opened its thirty-two-page report with these words: "Opposition to gay marriage has increased since the summer and a narrow majority of Americans also oppose allowing gays and lesbians to enter legal agreements that fall short of marriage."[59] Three findings stood out: (1) overall 59 percent of those surveyed opposed gay marriage, an increase of 6 percent since the previous survey in July; (2) much of the opposition to homosexuality in general and to gay marriage in particular was driven by religious belief, with those displaying a high level of religious commitment opposing gay marriage at the rate of 80 percent; and (3) supporters of President Bush were "largely of one mind on this issue." According to the survey: "More than three-quarters (76%) of voters who favor the president's reelection in 2004 oppose gay marriage; more than half (53%) *strongly* oppose the idea. But voters who prefer to see a Democrat elected in 2004 are divided—46% favor gay marriage, 48% oppose. A substantial minority of these Democratic-leaning voters strongly oppose gay marriage (25%)."[60] Doubtless the White House was doing its own polling on the issue as well.

Having made a rather subdued response to the Massachusetts decision, particularly in comparison with the responses from his orthodox allies, Bush waited almost a month before weighing in again, a month in which he was pilloried by conservatives for not immediately endorsing a constitutional amendment, warned by the Religious Right that he risked losing their support, taken to the woodshed by certain columnists for not staking out a more definitive position, and warned by gay conservative Andrew Sullivan that if he endorsed the proposed amendment it would "make the position of gay Republicans essentially untenable and Bush would lose almost all the million gay votes he won in 2000."[61] Clearly Bush had to tread carefully whatever step he might take.

Finally, on December 16, Bush spoke out. In an interview with Diane Sawyer, the president said that he would support a constitutional amendment "if necessary." The qualification appeared to hinge on what the courts would do. As Bush explained: "Let me tell you, the court, I thought, overreached its bounds as a court. It did the job of the legislature. It was a very activist court in making the decision it made. As you know, I'm a person who believes in judicial restraint, as opposed to judicial activism that takes the places of the legislative branch."[62] Bush went on to note that he preferred that the issue be dealt with at the state level, saying: "The position of this administration is that whatever legal arrangements people want to make, they're allowed to make, so long as it's embraced by the state or at the state level. Except and unless judicial rulings undermine the sanctity of marriage; in which case we may need a constitutional amendment."[63]

Not surprisingly, both extremes in the culture war found the statement objectionable. From the orthodox camp, Tony Perkins, president of the Family Research Council, said of Bush: "I'm concerned that the president thinks that counterfeit institutions such as same-sex unions are OK, that he doesn't see that they threaten to devalue the real thing."[64] Matt Foreman, executive director of the NGLTF, was outraged: "We consider this a declaration of war on gay America. . . . We cannot and will not be silent in the face of this attempt to enshrine our community with second class citizenship in this nation's most sacred document. The President is clearly pandering to the political and religious extremists that are his base."[65]

In a pattern that has characterized all of Bush's comments on same-sex marriage, he waited another month before making further comment. But this time the comments came in the most widely watched speech of the year—the State of the Union address. In a speech that many observers called a blueprint for the 2004 campaign, Bush said:

> A strong America must also value the institution of marriage. I believe we should respect individuals as we take a principled stand for one of the most fundamental, enduring institutions of our civilization. Congress has already taken a stand on this issue by passing the Defense of Marriage Act, signed in 1996 by President Clinton. That statute protects marriage under federal law as the union of a man and a woman, and declares that one state may not redefine marriage for other states.
>
> Activist judges, however, have begun redefining marriage by court order, without regard for the will of the people and their elected representatives. On an issue of such great consequence, the people's voice must be heard. If judges insist on forcing their arbitrary will upon the people, the only alternative left to the people would be the constitutional process. Our nation must defend the sanctity of marriage.
>
> The outcome of this debate is important, and so is the way we conduct it. The same moral tradition that defines marriage also teaches that each individual has dignity and value in God's sight.[66]

Several elements of this passage deserve comment. First, Bush brackets the whole section with the terms *respect* (at the opening) and *dignity and value* (at the close), once again pairing terms of approbation for gay individuals with what he calls a "principled stand" against same-sex marriage. He grounds that approbation in "the same moral tradition" that has led him to take this stand, thus identifying gays as part of God's economy. Second, he references the 1996 Defense of Marriage Act and points out that it was signed by President Clinton. This passage functions in two ways—first to identify Bush's stance with that already endorsed by the Congress, and second to identify Bush with Clinton, the person who signed the act. This again appears to expand the range of public opinion that Bush represents by his "principled stand." Third, Bush focuses his attack on "activist judges," thus picking an enemy that is, by definition, outside the political process. He could have attacked gay activists, progressivist proponents of the homosexual agenda, the numerous Democratic presidential candidates who had criticized him on the issue, moral laxity in general, or any combination of these. But he chooses to pick a fight with the courts. This had, of course, been foreshadowed in his December 16 interview. It now emerges as the centerpiece of his rhetorical appeal. Note also that in this middle paragraph the president uses the ideograph of the "people" four times. It is not so much Bush himself who opposes the activist judiciary, but Bush as embodiment of the people. If the people are offended by this legislating from the bench, then it is the people's right to engage in a "constitutional process." It is entirely possible that this is a rhetorical precursor to a particular stance: the president will step back and let the people and the process go on as mandated by the Constitution. He will support the people's right to exercise their constitutional prerogatives, but he will not lead the parade. Indeed, he may well choose to watch from the sidelines while the process plays itself out.

Finally, Bush notes that "the way we conduct the debate" is important. And here I return to my third argument—that Bush's way of speaking about the debate and the way he proposes to conduct it may be one way of encompassing, through rhetorical performance, Hunter's call for a more deliberative way through the culture wars. According to Hunter, there are several things that must happen before any kind of resolution to the culture wars can be found. First, there must be a toning down of what he labels the "distortions of rhetoric."[67] Second, there must be a willingness to listen to the other side. Third, there must be a real attempt to listen to the public and to fashion public positions that reflect the vast middle rather than either of the extremes. And, finally, there must be a willingness to compromise.

Whatever else may be said about Bush's rhetoric on same-sex marriage, one cannot accuse him of using name calling or hyperbole—the kind of rhetoric characteristic of both extremes. His rhetorical discourse grows out of a worldview committed to love of neighbor, particularly the neighbor whom others find unlovable. Bush's willingness to listen to gay Americans was signaled as early as the 2000 campaign when he met privately with a group of gay Republicans. He refused to remove the Arizona Republican and openly gay Representative Jim Kolbe from his speaking slot at the Republican National Convention, even though loud voices on the Right insisted that he do so. And while he reached his decision on same-sex marriage long before any of the recent national surveys were conducted, it is a fact that Bush's position does represent the views of a strong majority of Americans. Even so, he has not foreclosed the possibility of compromise at the state level. He has never disavowed, for example, the comments made by Dick Cheney during the 2000 campaign, when the then vice presidential candidate said: "I think different states are likely to come to different conclusions, and that's appropriate. I don't think there should necessarily be a federal policy in this area."[68] Despite intense opposition to civil union or domestic partnership laws from both the Religious Right and the Vatican, Bush has held open compromise positions, if properly enacted by state legislatures. But the extremes do not want compromise at any level.

Bush has been repeatedly assaulted from both orthodox and progressive sides after each of his major statements on same-sex marriage. The State of the Union was no exception. No sooner had he finished speaking than Tony Perkins of the FRC proclaimed that social conservatives were "disappointed" in the president.[69] The Parents, Families and Friends of Lesbians and Gays (PFLAG) issued a statement accusing Bush of promoting "a partisan homophobic agenda."[70] And the *Washington Post,* in an editorial on January 26, 2004, referred to the speech as a "not-so-artful dodge on the subject of gay marriage" that was filled with "verbal Pablum about the 'sanctity of marriage.'"[71] That the phrase "sanctity of marriage" should strike the editorial writer as "Pablum" is a sure indicator that the *Post* is more interested in being a partisan participant in the culture war than in being a source of reasoned compromise. Much the same might be said of the judiciary. Indeed, Hunter himself points a finger at the third branch of government when he writes:

> The judiciary has not helped matters. Though by its very nature it is immune from democratic process, it is still capable of providing a highly visible forum for an elevated public moral debate, one that links competing legal reasonings and judgments to the rich moral and philosophical (even if opposing) presuppositions upon which they are based and upon which most citizens implicitly ground their own views. The tendency of judicial actions over recent decades, however, has been to divorce legal reasoning and judgment from moral argument altogether. Here, too, power is wielded without meaningful connection to the various cultural traditions reflected in democratic pluralism.[72]

One can only imagine what Hunter might think of Justice Kennedy's opinion in the *Lawrence* decision, an opinion that completely severs law from moral consensus.

Of course, any conclusive proof of my third argument must await the outcome of the debate over same-sex marriage. But it seems clear that Bush is trying to practice a rhetoric that, while well within the bounds of orthodoxy, nonetheless is an attempt to balance a "principled stand" against same-sex marriage with a message of "respect," "tolerance," and the intrinsic "value" of gay people. Even his decision, on February 24, 2004, to support the Federal Marriage Amendment illustrated this balanced approach. He began his announcement by noting that the Congress had overwhelmingly passed the Defense of Marriage Act (DOMA) in 1996 and then repeated his now standard complaint that "activist judges" were attempting to "redefine marriage." Bush then located his opposition to same-sex marriage in both American history and human experience:

> After more than two centuries of American jurisprudence and millennia of human experience, a few judges and local authorities are presuming to change the most fundamental institution of civilization. Their actions have created confusion on an issue that requires clarity.
>
> On a matter of such importance, the voice of the people must be heard. Activist courts have left the people with one recourse. If we are to prevent the meaning of marriage from being changed forever, our Nation must enact a constitutional amendment to protect marriage in America.[73]

Yet even at this decisive moment, a moment that Bush surely must have known would sever, perhaps permanently, his ability to build any kind of bridge to the homosexual community, he still called for respect and tolerance: "Our government should respect every person and protect the institution of marriage. There is no contradiction between these responsibilities. We should conduct this difficult debate in a manner worthy of our country, without bitterness or anger. In all that lies ahead, let us match strong convictions with kindness and good will and decency."[74]

From February 24, 2004, until election day on November 2, 2004, the issue of same-sex marriage would continue to roil the electorate. But following a long-established pattern, Bush would speak only infrequently about the proposed constitutional amendment, though he would regularly state his support for the institution of traditional marriage and his intention to appoint judges who would "interpret" the law rather than "legislate from the bench." Indeed, between February 24 and November 2, 2004, Bush mentioned the amendment only fourteen times. These mentions usually happened in one of three contexts—remarks before religious groups, answers to questions from a campaign-stop audience, or comments about legislative actions such as votes on the proposed amendment in the Senate or House.

In front of conservative religious audiences, Bush did speak more specifically and at greater length. For example, on March 11, 2004, he spoke by satellite connection to the annual meeting of the National Association of Evangelicals, telling the gathering:

> I will defend the sanctity of marriage against activist courts and local officials who want to redefine marriage. The union of a man and a woman is the most enduring human institution, honored and encouraged in cultures and by every religious faith. Ages of experience have taught humanity that the commitment of a husband and wife to love and to serve one another promotes the welfare of children and the stability of society. And Government, by recognizing and protecting marriage, serves the interests of all. It is for that reason I support a constitutional amendment to protect marriage as the union of a man and a woman.[75]

On May 26, the evangelical monthly *Christianity Today* published a long interview with the president, in which he said: "I want the American people participating in the process. I don't want this decided by judges. It's too big an issue. And the constitutional process is a sure enough way to get people involved through the amendment process."[76] This was followed on June 15 by a speech via satellite to the Southern Baptist Convention and an August 3 address to the annual convention of the Knights of Columbus, a Catholic fraternal organization. In all of these speeches and interviews Bush highlighted his support of the proposed amendment. But as the fall campaign began on September 2, with the president's nomination acceptance address at the Republican National Convention, his support for the amendment faded into the background and his defense of marriage took center stage.

In his nomination acceptance address, Bush introduced the three elements that would form the core of his argument about same-sex marriage over the course of the fall campaign—protection of traditional marriage, opposition to activist judges, and recitation of the congressional vote supporting the Defense of Marriage Act (DOMA), a recitation that Bush would use as a weapon with which to attack John Kerry.

Throughout the fall campaign, "values" was one of five issue areas used by Bush to distinguish himself from his opponent. On October 2, for example, campaigning in Mansfield, Ohio, Bush proclaimed: "We stand for a culture of life in which every person matters and every person counts. We stand for marriage and family, which are the foundations of this society. I also stand for putting Federal judges on the bench who know the difference between their personal opinion and the strict interpretation of the law."[77] This was the standard refrain in all of Bush's stump speaking. On only one occasion, the third presidential debate on October 13, did Bush depart from his scripted comments. Asked about whether he thought homosexuality was a "choice," Bush replied:

> You know, Bob [Schieffer], I don't know. I just don't know. I do know that we have a choice to make in America, and that is to treat people with toleration and respect and dignity. It's important that we do that. I also know, in a free society, people, consenting adults, can live the way they want to live. And that's to be honored.
>
> But as we respect someone's rights and as we profess tolerance, we shouldn't change—or have to change—our basic views on the sanctity of marriage. I believe in the sanctity of marriage. I think it's very important that we protect marriage as an institution between a man and a woman.
>
> I proposed a constitutional amendment. The reason I did so was because I was worried that activist judges are actually defining the definition of marriage. And the surest way to protect marriage between a man and a woman is to amend the Constitution. It has also the benefit of allowing citizens to participate in the process. After all, when you amend the Constitution, State legislatures must participate in the ratification of the Constitution.
>
> I'm deeply concerned that judges are making those decisions and not the citizenry of the United States. You know, Congress passed a law called DOMA, the Defense of Marriage Act. My opponent was against it. It basically protected States from the action of one State to another. It also defined marriage as between a man and a woman. But I'm concerned that that will get overturned, and if it gets overturned, then we'll end up with marriage being defined by courts. And I don't think that's in our Nation's interest.[78]

Bush would continue to use DOMA against Kerry throughout the campaign.

Following his victory in November, Bush said very little about same-sex marriage or the constitutional amendment, now dubbed the Marriage Protection Amendment. Indeed, when the legislative agenda for the second term was announced publicly on January 18, 2005, Bush explicitly recognized that the amendment would not be a top priority because the votes were not currently present to reach the needed two-thirds majority in either the House or the Senate. Social conservatives were livid. In a letter to the president dated January 18, the Arlington Group, an umbrella organization of social and religious conservatives, wrote:

> We couldn't help but note the contrast between how the president is approaching the difficult issue of Social Security privatization where the public is deeply divided and the marriage issue where public opinion is overwhelmingly on his side. . . . Is he prepared to spend significant political capital on privatization but reluctant to devote the same energy to preserving traditional marriage? If so it would create outrage with countless voters who stood with him just a few weeks ago, including an unprecedented number of African-Americans, Latinos and Catholics who broke with tradition and supported the president solely because of this issue.[79]

Once again, Bush reassured his supporters that he was with them philosophically, but that he would not lead the effort to pass the amendment. This was to be the people's issue and the people would have to speak to the issue either by convincing their elected representatives in Congress or through state-by-state ballot initiatives designed to restrict marriage to one man and one woman. And that is precisely what the people did. By the fall of 2006, forty-five out of the fifty states had restricted marriage to one man and one woman either through statute or through amendment of the state constitution. The effort to pass a federal amendment continues but with no discernable progress toward securing the needed two-thirds vote in Congress. And George W. Bush continues to speak about the topic only on rare occasions, preferring to let the constitutional process work itself out, a process that he had to know would take years and would have only the remotest chance of success.

Conclusion

I have tried to show that George Bush's response to the debate over same-sex marriage has been influenced primarily by his Christian worldview, that his worldview contributes substantially to the way Bush speaks about same-sex marriage, and that his way of speaking and acting may be one way of performing Hunter's call for a reasoned and more civil way through the culture wars.

I do not deny that Bush is also a political animal, or that his administration often runs by raw political calculation rather than principle, or that at some level principle and calculation may be difficult, if not impossible, to separate. All of that is true. I do hold, however, that the debate would be more volatile, the language coarser, and the strategies employed more divisive were it not for Bush's orthodox faith commitments. It was precisely because of that commitment that Bush could say: "Let me encourage everybody, as we debate this issue, to do so with the utmost of respect. I mean this is an issue that requires thoughtful dialog. It's a serious issue. And it's one that I hope we can have a debate [about] in a way that is uplifting and not tearing people down on either side of the issue."[80]

Much of Bush's rhetoric on the subject of same-sex marriage—and many other subjects as well—cannot be fully appreciated without recourse to his ideological orthodoxy. To understand George W. Bush, one must take seriously his commitment to an orthodox worldview. As he told the interviewer from *Christianity Today*: "But I'm the kind of person who doesn't change. The best thing I can do is to be myself so that when I finish my job here I will say I was comfortable with who the world saw. I think others will have to reflect upon what it means where there's a worry that somebody holds the office that also understands there's a higher power. We'll let others reflect upon that for history's sake."[81]

NOTES

1. James Davison Hunter, *Culture Wars: The Struggle to Define America* (New York: Basic Books, 1991), 34.
2. Hunter, *Culture Wars*, 42–43.
3. Hunter, *Culture Wars*, 120.
4. Hunter, *Culture Wars*, 123.
5. Hunter, *Culture Wars*, 123.
6. Hunter, *Culture Wars*, 125–26.
7. Hunter, *Culture Wars*, 130.
8. Hunter, *Culture Wars*, 131.
9. Torie Osborn quoted in "About NGLTF: Three Decades of Fighting for Freedom, Justice and Equality," *National Gay and Lesbian Task Force*. Online at http://www.ngltf.org/about/highlights.htm.

10. Defense of Marriage Act, 110 Stat. 2419 (1996). Online at http://www.unix.oit.umass.edu/~leg450/doma.htm.

11. Anthony Kennedy writing for the majority in *Romer v. Evans*, quoted in "The American Gay Rights Movement: A Timeline." Online at http://print.infoplease.com/ipa/0/7/6/1/9/0/A0761909.html.

12. Elizabeth Toledo quoted in "About NGLTF: Three Decades of Fighting for Freedom, Justice and Equality," *National Gay and Lesbian Task Force*. Online at http://www.ngltf.org/about/highlights.htm.

13. Steve Gunderson quoted in Ron Hutcheson, "Bush Tries to Balance Gay Views," *Star-Telegram.com*. Online at http://www.dfw.com/mld/dfw/news/6628796.htm.

14. *Larry King Show*, February 15, 2000. Online at http://www.issues2000.0rg/News_Gay_Rights.htm.

15. Presidential Debate at Wake Forest University, October 11, 2000. Online at http://www.issues2000.0rg/News_Gay_Rights.htm.

16. Americans for Truth Pressroom, "Pat Buchanan Says Republicans Becoming 'Agnostic' on 'Gay,' Social Issues." Online at http://www.americansfortruth.com/PatB1.html.

17. "Double Standard," *Time*, October 19, 2000, 62. It is not clear where *Time* came up with this idea. During the South Carolina primary in February of 2000 Bush had said that "an openly known homosexual is somebody who probably wouldn't share my philosophy." He said nothing about homosexuals who did share his philosophy. See Julia Campbell, "Where Will He Stand? Bush Faces Difficult Issues on Gay Rights." Online at http://abcnews.com/sections/politics/DailyNews/Gays_Bush010117.html.

18. "Group Rails against Bush's 'Homosexual Activism,'" CNN Inside Politics, May 31, 2001. Posted online by Log Cabin Republicans at http://www.logcabinwa.com/archive/200105311811.shtml.

19. Robert Knight, quoted in "Group Rails against Bush's 'Homosexual Activism.'"

20. Ken Connor, "Bush Actions Advance Homosexual Agenda," September 27, 2001. Online at http://www.chuckbaldwinlive.com/bushhomosexualagenda.html.

21. Quoted in Lou Chibbaro Jr., "Mixed Reviews on Lesbian and Gay Rights for Bush's First Year," in *Rights at Risk: Equality in an Age of Terrorism* (Report by Citizens' Commission on Civil Rights, 2002), 219. Chibbaro's chapter was reprinted from the *Washington Blade*, January 18, 2002.

22. Lorri Jean quoted in Chibbaro, "Mixed Reviews," 219.

23. Chibbaro, "Mixed Reviews," 220. Bush was very conscious about his use of executive orders. On his first day in office, for example, he issued orders to stop funding for international organizations that provide abortions. Within the first week, he had issued orders for a "National Day of Prayer" and by the second week had created the White House Office of Faith-Based and Community Initiatives. It was not by accident that the Clinton-era executive orders remained in place—which is precisely why the Religious Right was so furious.

24. Larry Sabato quoted in Chibbaro, "Mixed Reviews," 225.

25. Chad Johnson quoted in Chibbaro, "Mixed Reviews," 225.

26. I have relied heavily on Stephen Mansfield, *The Faith of George W. Bush* (Lake Mary, Fla.: Charisma House, 2003), and David Aikman, *A Man of Faith: The Spiritual Journey of George W. Bush* (Nashville: W Publishing Group, 2004), for background on Bush's conversion to Christianity.

27. George W. Bush, *A Charge to Keep: My Journey to the White House* (New York: Harper Perennial, 2001), 136.

28. George W. Bush, "Commencement Address at Yale University," May 21, 2001. Online at http://frwebgate2.access.gpo.gov/cgi-bin/waisgate.cgi?WAISdocID=517693428972+0+0+&WAISaction=retrieve.

29. George W. Bush, "2000 Republican National Convention Nomination Acceptance Address," August 3, 2000. Online at http://www.presidentialrhetoric.com/speeches/08.03.00.html.

30. George W. Bush, "Inaugural Address," January 20, 2001. Online at http://www.presidentialrhetoric.com/speeches/01.20.01.html.

31. George W. Bush, "2003 State of the Union Address," January, 28, 2003. Online at http://www. presidentialrhetoric.com/speeches/01.28.03.html.

32. George W. Bush, quoted in Carter M. Yang, "Man of Faith: Religion Prominent in Bush Presidency." Online at http://abcnews.go.com/sections/politics/DailyNews/Bush_religion010521.html.

33. Quoted in Francine Kiefer, "The Private Faith of a Public Man: How Religion Shapes This Presidency," *Christian Science Monitor*. Online at http://www.csmonitor.com/2002/0906/p01s03-uspo.html.

34. "The President's News Conference," July 30, 2003, *Weekly Compilation of Presidential Documents*. Online at http://frwebgate1.access.gpo.gov/cgi-bin/waisgate.cgi?WAISdocID=93420723356+2+0+0&WAISaction=retrieve?

35. For an interesting interpretation of Bush's rhetorical use of the term *history* see James W. Ceaser, "Providence and the President: George W. Bush's Theory of History," *Weekly Standard*, March 10, 2003. Online at http://theweeklystandard.com/Content/Public/Articles/000/000/002/315mmrvy.asp.

36. Quoted in Lou Dubose, "Bush's Messiah Complex," *Progressive*, February 2003. Online at http://www.progressive.org/feb03/comm0203.html.

37. "President's Speech of September 20, 2001." Online at http://www.presidentialrhetoric.com/speeches/09.20.01.

38. "Bush Religious Freedom Remarks to American Jewish Committee," *Department of State Washington File*. Online at http://usembassy-austrailia.state.gov/hyper/2001/0503/epf406.htm.

39. Gregg Easterbrook quoted in Bill Keller, "God and George W. Bush," *Lebanon Wire*. Online at http://www.lebanonwire.com/0305/03051701NYT.asp.

40. Hunter, *Culture Wars*, 128.

41. Hunter, *Culture Wars*, 130.

42. Matthew 19:4–6. Revised Standard Version.

43. Anthony Kennedy's majority opinion in *Lawrence v. Texas* (02–102). Online at http://www.law.cornell.edu/supct/html/02-102.ZO.html.

44. Antonin Scalia's dissenting opinion in *Lawrence v. Texas* (02–102). Online at http://www.law.cornell.edu/supct/html/02-102.ZD.html.

45. Quoted in "Bush Uncertain about Gay Marriage Ban," *CNN Inside Politics*, July 2, 2003. Online at http://www.cnn.com/2003/ALLPOLITICS/07/02/bush.gay/index.html.

46. Genevieve Wood quoted in "Bush Uncertain about Gay Marriage Ban."

47. Robert Knight quoted in Evan Thomas, "The War over Gay Marriage," *Newsweek*, July 7, 2003. Online at http://www.newsweek.com.

48. Steven Waldman, "White House Word Play: Does Bush's Ambiguous Phrasing Reflect a Growing Acceptance of Gay Unions?" *Beliefnet*. Online at http://www.beliefnet.com/story/130/story_13037_1.html.

49. Colin Stewart quoted in "President Bush Promises to Preserve Traditional Marriage." Online at http://www.goodnewsetc.com/093FAM1.htm.

50. "The President's News Conference," July 30, 2003, *Weekly Compilation of Presidential Documents*. Online at http://frwebgate1.access.gpo.gov/cgi-bin/waisgate.cgi?WAISdocID =93420723356+2+0+0&WAISaction=retrieve.

51. "President's New Conference," July 30, 2003.

52. Sonego quoted in Jerry Falwell, "President Bush Denounced for 'Religion-Based' Comments." *NewsMax.com*, August 2, 2003. Online at http://www.newsmax.com/archives/articles/2003/8/1/135857.shtml.

53. "Proclamation 7697—Family Day, 2003," *Weekly Compilation of Presidential Documents*, August 28, 2003. Online at http://frwebgate1.access.gpo.gov/cgi-bin/waisgate.cgi?WAISdocID=93420723356+27+0+0+0&WAISaction=retrieve.

54. "Proclamation 7714—Marriage Protection Week, 2003." *Weekly Compilation of Presidential Documents,* October 3, 2003. Online at http://frwebgate1.access.gpo.gov/cgi-bin/waisgate.cgi?WAISdocID=93420723356+0+0+0&WAISaction=retrieve.

55. For comments by gay people who have known Bush well see Ron Hutcheson, "Bush Tries to Balance Gay Views." On Bush's attitudes about gay people, articulated in private conversations in 1998, see David D. Kirkpatrick, "In Secretly Taped Conversations, Glimpses of the Future President," *New York Times*, February 20, 2005. Online at http://www.nytimes.com/2005/02/20/politics/20talk.html?th=&pagewanted=print&position=.

56. Bush quoted in "Bush Condemns US Court Ruling Backing Gay Marriage," *Sydney Morning Herald*, November 19, 2003. Online at http://www.smh.com.au/articles/2003/11/19/1069027147337.html?from+storyrhs.

57. Evan Wolfson quoted in Carolyn Lochhead, "Massachusetts Court Allows Gay Marriage; Bush Says He Will Lead Fight to Ban Unions," *San Francisco Chronicle*, November 19, 2003. Online at http://sfgate.com/cgi-bin/article.cgi?file=/c/a2003/11/19/MARRIAGE.TMP&type=printable.

58. Center for Reclaiming America, "Dr. Kennedy Calls for Constitutional 'Firewall' to Protect Marriage," November 19, 2003. Online at http://www.reclaimamerica.org/Pages/pressreleasepage.asp?story=1460.

59. The Pew Research Center for the People and the Press, "Republicans Unified, Democrats Spilt on Gay Marriage." Online at http://www.people-press.org.

60. Pew Research Center, "Republicans Unified."

61. Andrew Sullivan, "Bush and Marriage: A Middle Way?" Online at http://www.andrewsullivan.com/main_article.php?artnum=20031210.

62. Bush quoted in Paul Johnson, "Bush Gay Marriage Remarks 'Act of War.'" Online at http://www.equality.org.za/news/2003/12/18bushantigay.php.

63. Bush quoted in Gary Younge, "Bush Backs Bar on Gay Marriage," *Guardian*, December 18, 2003. Online at http://www.guardian.co.uk/usa/story/0,12271,1109317,00.html.

64. Tony Perkins quoted in Susan Page, "Bush's Gay-Marriage Tack Risks Clash With His Base," *USA Today*, December 17, 2003. Online at http://usatoday.com/new/washington/2003-12-17-bush-gay-marriage_x.htm.

65. Matt Foreman quoted in Johnson, "Bush Gay Marriage Remarks 'Act of War.'"

66. George W. Bush, "2004 State of the Union Address," January 20, 2004. Online at http://www.presidentialrhetoric.com/speeches/01.20.04.html.

67. James Davison Hunter, *Before the Shooting Begins: Searching for Democracy in America's Culture War* (New York: Free Press, 1994), 45–82.

68. Cheney quoted in Tom Musbach, "Vice President Backs Bush over Gay Marriage." Online at http://ok.gay.com/printit/headlines/5642.

69. Tony Perkins quoted in Randall Mikkelsen, "Bush Stops Short on Constitution Gay Marriage Ban." Online at http://www.reuters.com/printerFriendlyPopup.jhtml?type=politics News&storyID=4172520.

70. Quoted in Mikkelsen, "Bush Stops Short."

71. "State of Gay Unions," *Washington Post*, January 26, 2004. Online at http://www.washingtonpost.com/ac2/wp-dyn/A47627-2004Jan25?language=printer.

72. Hunter, *Before the Shooting Begins*, 221.

73. George W. Bush, "Remarks Calling for a Constitutional Amendment Defining and Protecting Marriage," *Weekly Compilation of Presidential Documents*, February 24, 2004. Online at http://frwebgate3.access.gpo.gov/cgi-bin/waisgate.cgi?WAISdocID=82204416928+2+0+0+0&WAISaction=retrieve.

74. Bush, "Remarks Calling for a Constitutional Amendment."

75. George W. Bush, "Satellite Remarks to the National Association of Evangelicals Convention," *Weekly Compilation of Presidential Documents*, March 11, 2004. Online at http://frwebgate4.access.gpo.gov/cgi-bin/waisgate.cgi?WAISdocID=13833117502+48+0+0&WAISaction=retrieve.

76. Bush quoted in Sheryl Henderson Blunt, "Bush Calls for 'Culture Change,'" *Christianity Today*, May 28, 2004. Online at http://www.christianitytoday.com/ct/2004/121/51.0.html.

77. "Remarks in a Discussion in Mansfield, Ohio," *Weekly Compilation of Presidential Documents*, October 2, 2004. Online at http://frwebgate1.access.gpo.gov/cgi-bin/waisgate.cgi?WAISdocID=141935312239+66+0+0&WAISaction=retrieve.

78. "Presidential Debate in Tempe, Arizona," *Weekly Compilation of Presidential Documents*, October 13, 2004. Online at http://frwebgate3.access.gpo.gov/cgi-bin/waisgate.cgi?WAISdocID=82204416928+1+0+0+0&WAISaction=retrieve.

79. Quoted in David D. Kirkpatrick and Sheryl Gay Stolberg, "Backers of Gay Marriage Ban Use Social Security as Cudgel," *New York Times*, January 25, 2005. Online at http://www.nytimes.com/2005/01/25/politics/25marriage.html?ex+1264395600&en=81d86605d289bf51&ei=5088%partner=rssnyt.

80. "Remarks in a Discussion at Eclipse Aviation in Albuquerque, New Mexico," *Weekly Compilation of Presidential Documents*, August 11, 2004. Online at http://frwebgate1.access.gpo.gov/cgi-bin/getdoc.cgi?dbname=2004_presdiential_documents&docid=p0116au04_txt_12.

81. Bush quoted in Blunt, "Bush Calls for 'Culture Change.'"

CHAPTER 10

THINKING HARDER ABOUT PRESIDENTIAL DISCOURSE

The Question of Efficacy

Roderick P. Hart, University of Texas at Austin

The chapters in this book were originally presented at the tenth Texas A&M conference on presidential rhetoric. So I begin by thanking Marty Medhurst, who oversaw those ten conferences and whose vision and energy sustained them. Readers should also be grateful to Jim Aune for having overseen the tenth annual conference and for his contribution to the study of rhetoric and politics writ large. Together, Marty and Jim model professionalism in its highest key.

This volume's essays mark another anniversary as well. Ten years before they were delivered, a certain professor of political science offered a disquisition about the effects of presidential discourse, arguing that rhetorical scholars had habitually inflated its range and function and had not proven the causal claims they made. Because of a sudden death in my family, I could not attend that first conference, although I did present a paper via the kind offices of Vanessa Beasley. My guess is that if I had been present at the conference it would not have intimidated George Edwards from giving his paper. No, George was determined to question rhetorical study of the presidency broadly, even the work produced by its avatars—David Zarefsky, Karlyn Campbell, Jim Andrews, and Kathleen Hall Jamieson.

The story gets worse. Inspired by the rousing reception he received at the conference, the good professor began a set of systematic studies to measure the empirical impact of what presidents say. Some years later, his work culminated in the publication of *On Deaf Ears: The Limits of the Bully Pulpit.*[1] Edwards's book is an exhaustive analysis of the available quantitative data on rhetoric's impact. His book runs to 254 pages in length (exclusive of endnotes); seventy-six of those pages consist of charts and tables.

What does Edwards find? He finds that presidents affect public opinion in only episodic and indirect ways. He discovers that rhetoric has some impact on a president's personal popularity and policy preferences but no overall, systematic effect. He reports that the concept of charisma, a concept that many in this room cherish, "does not appear to be either salvageable analytically or helpful empirically."[2] He notes that the president has only modest ability to focus the electorate on his policy priorities, in part because the president has too much informational competition from his political opponents and the working press. Equally, a president has only limited ability to "frame" the political debate or to "prime" voters to pay attention to this matter and not that. To make matters worse, Edwards finds that audiences for presidential speech are getting smaller, and when they do hear a president speak, listeners often do not understand what he has said or, if they do understand it, often forget it.

Why do presidents go public in that case? He answers thus: (1) because of routine, (2) for a chance to address the already converted, and (3) to influence elites. On the flyleaf of Edwards's book, the estimable (and much mourned) Richard Neustadt calls it "a bold, convincing challenge to both thirty years of literature and the conventional wisdom of 'Going Public' from the White House."

On Deaf Ears turned out to be an important book. In it, Edwards exhaustively researched the question of effect and took his potential detractors—the essayists in this volume—quite seriously. He took none of the cheap shots that empirical social scientists often take at critics and historians and never settled for a single statistical test when probing a complex matter. Instead, he turned the relevant questions around and around, looking at them from multiple vantage points. He also instigated conversations with rhetorical critics, often by anticipating their objections and then answering these.

Speaking as one who has attended two political science conferences a year for the past twenty years and who counts scores of political scientists among his closest colleagues, I find this to be an exceptional book. I have read virtually everything George has written on the American presidency and I have great respect for his work. George Edwards is a gifted scholar and my friend.

But he is not perfect, and his book is not the last word on the matters it treats. Indeed, its main value may be to help us reimagine the entire question of rhetorical efficacy. But for us to do so we must first come to grips with Edwards's seventy-six pages of quantitative data, for they can be intimidating indeed. Edwards culls the findings of the best polling operations in the United States and so he stands on solid ground. Or so I thought until I heard the tale of a rather strange fellow from the state of Michigan. His story is entitled . . .

DODDS'S REVENGE

The first news report was buried innocently enough on page sixteen of the Ann Arbor paper. A sixty-seven-year-old functionary in one of the research units at the University of Michigan had been fired for unprofessional conduct.[3] The university was considering suing him, although given his age and modest salary, that hardly seemed worth it. The gentleman in the eye of the storm, one William P. Dodds, was not interviewed for the article, nor was his supervisor, a rather bewildered-looking woman named Madeline whose photograph in the newspaper bore the subtle markings of stark terror.

The second news story appeared two days later (this time on the first page of the city section). Dodds, as it turns out, had indeed been a factotum in one of the social science research units (the one dealing with politics or something) and had been continuously employed by the university since 1951. The immediate cause of his dismissal was still unclear, but the suspicion was that he had altered some computer tapes. His supervisor, Madeline, was not taking calls.

The third story was a blockbuster. It came three days later, right on page one of the Sunday edition, and it appeared in the Detroit paper as well. Dodds had now been formally charged by the university with malicious tampering and was dismissed from his job. His supervisor, Madeline, had requested an indefinite leave of absence but agreed to appear at a news conference the next day.

Mondays in Ann Arbor can be glorious, especially with snow on the ground, but this was no ordinary Monday. The university president began the press conference by giving a quick synopsis of recent events. Dodds turned out to be William P. Dodds Jr., the disaffected son of a disaffected university employee who had been fired in 1954 for drinking on the job. Dodds Sr.'s premature retirement led to his premature suicide—and to a very despondent son. But Dodds Jr. turned out to be a patient young man and, as he aged, a patient old man. Throughout his fifty years at the university he worked in just one research unit—the one dealing with politics or something. His perfidy had just come to light.

The university president then turned over the microphone to Madeline, she of the ashen hue, who spelled out the details: Dodds Jr. had been solely responsible for maintaining the data files in the Politics or Something Unit. Most people in the unit ignored Dodds (he had several odd facial tics and certain erratic hand movements) except when they gave him the polling data they collected each day, each month, each year, each decade, whereupon Dodds Jr. would load them onto the mainframe (later, the server) and then set up the Very Large Search Routines for which the polling unit had become justifiably famous.

Madeline then continued (one could tell it was painful for her): "I never liked the cretin," she said, "but he knew where all the statistical bodies were buried so we kept him around. In any event, it turns out that Dodds was intent on sabotaging us right from the beginning and a week ago Tuesday we found out about it. What he had been doing over the years was eliminating all the 3's in our datasets and replacing them with either 6's or 7's. We have not been able to find out why he removed the 3's but we suspect it had something to do with his being the youngest of three children. Anyway, that's what he did in the 1950s. In the 1960s he replaced all the 2's with the square root of Pi and in the 1970s he put an encrypted form of 'Hail to the Victors' where the open-ended survey responses should have been. In the 1980s he stored the tapes in mayonnaise jars which naturally corroded all the ethnic data. So far, we have not been able to track down the damage he did in the '90s but we know it was guided by his growing feminist consciousness."

Madeline finally concluded (one could detect the earliest signs of a migraine). For their parts the reporters were nonplussed. "What does all this mean?" asked one. "Why are we here?" asked another. "Don't you get it?" Madeline responded (she tended to pull on her ear when irritated). "All the survey data gathered here about the American voter since 1952 are completely worthless. Totally untrustworthy. All those dissertations. All those Yale books. Worthless. Tenure is going to be revoked throughout the United States because of this one, stupid moron. Political science is dead as a discipline. Washington, D.C., just lost one of its biggest conventions for 2008."

"What's the big deal?" asked the rumpled reporter from Detroit. "Is this about some professors or something?" inquired another. "What's the big deal?"

Madeline mimicked. "What's the big deal? I'll tell you what's the big deal. This place used to be the Taj Mahal of data. Now we've got nothing. Zero. Zip. Nada. Now we don't know a damned thing about American politics."

"We've still got George Will," volunteered one of the reporters. "And that fellow at Princeton who writes about presidents," said another. "Yeah, and don't forget that guy Larry from Virginia, the slick-haired guy on all the talk shows?" said a third. "But don't you see?" Madeline wailed to nobody in particular, "now there's no science in political science. Now we're just (the words came hard for her)—just History or Journalism or . . ." (her voice trailed off, infinitely one presumes).

It had been a hard couple of weeks at the university, but then the Boilermakers came to town for the big game. The Wolverines lost a heartbreaker on Saturday, 85–83. For his part, Dodds had gotten on with his life and taken a new job—working the scoreboard.

BUT WHAT IF IT WERE TRUE?

Indeed, what if it were true? What if, just to be obstreperous, we forsook survey data entirely? What if, just for the sake of argument, we refused to genuflect when hearing the phrase "public opinion data"? What if we treated survey research as more art than science? What if we took seriously the critiques presented by Lisbeth Lipari and Susan Herbst?[4] For her part, Lipari has studied the wording of the questions pollsters have used over the years and finds them to be largely rhetorical in character, carefully inscribing Statist values into the research enterprise. If you cannot trust the objectivity of the questions, Lipari asks, how can you trust the answers public opinion research provides?

And, asks Herbst, why should survey data be labeled "public opinion" at all? There are countless sources of public opinion in the world, she observes, and Messrs. Gallup and Roper have only one version and not a very smart version at that. Herbst attributes Americans' love of polls to their modernist tendencies, to the belief that something inchoate can be made transparent via stipulation. Aggregating the private responses of private persons and then calling the results "public," says Herbst, is a constructivist enterprise that conceals more than it reveals. We might ask Herbst's question this way: If the Pew Research Center for the People and the Press declared that 59 percent of the American people liked jelly better than peanut butter, would you stake your life on that claim? Well, would you?

John Zaller also asks uncomfortable questions about survey data, even though he himself is an astute practitioner of the art.[5] Zaller notes that survey respondents reveal only as much about themselves as surveyors think to ask (how many times have you filled out a survey that had more than few demographic questions, for example?). People expose themselves to public matters differentially, says Zaller, and so they vary considerably in critical astuteness. Too, he notes that few people have fixed attitudes on most issues; people often make them up on the fly (as, for example, when filling out survey forms). Even then, says Zaller, they only respond to things they care about *now*; tomorrow, they may not give a damn.

Among the things survey researchers are particularly keen about are time-series analyses that track people's responses to the same questions, survey after survey. Unfortunately, few questions have been worded in the same way consistently (even the vaunted National Elections Study and National Opinion Research Center databases have only a handful of such questions). But the problems do not end there, for even identical wording cannot keep things stable. For example, if respondents were asked in 1950 if they thought "American capitalism were the envy of the world" they would surely have said yes. But what does "capitalism" mean to Americans today in a world bedeviled by colossal economic imbalance? How many Americans today are proud of being envied? Is this survey question not itself an answer, at least in part?

In short, there is a rhetoric to public opinion research. Rhetoric guides the survey questions that researchers choose, and it guides the subject populations they deem appropriate. How large a sample will the journal editors accept? How many call-backs will they demand? How can I explain missing data? Which of the thousand facts unearthed are most important? Which data should be put in the tables, which in footnotes, which can be safely ignored?

Survey researchers are also condemned to paradox. Was Respondent A even thinking about President Bush before the surveyor brought up the matter? Did having to take the survey force Respondent B to make a premature judgment about Bush? Does Respondent C think about Bush in terms of a seven-point scale or would a two-point scale do just as well: love him or leave him? Polling researchers, it can be argued, invent the world they study, as do we all.

Enough. My purpose here is not to question the integrity of survey research. I have learned an enormous amount from it and often use it as a kind of North Star to tell me when my impressionistic work with rhetorical texts has gone off course. I admire survey researchers' rigor as well as their persistence and reflexivity. But because so much of what we know about the presidency is based on survey data, it needs to be scrutinized carefully. Scholars more talented than I have worried lately about the growing disinclination of people to fill out survey forms, about the demand characteristics of the instruments being used, and about polling's modest record of political prediction. A survey is a fine thing but it is not everything.

WHAT ELSE DO WE HAVE?

We have rhetorical studies, the kinds of studies presented in this volume. But rhetorical critics should not become boosterish or provincial. Indeed, I would like this essay to be seen as homage to George Edwards, for he has done something he did not have to do: he took his critics seriously. George listened to what they had to say and he listened intently. He has also listened critically, but critical listening is surely a boon.

How can we best honor George in return? By taking his challenges seriously as well. It is not enough for us to contend that survey researchers are pedestrians and critics Apollonian. As David Zarefsky opined recently, George has sensitized us to the careless claims of causality rhetorical scholars tend to make.[6] We should shudder when our colleagues blithely declare that a given discourse has "unleashed a whirlwind of hegemony" or "reinscribed a postcolonial orthodoxy" or "instantiated rhizomes of disciplinarity." Statements like that unnerve me. They are too grand, too sweeping, too sterile, too unproven, and worse, too unprovable. We can, of course, enter our various salons and say such things to one another, the wisest among us wandering to and fro speaking of Michelangelo, but it seems better to become smarter, more layered, and more precise about rhetorical effects.

The chapters in this volume move us along that path. Collectively, they tell us that rhetoric's effects are broader and deeper than can be captured by paper and pencil measures. For example, it seems clear that presidential rhetoric often *changes the national conversation,* causing us to talk about public problems in new ways. The "secondary discourses" presidents inspire constantly swirl about us in the public marketplace. A while back, for example, many Americans were in a dither about Janet Jackson's "wardrobe malfunction" and scientists' stem-cell research, effects that might reasonably have been attributed to the fellow currently sitting in the Oval Office. Because presidents often label things first—whipped inflation, a national malaise, the death tax—they *crystalize vague concepts* and thus put new issues on the national agenda.

Presidents can also *alter the national imagination* and get us to think of possibilities—relations with Red China, the Interstate highway system—that only specialists had imagined before. Carol Winkler explains how that has been done in the war on terrorism, with an old and comfortable narrative of Cold War perfidy being retrofitted for a new age and a new purpose. Presidents often *change our definitional habits* in these ways, getting us in 1950 to think of the Korean conflict as a "police action" and, fifty years later, to find compassion in conservatism.[7] Perhaps most powerfully, presidents can *change people's presuppositions*—that which they take for granted, that which they would be hard-pressed to defend if asked to do so. Prior to the Clinton years, for example, who would have thought that a Democratic president could snub the unions and, simultaneously, sit down with the Wall Street bankers? A bit earlier, who would have thought that blue-collar workers in the Midwest would queue up at a Ronald Reagan rally or, later, that suburban women would desert the first George Bush in droves?

Presidential rhetoric has additional effects. John Murphy tells us, for example, that such rhetoric can *relocate sources of authority*, as when George W. Bush married identity appeals with religious appeals to get people to cede more power to the federal government. John Murphy and Marouf Hasian have told us that presidents can *change the arc of time*, making us feel it is earlier, or later, than it really is. Murphy explains how inaugural addresses make us live in a "time out of time," thereby empowering us. On the other hand, President Bush's rhetoric on Afghanistan, says Hasian, made banal exigences seem emergencies, thereby encouraging precipitousness on our part.

Presidential rhetoric can also *change the arc of space*, making some things seem closer than they really are (Mars, for example) or farther away (Haiti, for example). A powerful rhetoric can make us feel restrained (crowded out by illegal immigrants, for example), or it can emancipate us and turn the world into a neighborhood (the Peace Corps campaign, for example). But if rhetoric can make our conceptions broader, it can also narrow them. As Jim Aune shows, rhetoric sometimes *shortens the political agenda*, convincing us that some things are settled when they are not (civil rights, for example) or that other persons are more qualified to deal with our problems than are we (the rhetoric of the Federal Reserve, for example).

Trevor Parry-Giles shows that presidential discourse can *shift the locus of controversy* by claiming that a president's appointive powers are more important than the qualifications of those sitting on the nation's highest court. The power of the presidency can also *alter political metrics*. That is, it is one thing for a president to endorse a particular solution to the nation's problems and quite another to calibrate the gravity of those problems. As Marilyn Young reports, when George W. Bush replaced continua with binaries in foreign policy, he invited us to think differently, perhaps dangerously, about international relations.

As Marty Medhurst notes, though, rhetorical scholars should avoid becoming unduly abstract about political matters, for presidents-as-persons often *model particular attitudes,* thereby becoming the embodiments of otherwise abstract ideas and virtues. On television, Mr. Rogers performed that function for a generation of young Americans and Oprah Winfrey did the same when they grew up. As Medhurst argues, the current President Bush performed similarly in the area of gay rights, being vigilant about what his rhetoric walled in and walled out. Leroy Dorsey pushes this one step further, showing how such modeling *instantiates new possibilities* for a people. If a president fails to perform that function, says Dorsey, a nation's myths and realities become disentangled, leading to complacency during happy times, corrosive cynicism when times are tough.

Conclusion

I have just adduced twelve specific effects of presidential rhetoric, any one of which would make Edwardians blush. They would be nervous for many reasons but primarily because such effects are not easy to measure. Rhetorical critics, I suppose, are condemned to that fate, in part because they operate at such a high level of abstraction and in part because they feel invited to participate in the conversations they study. Social scientists rarely feel invited in these ways and so they stand back, observing. This does not make critics better than social scientists, but it does make them different.

In the preceding remarks, I have argued that presidential rhetoric (1) crystalizes vague concepts, (2) alters the national imagination, (3) changes definitional habits, (4) shifts people's presuppositions, (5) relocates sources of authority, (6) changes the arc of time and (7) space, (8) shortens the political agenda, (9) shifts the locus of controversy, (10) alters our political metrics, (11) models specific attitudes, and (12) instantiates new possibilities. These are not small matters. These are large and encompassing matters.

A dozen years ago, George Edwards asked rhetorical critics to prove all this, and I renew that call. I believe it is possible for critics to pursue the work they love and to be more precise than they have been in the past. Making vacuous causal statements about political effects profits no one. It becomes cant, not interrogation; ideology, not scholarship. Rhetorical critics need to be humbler when advancing their claims. Doing so will make their scholarship better and earn them the kingdom of heaven as well.

As I have argued previously, rhetorical scholars often become short-sighted when seizing on some specific persona, artifact, or historical anomaly rather than asking case-transcendent questions.[8] How much more exciting it would be if we launched a program of research centered on rhetorical efficacy itself. We might ask, for example, how political concepts become crystalized across time and circumstance or which definitional habits are amenable to change and which are not? We could also ask which agents are best able to shift our presuppositions—the president, the mass media, the church, the schoolroom, popular culture? Too, we could investigate whether Democrats or Republicans, young politicians or their elders, southerners or northerners, are most adept at modeling specific attitudes or instantiating new possibilities? Starting with questions like these—and then examining situated discourses for the answers—would make our work less parochial, requiring scholars from across the academy to deal with our ideas, ideas rooted in data but ideas that go beyond those data as well.

However we study rhetorical effect, I doubt we will find, as did George Edwards, that presidential discourse falls on deaf ears. We may find that it falls on slow ears, for it often takes time for a president's remarks to insinuate themselves into the national mainstream. Presidential rhetoric probably falls on busy ears as well, for it is only one of many inputs the average American deals with each day. Presidential discourse also falls on elite ears as it courses through a social network superintended by the mass media and a gaggle of opinion leaders. A modern society like ours is filled with slow ears, busy ears, and elite ears, but a good deal of listening still gets done. I allege this to be true, but it is up to rhetorical critics–and their colleagues in the social sciences—to see if it is true in fact. But this surely seems true: critics will operate at their own peril if they ignore the questions George Edwards asked them some time ago and renewed more recently.

Notes

1. George C. Edwards III, *On Deaf Ears: The Limits of the Bully Pulpit* (New Haven: Yale University Press, 2003).

2. Edwards, *On Deaf Ears*, 105.

3. An earlier version of this tale was told by me during an informal convocation of scholars that lead to the publication of L. Bennett and R. Entman (eds.), *Mediated Politics and the Future of Democracy* (New York: Cambridge University Press, 2001). The story has not appeared in print before.

4. Lisbeth Lipari, "Voice, Polling, and the Public Sphere," in R. P. Hart and B. Sparrow (eds.), *Politics, Discourse, and American Society: New Agendas* (Boulder: Rowman and Littlefield, 2001), pp. 129–150. Susan Herbst, *Numbered Voices: How Opinion Polling Has Shaped American Politics* (Chicago: University of Chicago Press, 1995).

5. John R. Zaller, *The Nature and Origins of Mass Opinion* (New York: Cambridge University Press, 1992).

6. David Zarefsky, "Presidential Rhetoric and the Power of Definition," paper presented at the Conference on Researching the Public Presidency, Texas A&M University, February 28, 2004.

7. For more on the rhetoric of definition see Zarefsky, "Presidential Rhetoric."

8. If nothing else, I have been persistent in making this argument. See "Doing Criticism My Way: A Reply to Darsey," *Western Journal of Communication* 58 (1994): 308–12; "Wandering with Rhetorical Criticism," in *Critical Questions: Invention, Creativity, and the Criticism of Discourse and the Media*, ed. W. Nothstine, C. Blair, and G. Copeland (New York: St. Martins, 1994), 71–81; "Contemporary Scholarship in Public Address: A Research Editorial," *Western Journal of Communication* 50 (1986): 283–95; and "Theory-Building and Rhetorical Criticism," *Communication Studies* 27 (1976): 70–77.

PART 2
Task Force Reports

CHAPTER 11

REPORT OF THE NATIONAL TASK FORCE ON THE PRESIDENCY AND DELIBERATIVE DEMOCRACY

Chair: Vanessa B. Beasley, Southern Methodist University
Robert Asen, University of Wisconsin, Madison
Diane M. Blair, California State University, Fresno
Stephen J. Hartnett, University of Illinois, Champaign-Urbana
Karla K. Leeper, Baylor University
Jennifer R. Mercieca, Texas A&M University, College Station

The idea of deliberation looms large in the American imaginary. On one hand, it is impossible to consider U.S. history without also imagining lively public conversations, debates, protests, and demonstrations. In such imaginings, America's charter was born from the Founders' deliberations, with subsequent events such as the Lincoln-Douglas debates, civil rights rallies, and war protests attesting to that charter's tolerance for public rhetoric and dialogue. On the other hand, there have also been times when these same types of exchanges have been feared by both the American people and their leaders. Centuries after Plato's warnings that democracy and its tool of rhetoric would surely bring ruin to ancient Greece, the

Founders were similarly concerned about how to mitigate popular will in the United States. This concern has endured into the twenty-first century. As Robert Ivie has noted, "prevailing American political culture teaches Americans to elect their betters, preferably indirectly, to represent and deliberate for them."[1]

Given the ongoing tension between nostalgia and anxiety about democratic deliberation in the United States, one might wonder how the presidency figures into the mix. Have U.S. presidents encouraged democratic deliberation, for example? Are they supposed to be responsive to it? If so, how? When? And why? In this report we investigate the past relationships between the presidency and democratic deliberation in the United States by offering an overview of four "snapshots" of specific historic periods in the development of the institution of the U.S. presidency: the Founding, the antebellum period, the budding rhetorical presidency, and the mature rhetorical presidency. As we examine each of these periods, we ask if practices of democratic deliberation have changed as the U.S. presidency has changed, or vice versa.

In attending to history, we also hope to shed light on some larger conceptual and normative issues, and at the end of this report, our recommendations link some of our findings to these sorts of concerns. At this point, however, it is worth mentioning that at least five clusters of questions recurred throughout our discussions: (1) *Ontology*—what is democratic deliberation? (2) *Worth*—what is the value of democratic deliberation? (3) *Accountability*—who is the audience for democratic deliberation, and should that audience be responsible for attending or responding to it? (4) *Agency*—who participates and under what conditions? And (5) *Distribution*—who distributes, monitors, and/or facilitates deliberative practices? Although each of us does not answer all of these questions in the same way, we begin by offering the broad definition of democratic deliberation used in this report.

A useful stipulative definition of deliberative democracy, written by Joshua Cohen, is "an association whose affairs are governed by the public deliberation of its members."[2] Likewise, drawing from the work of both John Dryzek and Darrin Hicks, we imagined that such an association would derive its political legitimacy from participants' "capacity to underwrite or destabilize collective outcomes."[3] Thus, although a wide range of discursive activities could fit under the rubric of deliberation, we took the concept of *democratic deliberation* to have at its core any communicative practices conducted by citizens in order to influence elite decision making, particularly with regard to public policy. Although most of us agreed that such an idealized form of a more or less direct democracy does not exist today, we presumed that democratic deliberation, with its assumed public exchange of ideas, is in itself an inherent good.

At this point we should also acknowledge that some of the larger questions we asked about the relationship between the presidency and democratic deliberation are not new. Scholarship on democratic deliberation has thrived within the past few decades, with at least two strains of this work directly implicating the executive office in general and presidential rhetoric in particular. First, much of the recent interest in democratic deliberation can be explicitly linked to the twentieth-century "rhetorical presidency" bemoaned by political scientists. For these scholars as well as other contemporary liberal theorists, the "rise of the rhetorical presidency" has been troubling, particularly to the extent that it may cause politicians to seek popularity rather than to pursue more noble forms of statecraft. To strengthen democratic politics in the face of such developments, some of these thinkers have tried to "reconcile democracy and deliberation" through organized exercises such as James Fishkin's deliberative opinion polls, in which citizens are formally invited to assemble and discuss political questions.[4]

In the second case, the link to presidential rhetoric has been far less explicit and yet increasingly important. Numerous legal scholars and political philosophers have written about deliberative democracy within the context of democratic legitimacy. Indeed, this is the context for the Cohen definition mentioned ("an association whose affairs are governed by the public deliberation of its members"), and although Cohen published this definition in 1997, its relevance to both the presidency and presidential rhetoric has become more obvious in recent years.[5] Through events ranging from the Supreme Court's deciding ruling in the 2000 presidential election to the more recent concerns about George W. Bush's public justifications for sending troops to Afghanistan in 2001 and Iraq in 2003, the American people have been increasingly concerned with questions of political legitimacy and the impact of public opinion on political decision making.

In sum, there has been no shortage of recent theoretical, philosophical, and normative frameworks to inform the thinking of our task force. What has been missing, however, was an accounting of the historic relationship between the presidency and democratic deliberation. In the four sections that follow, we have compiled a broad historical overview that emphasizes the ways in which the presidency has functioned vis-à-vis democratic deliberation at specific times in its institutional development. To our minds, the record shows that this relationship has been uneasy, awkward, and at times even contradictory. In fact, if we go back to the nation's founding, we can see that perhaps the presidency and democratic deliberation were never intended to have a relationship at all.

THE FOUNDING AND EARLY REPUBLIC, CIRCA 1787–1828

At the nation's founding *democracy* was a word that connoted chaos, turbulence, and leveling of the social hierarchy—a word that sent shudders of fear through America's elite. As James Madison argued in *Federalist* 10, the proposed constitution was specifically not a democracy but was rather a republic. According to Madison, a republican form of government would provide the most protection from the threat of a faction, which was said to result whenever what we would now call democratic deliberation, conceived as citizens assembled to administer their government, took place. Thus, if the United States Constitution was designed as a republic specifically to temper the threat of democracy, then the government as proposed and adopted was specifically meant to *prevent* actual democratic deliberation. But then how did the Founders envision that the people would participate in the political process?

The Constitution is silent on democratic deliberation and on suffrage. Yet the Constitutional Convention did order each state to hold ratifying conventions so that the people could decide for themselves if the proposed republic was the best form of government. The convention delegates understood that if the Union was going to replace the Confederacy, then the people had to deliberate and agree to support the new government. In short, the Founders believed that democratic deliberation was required to grant the new Union legitimacy. The founding of the United States thus highlights some of the ambiguities of democratic deliberation. Is democratic deliberation required to confer legitimacy on political decisions? In a republic in which the people rule through a representative, what is the proper role of democratic deliberation in the representative's decision making? Even more specifically, what role, if any, was democratic deliberation supposed to have in the president's decision-making process?

Article II, section 3, of the Constitution requires that the president "shall from time to time give to the Congress Information of the State of the Union, and recommend to their Consideration such Measures as he shall judge necessary and expedient," but this requires only that the president give "information" and "recommend" policies to Congress—not to the people—and the Constitution does not explicitly grant Congress the right to respond (although by custom it has). The Constitutional Convention delegates meant for the lower branch of Congress to be the site of democratic deliberation, thus the House of Representatives was granted the powers to originate laws, levy taxes, conduct war, and control the budget in the name of the people. In early congressional practices the House was accessible to the average citizen; petitions were read on an almost daily basis from citizens throughout the new nation on such questions as owed Revolutionary War debts, land grants, memorials, and public support for the infirm and poor. By 1836, however, increased controversy over slavery resulted in the Gag Rule, which attempted to save the Union by tabling all petitions without entering them into the public record, and thus greatly limited the average citizen's ability to enter directly into the congressional debates.

All of this seems to point to the fact that the Founders created a nation that accorded a small role, if any, to the influence of democratic deliberation over the government. Nevertheless, does that mean that nonpoliticians did not exercise any influence over the government or its representatives? The simple answer is no. The people *did* influence the government's decisions. Newspapers and private letters served as the main method of conveying information between people and places, and along with the town meeting, newspapers functioned as a deliberative space for some citizens to debate local and sometimes national policy decisions. Politicians paid very close attention to these debates; the private letters of political elites from 1787 to 1828 were constantly focused on how "the public will" regarded governmental action. Yet partisan presses dominated the American public sphere in an effort to control how newspapers portrayed elites and governmental action and, thus, in an effort to influence public perceptions. Every president from George Washington to John Quincy Adams attended to, or in some cases obsessed over, the public's perception of his presidency. But presidential concern over perceived republican honor is not true dialogue between the president of the United States and the *demos*.

The question of the presidency and democratic deliberation during the early national period is thus virtually unanswerable. If we are to define democratic deliberation as James Madison did, as citizens "assembl[ing] and administer[ing] the government in person," and then we look for the role of democratic deliberation in the Constitution, we find nothing to indicate that it was institutionally encouraged—except for Ratification. When we examine the limited space for entering public debates in the House of Representatives, we find that democratic deliberation was easily sacrificed to the stability of the Union with the Gag Rule. When we hunt for democratic deliberation in the town meetings, newspapers, and letters of the period, we find that while there may have been robust deliberation in some spheres of public life, these debates affected the president only in the most minimal of ways. Still, there were citizens who spoke, wrote, assembled, and in other ways entered into public dialogue with other citizens and elected officials. In some ways we find democratic deliberation despite the best efforts of the government to prevent it; in other instances we find democratic deliberation to be deliberation for deliberation's sake alone, without the power to "administer" the government—deliberation for legitimacy without the institutional power to effect a single policy in a single sphere of the national government. If we could ask the Founders what they thought of the role of the president in democratic deliberation, they would likely think the question to be very odd and even incompatible with their republican form of government.

The Presidency in Antebellum America, circa 1828–61

During this period, the presidency played a paradoxical—one might even say contradictory—role vis-à-vis the practice of democratic deliberation. On one hand, the presidency was crucially important, even central and generative, to many of the public debates, arguments, songs, poems, and other forms of public commentary and deliberation that rendered the antebellum period a veritable laboratory of democratic deliberation. On the other hand, the presidency was equally responsible for fostering policies that squashed the practice of democratic deliberation, sometimes going so far as to invoke powers that were dictatorial rather than democratic and often functioning in modes more unilateral then deliberative. Moreover, summarizing the relationships and mutual impacts between the presidency and democratic deliberation is a slippery proposition because throughout this period the nature of the presidency was in constant change, as were the various practices that one might choose to label democratic deliberation. Nonetheless, following are some cursory observations, focusing on exemplary moments that may function synecdochically, as representative parts that illustrate some of the complexities of the period as a whole.[6]

It is important to begin by foreswearing any nostalgia for some supposedly unsullied past. Much like contemporary America, antebellum America was a cacophonous circus of competing genres of communication, some of them enchantingly eloquent and noble but most of them either hilariously comic or embarrassingly crude. The presidency was therefore the subject of both veneration and disgust, as it functioned as a catch-all *topos* across which just about any political agenda could be written, either in the form of support for or critique of the president, either celebration of the nation in general or mockery of its overstuffed politicians in particular. It was not the president's task to engage in democratic deliberation so much as to trigger its practice by others; presidents were not expected to speak with the people so much as to them, at them, and for them. The people spoke back in volumes, but these responses were rendered not as part of a dialogue between leader and the led so much as between local advocates and critics of the president's words.[7]

For example, consider the antebellum State of the Union address. At this time it was standard for the president's address to be read into the congressional record by his secretary or other chosen mediator. The president had no technological means of speaking directly to the people, and speaking before Congress could be a harrowing affair for many presidents, so this mediated delivery system granted the president personal cover while draping his words in a distanced authority. This physical and rhetorical distance conveyed the sense that the president was above the fray of congressional give-and-take, literally an executive power speaking from on high. The address would then be printed widely, triggering waves of rebuttals and retorts, celebrations and salutations. Unlike today, Congress dedicated long sessions considering the particularities of the address. Hence, while the president never spoke his State of the Union address in public, and while it was considered beneath him to make any public comments regarding its reception, his words triggered a massive round of deliberation in local papers, in local taverns, and in Congress. The president thus initiated democratic deliberation without directly engaging in it himself.

Or consider the rhetorical history of the proclamation. The device was used sparingly and generally only in moments of crisis; when the president felt the need to speak directly to the people, he could release a proclamation. Drawing upon age-old traditions of executive—and some argued monarchical—privilege, such presidential proclamations were not invitations to engage in democratic deliberation but authoritarian thunderbolts flung from on high. While historians have come to venerate certain proclamations, such as Lincoln's 1862 Emancipation Proclamation, they have tended to avoid the majority of proclamations because these actions so obviously destroy any sense of what we have come to call democratic deliberation. For example, President Franklin Pierce's February 11, 1856, "Proclamation" was an authoritarian polemic attacking abolitionists and thus sanctioning pro-slavery vigilante violence in Kansas. The Proclamation was widely received as damning evidence that the president had become a proponent of an extremist pro-slavery version of states' rights. Like the State of the Union address, then, proclamations were often less attempts to engage in democratic deliberation than unilateral executive pronouncements that triggered responses, sometimes with dramatic consequences.[8]

The presidency's relationship to democratic deliberation was therefore tenuous at best during this period; rather than acting as a special participant in a national dialogue, the president was both an instigator and a squasher, a promoter and a censor—but in both cases he served from a distance, he ruled from a distance, and he spoke from a distance, less a representative of the people's will than a puppeteer arranging discourse from afar. This is not a critique of democratic deliberation per se, which we have already noted flourished during the antebellum period; rather, it is a cautionary reminder that democratic deliberation and the presidency circulated in different realms of power—the former serving as a necessary balm to the masses, the latter serving at the behest of elites.

The Increasingly Rhetorical Presidency, circa 1865–1920

The period of 1865 to 1920 was one of incredible transition in the nation as well as in the role of the presidency with respect to democratic deliberation. Even if the late nineteenth century and early twentieth can be regarded as the beginnings of the rhetorical presidency, for most of this period, the president did not talk to or with the people but instead tried to influence his own party, the media, and Congress.

At the beginning of this period, the presidency's position relative to Congress was weakened by several factors, including Lincoln's assassination, the struggle over Reconstruction, and the reconstitution of the Union. Many in government subscribed to a constitutional philosophy that an executive that was too strong bordered on tyranny, and a few observers even pointed to Lincoln's actions during the Civil War as evidence. Such weakness meant that the presidency did not participate significantly in public debate from the Johnson Administration through the second Cleveland Administration in 1896. The exception proves the norm: when Andrew Johnson broke with this tradition during his "Swing around the Circle" tour in 1866, his attempt to take his case for his legislative agenda to the public was received poorly. He was accused of hurting the dignity of the office of the president, and his opponents won huge gains in the congressional election of 1866.

Even if presidents did not participate in public debates, they did try to influence the deliberations of their party's elites. During this era, political parties were believed to be the primary vehicle by which the public could influence the legislative agenda. Parties were viewed as a buffer between the executive and legislative branches and the whims of an uninformed and inexperienced public.[9] One primary means by which the president repaid his debt to the party was through the exercise of appointment power. Politicization of the civil service was the source of a tremendous amount of corruption in government, and highly publicized scandals created a sense that representative government was in trouble.

This sense, along with the corruption itself, was brought to public attention by the burgeoning print media of the time. Before and immediately after the Civil War, the press was highly partisan, but soon newspapers took on a more independent existence as better printing methods were developed and readership and advertising grew. In a battle for circulation, yellow journalism rose to prominence. Searching for a new story, the press focused on the partisan battles in Congress and some colorful characters in the White House for inspiration.

The administration of William McKinley was the first actively to attempt to use press coverage of events to its advantage; therefore we might say that the McKinley Administration was the first to use the media specifically to impact democratic deliberation. McKinley met with correspondents personally and worked to cultivate their goodwill, anticipated and shaped press coverage of the president's position on issues with announcements timed to influence the agenda, and established a procedure for press coverage within the building that housed the president.[10] His successors institutionalized and expanded this relationship. Woodrow Wilson believed that the press should be used to educate the public on what its government was doing and that the public would be capable of sorting out the good policies from the bad ones, the responsible officials from the demagogues.[11] When the press could not get the job done, the presidency began to develop its own public relations arm, the Committee on Public Information. The office of the presidency was changing to encourage a more direct connection between the president and the public in an effort to go over the heads of Congress.

Finally, the way in which the presidents addressed Congress changed. The veto was widely used during this period as a way to publicize an issue on which the president differed from Congress. While the veto may not have been a speech, the exercise of one of the most significant presidential powers drew enormous attention from the news-hungry press. The veto allowed the president to participate in congressional debate over legislation and to signal his position to the public. Apart from the veto, presidents used other public messages to engage Congress. Taft was the first president to provide a specific list of legislative objectives to the Congress, for example, and Woodrow Wilson called a special session of Congress to present his State of the Union message in person. As these examples illustrate, the presidency was discovering its ability to engage in legislative debate and to find ways to speak directly to both Congress and, later, the public.

THE MATURE RHETORICAL PRESIDENCY, CIRCA 1920–2004

Many scholars agree that Wilson's presidency marked a significant turning point indeed. Jeffrey Tulis writes that for all of Wilson's successors, "popular or mass rhetoric has become a principal tool of presidential governance," as presidents routinely "'go over the heads' of Congress to the people in support of legislation and other initiatives."[12] For Tulis, Samuel Kernell, and others, this move of "going public" is especially problematic because "the doctrine that a president ought to be a popular leader has become an unquestioned premise of our political culture."[13] While this shift can be viewed as having many implications, our task force wondered if one of the main consequences has been an expectation related to this presumed popularity and its importance for deliberative democracy.

Simply put, if it is true that rhetorical presidents speak directly to the people, is it also true that they listen to the people? In one sense, the answer is clearly affirmative, as there can be little doubt about the growing use of public opinion data within executive decision making throughout the twentieth century. Yet there are plenty of other ways that the American people have made their wishes, demands, and concerns known, and many of these would be considered deliberative activities, such as organized debates, forums, speeches, and even protests and demonstrations. In fact, if we define deliberation broadly, there has been so much of it throughout the twentieth century that in this report we have space to focus on only three issue trajectories as examples: women's rights, poverty, and race. With the growing influence of mass media, deliberation surrounding these issues certainly became more public and more democratic, at least in the sense of inclusiveness and distribution, as the century progressed. But have rhetorical presidents promoted or reacted to democratic deliberation? Or have they done both? Or neither?

Women's Rights as an Issue Trajectory

Measured purely in terms of public policy furthering women's rights, the track record of most twentieth-century U.S. presidents is less than inspiring, as most either ignored the issue entirely or sought to avoid it whenever possible. In many cases, it was first ladies who participated in and facilitated public deliberation on women's rights.

It was not until the twentieth century that women's rights become a presidential issue. When Woodrow Wilson was inaugurated in 1913, the tenacious

Alice Paul began a suffrage campaign that included picketing the White House. Paul's use of public protest, including hunger strikes and force feeding, and her arrest (along with arrests of hundreds of other women) were contributing factors in Wilson's decision to support the federal woman's suffrage amendment. In this case, then, democratic deliberation may have influenced presidential decision making.

Yet this type of influence would not be as obvious in the public policy of several of Wilson's successors. Within Franklin Roosevelt's administration, women were appointed to high office and cabinet positions in unprecedented numbers, but his presidential policies were a mixed bag for women. Women's rights advocates did have a loyal friend in the White House, as First Lady Eleanor Roosevelt frequently used her press conferences as a platform for herself and other female political leaders. But it would not be until John F. Kennedy's administration that women's rights issues were given a prominent place in a presidential policy agenda with the establishment of the President's Commission on the Status of Women in 1961, with former first lady Eleanor Roosevelt as its head. As a result of the commission's investigation, Kennedy signed into law the Equal Pay Act before his assassination in 1963.

Kennedy's successor Lyndon B. Johnson appointed women to seventy-five executive positions in his administration, a new record. He also repeatedly used the bully pulpit to argue that women were a national resource that should be utilized. With the Nixon Administration, women's rights were once again relegated to the back burner in his policies as well as in his public rhetoric. Nixon made no effort to continue Johnson's policy of recruiting women into high government positions, and he also refused to consider well-qualified women when he had the opportunity to replace two Supreme Court justices in 1971. Similarly, Gerald Ford's presidency approached women's rights and the women's liberation movement as a nonissue. It was First Lady Betty Ford who would take up the topic of women's rights during her husband's presidency. Betty Ford appeared publicly with campaign buttons that read "Ratify ERA in 1975," and she lobbied both publicly and privately on behalf of the controversial amendment.

As these examples indicate, within the mid-twentieth century at least, it has often been first ladies and not presidents who have promoted public deliberation on women's rights. First ladies have also used their positions to bring other social issues into the public spotlight. For example, Ellen Wilson's public advocacy as first lady brought attention to the need for housing reform measures, and she actively lobbied on behalf of the Slum Clearance Bill, also known as the "Mrs. Wilson bill." Eleanor Roosevelt's advocacy went far beyond her husband's public agenda, especially in the case of civil rights for black Americans. While her husband avoided making public statements on the issues of a federal antilynching law and the elimination of the poll tax, Eleanor Roosevelt spoke out often on behalf of civil rights. Likewise, in addition to their advocacy on behalf of the ERA, both Betty Ford and Roslyn Carter gave voice to important issues of public health: Ford spoke out about breast cancer, and Carter spoke out about mental health. Stating that her explicit goal was to promote public awareness and discussion, Carter lobbied heavily for the passage of the Mental Health Systems Act of 1980. Hillary Rodham Clinton took deliberation on matters of public health one step further as the appointed chair of the President's Task Force on Health Care Reform. More recently, Laura Bush has testified before the Senate Committee on Health, Education, Labor and Pensions arguing that "educational" concerns represent a "significant public health problem."

If it were not for the first ladies of the twentieth century, presidential rhetoric on the issue of women's rights would be scarce indeed. In a sense, then, presidential rhetoric itself cannot be viewed as promoting democratic deliberation on this issue, as many recent chief executives have seemed content either to avoid or to ignore the issue themselves. Instead, they have chosen to delegate—or perhaps relegate—public discussions of the issue to their presidential partners, many of whom have also used their position to increase awareness and thus potentially promote democratic deliberation of other social issues as well.

Poverty as an Issue Trajectory

Overall, both presidential and public attention to poverty as a matter of national interest increased during the twentieth century. Prior to this period, poverty had been viewed as a local matter best handled by individual communities. Yet the economic dislocations of the Great Depression and the rapid nationalization of the economy confounded local approaches to poor relief. In terms of presidential discourse, the word *poverty* appeared in presidential inaugurals and annual messages to Congress only seventeen times between 1789 and 1932. Since 1933, presidents have uttered the word ninety-five times in these two speech genres.[14] It is difficult to determine, in a general sense, whether presidents responded to heightened public concern, whether presidential attention spurred public concern, or whether presidential and public concern were mutually informative. It does seem safe to say, however, that neither presidents nor publics could ignore the socioeconomic events of the mid-twentieth century. Moreover, once the issue of poverty entered the national agenda, it stayed there in various guises and at different levels of attention through good economic times and bad.[15]

When considering the issue of poverty as a topic for both democratic deliberation and the presidency, one lesson to be learned is how presidents provide problem-solving frames for topics of public deliberation. In Franklin Delano Roosevelt's first Fireside Chat of 1935, for example, while addressing a nation still ravaged by the Great Depression, the president insisted that solutions to pressing social and economic problems lay in the initiatives of federal, state, and local governments. He explained that "long experience in government has taught me that the exceptional instances of wrong-doing in Government are probably less numerous than in almost every other line of endeavor."[16] For FDR and many of his contemporaries, competency, efficiency, and integrity were attributes of public institutions. Private enterprises, in contrast, raised concerns about rapacity, corruption, and bias. Yet this frame was subject to change over time. By 1981, when self-avowed FDR supporter Ronald Reagan delivered his Inaugural Address as the fortieth president of the United States, he completely reversed FDR's value hierarchy. President Reagan also addressed a country facing economic troubles, albeit not as severe as those of the Great Depression. For Reagan, the solutions to these problems lay outside government. He insisted that "government is not the solution to our problem; government is the problem."[17] Competency, efficiency, and integrity resided in private enterprise. Of course, many important and complex events occurred between 1935 and 1981, so it would be a dramatic oversimplification to say that the path from FDR to Reagan on poverty was direct and unmediated. Yet comparing their statements does demonstrate that presidents seek to frame matters of democratic deliberation.

A second lesson to be gleaned from discussions of poverty suggests that presidents may attempt to define problems themselves. In 1969, after his predecessor sought to wage war on poverty, Richard Nixon called for a new approach to federal social policy. Yet this approach did not take as settled the problems identified by the Johnson Administration. President Nixon presented an alternative set of problems for his administration to address. Here, too, a president addressed the nation in times of perceived crisis. A centralization of social policy in the nation's capital had engendered "a crisis of confidence in the capacity of government to do its job."[18] The failures of government policies had been "tragically apparent" in the government's efforts to help the poor. Nixon judged the nation's welfare system a "colossal failure": "its effect is to draw people off payrolls and onto welfare rolls—just the opposite of what government should be doing."[19] Yet this was not only a call to redirect the locus and aims of federal social welfare policy; it was also an identification of a different social problem: welfare, not poverty. Too many people received public assistance, so he sought to reduce the number of public assistance recipients. Exhibiting both problem-identification and problem-solving functions, Bill Clinton ratified the moves of Nixon and Reagan in supporting legislation in 1996 that repealed Title IV of the 1935 Social Security Act: the Aid to Dependent Children program. In his 1996 State of the Union address, Clinton called for a new approach to governance by acknowledging that "we know big government does not have all the answers. We know there's not a program for every problem. . . . The era of big government is over."[20] In this situation, perhaps the president was affirming prevailing sentiments expressed by citizens in democratic deliberation.

Race Relations as an Issue Trajectory

The topic of race relations has clearly been at the forefront of national politics in the United States throughout much of the twentieth century. However, to discuss this topic vis-à-vis the relationship between the executive office and democratic deliberation, we might also ask not what certain presidents have said about race but rather if and how they have attended to public deliberation on race. On this latter set of questions, the historical record is not necessarily impressive. In short, U.S. presidents typically did not encourage public deliberation on race in the twentieth century. To be sure, at times they stimulated it by their actions or, more often, by their inaction. Yet instead of proactively initiating deliberation on racial matters, twentieth-century presidents—with one notable exception—were more likely to adopt one or both of two primary modes: monitoring and/or reacting to public deliberation.

First, the majority of twentieth-century presidents tried to constrain the ways in which the public could talk about race by monitoring and censuring blacks and other supporters of civil rights—a practice that goes at least as far back as Teddy Roosevelt. During his 1900 campaign for the vice presidency, for example, Roosevelt defended himself against charges of racism by noting that his children "sat in the same school with colored children" and that he allowed black men to "eat at my table and sleep in my house."[21] Yet the fact that Roosevelt was charged with racism is perhaps more important than his response, as it demonstrates that racism was part of the public discourse surrounding the twentieth century's first presidential election.

No matter what Roosevelt said in public to defend himself as a candidate, once he was elected, he became the first of a long line of twentieth-century presidents who used the relative privacy of the executive office to sanction the organized surveillance and punishment of "those who promoted visions of racial justice too greatly exceeding the established conventions of the day," according to Russell Riley.[22] In this sense, Roosevelt thus initiated the systematic limitation of which voices and what arguments could become part of public discourse on race. Even though critics in Congress complained that Roosevelt was developing a "Federal secret police," there was little they could do to stop the FBI in particular from the "surveillance and harassment of political agitators in the private sector, including black Americans."[23]

By 1919, Riley reports, J. Edgar Hoover had already "defined political movements within the black community as a permanent field of investigation for his Radical Division."[24] The Wilson Administration was especially concerned with the "Black radicalism" associated with Marcus Garvey.[25] Under the Hoover Administration, the FBI was encouraged to increase its surveillance of the NAACP.[26] During the Truman and Eisenhower administrations, popular black entertainers including Louis Armstrong, Josephine Baker, and Paul Robeson were the subjects of FBI investigations as well as intense public criticism from the State Department for their very public criticisms of racial politics in the United States.[27] And while the Kennedy Administration courted the favor of Martin Luther King Jr. and his supporters, its support for J. Edgar Hoover's widespread investigations of MLK was thinly veiled.[28] Throughout the first half of the twentieth century, even as black Americans were slowly gaining demographic and political power, they were increasingly on the radar of various presidents and their administrations, which clearly worried about the influence of such voices on public sentiment.

Despite these executive efforts at surveillance and control, activist voices could not be silenced, and presidents increasingly went into a second mode: reacting. Historians of the civil rights movement routinely bemoan the absence of presidential leadership on racial matters until the Johnson Administration, and even he and his successors have been criticized for not being proactive enough.[29] If presidents have appeared to be largely reactive to racial matters, however, perhaps this collective stance reflects the conflicted and even fearful nature of their constituents regarding racial politics.

For example, today many view Lyndon Johnson's 1965 pledge that "We Shall Overcome" as a triumphant example of socially progressive rhetoric that prompted equally progressive public deliberation on race, as it surely did. But we should also remember that it took a bloody Sunday in Selma, and the resulting outrage of white voters, for Johnson to utter those words. Garth Pauley suggests that it also took some calculated political reassurance, as "active public support" for such policies did not "mature" until after Selma.[30] From the standpoint of democratic deliberation on race, the pressing question is whether great moments in presidential rhetoric on this topic can occur on their own, without needing to be prompted by racial violence or any other type or crisis. As Pauley has noted, "it seems uncertain whether civil rights has yet become part of normal politics or normal political discourse."[31] Even Bill Clinton's Initiative on Race and Reconciliation, introduced in 1997 to promote public deliberation on racial matters, seemed to beg the question: would—indeed, could—the American people have a "conversation" about race? To most observers, Clinton's initiative was not successful. Yet perhaps this perceived failure itself provides yet another lesson about the relationship between the rhetorical presidency and democratic deliberation: presidents cannot simply command the public to deliberate.

Summary

Taken together, the historic moments we have revisited here provide an interesting way of tracing the relationship between the U.S. presidency and democratic deliberation. In the nation's earliest years, the federal government in general was designed to minimize the impact of public deliberation and, in some cases, even prevent it. From about 1828 to 1861, we see a slight change, as presidents try to both trigger and suppress such activity. After the Civil War, the weakened presidency becomes almost irrelevant to democratic deliberation (and vice versa) even as the burgeoning media increasingly provide a new context for both types of discourse to thrive. As the century closes and the groundwork is being laid for the rhetorical presidency, we see the beginnings of a strengthened and more public executive office. Yet even if the twentieth century brought more opportunities for mediated forms of deliberation and the exchange of ideas, we see the presidency reacting with both ambivalence and savvy. Presidents largely ignore women's issues and/or let their wives promote these within the public sphere; they actively frame and define issues related to poverty so as to impose certain meanings or parameters on deliberation; and they both monitor and react to deliberation surrounding race.

Overall, then, it would seem that a rhetorical presidency is not necessarily the same thing as a responsive presidency. In fact, with regard to its view of democratic deliberation, the contemporary presidency may not have come all that far from the nation's earliest days. Consider this 1803 quote from New Hampshire Senator William Plumer:

Consistency, is not, I know a trait in democracy! When it suits there [*sic*]
purpose—when unanswerable arguments are opposed to democrats,
then our ears are stunned with the *people*, the *sovereign people*
demand it—the *public* will is in its favor—& we must bow submissive.
But these same men, when they pursue measures to which they conceive the
public mind is opposed, then tell us, that the people are *uninformed*—they are
a *rabble incapable of judging*—& good legislators will not consult them.[32]

What Plumer knew, and what much of our research reveals, is that U.S. politicians have tended to discount the public's deliberation when it went against their own policy choices. With that conclusion in mind, perhaps there are ways in which scholars can improve the situation. Even if we grant that an idealized model of deliberative democracy is impossible, there may be ways to educate citizens about the merits of deliberation and its potential impact on public policy. Likewise, we may also be able to draw attention to the emerging constraints, both institutional and political, which keep chief executives from being as responsive to public deliberation.

Recommendations

1. Scholars need to monitor the relationship (or lack thereof) between democratic deliberation and political institutions. There can be no democratic deliberation without a more worthy mass media, one more critical of executive branch decisions. Given that the media cannot police itself, we need a watchdog group committed to holding both the executive branch and the corporate media accountable, and communication scholars could be at the forefront of this effort. This type of involvement has the added advantage of not calling on others to change their behavior but of calling on us to be more active citizens. Part of the problem is that we, as public intellectuals, are not involved enough in the key decisions of our times. We need, then, to become National Public Radio commentators, newspaper editorial writers, and so on

for our local areas, so that what we do in the academy also provides the public with a higher level of discourse.

2. Scholars need to write more longitudinal accounts of the historic relationship between deliberative practices and the presidency. As we have demonstrated in this report, there has not always been a clear channel of deliberative opportunity and/or exchange between "the people" and their presidents. Indeed, for some of our task force members, this omission is so glaring as to bring the concept of democratic deliberation itself into question, with the suggestion that the record implies something more akin to republican deliberation only. In order to revisit such questions about the nature and health of democracy in the nation's past as well as its future, scholars need to continue to build a critical-historical record that can identify problems and patterns and thus help create a heuristic.

3. Scholars need to continue to expand our research in order to include influential voices that are both linked to and distinct from the presidency. First ladies, for example, are clearly part of presidential administrations, but at the same time they are frequently operating at the margins of presidential politics. In some cases, speaking from the margins may provide more opportunities for facilitating public deliberation. As Shawn Parry-Giles and Diane Blair note in their article on the rise of the rhetorical first lady, "certain first ladies facilitated the transformation of women's issues into national issues, evidencing the rhetorical power of the post and the public visibility of first ladies on important deliberative matters."[33] What other voices act as surrogates for the president? When and why are these surrogates deployed?

4. Scholars need to reconsider our assumptions about the rhetorical presidency. The presidency unquestionably has rhetorical power. However, that rhetorical power is not without limits: it is possible for the executive branch to squander its power or to have this usurped by another branch of government or the media. The influence of new technology on democratic practice, demographically driven changes in electoral politics, and increasing legislative incursions on presidential power are all developments that should encourage scholars and executives to rethink our old assumptions about the rhetorical presidency and, more specifically, whether being "rhetorical" means being in dialogue with constituents. Presidents and citizens who seek such an exchange may have to fight harder for a role in deliberative democracy, finding new ways to craft, influence, and respond to public argumentation.

5. Scholars need to remember also that the practice of democracy is greater than any one political institution. Given our task force's charge, we have focused our discussion on the relationships between political institutions, particularly the presidency, and public deliberation. This focus has also informed our recommendations. We wish to end our report, however, by pointing to the potential value of a distinction implied in the phrase "the presidency and democratic deliberation," namely, a distinction between the institutions of government and the practice of democracy. We believe that government and democracy cannot be equated; the practice of democracy exceeds any particular political institution. Sustaining a critical distinction between democracy and government thus offers heuristic value. In this spirit, John Dewey once wrote that "the heart and final guarantee of democracy is in free gatherings of neighbors on the street corner to discuss back and forth what is read in the uncensored news of the day, and in gatherings of friends in the living rooms of houses and apartments to converse freely with one another."[34] Indeed, however much the presidency may encourage, impede, engender, prevent, augment, or circumscribe democratic deliberation, the latter is not dependent on the former. Democratic deliberation proceeds whether presidents like it or not. As scholars of presidential rhetoric, we would do well to remember the incorrigibility of democratic deliberation.

NOTES

1. Robert L. Ivie, "Rhetorical Deliberation and Democratic Politics in the Here and Now," *Rhetoric & Public Affairs* 5 (2002): 280.

2. Joshua Cohen, "Deliberation and Democratic Legitimacy," in *Deliberative Democracy: Essays on Reason and Politics,* ed. James Bohman and William Rehg (Cambridge: MIT Press, 1997), 67.

3. Darrin Hicks, "The Promise(s) of Deliberative Democracy," *Rhetoric & Public Affairs* 5 (2002): 228.

4. Robert L. Ivie, "Democratic Deliberation in a Rhetorical Republic," paper presented at the 83rd meeting of the National Communication Association, Chicago, Illinois, November 22, 1997.

5. Joshua Cohen, "Deliberation and Democratic Legitimacy," 67.

6. On the ways democratic deliberation was changed in this period by women's petitions, see Susan Zaeske, *Signatures of Citizenship: Petitioning, Antislavery, and Women's Political Identity* (Chapel Hill: University of North Carolina Press, 2003); regarding both pro- and antislavery movements, arguments about national expansion, and the role of daguerreo-

types in transforming antebellum politics, see Stephen Hartnett, *Democratic Dissent and the Cultural Fictions of Antebellum America* (Champaign: University of Illinois Press, 2002); for examples of how antebellum democratic deliberation has been addressed by rhetorical critics, see Thomas W. Benson, ed., *Rhetoric and Political Culture in Nineteenth-Century America* (East Lansing: Michigan State University Press, 1997).

7. For evidence of these claims see the materials, both prose and visual, in almost any edition of *Harper's*, the *United States Magazine and Democratic Review*, the *National Intelligencer*, the *North American Review*, or any of the nation's other leading journals; for a compendium of the period's newspapers see Winifred Gregory, *American Newspapers, 1821–1936: A Union List of Files Available in the United States and Canada* (New York: Bibliographical Society of America, 1937).

8. Franklin Pierce, "By the President of the United States of America. A Proclamation," February 11, 1856, in *A Compilation of the Messages and Papers of the Presidents, 1789–1908*, vol. 5, ed. James Richardson (Washington, D.C.: Bureau of National Literature and Art, 1909), 390–91; for an extended rhetorical analysis of Pierce's presidency, see Stephen Hartnett, "Franklin Pierce and the Exuberant Hauteur of a Dying Age: A Love Letter to America in Six Tragicomic Movements," in *Before the Rhetorical Presidency*, ed. Martin Medhurst (College Station: Texas A&M University Press, forthcoming).

9. Michael Korzi, "The Seat of Popular Leadership: Parties, Elections, and the Nineteenth-Century Presidency," *Presidential Studies Quarterly* 29 (1999): 351–69.

10. Stephen Ponder, "The President Makes News: William McKinley and the First Presidential Press Corps, 1897–1901," *Presidential Studies Quarterly* 22 (1994): 823–36.

11. Jeffrey Tulis, *The Rhetorical Presidency* (Princeton, N.J.: Princeton University Press, 1987)

12. Tulis, *The Rhetoric Presidency*, 4.

13. Tulis, *The Rhetoric Presidency*, 4.

14. Elvin T. Lim, "Five Trends in Presidential Rhetoric: An Analysis of Rhetoric from George Washington to Bill Clinton," *Presidential Studies Quarterly* 32 (2002): 343.

15. By "stayed there," I mean that poverty remained as a potential agenda item, as public attention to issues of poverty waxed and waned over the second half of the twentieth century. Along these lines, David Zarefsky argues that President Johnson has to arouse public interest in ameliorating poverty in declaring war on poverty. See David Zarefsky, *President Johnson's War on Poverty: Rhetoric and History* (Tuscaloosa: University: University of Alabama Press, 1986). See also Robert Asen, *Visions of Poverty: Welfare Policy and Political Imagination* (East Lansing: Michigan State University Press, 2002).

16. Franklin D. Roosevelt, *The Public Papers and Addresses of Franklin D. Roosevelt: The Court Disapproves*, vol. 4 (New York: Random House, 1938), 137.

17. Ronald Reagan, *Public Papers of the Presidents of the United States: Ronald Reagan, 1981* (Washington, D.C.: Government Printing Office, 1982), 1.

18. Richard M. Nixon, "Address to the Nation on Domestic Programs," in *Public Papers of the Presidents of the United States: Richard M. Nixon, 1969* (Washington, D.C.: Government Printing Office, 1971), 637.

19. Nixon, "Address to the Nation," 639. See also Robert Asen, "Nixon's Welfare Reform: Enacting Historical Contradictions of Poverty Discourses," *Rhetoric & Public Affairs* 4 (2001): 261–79.

20. William J. Clinton, *Public Papers of the Presidents of the United States: William J.*

Clinton, 1996, bk. 1 (Washington, D.C.: Government Printing Office, 1997), 79.

21. Kenneth O'Reilly, *Nixon's Piano: Presidents and Racial Politics from Washington to Clinton* (New York: Free Press, 1995), 66.

22. Russell L. Riley, *The Presidency and the Politics of Racial Inequality* (New York: Columbia University Press, 1999), 130.

23. Riley, *The Presidency and the Politics of Racial Inequality,* 131.

24. Riley, *The Presidency and the Politics of Racial Inequality,* 132.

25. Riley, *The Presidency and the Politics of Racial Inequality,* 132.

26. On Hoover, see Riley, *The Presidency and the Politics of Racial Inequality,* 131–32. On the Kennedy Administration, see Riley, *The Presidency and the Politics of Racial Inequality,* 215.

27. Mary Dudziak, *Cold War Civil Rights: Race and the Image of American Democracy* (Princeton, N.J.: Princeton University Press, 2000), 61–77.

28. Riley, *The Presidency and the Politics of Racial Inequality,* 134.

29. Garth E. Pauley, *The Modern Presidency and Civil Rights* (College Station: Texas A&M University Press, 2001), 5.

30. Pauley, *The Modern Presidency and Civil Rights,* 181.

31. Pauley, *The Modern Presidency and Civil Rights,* 219.

32. *William Plumer's Memorandum of Proceedings in the United States Senate, 1803–1807,* ed. Everett Somerville Brown (New York: Macmillan, 1923), 87.

33. Shawn J. Parry-Giles and Diane Blair, "The Rise of the Rhetorical First Lady: Politics, Gender, and Women's Voices, 1789–2002," *Rhetoric & Public Affairs* 5 (2002): 587.

34. John Dewey, "Creative Democracy: The Task before Us," in *The Later Works, 1925–1953,* vol. 14: *1939–1941,* ed. Jo Ann Boydston (Carbondale: Southern Illinois University Press, 1991), 227.

CHAPTER 12

REPORT OF THE NATIONAL TASK FORCE ON PRESIDENTIAL COMMUNICATION TO CONGRESS

Chair: Mary E. Stuckey, Georgia State University
Michael A. Genovese, Loyola Marymount University
Sharon E. Jarvis, University of Texas at Austin
Craig Allen Smith, North Carolina State University
Craig R. Smith, California State University, Long Beach
Robert Spitzer, State University of New York, Cortland
Susan M. Zaeske, University of Wisconsin, Madison

Public misperception notwithstanding, the president is not the government but is part of a Madisonian system, designed to share power with other branches.[1] As Richard Neustadt noted in 1960, the Constitution created a system not of separated powers but of separate institutions sharing powers.[2] The distribution of partial powers among the several branches of government created the checks and balances of the American system of government.[3]

All relationships—marriages, friendships, and working arrangements—require the negotiation of needs and interests. In the constitutional context of shared powers, presidents have ranged from timid to aggressive in their efforts to have their way despite congressional opposition, and they have met with varied results. Leading successfully in a large system of shared powers requires careful coordination, and coordination entails communication among the various parts. Neustadt observed that in order to govern, presidents must both command (use their formal power) and bargain (use their informal power). Both of these tasks involve persuasion. In order to persuade, presidents use various means of communication.

Lester Seligman and Cary Covington suggest that a candidate mobilizes a winning electoral coalition, transforms it into a governing coalition, and then reconstructs a coalition for reelection while trying to maintain the governing coalition.[4] Importantly, these electoral and governing coalitions entail different people in different roles—the voters of Iowa and New Hampshire, for example, do not figure prominently in most governing coalitions. In addition to Congress, the president's governing coalition includes the executive staff and appointees, interest groups, the bureaucracy, the media, and the "general" public. All of these coalitions are forged through the rhetorical processes of presidential persuasion.

Some of this presidential communication attempts to unite that which the constitutional design separated (State of the Union addresses, judicial and other nominations, vetoes, *amicus curae* briefs); others serve as walls intended to keep those separations intact (executive orders, other administrative communications). Thus, presidential communication to Congress can be understood as either a dialogue or a monologue, as exchange or as a one-way street; it can be understood as talking with, to, at, or around Congress. Reflecting these imperatives, we have divided our discussion of presidential communication with Congress into three parts: presidential attempts to use the mass public as a means of persuading Congress, direct communication from the president to Congress, and presidential attempts to subvert Congress. We conclude with our thoughts concerning the state of the literature in each of these areas.

GOING PUBLIC

Presidents have been advised, as James Pfiffner put it, "to hit the ground running," to move quickly and decisively on a legislative agenda or risk losing potential effectiveness in office.[5] They are told that focus is imperative and are accustomed to having their legislative records critiqued after their first three months in office ("the first one hundred days") and then periodically throughout their term (reviews of executive and legislative box scores in the national press). In a sense, the modern presidency is judged by the amount and types of legislation the chief executive can get "through" Congress. And yet in this media-saturated age, a key way that modern presidents work to get their packages through Congress is by talking "around" them.

The first theme to be explored in this report is how recent presidents have appealed to public support to enhance their legislative successes in Washington, D.C., a practice that has changed the relationship between the executive and legislative branches and has, in the minds of some, made governing more volatile.[6]

The theorists of the rhetorical presidency contend that developing communication technologies, changes in electoral processes, and alterations in the party system helped to change the institution of the presidency, moving it from a constitutionally delimited office to one that depends on public support for success. These theorists do not necessarily argue that presidential persuasion was nonexistent prior to the twentieth century, only that it was rare and inconsistent with the prevailing understanding of the institution—that the contemporary institution *relies* upon mass persuasion in a way that its previous incarnations did not.

This model has not gone unchallenged. Several scholars, for example, have examined the premises of this work, and have decided that the rhetorical presidency—even in its most restricted institutional sense—may not be as new a phenomenon as the model suggests. There is considerable evidence that presidents worked very hard—through institutional means such as public appearances and quasi-institutional means such as the partisan press—to convey specific messages to the people in an attempt to influence important political debates as well as legislation. There is also evidence that such persuasive efforts were an integral part of the office from its earliest inception. There is thus considerable and healthy debate over the extent of presidential persuasion in the historical presidency and over its constitutional and institutional implications.[7]

However useful it may be for understanding the historical presidency, work on the rhetorical presidency has also been important in research that focuses on the contemporary institution. This model is most often paired with Samuel Kernell's work on *Going Public*, which calls attention to presidential persuasion in the contemporary era, particularly with regard to the presidential strategy of appealing to individuals outside the beltway to garner power over those inside it.[8] Two structural elements inherently complicate the strategy of going public in the twenty-first century. The first is that the act of "going over Congress's heads to the people" (as Nixon called it) communicates disrespect to the Congress as a body and to the individual legislators whose support the president needs.

The potential for congressional alienation is great, and it is not often wise to alienate the people with whom one shares power. If it is to be effective, then, a president's public persuasion must be combined with other more personal attempts to reach key legislators, if only to minimize the offensive potential of the public strategy.

The second structural problem with the strategy today is the fragmentation of the national audience as a result of emerging technologies. Although Tulis saw the rhetorical presidency emerging prior to radio, the age of radio and Roosevelt's presidency clearly combined to define a new kind of presidential leadership. It is now inconceivable that any president could command the attention of the entire nation as did FDR. This changing media environment may well produce a less informed general public even as it produces more pressure on Congress, more quickly, from the most vocal and committed and mobilized interests.

There is a healthy debate on the parameters, uses, and definitions of going public as well as on the relevance and strength of their institutional correlates. While the jury may still be out regarding the effects of going public in political science, the conceptual power of the argument holds currency in communication studies, where the emphasis is often on the means individual presidents use to persuade the public and the type of audience(s) constructed by such efforts.

One thing, at least, is clear: as Martin J. Medhurst has pointed out, there is a difference between presidential rhetoric and the rhetorical presidency, but this difference is all too often elided or ignored.[9] At the dawn of the twenty-first century, going public is not a strategy confined to the presidency, and when additional, competing voices enter the communicative arena, the president is likely to choose other options for legislative action.

DIRECT COMMUNICATION

Direct communication to Congress by the president—or more commonly, the president's people—is directly related to the subverting of Congress. That is, presidents frustrated with congressional delay or inaction on their legislative proposals may pursue nonlegislative avenues; they may threaten nonlegislative action to prod legislative action, or they may go ahead and act first in the nonlegislative arena, which may in turn prod Congress to react on its own.[10]

There are many forms of routine communication between the president and Congress. The Congressional Liaison Office handles most of that routine communication. Less frequent is direct communication between the president and Congress, although such communication can be productively studied.[11] In general, direct presidential communication to Congress can be understood as occurring in four main arenas: nominations and appointments, vetoes, the annual State of the Union address and other important policy speeches, and, less routinely, war and impeachment.

Nominations and Appointments

While the Cabinet is the earliest set of nominations and appointments to go from any president to Congress, much of that research concerns the particulars of a given presidency rather than theorizing about the appointments process in general. The vast majority of all nominees are eventually confirmed by the Senate, although there is evidence that a secretary-designate's chances of success can be influenced by the Senate's perceptions of nominees: Mary Ann Borrelli offers evidence that gender and insider versus outsider status matter.[12] James D. King and James W. Riddlesperger tell us that a nominee's perceived conduct relative to the Senate's standard of appropriateness can affect the success of a nomination.[13] According to Nolan McCarthy and Rose Razaghian, divided government may play a role, as some argue the nomination process is lengthened by delays created by sharp ideological disagreements.[14] While Gus Krutz, Richard Fleisher, and Jon Bond find no such relationship, arguing instead that the process is determined by the actions of "entrepreneurs," who can affect the process through the presentation of negative information argued with a clear rationale for defeating the nomination.[15] All of these possibilities are profoundly rhetorical, yet there is no research from communication scholars on this important aspect of national politics.

There is, however, considerable research on the Supreme Court nominations process, most of which focuses on the escalating partisanship and politicization.[16] From the defeats of Abe Fortas and Robert Bork to the contention between George W. Bush and Senate Democrats, the process has become more strident, more rhetorical, and much more political. There is little rhetorical analysis of these battles.[17] Presidential memoirs and biographies by administration personnel provide biased discussions of the nomination process. They often hide important details, embarrassments, and the extent of White House involvement in public relations efforts on behalf of nominees.

A survey of controversial cases and the research surrounding them indicates that White House congressional liaison officials need to be very careful about the candidates selected and the persuasive pressure brought to the scene. The research available yields several major points. First, congressional liaison officers are often supplemented with a media public relations campaign that extends the scope of the conflict to the public. This phenomenon tended to occur in the ideological cases more than in the other controversial types. Second, the personal persuasion of the president has been expanded since the Bork controversy. Every president since Reagan has felt obligated to endorse his nominee publicly. Third, any statements or publications by a nominee may damage the chances of nomination. Fourth, rulings on or participation in socially controversial issues may damage the chances of nomination. While the public may not understand the incorporation doctrine, or care much about the precept of original intent, they do care about abortion, drug use, sexual misconduct, and racism. The controversies surrounding the nominations of Douglas Ginsburg, G. Harrold Carswell, Clarence Thomas, and Robert Bork were expanded to the public because the nominees were perceived to have touched on these social issues. Fifth, the possible "appearance" of ethical impropriety in financial matters can also result in a failed nomination. Sixth, qualifications matter. Finally, sometimes it is the nominee who widens the scope of the controversy to the public. This phenomenon is likely to occur when the nominee seeks to save the nomination by bringing public pressure on senators. Both Hugo Black and Clarence Thomas broke through the screen of senators, handlers, and news media, to appeal directly to the public.

Thus, when a nominee is chosen, the screening process is crucial not only because it can generate arguments in favor of the nominee but because it can discover any potential Achilles' heel. The White House liaison office must then decide how to use the arguments in favor of the nominee. At first, such arguments are directed at the Senate Judiciary Committee, and then to the Senate itself. However, should the nomination run into trouble, the appeals may be expanded beyond Congress proper to the public. The liaison office may also expand the involvement of the administration to the departments in the Justice Department and the political wing of the White House. The same pattern with some modification is true of the opposition. Initially, opposing groups, usually special interest groups, focus their attention and testimony on the senators on the Judiciary Committee. If they are successful, they need not expand the scope of the controversy. However, should they fail, they expand the scope first to the Senate at large and then to the public.

At the president's disposal are several loci of persuasion. These include the White House Congressional Liaison Office and Communication Center, the Justice Department (particularly the Office of Legal Counsel), interest groups, and the party's national political apparatus. All of these can act in concert through various ad hoc groups to provide pressure on the Senate to confirm a nominee. They also do battle with the opposing interest groups and with the opposing party's political apparatus. Because the number of players has grown and because of media focus, the nomination process has become increasingly public. The role the Supreme Court played in the selection of the president in 2000 will undoubtedly up the stakes in the nomination process. Not only does the Supreme Court rule on crucial constitutional issues; it can select the person who will appoint the next members of the court, thus overcoming one of Madison's checks on a monolithic system.

Vetoes

As with other forms of direct presidential communication with Congress, the exercise of the presidential veto power offers a decisive example of the interplay between rhetoric and action. Recent studies by Robert Spitzer, Richard Watson, and Charles Cameron have demonstrated that the veto power is a driving force behind the president's relations with Congress and therefore behind the veto bargaining process that accompanies vetoes and veto threats.[18] Veto dynamics play an even greater role in executive-legislative relations during times of divided government, which have typified executive-legislative relations in the last four decades.

The rhetorical element of veto politics emerges particularly with veto threats, which, recent research demonstrates, has both public and private elements. Richard S. Conley's study of veto threats during the George H. W. Bush presidency found three types of veto threat patterns.[19] The first, private veto threats, were issued consciously outside of public view, and they generally succeeded in killing much minor legislation. A second category of veto threats began privately but later became public, usually through insider reporting, and generally led to compromise between the branches on routine legislative matters. The third category of threats began in the public realm and were focused on high visibility legislation. Of the three categories, presidential success was greatest in the first, private route. The third category of Kernell-style "going public" threats was that most likely to result in actual vetoes and high-stakes confrontation between Congress and the president. Thus, as the rhetorical tools and stakes escalate, so too do the political stakes for both sides; concomitantly, prospects for successful bargaining outcomes recede.

The causal relationship for this third and most significant category may function in two ways: presidents who decide to issue a highly public threat early in a bill's consideration may catalyze the opposition and invite conflict escalation. Presidents may initially seek compromise solutions, but find fierce resistance, prompting executive rhetorical escalation as the only option to the abandonment of the president's policy preferences.

State of the Union Addresses and Other Major Policy Speeches

The State of the Union address offers a significant instance of the role of rhetorical action in the emergence and maintenance of the modern presidency. Recent studies of the State of the Union address can be divided into three major categories: the role of the speech in defining the institution of the presidency; the content of the speech and how it has changed over time; and the impact of the speech on agenda setting and influencing public opinion.[20]

According to Todd Schaefer, the State of the Union constitutes "the most prominent and potentially influential weapon in the President's political arsenal."[21] Modern presidents rely on the State of the Union address as a major instrument to influence the public, members of Congress, and the media as well as to communicate with leaders of other nations. Communication scholars have studied these messages extensively and have produced a number of case studies on annual messages. In addition to the institutionally based analysis offered by Karlyn Kohrs Campbell and Kathleen Hall Jamieson, there have also been a number of case studies.[22] Consequently, we understand a good bit about these messages, how they work, and to what potential effect.

Given the transformation of the role of the State of the Union address from the nineteenth to the twenty-first century, scholars have inquired whether corresponding changes have occurred in the content of the message. Campbell and Jamieson provided a starting point for studying the content of Annual Messages and State of the Union addresses by identifying generic characteristics. Containing both ceremonial and deliberative elements, State of the Union addresses can be characterized by three processes: (1) public meditations on values, (2) assessments of information and issues, and (3) policy recommendations. In the course of executing these three processes, presidents "also create and celebrate national identity, tie together the past, present, and future, and sustain the institution of the presidency." Campbell and Jamieson note further that the messages they studied (1790–1989) were typically conciliatory in tone because they sought cooperation with Congress to enact legislation.[23]

Subsequent studies of the content of State of the Union addresses have identified, among other changes, a decrease in conciliatory words and an increase in assertive language, indicating a correlation between the strengthening of the institution of the presidency and presidential rhetoric. Elvin Lim's computer-assisted content analysis of all State of the Union and Inaugural addresses delivered from 1789 to 2000 resulted in identification of five significant changes in twentieth-century presidential rhetoric. Modern presidential rhetoric, he reports, has become more anti-intellectual, more abstract, more assertive, more democratic, and more conversational. These content changes, Lim concludes, support the general claim that a significant transformation of presidential rhetoric occurred in the early decades of the twentieth century.[24] Lim emphasizes the decrease in words implying submission to power as well as those implying uncertainty, along with an increase in words that imply greater confidence on the part of the president as leader of the nation. Lim cautions that there is a "dark side" to the growth of the president's rhetorical assertiveness: "While these rhetorical patterns have no doubt arisen because of the economic and technological progress of the nation and the emergence of the United States as a global power . . . , they have also emerged because of the institutional strengthening of the presidency vis-à-vis the other branches of government. More seriously, the increased confidence of presidential rhetoric reveals an increasing lack of humility in its rhetors."[25] Nonetheless, he offers five reasons to forestall condemnation of the state of contemporary presidential rhetoric, among them the observation that the shift to democratic rhetoric has brought the president, at least rhetorically, closer to the people.

Further content analysis has yielded the finding that since the early twentieth century, presidents have decreased the length of their State of the Union addresses and made increased attempts to identify with the American people. Ryan Teten, for instance, has found that the Annual Messages of George Washington and John Adams, delivered to Congress by the president in person, were short in length, not unlike the State of the Union addresses of modern presidents.[26] The length of written messages to Congress increased significantly in 1825 during the presidency of John Quincy Adams, then shrank precipitously in 1913 with Woodrow Wilson. Based on these findings, Teten offers a three-phased history of the State of the Union address: a founding period from 1790 to 1825, a traditional period from 1825 to 1913, and a modern period from 1913 to the present. Consequently, Teten challenges the prevailing traditional/modern paradigm of the American presidency.

A final strain of research on the State of the Union questions the efficacy of the State of the Union address in capturing the public's attention, conveying the president's message, and setting the administration's agenda. Building on studies finding that presidents target their messages for maximum effect in the media, Schaefer analyzed editorial coverage of State of the Union addresses of presidents Nixon through Clinton (1970–95). He found that the "actual" state of the union (based on unemployment and inflation figures as well as positive and negative events) had little influence on editorial coverage of the president's State of the Union message.[27] Rather, the factor that had the greatest influence on media assessment of a given State of the Union address was the popularity of the president at the time the speech was delivered. Schaefer concluded: "Although the President may now speak directly to the public through television, and conversely Americans may now be able to witness presidential speeches first hand, the meaning and interpretation of presidential messages is still largely in the hands of the 'professional persuaders' in the mass media."[28]

Further doubt has been cast on the power of the State of the Union address and the "bully pulpit" more generally to mobilize the citizenry. A study of four of President Ronald Reagan's televised addresses, including the 1982 and 1983 State of the Union addresses, found that 40 percent of the American public neither saw nor read about the speeches. Of those who viewed the address, only 25 percent or less could recall three points from the speech.[29] More generally, Reed Welch found that during the past twenty years the audience for televised presidential addresses has been shrinking. He concluded that "the bully pulpit might not be as powerful as some think." "Far from the heroic picture engendered by political folklore through the years in which the president is guaranteed success in capturing the public's attention and informing and even persuading people about his ideas and policies," Welch's findings show the president "as having limited success in even communicating his message to the public."[30]

Political scientists, of course, most notably George Edwards, tend to examine major policy addresses with an eye toward short-term changes in public opinion.[31] Unsurprisingly, they find little support for significant influence over public opinion. Rhetorical scholars, who tend to look more at the constitutive elements of such addresses, find more reasons to consider them worth significant analysis.[32] There are a number of such examples, and political scientists could improve their understanding of the policy process by referring more often to them.

War and Impeachment

When the Founders created a system of separated institutions sharing powers, they ensured macro-level struggles between the presidency and Congress. Especially important are two struggles that continue to play out over time, each of which is grounded in constitutional powers and each of which enables one branch of government to leverage its position relative to the other. Those two struggles entail the commitment of American military forces and the investigation of presidential conduct.

The first struggle is between the president's role as commander in chief of the armed forces and the Senate's power to declare war.[33] The founders imagined twenty-six senators deliberating matters of war behind closed doors. Their idea of a president was General Washington, and Ben Franklin was the press corps. Nearly four-score years later, President-Elect Lincoln would decline to comment on the impending war, saying it was not the president's jurisdiction. When Congress refused to fund Theodore Roosevelt's plan to send the fleet around the world, he sent them halfway and forced Congress to approve the funds to bring them back. And when a Vietnam-weary Congress passed the War Powers Act intended to limit presidents' ability to wage war without them, their mechanism had the president himself start the War Powers clock that limits his power. At this writing, it has been more than sixty-three years since a president (of either party) has asked a Senate (controlled by either party) for a declaration of war. Is a declaration of war likely in the future if 9/11 did not produce one against the Taliban regime in Afghanistan for supporting the terrorists who attacked New York and Washington? Clearly, the leverage in this struggle has shifted from Congress to the president, and there are important communication issues involved.

There are costs to bypassing authorization. Although President Bush sought and received congressional support for the war in Iraq, questions have already arisen as to whether the war was about weapons of mass destruction (and whether they existed), or the elimination of an evil dictator, or both. President Bush may eventually find that it would have been preferable to have had formal declarations of war against the governments of Afghanistan and Iraq to sanction constitutionally the war on terror.

The second communication issue is that presidents' leverage has been enhanced by the narrative force of the rhetorical presidency. Thirty years ago Theodore Windt identified a presidential genre in which the president (1) asserts the existence of a new situation over which he alone has mastery, (2) provides a narrative of the new situation as part of a larger global or historic struggle in which "ideological angels do mortal and moral combat with ideological devils," and (3) support for the president's announced response is a mark of honor and character for the American people.[34] This is a rhetorical genre with which a deliberative body cannot compete, and there is no voice that has standing comparable to that of the president. Other scholars have analyzed this narrative tradition and its uses for the contemporary institution.[35] There is a fair amount of important scholarship in this area, which provides a solid basis for the continuance of a scholarly conversation on narrative, war, and presidential power and authority.

If the first struggle over the deployment of military forces has advantaged presidents relative to Congress, the second provides an increasing congressional check on presidents. For the narrative and symbolic power of the individual president personifying and embodying the nation can be checked by the congressional power to impeach. The second struggle is thus between the president's symbolic power to personify the nation and congressional power to investigate and impeach the person who is president. Political scientists have already had much to say about impeachment, and communication scholars are beginning to contribute to the conversation as well.[36] Presidents Andrew Johnson and Bill Clinton were impeached and remained in office, but their efforts to forestall removal greatly hampered their administrations. Even more important are the many instances in which Congress investigated presidential activities: Did Roosevelt know about Pearl Harbor? Did Nixon know about Watergate? Did Ford make a deal to pardon Nixon? Did Reagan trade arms for hostages? Did Bush plan an "October surprise"? Did Clinton invest improperly in Whitewater? As the office of the presidency has been elevated by the focus of modern communication media on the presidential personage, Congress has found that it can undermine a president's personal legitimacy with the degradation rituals of investigation, scandal, and in some cases impeachment. At the very least, such investigations distract the president from his legislative agenda and keep the public focused on nonlegislative matters.

Both struggles—military engagement and investigation—are made to order for the modern news media. Bill Kovach and Tom Rosenstiel tell us that as public attention to national news media has fragmented in the cable and Internet age, the national media relish "blockbuster stories."[37] Celebrity trials provide this, but no news hook can compare to war or congressional investigation of a president. Thus the struggles between president and Congress seem likely to continue to play out as struggles over the president's commitment of troops and congressional investigations of presidential conduct.

Subverting Congress

Increasingly, presidents are drawn to the one-way street of administrative means to power.[38] Designed to bypass Congress, the rise of the administrative presidency signals an effort by presidents to gain power by expanding the independent, managerial authority of the presidency. Such efforts have been largely successful, and political scientists have dedicated a sizable amount of time and effort to studying the administrative presidency. We now know a good deal about its origins and development, its influence, and its consequences.

As presidents fail to get Congress to respond favorably to their legislative proposals, ways are sometimes found to "go around" Congress. Frustrated by congressional nay-saying, presidents look for ways to achieve their policy goals without going through the difficult and cumbersome legislative arena. As Charles Walcott and Karen Hult have noted, the strategic approach popular with recent presidents is to devise an administrative agenda for governing.[39] Presidents try to employ managerial or administrative means to policy ends. As Robert Durant and Adam Warber describe it,

> the administrative presidency is premised on three assumptions. First, congressional opposition to presidential legislative initiatives is the rule rather than the exception. Second, federal agencies make policy as they exercise bureaucratic discretion when implementing status. Consequently, presidents have another opportunity to "legislate" that does not require them to mobilize legislative majorities in Congress. Third, and premised on conventional notions of hierarchical control, presidents indirectly can influence policy by naming political appointees to agencies who either substantively or ideologically share their policy agendas. These appointees, in turn, can change agency rules, budgets, structures, and personnel requirements to suit presidential policy goals. In contrast to this more "indirect" (or "contextual") approach of acting through agents, presidents can take a more direct (or "unilateral") approach. They do so when issuing executive orders, proclamations, presidential signing statements, national security directives, and presidential memoranda.[40]

Increasingly, presidents use these administrative devices to make policy. Using executive orders, memoranda, signing statements, and a variety of other administrative devices, presidents have been able to make policy without legislative approval and sometimes even against the will of Congress, as the case of George W. Bush's Executive Order 13233, limiting access to presidential papers, attests. The Supreme Court has held that executive orders, under most circumstances, have the full force of law (see *Jenkins v. Collard*, IAS U.S. 557, 560–561 [1891]). Richard Nixon is credited with "inventing" this strategy, but it did not fully blossom until the Reagan presidency. Reagan aggressively employed a strategy that politicized the managerial side of the presidency in an effort to circumvent Congress and govern on his own terms. President Clinton, learning the lesson well, continued using an administrative strategy to govern, especially after the 1995 Republican takeover of Congress.

An executive order is a directive issued by the president of the United States. Its purpose is to assist the president in the capacity of chief executive of the nation. Originally, the executive order was intended for rather minor administrative and rule-making functions, to help the nation's chief administrative officer administer the laws more efficiently and effectively. Over time, however, the executive order has become an important and sometimes controversial tool for a president to make policy without obtaining the consent of Congress, as required by the Constitution. The executive order is an "implied" power, not specifically mentioned in the Constitution but deemed essential for the effective and efficient functioning of government. George Washington issued the first executive order on June 8, 1789. It instructed heads of departments (cabinet officers) to make a "clear account" of their departments. Under the National Administrative Procedure Act of 1946, all executive orders must be published in the *Federal Register*. Congress, if it wishes, can overturn an executive order. Executive orders can also be challenged in court on the ground that they may violate the Constitution.

Over time, presidents have gone beyond the use of executive orders for merely administrative matters and have begun to use orders to "make law" on more substantive and controversial matters. Such efforts bypass Congress and sometimes overstep the bounds of what is an appropriate use of the administrative tools of the office. Presidents have been accused, with some justification, of "going around" Congress and "legislating" independently of Congress.

Presidents have used executive orders to implement some very controversial policies. In 1942, during World War II, Franklin Roosevelt interned Japanese Americans in detention centers. In 1948, Harry S. Truman integrated the military. In 1952, Truman attempted to seize control of steel mills. In 1992, Bill Clinton directed the U.S. Coast Guard to return Haitian refugees found at sea to Haiti. In 2001, George W. Bush issued a series of orders aimed at undermining terrorist organizations in the United States and abroad. All these acts were accomplished through executive orders.

Some presidential efforts have been challenged in court. In general, the courts have recognized the legitimacy and legality of executive orders, but not all orders pass the test of constitutionality. In 1952, for example, during the Korean War, President Truman seized control of the nation's steel mills to prevent a work stoppage that might have had a negative impact on the war effort. The Supreme Court, in *Youngstown Sheet and Tube Co. v. Sawyer*, decided that the president's actions were unconstitutional. Truman was forced to back down, but such limitations are the exception. Overall, presidents have been able to take control of a variety of significant policy areas through the use of administrative tools such as the executive order, signing statements, proclamations, and rulemaking decisions. These administrative tools have become an important weapon in the president's arsenal and are likely to remain so.

Presidential unilateralism may be furthered by an increasing executive predilection for what Richard Rose calls "going international."[41] Rose is referring to the tendency of presidents to negotiate directly with foreign leaders in the making of international policy. There is some evidence that, rhetorically, there may be "two presidencies" developing—one dedicated to various attempts to persuade or subvert Congress on domestic matters, and another dedicated to the use of international publics and foreign leaders in an attempt to persuade or subvert Congress in international policy areas.[42]

While a number of scholars are drawing our attention to the increase in administrative authority being exercised by presidents, there are still glaring holes in the research that need to be filled. First, what is the source of this authority? Is it to be found in Article II, section 1 of the Constitution, which states: "The executive Power shall be vested in a President of the United States of America"? Or in delegated powers granted by Congress? Is it merely a presidential "fait accompli"? Second, what are the limits of this authority? Third, what can and should be the congressional response to usurpations of authority based on the assumption of presidential administrative authority? Finally, what can scholars contribute to this question?

Conclusion

We have located three main areas of research into presidential communication to Congress. All of them involve ways in which presidents attempt to increase their ability either to bargain or to command. The first area is "going public," or using the mass public to sway Congress; the second is direct communication to Congress in the form of nominations, vetoes, State of the Union and other important policy addresses, war, and impeachment; and the third includes administrative attempts to subvert Congress. The state of the literature on the three is mixed, with only the first characterized by a productive debate in both communication and political science.

The model of the rhetorical presidency, and its companion, going public, have provided a strong impetus for research in both political science and communication. Scholars in both fields have examined the usefulness of the model and have applied it to a variety of cases. The debate over the history and parameters of the rhetorical public is a vibrant one that appears to be proceeding along parallel tracks, with little attention paid by communication scholars to the institutional influences and implications of their work, and little real understanding of the actual communication of presidents by political scientists. We recommend continuing these conversations, although we believe it would be more productive if scholars in each discipline understood it as a single conversation rather than as two distinct ones.

In the area of direct presidential communication to Congress, there is less research, it is less interdisciplinarily informed, and in all but two of its elements, communication scholars have all but ceded this important area to political scientists. There is almost no important work by a communication scholar on either Cabinet or Supreme Court nominations. There is no important work by a communication scholar on vetoes or on veto threats. Political scientists understand the importance of these areas for national politics; they devote considerable time and effort to studying them. They are worth the attention of communication scholars as well. We therefore recommend that communication scholars move into this potentially productive area of research.

Rhetoricians do much better at other areas of direct communication. We know quite a lot about the rhetoric of war and crisis, both in its macro uses and in individual cases. Political scientists could learn a great deal from this research, and we recommend that they begin to study this area with an eye toward the importance of rhetoric. Scholars are also well informed about State of the Union and other important policy addresses and how they function both instrumentally and constitutively; as with the rhetorical presidency and going public, it would be productive if this area became more truly interdisciplinary. Impeachment is more of a mixed bag; there is considerable research from political scientists on the recent Clinton impeachment but less as yet from communication scholars. Both groups of scholars would do well to heed to the contributions of the other.

Finally, presidents increasingly use administrative means to subvert the will of Congress, and here, communication research is almost nonexistent. Presidential administrative rhetoric merits considerably more attention than it has received thus far. Presidential secrecy is also an increasingly important concern, and rhetoricians are well suited to contribute to scholarly conversations on this topic. We recommend that they begin work in this area.

The research in all of these areas seems to be confined either to one discipline or to the other, or it is proceeding along parallel tracks. There is a need for more truly interdisciplinary research that can both appreciate the institutional context and apply theories aimed at understanding the persuasive and constitutive elements of that institutionally based communication. As we noted at the beginning of this report, it is tempting to view the presidency as the entire government. Working together, political scientists and communication scholars can help to refine our understanding of the inter-institutional communication processes to improve our understandings of the presidency, Congress, and the relationships between them.

RECOMMENDATIONS

1. Scholars in the disciplines of political science and communication should continue to work on refining and articulating the model of the rhetorical presidency and should do so as participants in a joint conversation rather than in two separate ones.

2. Communication scholars should join the ongoing conversations in political science on presidential nominations, vetoes, and veto threats, and other areas of direct presidential communication to Congress.

3. Political scientists should take seriously the important work done by communication scholars on State of the Union and other major policy addresses.

4. Both political scientists and communication scholars should devote significant attention to the communicative aspects of the administrative presidency.

NOTES

1. Charles O. Jones, *The Presidency in a Separated System* (Washington, D.C.: Brookings Institution, 1994).

2. Richard Neustadt, *Presidential Power: The Politics of Leadership* (1960; New York: Wiley, 1980).

3. For an overview of the president and the political system, see Michael A. Genovese, *The Presidential Dilemma* (New York: Longman, 2003); Michael A. Genovese, *The Paradoxes of the American Presidency* (New York: Oxford University Press, 2004).

4. Lester M. Seligman and Cary R. Covington, *The Coalitional Presidency* (Homewood, Ill.: Dorsey Press, 1989).

5. James. Pfiffner, *The Strategic Presidency: Hitting the Ground Running* (Lawrence: University Press of Kansas, 1996).

6. For the germinal book on the rhetorical presidency, see Jeffrey Tulis, *The Rhetorical Presidency* (Princeton, N.J.: Princeton University Press, 1987). For the germinal work on going public, see Samuel Kernell, *Going Public: New Strategies of Presidential Leadership*. (Washington, D.C.: Congressional Quarterly Press, 1997).

7. There is considerable debate on the merits and limitations of the rhetorical presidency

as a model. See, among others, Matthew A. Bodnick, "'Going Public' Reconsidered: Reagan's 1981 Tax and Budget Cuts, and Revisionist Theories of Presidential Power," *Congress and the Presidency* 17 (1990): 13–29; Matthew Corrigan, "The Transformation of Going Public: President Clinton, the First Lady, and Health Care Reform," *Political Communication* 17 (2000): 149–69; George C. Edwards III, *At the Margins: Presidential Leadership of Congress* (New Haven, Conn.: Yale University Press, 1989); George C. Edwards III, *On Deaf Ears* (New Haven, Conn.: Yale University Press, 2003); Roderick P. Hart, *The Sound of Leadership: Presidential Communication in the Modern Age* (Chicago: University of Chicago Press, 1987).

8. Paul Brace and Barbara Hinckley, *Follow the Leader* (New York: Basic Books, 1992); Jeffrey Cohen, "Presidential Rhetoric and the Public Agenda," *American Journal of Political Science* 39 (1995): 87–107. Edwards, *At the Margins;* Edwards, *On Deaf Ears;* Karen S. Hoffman, "Going Public in the Nineteenth Century: Grover Cleveland's Repeal of the Sherman Silver Purchase Act," *Rhetoric & Public Affairs* 5 (2002): 57–77; Mel Laracey, *Presidents and the People: The Partisan Story of Going Public* (College Station: Texas A&M University Press, 2002); Brad Lockerbie and Stephan A. Borrelli, "Getting Inside the Beltway: Perceptions of Presidential Skill and Success in Congress," *British Journal of Political Science* 19 (1989): 97–106; Richard J. Powell, "Going Public Revisited: Presidential Speechmaking and the Bargaining Setting in Congress," *Congress and the Presidency* 26 (1999): 153–70; Lyn Ragsdale, "The Politics of Presidential Speechmaking," *American Political Science Review* 78 (1984): 971–84;

9. Martin J. Medhurst, "Introduction: A Tale of Two Constructs: The Rhetorical Presidency versus Presidential Rhetoric," in *Beyond the Rhetorical Presidency*, ed. Martin J. Medhurst (College Station: Texas A&M University Press, 1996).

10. For work on the presidency and Congress see, among many others, Jon Bond and Richard Fleisher. *The President in the Legislative Arena* (Chicago: University of Chicago Press, 1990); Calvin Mouw and Michael MacKuen, "The Strategic Configuration, Personal Influence, and Presidential Power in Congress," *Western Political Quarterly* 45 (1992): 579–608.

11. See Roderick P. Hart and Kathleen E. Kendall, "Lyndon Johnson and the Problem of Politics: A Study in Conversation," in *Beyond the Rhetorical Presidency.*

12. Marianne Borrelli, "Gender, Credibility, and Politics: The Senate Nomination Hearings of Cabinet Secretaries-Designate, 1975 to 1993," *Political Research Quarterly* 50 (1997): 171–97.

13. James D. King and James W. Riddlesperger Jr., "Senate Confirmation of Cabinet Nominations: Institutional Politics and Nominee Qualifications," *Social Science Journal* 33 (1996): 273–88.

14. Nolan McCarty and Rose Razaghian, "Advice and Consent: Senate Responses to Executive Branch Nominations, 1885–1996," *American Journal of Political Science* 43 (1999): 1122–43.

15. Gus Krutz, Richard Fleisher, and Jon Bond, "From Abe Fortas to Zoe Baird: Why Some Presidential Nominations Fail in the Senate," *American Political Science Review* 92 (1998): 871–81.

16. See Henry J. Abraham, *Justices, Presidents and Senators*, 4th ed. (Lanham, Md.: Rowan and Littlefield, 1999); Susan Low Bloch and Thomas G. Krattenmaker, *Supreme*

Court Politics: The Institution and Its Procedures (St. Paul, Minn.: West Publishing, 1994); John Anthony Maltese, *The Selling of the Supreme Court Nominees* (Baltimore, Md.: Johns Hopkins University Press, 1995); David Alistair Yalof, *Pursuit of Justices: Presidential Politics and the Selection of Supreme Court Nominees* (Chicago: University of Chicago Press, 1999).

17. Please note, however, Trevor Parry-Giles's chapter in this volume.

18. Charles M. Cameron, *Veto Bargaining* (New York: Cambridge University Press, 2000); Robert J. Spitzer, *The Presidential Veto* (Albany, N.Y.: SUNY Press, 1988); Robert J. Spitzer, *Presidential Veto: Touchstone of the American Presidency* (Albany, N.Y.: SUNY Press, 1988); Richard A. Watson, *Presidential Vetoes and Public Policy* (Lawrence: University Press of Kansas, 1993).

19. Richard S. Conley, "George Bush and the 102nd Congress: The Impact of Public and 'Private' Veto Threats on Policy Outcomes," *Presidential Studies Quarterly* 33 (2003): 730–49.

20. Other studies, though an insubstantial number to constitute a major category, have focused on the writing of the State of the Union address. See Meena Bose, "Words as Signals: Drafting Cold War Rhetoric in the Eisenhower and Kennedy Administrations," *Congress and the Presidency* 25 (1998): 23–41; and Charles J. G. Griffin, "Dwight D. Eisenhower: The 1954 State of the Union Address as a Case Study in Presidential Speechwriting," in *Presidential Speechwriting: From the New Deal to the Reagan Revolution and Beyond*, ed. Kurt Ritter and Martin J. Medhurst (College Station: Texas A&M University Press, 2003).

21. Todd M. Schaefer, "Persuading the Persuaders: Presidential Speech and Editorial Opinion," *Political Communication* 14 (1997): 97–11.

22. See, for instance, Dan F. Hahn and Justin J. Gustainis, "Anatomy of an Enigma: Jimmy Carter's State of the Union Address," *Communication Quarterly* 33 (1985): 43–49, and David Zarefsky, "Lincoln's 1862 Annual Message: A Paradigm of Rhetorical Leadership," *Rhetoric & Public Affairs* 3 (2000): 5–14.

23. Karlyn Kohrs Campbell and Kathleen Hall Jamieson, *Deeds Done in Words: Presidential Rhetoric and the Genres of Governance* (Chicago: University of Chicago Press, 1990), 54.

24. Elvin T. Lim, "Five Trends in Presidential Rhetoric: An Analysis of Rhetoric from George Washington to Bill Clinton" *Presidential Studies Quarterly* 32 (2002): 332.

25. Lim, "Five Trends," 337.

26. Ryan L. Teten, "Evolution of the Modern Rhetorical Presidency: Presidential Presentation and Development of the State of the Union Address," *Presidential Studies Quarterly* 33 (2003): 333–46.

27. Schaefer, "Persuading the Persuaders," 97; Thomas J. Johnson, Wayne Wanta, John T. Byrd, and Cindy Lee, "Exploring FDR's Relationship with the Press: A Historical Agenda-Setting Study," *Political Communication* 12 (1995): 157–72.

28. Schaefer extended the findings of his study of media coverage of State of the Union addresses from 1970 to 1995 with a subsequent analysis of *New York Times* coverage of State of the Union addresses from Eisenhower through Clinton's first term (1953–96). He again found that "greater political support for the President, as measured through approval polls and partisan elites' statements, produces more favorable coverage. Thus, it appears the President's political standing in Washington as well as with the public, colors the way the

media treat his message." Todd M. Schaefer, "The 'Rhetorical Presidency' Meets the Press: The *New York Times* and the State of the Union Message," *Journalism and Mass Communication Quarterly* 76 (1999): 523.

29. See Matthew C. Moen, "The Political Agenda of Ronald Reagan: A Content Analysis of the State of the Union Messages," *Presidential Studies Quarterly* 18 (1988): 775–86; Wayne Wanta, "How Presidents' State of the Union Talk Influenced News Media Agendas," *Journalism Quarterly* 66 (1989): 537–41; Reed L. Welch, "Is Anybody Watching? The Audience for Televised Presidential Addresses," *Congress and the Presidency* 27 (2000): 41–58; Darrell West, "Television and Presidential Popularity in America," *British Journal of Political Science* 21 (1991): 199–214.

30. Reed L. Welch, "Presidential Success in Communicating with the Public through Televised Addresses," *Presidential Studies Quarterly* 33 (2003): 362. See also Randy E. Miller and Wayne Wanta, "Sources of the Public Agenda: The President-Press-Public Relationship," *International Journal of Public Opinion Research* 8 (1996): 390–402; Edwards, *On Deaf Ears*.

31. Edwards, *At the Margins*.

32. David Zarefsky has produced interesting work on Lyndon Johnson's War on Poverty, for example David Zarefsky, *President Johnson's War on Poverty: Rhetoric and History* (Tuscaloosa: University of Alabama Press, 1986); and others have productively studied Ronald Reagan's economic rhetoric. See Richard L. Johannesen, "Ronald Reagan's Economic Jeremiad," *Central States Speech Journal* 37(1986): 79–89; Amos Kiewe and Davis Houck, *A Shining City on a Hill: Reagan's Economic Rhetoric, 1951–1989* (Westport, Conn.: Praeger, 1991).

33. For some examples of work done on war rhetoric, see, among many others, Robert L. Ivie, "Presidential Motives for War," *Quarterly Journal of Speech* 60 (1974): 337–45; Robert L. Ivie, "Images of Savagery in American Justifications for War," *Communication Monographs* 47 (1980): 279–94; Mary E. Stuckey, "Competing Foreign Policy Visions: Rhetorical Hybrids After the Cold War," *Western Journal of Communication* 59 (1995): 214–27; Philip C. Wander, "The Rhetoric of American Foreign Policy," *Quarterly Journal of Speech* 70 (1984): 339–361.

34. Theodore O. Windt, "The Presidency and Speeches of International Crises: Repeating the Rhetorical Past," in *Essays in Presidential Rhetoric,* 3rd edition, ed. Theodore Otto Windt and Beth Ingold (Englewood Cliffs, N.J.: Prentice Hall, 1992), 91–100. For other important work on crisis rhetoric, see Denise M. Bostdorff, *The Presidency and the Rhetoric of Foreign Crisis* (Columbia: University of South Carolina, 1993); Amos Kiewe, ed., *The Modern Presidency and Crisis Rhetoric* (Westport, Conn.: Praeger, 1994).

35. See for example, G. Thomas Goodnight, "Reagan, Vietnam, and Central America: Public Memory and the Politics of Fragmentation," in *Beyond the Rhetorical Presidency;* David Henry, "Ronald Reagan and Aid to the Contras: An Analysis of the Rhetorical Presidency," in *Rhetorical Dimensions in Media,* 2nd edition, ed. Martin J. Medhurst and Thomas W. Benson (Dubuque, Iowa: Kendall/Hunt, 1991), 73–88; William Lewis, "Telling America's Story: Narrative Form and the Reagan Presidency," *Quarterly Journal of Speech* 73 (1987): 280–302; Janice Hocker Rushing, "Ronald Reagan's 'Star Wars' Address: Mythic Containment of Technical Reasoning," *Quarterly Journal of Speech* 72 (1986): 415–33.

36. For work on impeachment from a political science perspective, see Raoul Berger, *Impeachment: The Constitutional Problems* (Cambridge: Harvard University Press, 1974);

Michael J. Gerhardt, *The Federal Impeachment Process: A Constitutional and Historical Analysis* (Chicago: University of Chicago Press, 2000); Nancy Kassop, "Impeachment," in *The Encyclopedia of the American Presidency*, ed. Michael A. Genovese (New York: Facts on File, 2004). For work dealing with impeachment from a communication perspective, see Robert E. Denton Jr., "William Jefferson Clinton and the Symbolic Dimensions of the American Presidency: Issues of Character and Trust," in *Images, Scandal, and Communication Strategies of the Clinton Presidency*, ed. Robert E. Denton Jr. and Rachel L. Holloway (Westport, Conn.: Praeger, 2003); Shawn J. Parry-Giles and Trevor Parry-Giles, *Constructing Clinton: Hyperreality and Presidential Image-Making in Postmodern Politics* (New York: Peter Lang, 2002).

37. Bill Kovach and Tom Rosenstiel, *Warp Speed: America in the Age of Mixed Media* (New York: Century Foundation Press, 1999).

38. For work on the administrative presidency, see Peri Arnold, *Making the Managerial Presidency: Comprehensive Reorganization Planning 1905–1996* (Lawrence: University Press of Kansas, 1998); Phillip J. Cooper, *By Order of the President: The Use and Abuse of Direct Action* (Lawrence: University Press of Kansas, 2002); Robert F. Durant, *The Administrative Presidency Revisited: Public Lands, the BLM and the Reagan Revolution* (Albany, N.Y.: SUNY Press, 1992); William G. Howell, *Power without Persuasion: The Politics of Direct Presidential Action* (Princeton, N.J.: Princeton University Press, 2003); Kenneth R. Mayer, *With the Stroke of a Pen: Executive Orders and Presidential Power* (Princeton, N.J.: Princeton University Press, 2001); Richard P. Nathan, *The Administrative Presidency* (New York: Wiley Mayer, 1993).

39. Charles E. Walcott, and Karen M. Hult, *Governing the White House: From Hoover through LBJ* (Lawrence: University Press of Kansas, 1995).

40. Robert F. Durant and Adam L. Warber, "Networking in the Shadow of Hierarchy: Public Policy, the Administrative Presidency and the Neo Administrative State," *Presidential Studies Quarterly* 31 (2001): 221–45.

41. Richard Rose, *The Postmodern President: George Bush Meets the World* (Chatham, N.J.: Chatham House, 1991); Michael J. Smith, "Going International: Presidential Activity in the Post-Modern Presidency," *Journal of American Studies* 31 (1997): 219–33.

42. David Lewis, "The Two Rhetorical Presidencies: An Analysis of Televised Presidential Speeches, 1947–1991," *American Politics Quarterly* 25 (1997): 380–95.

CHAPTER 13

REPORT OF THE NATIONAL TASK FORCE ON THE PRESIDENCY AND PUBLIC OPINION

Chair: J. Michael Hogan, Pennsylvania State University, University Park
George C. Edwards III, Texas A&M University, College Station
Wynton C. Hall, Bainbridge College
Christine L. Harold, University of Georgia, Athens
Gerard A. Hauser, University of Colorado, Boulder
Susan Herbst, Temple University
Robert Y. Shapiro, Columbia University
Ted J. Smith III, Virginia Commonwealth University

The National Task Force on the Presidency and Public Opinion was charged with assessing scholarship at the nexus of two topics that have produced large, interdisciplinary bodies of literature: the presidency and public opinion. Under the space constraints of this report, we cannot possibly review all of that literature, much less provide definitive answers to all of the questions raised by scholars, journalists, and concerned citizens. In what follows, we focus on those issues that we believe have been central to inquiry into the *relationship* between the presidency and public opinion and that we believe will guide research in the future.

We begin with a brief review of the presidency and public opinion in history and democratic theory. We then focus on the rise of polling and the instrumental use of polling by presidents and presidential candidates. In the third section of the report we focus on media polling and the impact of public polls on electoral politics and presidential leadership. Finally, we discuss the future of research on the presidency and public opinion, reviewing the empirical questions that remain to be resolved and sketching some new directions for research on the topic.

The Presidency and Public Opinion in History and Democratic Theory

Presidential leadership of public opinion, as Richard J. Ellis has written, is "nowhere mentioned" in the Constitution.[1] During the debates over the Constitution, Alexander Hamilton argued for a strong executive insulated from popular opinion, and the indirect election of the President, a fixed term of office, and the separation of powers were all designed, at least in part, to insulate the presidency from public opinion. Fears of demagoguery animated many of the Founders, as they regarded manipulation of the masses and majority tyranny as "the peculiar vice to which democracies were susceptible."[2] The Founders wrote no rules for popular leadership into the constitutional presidency, but their theory *implied* a rhetorical doctrine that severely limited the president's direct communication with the people. In the nineteenth century, two general proscriptions on presidential rhetoric reflected that doctrine: that appeals to the public ought to be limited to ceremonial addresses and formal proclamations, and that specific policy proposals ought not be advocated publicly but should be communicated to Congress *in writing*.[3]

Throughout the nineteenth century, a few presidents pushed the boundaries of these informal limitations on popular speech, and after the Civil War presidents spoke in public much more frequently. For the most part, however, even such "popular" presidents as Andrew Jackson rarely addressed the public, and those who did delivered mostly greetings, patriotic orations, or other ceremonial addresses. The one nineteenth-century president who *did* promote himself and his agenda in public, Andrew Johnson, was excoriated in the press and impeached on charges that, among other things, he brought "contempt, ridicule, and disgrace" upon the high office of the president with his "intemperate, inflammatory, and scandalous harangues."[4] Recently, a number of scholars have argued that the transition to the modern, rhetorical presidency was "less abrupt and more complex and multi-faceted" than Tulis suggested, yet all agree that the relationship between presidents and public opinion changed dramatically in the twentieth century and that "presidential modes of popular communication look radically different today than they did in 1787 or even 1887."[5]

Theodore Roosevelt, of course, played a major role in the rise of the modern, "rhetorical" presidency. Campaigning publicly for the Hepburn Act, Roosevelt successfully appealed "over the heads" of Congress, and throughout his presidency he exhorted the public to embrace not only his policies but also his philosophical and social values. Reflecting on his own leadership, Roosevelt articulated no grand theory of "going public," but he did attribute much of his success as president to his exploitation of the "bully pulpit." As he recalled in his *Autobiography*, TR made a "resolute effort" to persuade congressional leaders to embrace his program of progressive reform, but eventually he found it necessary to go directly to the people: "Gradually, . . . I was forced to abandon the effort to persuade them to come my way, and then I achieved results only by appealing over the heads of the Senate and House leaders to the people, who were the masters of both of us."[6]

That left it for Woodrow Wilson—the presidential scholar—to develop a philosophical and theoretical rationale for the rhetorical presidency. And while Jeffrey Tulis may be correct that Wilson radically revised the Founders' constitutional theory, he did *not* advocate that presidents routinely go over the heads of Congress, nor did he envision the modern rhetorical presidency—the presidency of sound bites and spin, of focus groups and polling.[7] To the contrary, Wilson shared the Founders' concerns about demagogic speech, and he embraced a classical model of oratorical statesmanship that, like the Founders' constitutional theory, implied strict limitations on the president's communication with the public. Wilson never suggested that "public opinion leadership" should be "the sole, or even the primary, mode of leading Congress"; it had "to complement—it could not replace"—more "intimate communication" with Congress.[8] Moreover, Wilson's ideal president delivered only reasoned and ethically sound speeches, eschewing personal, partisan, or emotional appeals to public opinion. Envisioning rhetorical presidents who both led and followed public opinion by engaging the people in "common counsel," Wilson observed in *Constitutional Government* that the "nation as a whole" chose the president and that the president served as the "political spokesman" for *all* the people. When the president "rightly" interpreted "the national thought" and "boldly" insisted upon it, Wilson concluded, he was politically "irresistible." But if he failed to voice the "real sentiment and purpose of the country," he lost his moral authority and political effectiveness.[9]

The theory of the rhetorical presidency—and the related ideas that presidents govern by going public or through "permanent campaigns"—has framed much of the scholarship on the presidency and public opinion. At least in studies of twentieth-century presidents, scholars generally have assumed that modern presidents govern not by traditional means of bargaining and compromise but by exploiting the bully pulpit to "promote themselves and their policies before the American public."[10] In a recent book, however, George Edwards III has challenged this conventional wisdom. Arguing that presidential efforts to lead public opinion "almost always fail," Edwards argues that even the most rhetorically skilled presidents have rarely succeeded in boosting their own approval ratings or in promoting their political agenda by addressing the public. According to Edwards, even the "Great Communicator," Ronald Reagan, was "less a public relations phenomenon than the conventional wisdom indicates."[11] If Edwards is correct, then the theory of the rhetorical presidency would seem to miss the point of why presidents go public, and scholars of presidential rhetoric will need to reconfigure their work to address the obvious question: if presidential rhetoric makes no difference, then why do presidents devote so much time and energy to speaking in public?[12]

Beyond empirical questions about the effects of presidential rhetoric, democratic theory raises philosophical and normative questions about the presidency and public opinion. *Should* presidents defer to public opinion? Should they aspire only to interpret and give voice to public opinion, articulating prevailing beliefs and values and speaking *on behalf* of "the people"? Or should they rely upon their own best judgment in governing? Should presidents be active leaders and educators of public opinion? Or are such efforts inherently manipulative and antidemocratic? These questions, rooted in the tension between "delegate" and "trustee" models of representative representation, undergird much of the research on the history and theory of presidential leadership.[13] In the view of the task force, however, both the delegate and the trustee models oversimplify the complex relationship between the presidency and public opinion. In practice, presidents both lead and follow public opinion, depending on the issues at stake, the public's interest in those issues, the historical context, and other factors.

From the general question of whether presidents ought to lead or follow public opinion arise other, equally difficult questions. Is the public sufficiently attentive and knowledgeable about politics to provide guidance to presidents in day-to-day governing?[14] To what extent do presidents *need* public support to govern effectively? Do efforts to gauge and respond to public opinion distract from the real business of governing? Or is going public itself a mode of governing, no less legitimate than more traditional approaches? How might we distinguish efforts to inform or educate from attempts to deceive and manipulate public opinion? And how can presidents assure the best policy outcomes while maintaining a concern for the democratic character of policies?

These are just a few of the many questions about the relationship between the presidency and public opinion that will continue to inspire research in the years to come. In history and democratic theory, both empirical and normative questions about that relationship remain to be answered, and many of those questions are complicated by debates over *how* public opinion is defined and measured. In the next section, we discuss some of the controversies that have surrounded the dominant measure of public opinion since the 1930s: the public opinion poll. We then turn to the question of how presidents have *used* polling as a political tool, reviewing the emerging literature on presidential polling.

THE RISE OF SCIENTIFIC POLLING AND THE PRESIDENTIAL POLLSTER

Since the 1930s, public opinion has been defined, as a practical matter, as poll results. For some, this represents the inevitable triumph of "science" over crude, unscientific methods of gauging public opinion. For others, the rise of polling was more a triumph of public relations than of science, and the rise of polling has had a number of deleterious effects on the democratic process and public deliberation. In this section of our report, we touch upon the history of polling and consider some of the controversies that have surrounded the quantification of public opinion. We then discuss the instrumental use of polling by U.S. presidents, summarizing the research on *how* and *why* presidents have employed private pollsters.

The early history of polling has inspired a substantial literature, as have questions about sampling methods and other technical matters. Indeed, as Susan Herbst has observed, "there are so many histories of polling, and so many methodological tracts about survey research, that students and amateur pollsters are often overwhelmed by the sheer size of this literature."[15] Not surprisingly, polling practitioners, who founded their own journal in 1937 (*Public Opinion Quarterly*) and their own professional organization (the American Association for Public Opinion Research, or AAPOR) a decade later, have contributed much of this literature. Among the most prolific of the pollsters writing about their own methods and contributions was George Horace Gallup, who published several books and more than a hundred articles on polling between the late 1930s and the 1970s.

As polling's most visible champion for half a century, Gallup made three major contributions to the polling literature. First, he helped create the historical folklore of the industry by telling the story of polling's remarkable progress from "a glorified kind of fortunetelling into a practical way of learning what the nation thinks."[16] Gallup's version of history, which included a misleading account of the pollsters' triumph over the *Literary Digest* poll in 1936 and an interpretation of their 1948 miscall that transformed the industry's greatest embarrassment into a "blessing in disguise," remains prominent in textbooks and popular histories of polling.[17] Second, Gallup campaigned tirelessly to establish the pollsters' claim to "science," defending their methods and boasting of their statistical record in predicting elections. Dismissing polling's critics as "arm-chair philosophers" who knew "nothing about research procedures," Gallup diverted attention from the pollsters' most troublesome technical problems by emphasizing what they did best: sampling, data collection, and statistical analysis.[18] Finally, Gallup celebrated polling as a technology that empowered ordinary citizens and made "democracy work more effectively."[19] Celebrating the wisdom of the common folk, Gallup portrayed polling as an antidote to special interests and a weapon in the larger struggle between those "who would place more power in the hands of the people" and those "who are fearful of the people and would limit that power sharply."[20]

Today echoes of Gallup's celebratory attitude toward polling can still be heard in such works as Kenneth Warren's *In Defense of Polling*.[21] For the most part, however, today's pollsters acknowledge the technical problems and limitations of polling, and they are often among the toughest critics of their industry's own performance in forecasting elections and assessing public opinion on the issues of the day.[22] Outside the industry, critics of polling have raised even more fundamental questions, challenging not only its track record and its legitimacy as a social science but also its role in the democratic process. Polling's critics generally do not dispute that the pollsters have become adept at sampling and other technical procedures; many also concede that they have become quite good at forecasting elections.[23] Yet critics still question whether polls can provide meaningful portraits of public opinion on public policy issues, particularly those that involve complicated technical questions or are not highly salient to most Americans.[24] In recent years, more and more scholars have even questioned whether polls measure "public opinion" at all.[25] Is an aggregation of opinions expressed privately and confidentially to a pollster a meaningful measure of "public opinion"? Does it make sense to define "the public" as an undifferentiated mass that includes large numbers of disengaged and uninformed citizens? In short, *should* "the public" be defined to include *all* citizens or only those who are somehow engaged in the civic life of their community?[26] These are just some of the questions raised by the most ardent critics of polling.

In recent years, much of the scholarly debate has focused on polling's *effects* on political leadership. Reflecting fears that presidents and other politicians pander to the polls or avoid tough choices that might be unpopular, one study compared the behavior of politicians to "antelopes in an open field" and concluded: "When politicians perceive public opinion change, they adapt their behavior to please their constituency."[27] Another critic, John G. Geer, has likewise argued that "polls have altered in systematic and important ways the behavior of elected politicians," encouraging the "rational" politician to follow rather than lead public opinion, particularly on highly salient issues.[28] In an influential study published in 2000, however, Lawrence Jacobs and Robert Shapiro disputed the view that politicians "pander" to public opinion, arguing that in the past two decades, at least, politicians generally have tracked public opinion "not to make policy but rather to determine how to craft their public presentations and win public support for the policies they and their supporters favor."[29] Nevertheless, the concern that polls encourage politicians to "pander" to rather than to lead public opinion remains prominent in both the scholarly literature and popular commentary. Americans apparently want it both ways: we want our presidents to be accountable, but we do *not* want presidents who decide what to do based on the latest poll.[30]

Finally, some scholars have worried that polls undermine democratic deliberation in various ways. Some see polling as focusing public discussion on the polls themselves rather than on substantive issues.[31] Other worry that polls limit other forms of public expression or even create "the illusion that the public has already spoken in a definitive manner," thereby rendering debate "superfluous."[32] Still others have argued that polling functions as a form of "social control" by disciplining or silencing those outside the political mainstream, or by allowing elites to identify the discontented and to domesticate or pacify dissent.[33] Going still further, Justin Lewis has even argued that polling helps to sustain a dominant conservative ideology by skewing public opinion toward the right. According to Lewis, media representations of polls routinely exclude the more "progressive" dimensions of public opinion, thereby helping to sustain "public acquiescence to the procorporate, center-right hegemony in U.S. politics."[34]

Thus, the critical literature on polling has gone well beyond the technical and political issues raised by polling's early critics. Scholars no longer question whether it is possible to generalize from a small sample to a large population, nor do they accuse the public pollsters of rigging their preelection polls to favor particular candidates, as they did after the 1948 miscall.[35] Critics today *do* wonder whether polls provide an accurate and meaningful measure of "public opinion," especially on political and social issues of low salience or high complexity, and they worry about the impact of polling on political leadership and democratic deliberation. Not surprisingly, these larger concerns with how polls *function* in a representative democracy have been especially pronounced in the literature on presidential polling—a literature examining the *instrumental* use of *private* polls by presidents and presidential candidates.

Presidential candidates, of course, have long used private pollsters to help them get elected. In 1976, Michael Wheeler told the story of how pollster Lou Harris became famous as "the president's pollster" after he worked for the Kennedy campaign in 1960, despite his rather "spotty" performance.[36] Twenty years later, David Moore told a somewhat different version of Harris's "decisive" role in the Kennedy campaign, along with accounts of the increasingly important role of private pollsters in the presidential campaigns of the 1970s and 1980s. Moore's account was largely descriptive, yet he lamented how polls had "enhanced the ability of candidates to manipulate public opinion and the press," and he even blamed pollsters for much of the negative campaigning of the past three decades. In conclusion, Moore worried about how polling had become "not just an important part, but a dominant part, of the political process in America," dictating "virtually every aspect of election campaigns, from fund-raising to electoral strategy to news coverage."[37]

Today polling has evolved into an accepted and routine part of presidential campaigning. Rather than hide their activities, many pollsters publicly boast about their role in getting presidents elected, and some, like Lou Harris, Patrick Cadell, and Dick Morris, have become political celebrities. Less is known, however, about the role of presidential pollsters *after* the election—that is, the use of polls in presidential governance. Since Harris worked for Kennedy, presidential pollsters have not only helped elect presidents but also have served those presidents as top policy advisers. Yet specifically *how* polls have been used by presidents has been shrouded in secrecy over the years, and scholars have just begun to shed light on that topic through interviews and archival research.

Jacobs and Shapiro were among the first to conduct systematic research into the role of presidential pollsters. Based upon interviews and archival research on the Kennedy, Johnson, and Nixon administrations, they showed how a "public opinion apparatus" had evolved into an important institutional component of the presidency.[38] In *Politicians Don't Pander,* the same authors elaborated on how the White House and others involved in the health care debate of 1993–94 "tracked public opinion in order to carefully craft their preferred policy options in order to win (rather than follow) public opinion."[39] Along the same lines, Diane Heith has shown how the growing involvement of senior advisors in the "public opinion apparatus" of the Nixon, Ford, Carter, and Reagan administrations institutionalized opinion research within the presidency.[40] Finally, in 2003, Robert Eisinger published the first comprehensive survey of the evolution of presidential polling from FDR to Clinton. Arguing that presidential polling has historically been motivated by a desire for institutional autonomy, Eisinger observed that "it is now considered commonplace and acceptable for presidents to conduct private polls." Unlike early critics, however, Eisinger sensed nothing sinister or dangerous in this development. To the contrary, he concluded that presidential polling has "enhanced accountability" by providing presidents with more "reliable means to ascertain what concerns the mass citizenry."[41]

The question of whether presidential polling promotes accountability or the manipulation of public opinion will remain a vibrant area of scholarly research in the years to come, especially as archival sources from the Reagan, Bush, and Clinton administrations become more available. George W. Bush will someday provide an especially intriguing case study in presidential polling, given his denunciations of poll-driven leadership during the 2000 presidential campaign. In the most recent studies, the notion that presidential polling promotes accountability has been challenged by the finding that Presidents Reagan and Bush used polling primarily to fashion politically "safe" rhetorical appeals.[42] In a book published in 2004, Michael J. Tole has even suggested that Truman, Johnson, and Carter became "out of touch" as a result of the polls, as their declining approval ratings led them to become dismissive and distrustful of public opinion.[43] How have other presidents used or responded to polling data? The answer to that question awaits further archival research. In the meantime, scholars interested in the most recent presidents will have to be content with studies of the public or media polls. In the next section of this report, we turn to some of the work that has already been already been done on that subject, focusing on the two best-known media polls directly involving the presidency: preelection polling and presidential approval polls.

MEDIA POLLING AND THE PRESIDENCY

Polls about presidential elections have always been "news"; newspapers "actually may have originated polling," as Mann and Orrin have observed.[44] "Straw polls" measuring candidate preferences date back to the early nineteenth century.[45] In 1916, the *Literary Digest* began its surveys of presidential preferences, and in the 1930s even the "scientific" pollsters sold their results to newspapers. For George Gallup, media syndication offered a way both to profit from his polls and to assure the public of their integrity. Since his polls appeared in newspapers of "all shades of opinion," Gallup argued in 1938, syndication offered "a pretty realistic guarantee" of their honesty.[46]

Since the 1970s, media syndication has given way to direct media sponsorship of polls, and this media "takeover" of polling has raised new concerns. As Everett Carll Ladd observed in 1980, there is a "clash of institutional imperatives" between journalism and polling, as journalism's demand for timely and dramatic news conflicts with polling's interest in "scientific" accuracy. So serious is this "clash"—so different are the requirements of a good news story and sound polling, according to Ladd—that the proliferation of media-sponsored polls in the 1970s and 1980s raised "serious questions as to whether opinion research does, or even can, enhance the democratic process."[47]

Preelection polling has long caused the most concern among critics of media polling. Even George Gallup himself conceded that such polls had "no great social value," calling election forecasts the "least socially useful function that the polls perform." Instead emphasizing how polls might provide guidance to policy makers on the issues of the day, Gallup claimed to conduct issue polls only to test his procedures and prove the reliability of his methods.[48] Nevertheless, presidential preference polls have become something of a media obsession, with news organizations quick to report any and all polls relating to the election, "no matter how irrelevant and inane."[49] In recent years, the sheer volume of preelection polling has become astonishing. Between January 1 and election day 2000, for example, the media pollsters asked some two thousand questions about voting and more than six hundred separate questions pitting Al Gore against George W. Bush. The number of news stories referring to election polls during that period numbered in the tens of thousands, with 1,590 stories referring to CBS News polls alone and 4,559 more citing Gallup polls.[50]

Twenty or thirty years ago "horserace" journalism actually had its defenders. In 1980, for example, Anthony Broh argued that polls increased public interest in campaigns and provided reporters with reliable means for predicting the outcome. Declaring the emphasis on polls "generally beneficial" and only "occasionally harmful," Broh sounded only a minor "note of caution" as he worried that some reporters might distort the results of polls or that the polls might focus attention "on exciting, but ultimately irrelevant aspects of a campaign."[51] Today, however, scholars point to a variety of potentially harmful effects from the emphasis on polls in campaign news. Some worry about the direct effects of preelection polls on voters and elections, while others emphasize the more subtle, indirect effects of polling on the character and quality of campaign discourse.

Polling's critics have long worried about a possible "bandwagon" effect from preelection polling. Over the years the pollsters have tended to dismiss this concern, yet in 1991 Albert Cantril warned that bandwagon effects could "no longer be dismissed as unproven" and called for "more comprehensive research."[52] Today, that research remains inconclusive, undoubtedly because of the difficulty of assessing bandwagon effects independently of other events and influences upon voter preferences. As Traugott and Lavrakas have summarized the literature, experimental studies have shown that poll reports can influence voters with weak candidate preferences or weak party affiliations, but they have also suggested that "bandwagon and underdog effects are present simultaneously in the electorate" and tend to be offsetting.[53] Similarly, Herbert Asher has concluded that bandwagon and underdog effects "can and do occur, but their magnitude is small and probably inconsequential."[54]

While many have noted the potential for polling to affect voter turnout, research on that topic also remains inconclusive. A classic study of the 1964 presidential election found that reports of Lyndon Johnson's probable landslide discouraged voting by supporters of both LBJ and Goldwater.[55] Yet there have been few attempts to assess, in general, in the impact of polling on voter turnout. A number of studies have focused specifically on the impact of the exit polls that networks use to make early projections. Following the 1980 election, for example, several studies produced evidence that the networks' early projections had, in fact, depressed voter turnout.[56] Some of those studies were criticized on methodological grounds.[57] However, and the research remains "far from definitive."[58] Nevertheless, concerns over the *potential* for early projections to depress voter turnout has prompted continued debate over possible solutions to the problem.[59]

Another area of research focuses on the effects of preelection polling on the quantity and quality of campaign news coverage. Studies have shown that candidates ahead in the polls receive a disproportionate share of the media coverage, particularly during the primary season, and that those ahead in the polls also get better, more positive media coverage.[60] As Kathleen Hall Jamieson has argued, polls not only provide "the trip wire that activates the discussion of strategy"; they also "determine how reporters treat the candidates." Candidates doing well in the polls are typically portrayed as doing things *correctly*, while those behind in the polls are disparaged for "what they are doing *wrong*." Not only are candidates ahead in the polls taken more seriously; they are also likely to see "segments of their ads run in news to illustrate the effectiveness of their communication strategies."[61] As Jamieson concludes, media polls may thus create a self-fulfilling prophecy: those leading in the polls get more and better news coverage, which in turn increases their chances of winning.[62] Perhaps more important, candidates leading in the polls have an easier time raising money and recruiting campaign staff and volunteers.[63]

Whatever the direct or indirect effects of media polling on elections, the heavy emphasis on polls and the horserace aspects of presidential campaigns in campaign news troubles many students of presidential politics. Indeed, Thomas Patterson has argued that the media's role in deciding who is and who is not a "serious" candidate has fundamentally corrupted the whole electoral process.[64] There is little doubt that the rhetoric of horserace journalism trivializes campaigns, and the media's obsession with the horserace has also encouraged the proliferation of dubious "overnight polls" and a variety of pseudoscientific measures of public opinion, such as call-in or Internet "polls" and on-air "focus groups." All this might make presidential campaigns more exiting and entertaining for some, but it also raises serious questions about the impact of polling on the character and quality of campaign discourse.

After preelection polls, presidential approval polls have attracted the most scholarly attention. Ostensibly designed to separate evaluations of job performance from mere "liking" of the president, approval polls also date back to the 1930s, with most pollsters still using a question that George Gallup settled on in 1945: "Do you approve or disapprove of the way [the incumbent] is handling his job as President?" In a study of polls in the news in the 1970s, Paletz and his colleagues observed that presidential approval ratings were the most commonly reported nonelection polls, and since that time the number of presidential approval polls has increased dramatically.[65] During Ronald Reagan's two terms in office, the Gallup poll asked the presidential approval question an average of just under seventeen times per year, but that average rose to more than twenty-five times per year during Clinton's first term in office. Reflecting the media "feeding frenzy" during the Monica Lewinsky scandal, there was another dramatic increase in the number of presidential approval polls during Clinton's second term. Between the day the Lewinsky story broke (January 21, 1998) and the end of April the following year, the Gallup poll alone asked the presidential approval question fifty-eight times, or about twice as frequently as normal. During the fourteen months that the scandal was in the news, nine different pollsters asked the question a total of some 217 times, or about every other day on average.[66]

According to the director of surveys at CBS News, Kathleen Frankovic, presidential approval polls can provide a "fever chart" of public reactions to speeches, debates, and scandals.[67] Scholarship on the approval rating would seem to suggest otherwise, however, as the measure appears to tap deeply rooted sentiments and commitments more than reactions to day-to-day events. According to Edwards and Gallup, for example, long-term "predispositions" such as party identification "provide the foundations of presidential approval and furnish it with a basic stability." Edwards and Gallup also dispute the conventional wisdom that approval ratings reflect people's personal economic circumstances and respond most dramatically to international crises, or "rally events."[68] Other studies seem to confirm that presidential approval ratings generally remain quite stable over time. Studies of the effects of major televised addresses on presidential approval ratings have shown only small, short-term effects.[69] A recent study revealed that Clinton's approval ratings during the Lewinsky scandal were "remarkably stable and reflected little responsiveness to day-to-day developments in the scandal."[70]

However responsive presidential approval ratings may be to presidential speeches or dramatic events, presidents "devote an impressive amount of time, energy, and money" to securing public approval, and some, like Bill Clinton, have pursued an "explicit strategy" of raising their approval ratings "in order to create public support for . . . specific proposals."[71] As Edwards explains: "Presidents and their aides firmly share the view that public support for the president is an important asset for obtaining votes in Congress and that it is difficult for others who hold power to deny the legitimate demands of a president with popular support. A president who lacks the public's support, on the other hand, is likely to face frustration and perhaps humiliation at the hands of his opponents."[72] Of course, not all presidents have embraced this view of presidential leadership, and presidents also rely upon other sorts of evidence to assess their public approval. Yet as long as the presidential approval poll remains the chief index of a president's performance in office, scholars will continue to investigate both its nature and behavior as a measurement tool and its significance as a symbolic resource in political debates.[73]

Finally, we need more research on how presidents have tried to influence their approval ratings and other media polls, not by going public but by manipulating the polls themselves. At least since Michael Wheeler's exposé of the Nixon Administration's "unprecedented attempt . . . to manipulate the public opinion polls," scholars have documented how some presidents have been obsessed with their poll numbers and have, on occasion, gone to extraordinary lengths to influence the polls.[74] Lyndon Johnson, for example, apparently had "poll fever."[75] His administration not only surreptitiously requested data and suggested questions to the media pollsters but also schemed to discredit George Gallup when his polls proved unfavorable.[76] The Nixon Administration went even further, with H. R. Haldeman spearheading a "top priority" effort to discredit Lou Harris and other pollsters deemed "enemies" of the administration.[77] Whether later presidents engaged in similar schemes awaits further archival research, but we do know that presidential pollsters now routinely appear on news and talk shows in efforts to put their own spin on the polls. Thus, the formerly secretive business of presidential polling has itself gone public, further blurring the lines between private and public polls, and between research and public relations.

Scholarship on the presidency and media polling will continue to focus on preelection and presidential approval polls. Yet we also need more studies of how presidents have manipulated the public polls, either through blatant attempts to intimidate the pollsters or through more subtle efforts to put a favorable spin on the media polls. Presidents do not use polls merely to "read" public opinion. Especially on low-salience issues, they also can exploit the symbolic and rhetorical authority of polls, as Herbst has suggested, to "manipulate public preferences."[78] If a president can show that the public is behind him, it becomes easier to pursue a particular course of action, whatever its merits. We need more studies of how presidents and their surrogates talk *about* polls and the implications of that talk for public deliberation and policy making.

THE FUTURE OF RESEARCH ON THE PRESIDENCY AND PUBLIC OPINION

The preceding review has suggested a number of the questions and controversies that will continue to inspire research on the presidency and public opinion in the years to come. The theory of the rhetorical presidency will undoubtedly remain prominent in the literature, as scholars grapple with new challenges to that theory raised by both historical and empirical research. What does it mean for a president to "go public"? When did presidents begin appealing to public opinion, and why do they devote so much time and energy to such efforts? What are the effects of presidential rhetoric on public opinion, and what are the limitations or constraints on the president's ability to rally the public behind his agenda? The answers to these questions are not so clear any more, as the whole paradigm of the rhetorical presidency has come under attack.

Democratic theory also will continue to inspire research on the presidency and public opinion, as scholars continue to investigate normative and empirical questions rooted in the delegate and trustee models of political representation. To what extent *should* presidents be concerned with public opinion? Is the public sufficiently engaged and informed to provide guidance to presidents? Do presidents *need* public support to govern effectively? Or do efforts to go public distract from the real business of governing or even represent antidemocratic efforts to manipulate public opinion? These are just a few of the persistent questions about the presidency and public opinion that arise directly out of democratic theory.

Research on polling will continue to revolve around historical and empirical questions about how quantification has changed our understanding of public opinion and its role in the political process. Within the industry, researchers will continue to look for answers to polling's most troubling methodological challenges, including rising refusal rates and problems of question wording. Outside the industry, critics of polling will continue to pursue broader questions about its legitimacy as a measure of public opinion as well as questions about its impact on political leadership and public deliberation. An especially exciting line of research makes use of archival evidence and interviews to shed light on how presidents have used private polling as a tool of leadership. With much of that research already suggesting that presidents poll primarily to help craft speeches and other public messages, we need more research specifically on *how* presidents and their speech writers use polls as an inventional resource. We also need to contemplate further the ethical and political implications of poll-driven presidential rhetoric.

Finally, the literature on media polling suggests not only some new lines of future research but also some possible reforms in the ways news organizations use polling data. As journalists continue to obsess over horserace and presidential approval polls, researchers will continue to illuminate how such polls trivialize presidential politics or, worse, subvert the electoral process and public deliberation. Recalling George Gallup's pioneering vision of polls as "sampling referenda," scholars might encourage journalists and pollsters to focus on substantive issues rather than the "game" of politics. By illuminating the relationship between the president's and the public's policy agendas, for example, media polling *could* promote political accountability. In addition, news organizations might guard more vigilantly against the partisan manipulation or "spinning" of polls, especially by the "pundit pollsters" who have become increasingly prominent on cable news and radio talk shows.[79] Finally, journalists might better educate their audiences about the limitations and possible sources of error in the polls they report, especially methodologically dubious call-in, Internet, and "overnight" polls.[80]

Beyond the lines of research suggested by the existing literature, several new avenues of investigation offer exciting possibilities. Some of these relatively unexplored approaches conceive of public opinion as a discursive phenomenon and invite qualitative rather than quantitative approaches—the methods of participant observation, ethnography, and rhetorical criticism. Going beyond poll results, for example, scholars might investigate the informal dialogue among citizens and between citizens and their leaders, including the president. Through such studies we might begin to answer questions that cannot be answered through survey research: Do presidents "listen" to the reasons *behind* the opinions of ordinary citizens? What are the discursive structures through which the public communicates the beliefs and values that underlie public opinion? Qualitative research also might be used to answer questions about how citizens understand and respond to presidential rhetoric. How do the president's words circulate among the people? How do they connect to people's lives and influence their choices and actions? How do citizens appropriate and act upon the images and arguments of presidential rhetoric?

Rhetorical criticism and other qualitative methods might also help shed more light on how presidents *use* public opinion to promote their political agendas. Citing not only polls but also letters and conversations with ordinary citizens, presidents routinely justify their actions and policies in terms of public opinion. Some presidents, like Woodrow Wilson, claimed to speak for the public without citing any quantitative or anecdotal evidence at all. How have these presidential "portraits" of public opinion been constructed at various times in our history? How have they changed over time, and what role have they played in justifying particular policies? What role, if any, do these presidential portraits of public opinion play in legislative debates or public deliberation? We have learned much in recent years about how presidents *assess* public opinion, but we are just beginning to understand how they *invoke* or even *construct* public opinion as a warrant for political action.

Finally, generational differences in political attitudes and behaviors have given rise to a number of questions that might be addressed through quantitative and qualitative opinion research. Given survey data showing low levels of political knowledge and interest among America's young people, we need to understand better the processes of political learning and how they have been affected by new technologies and cultural trends. We need to understand better how people of differing demographic characteristics—not only age but also race, class, and gender—form their understandings of politics and the political system. What narratives and arguments do people of different demographic categories draw upon to link events and public controversies to their own frames of reference? How do different people gauge the relevance of politics to their personal lives? What role does presidential rhetoric—as opposed to peer influence, journalistic opinion, or even popular culture—play in these processes? It is undoubtedly significant that the rising generation may be the most technologically savvy in history, and the consumer culture of young people has undoubtedly shaped how they view their role as citizens. Yet many questions about the politics of young people remain unanswered. How have Internet chat rooms, weblogs, and other "virtual" public spaces affected the ways in which young people learn and communicate about politics? How has the culture of mass marketing affected how young people relate to politics and to political leaders? What does it *mean* to today's young people to be engaged in civic affairs or to participate in "politics"? These are just a few questions that will become even more important to political researchers in the years to come.

The presidency and public opinion are two topics that cover a broad terrain of interdisciplinary studies. In this report, we have touched upon a number of issues at the nexus of those two topics, but our review is by no means exhaustive and it reflects the particular interests and biases of the task force members. Due to space constraints, we also could not address at sufficient length the practical implications of this research for politicians, pollsters, journalists, and political reformers. In the years to come, we hope that not only scholars but also ordinary citizens will continue to discuss and debate the issues raised in this report. The relationship between the presidency and public opinion should be of concern to *all* Americans, not just scholars.

Recommendations

1. Scholars need to revise the theory of the rhetorical presidency to take account of recent scholarship on the history of presidential rhetoric and the effects of that rhetoric on public opinion. We need to continue efforts to illuminate the various ways that presidents throughout history have gone public and to understand better the variety of effects that presidential rhetoric might have. We also need to develop more satisfying accounts of why presidents spend so much time and energy going public.

2. Scholars need to develop both descriptive and normative alternatives to the delegate and trustee models of the relationship between the presidency and public opinion. We need to illuminate more precisely the circumstances under which presidents lead or follow public opinion and investigate the implications of that relationship for the business of governing. We also need to develop theories prescribing the circumstances under which presidents *should* be more or less concerned with public opinion.
3. Both scholars and journalists need to shift the emphasis in polling research from technical or methodological concerns to larger questions about how polling has affected the political process and the public's understanding of public opinion itself. We need to expand the use of archival research to illuminate the political and ethical implications of how presidents have used private polling as a decision-making tool or as an inventional resource in developing rhetorical strategies. We need much more reflection by all concerned—scholars, media, and the general public—on the implications for both the theory and practice of democracy of defining public opinion as an aggregation of individual opinions expressed privately and anonymously to a pollster.
4. Scholars need to explore the proliferation of *media* polling in the past quarter century, including large-scale investigations of the effects of media polling on presidential elections, public deliberation, and presidential leadership. Both journalists and scholars need to develop guidelines for the responsible use of polling data by media organizations. We also need to devise ways to educate the public to be more critical consumers of media polling.
5. Scholars need to develop alternatives to the quantification of public opinion by exploring how new technologies and cultural trends may have changed the processes of opinion formation and expression. We must encourage the use of qualitative, as well as quantitative, methods to investigate public opinion as a *discursive* phenomenon, including how presidents and other political actors *construct* public opinion rhetorically and how ordinary citizens understand and respond to presidential rhetoric. Finally, we need to undertake large-scale investigations of how the Internet and other new technologies may be affecting the ways in which people perceive and respond to public opinion.

Notes

1. Richard J. Ellis, "Introduction," in *Speaking to the People: The Rhetorical Presidency in Historical Perspective*, ed. Richard J. Ellis (Amherst: University of Massachusetts Press, 1998), 1.
2. Jeffrey Tulis, *The Rhetorical Presidency* (Princeton, N.J.: Princeton University Press, 1987), 28.
3. Tulis, *The Rhetorical Presidency*, 46–47.
4. Quoted in Tulis, *The Rhetorical Presidency*, 91.
5. Ellis, "Introduction," in *Speaking to the People*, 2.
6. Theodore Roosevelt, *An Autobiography* (New York: Charles Scribner's Sons, 1924), 352.
7. See Tulis, *The Rhetorical Presidency*, 117–44.
8. Daniel Stid, "Rhetorical Leadership and 'Common Counsel' in the Presidency of Woodrow Wilson," in *Speaking to the People*, 166–67.
9. Woodrow Wilson, *Constitutional Government in the United States*, in *The Papers of Woodrow Wilson*, ed. Arthur S. Link, 69 vols. (Princeton, N.J.: Princeton University Press, 1966–93), 18:114.
10. Samuel Kernell, *Going Public: New Strategies of Presidential Leadership*, 3rd ed. (Washington, D.C.: Congressional Quarterly Press, 1997), ix.
11. George C. Edwards III, *On Deaf Ears: The Limits of the Bully Pulpit* (New Haven, Conn.: Yale University Press, 2003), xi, 72.
12. Edwards actually suggests part of the answer and, in the process, echoes the view of most rhetorical scholars that presidents typically lead not by radically changing public opinion but by articulating *existing* beliefs and values. Edwards is no doubt correct that presidents rarely "direct" public opinion, leading the public "where it otherwise refuses to go" and reshaping the "contours of the political landscape." Rather, presidents function as "facilitators who reflect, and may intensify, widely held views." Edwards, *On Deaf Ears*, 74.
13. In the "delegate" model of representation, elected representatives are presumed to defer to the will of their constituents on policy matters. In the "trustee" model, representatives are presumed to be accountable to the popular will at election time, but in day-to-day policy making they are presumed to use their own best judgment. The latter view was perhaps most famously expressed in Edmund Burke's letter to the electors of Bristol: "Your representative owes you not only his industry but also his judgment, and he betrays rather than serving you if he sacrifices it to your opinion."
14. This question, of course, has been at the heart of a long tradition of empirical scholarship on voter characteristics and behaviors. See, for example, Angus Campbell, Philip E. Converse, Warren E. Miller, and Donald E. Stokes, *The American Voter* (New York: Wiley, 1960); Norman H. Nie, Sidney Verba, and John R. Petrocik, *The Changing American Voter*, enlarged ed. (Cambridge, Mass.: Harvard University Press, 1979); Samuel L. Popkin, *The Reasoning Voter: Communication and Persuasion in Presidential Campaigns* (Chicago: University of Chicago Press, 1991); Benjamin I. Page and Robert Y. Shapiro, *The Rational Public: Fifty Years of Trends in Americans' Policy Preferences* (Chicago: University of Chicago Press, 1992); and Warren E. Miller and J. Merrill Shanks, *The New American Voter* (Cambridge, Mass.: Harvard University Press, 1996).

15. Susan Herbst, *Numbered Voices: How Opinion Polling Has Shaped American Politics* (Chicago: University of Chicago Press, 1993), 113.

16. George Gallup and Saul F. Rae, *The Pulse of Democracy: The Public Opinion Poll and How It Works* (New York: Simon and Schuster, 1940), 5.

17. See J. Michael Hogan, "George Gallup and the Rhetoric of Scientific Democracy," *Communication Monographs* 64 (1997): 162–65.

18. George Gallup, "A Reply to 'The Pollsters,'" *Public Opinion Quarterly* 13 (1949): 179–80.

19. Gallup and Rae, *The Pulse of Democracy*, 11.

20. George Gallup, "Polling Public Opinion," *Current History* 51 (February 1940): 57.

21. Kenneth F. Warren, *In Defense of Public Opinion Polling* (Boulder, Colo: Westview Press, 2001).

22. Despite dedicating the book to "four of the founders" of the polling industry, for example, Albert Cantril's 1991 book *The Opinion Connection* discussed many of the technical criticism of polls, reflected thoughtfully on concerns about how journalistic imperatives might have corrupted polling, and even took seriously questions about whether polls really measured "public opinion" at all. Cantril also concluded by considering whether polls contribute anything useful to the democratic process. More recently, Irving Crespi, a former executive in both the Gallup Organization and the Roper Organization, likewise conceded that many of the methodological criticisms of polling are "justified" and seriously considered arguments that polls not only fail "to capture the complexity and dynamics of public opinion" but also pose potential threats to democratic processes. See Albert H. Cantril, *The Opinion Connection: Polling, Politics, and the Press* (Washington: Congressional Quarterly Press, 1991); Irving Crespi, *The Public Opinion Process: How the People Speak* (Mahwah, N.J.: Lawrence Erlbaum Associates, 1997), 156–59. The polling industry's self-critical attitude may also be seen in many of the postings on AAPOR's listserv, AAPORnet, and in the papers presented at AAPOR's annual convention.

23. One exception is Michael Wheeler, who argued in his 1976 book *Lies, Damn Lies, and Statistics* that the pollsters' record in predicting elections, like most "parlor tricks," is "impressive until you see how it is done." According to Wheeler, the pollsters typically increase their sample size and tighten up their other procedures in final election polls, since those are the only polls that can be proven wrong, and they still have correctly predicted only the obvious landslides. Since Wheeler's study, as Hogan has pointed out, the pollsters have done even worse, completely missing the Reagan landslide in 1980 and making their most inaccurate prediction since 1936 in the 1992 election. In 1996, the pollsters again significantly missed the mark in their final vote projections, although in 2000 most correctly suggested an outcome too close to call. See Wheeler, *Lies, Damn Lies, and Statistics*, 37–40; and Hogan, "George Gallup and the Rhetoric of Scientific Democracy," 166–67; Warren J. Mitofsky, "Was 1996 a Worse Year for the Polls than 1948?" *Public Opinion Quarterly* 62 (Summer 1998): 230–49; and Michael W. Traugott, "Assessing Poll Performance in the 2000 Election," *Public Opinion Quarterly* 65 (2001): 389–419.

24. See, for example, J. Michael Hogan and Ted J. Smith III, "Polling on the Issues: Public Opinion and the Nuclear Freeze," *Public Opinion Quarterly* 55 (1991): 534–69.

25. See, for example, Gerard A. Hauser, *Vernacular Voices: The Rhetoric of Publics and Public Spheres* (Columbia: University of South Carolina Press, 1999), esp. 190–93.

26. As Michael Schudson has argued, polls "give more credit to the silent and the apathetic

than do other measures" of public opinion, and they often evoke "opinions" where people in fact "have no opinion or no strong opinion but feel obligated to say something." Michael Schudson, *The Power of News* (Cambridge, Mass.: Harvard University Press, 1995), 140.

27. James A. Stimson, Michael B. MacKuen, and Robert S. Erikson, "Dynamic Representation," *American Political Science Review* 89 (1995): 545, 559.

28. John G. Geer, *From Tea Leaves to Opinion Polls: A Theory of Democratic Leadership* (New York: Columbia University Press, 1996), xiii, 8–13.

29. Lawrence R. Jacobs and Robert Y. Shapiro, *Politicians Don't Pander: Political Manipulation and the Loss of Democratic Responsiveness* (Chicago: University of Chicago Press, 2000), xiii.

30. Jacobs and Shapiro find the anti-pandering attitude especially odd. To the extent that politicians *do* respond to the polls, they ask: "Why has the derogatory term 'pander' been pinned on politicians who respond to public opinion? . . . It is surely odd in a democracy to consider responsiveness to public opinion as disreputable." See Jacobs and Shapiro, *Politicians Don't Pander,* xiv.

31. See, for example, J. Michael Hogan, *The Nuclear Freeze Campaign: Rhetoric and Foreign Policy in the Telepolitical Age* (East Lansing: Michigan State University Press, 1994), 119–37.

32. Herbst, *Numbered Voices,* 166.

33. See, respectively, Elisabeth Noelle-Neumann, *The Spiral of Science: Public Opinion—Our Social Skin,* 2nd ed. (Chicago: University of Chicago Press, 1993), and Benjamin Ginsberg, *The Captive Public: How Mass Opinion Promotes State Power* (New York: Basic Books, 1986).

34. Justin Lewis, *Constructing Public Opinion: How Political Elites Do What They Like and Why We Seem to Go Along With It* (New York: Columbia University Press, 2001).

35. See, for example, Lindsay Rogers, *The Pollsters: Public Opinion, Politics, and Democratic Leadership* (New York: Alfred A. Knopf, 1949).

36. Wheeler, *Lies, Dam Lies, and Statistics,* 62–74.

37. David W. Moore, *The Superpollsters: How They Measure and Manipulate Public Opinion in America* (New York: Four Walls Eight Windows, 1995), xii, 359.

38. Lawrence R. Jacobs and Robert Y. Shapiro, "The Rise of Presidential Polling: The Nixon White House in Historical Perspective," *Public Opinion Quarterly* 59 (1995): 163–95.

39. Jacobs and Shapiro, *Politicians Don't Pander,* xviii.

40. Diane J. Heith, "Staffing the White House Public Opinion Apparatus: 1969–1988," *Public Opinion Quarterly* 62 (1998): 165–89. See also Diane J. Heith, "Presidential Polling and the Potential for Leadership," in *Presidential Power: Forging the Presidency for the Twenty-First Century,* ed. Robert Y. Shapiro, Martha Joynt Kumar, and Lawrence R. Jacobs (New York: Columbia University Press, 2000), 380–407.

41. Robert M. Eisinger, *The Evolution of Presidential Polling* (Cambridge: Cambridge University Press, 2003), 182, 185. Eisinger acknowledges concerns that polling may undermine the "deliberative nature of public opinion" and is often used by presidents "for public relations purposes," yet he still dismisses those like Hitchens, Ginsberg, and Herbst who have "described polls as potentially debilitating forces in democracy" (184).

42. See Wynton C. Hall, "The Invention of 'Quantifiably Safe Rhetoric': Richard Wirthlin and Ronald Reagan's Instrumental Use of Public Opinion Research in Presidential

Discourse," *Western Journal of Communication* 66 (2002): 319–46; and Wynton C. Hall, "'Reflections of Yesterday': George H. W. Bush's Instrumental Use of Public Opinion Research in Presidential Discourse," *Presidential Studies Quarterly* 32 (2002): 531–58.

43. Michael J. Tole, *Out of Touch: The Presidency and Public Opinion* (College Station: Texas A&M University Press, 2004).

44. Thomas E. Mann and Gary R. Orrin, "To Poll or Not to Poll . . . and Other Questions," in *Media Polls in American Politics*, ed. Thomas E. Mann and Gary R. Orrin (Washington: Brookings Institution, 1992), 1.

45. See Tom W. Smith, "The First Straw? A Study of the Origins of Election Polls," *Public Opinion Quarterly* 54 (1990): 21–36.

46. George Gallup, "Government and the Sampling Referendum," *Journal of the American Statistical Association* 33 (1938): 138.

47. Everett Carll Ladd, "Polling and the Press: The Clash of Institutional Imperatives," *Public Opinion Quarterly* 44 (1980): 575.

48. Quoted in Hogan, "George Gallup and the Rhetoric of Scientific Democracy," 166.

49. David L. Paletz, Jonathan Y. Short, Helen Baker, Barbara Cookman Campbell, Richard J. Cooper, and Rochelle M. Oeslander, "Polls in the Media: Content, Credibility, and Consequences," *Public Opinion Quarterly* 44 (1980): 499.

50. Monika L. McDermott and Kathleen A. Frankovic, "Horserace Polling and Survey Method Effects: An Analysis of the 2000 Campaign," *Public Opinion Quarterly* 67 (2003): 244.

51. C. Anthony Broh, "Horse-Race Journalism: Reporting the Polls in the 1976 Election," *Public Opinion Quarterly* 44 (1980): 514–29.

52. Cantril, *The Opinion Connection*, 216.

53. Michael W. Traugott and Paul J. Lavrakas, *The Voter's Guide to Election Polls*, 2nd ed. (New York: Chatham House, 2000), 18–19. See also Paul J. Lavrakas, Jack K. Holley, and Peter V. Miller, "Public Reactions to Polling News during the 1988 Presidential Election Campaign," in *Polling and Presidential Election Coverage*, ed. Paul J. Lavrakas and Jack K. Holley (Newbury Park, Calif.: Sage, 1991), 151–83.

54. Herbert Asher, *Polling and the Public: What Every Citizen Should Know*, 4th ed. (Washington: Congressional Quarterly, 1998), 139. Also see Diana A. Mutz, *Impersonal Influence: How Perceptions of Mass Collectives Affect Political Attitudes* (New York: Cambridge University Press, 1998), esp. 187–90.

55. See, for example, Kurt Lang and Gladys Engel Long, *Voting and Nonvoting: Implications of Broadcast Returns before Polls are Closed* (Waltham, Mass.: Blaisdell Publishing, 1968); Laurily K. Epstein and Gerald Strom, "Election Night Projections and West Coast Turnout," *American Political Science Quarterly* 9 (1981): 479–91; Paul Wilson, "Election Night 1980 and the Controversy over Early Projections," in *Television Coverage of the 1980 Presidential Campaign*, ed. William C. Adams (Norwood, N.J.: Ablex, 1983), 141–60.

56. See Raymond Wolfinger and Peter Linquiti, "Tuning in and Turning out," *Public Opinion* 4 (1981): 56–60; John Jackson and William H. McGee III, "Election Reporting and Voter Turnout," Report of the Center for Political Studies, University of Michigan, Ann Arbor, 1981; John Jackson, "Election Night Reporting and Voter Turnout," *American Journal of Political Science* 27 (1983): 615–35; Michael X. Delli Carpini, "Scooping the Voters? The Consequences of the Networks' Early Call of the 1980 Presidential Race," *Journal of Politics* 46 (1984): 866–85.

57. See Seymour Sudman, "Do Exit Polls Influence Voting Behavior?" *Public Opinion Quarterly* 50 (1986): 331–37.

58. Cantril, *The Opinion Connection,* 217.

59. See Asher, *Polling and the Public,* 120–21.

60. See, for example, J. W. Rhee, "How Polls Drive Campaign Coverage: The Gallup/CNN/USA Today Tracking Poll and USA Today's Coverage of the 1992 Presidential Campaign," *Political Communication* 13 (1996): 213–29.

61. Kathleen Hall Jamieson, *Dirty Politics: Deception, Distraction, and Democracy* (New York: Oxford University Press, 1992), 175–80.

62. See Kathleen Hall Jamieson, *Everything You Think You Know about Politics . . . and Why You're Wrong* (New York: Basic Books, 2000), 206–10.

63. See Michael W. Traugott, "The Impact of Media Polls on the Public," in *Media Polls in American Politics,* 128–29. According to Albert Cantril, however, preelection polling actually has "less impact on contributions to presidential campaigns than on contributions to campaigns for other offices," both because of the availability of federal matching funds for presidential candidates and because the unfolding of the primary season creates a dynamic that has greater impact on potential contributors than do poll standings. See Cantril, *The Opinion Connection,* 220–21.

64. See, for example, Thomas Patterson, *Out of Order* (New York: Vintage Books, 1994).

65. Paletz et al., "Polls in the Media," 499.

66. J. Michael Hogan, "The Rhetoric of Presidential Approval," in *Images, Scandal, and Communication Strategies of the Clinton Presidency,* ed. Robert E. Denton Jr. and Rachel L. Holloway (Westport, Conn.: Praeger, 2003), 271–72.

67. Kathleen A. Frankovic, "Public Opinion and Polling," in *The Politics of News and the News of Politics,* ed. Doris Graber, Denis McQuail, and Pippa Norris (Washington: Congressional Quarterly Press, 1998), 150.

68. George C. Edwards III and Alec M. Gallup, *Presidential Approval: A Sourcebook* (Baltimore: Johns Hopkins University Press, 1990), 134, 138–52.

69. See, for example, Lyn Ragsdale, "The Politics of Presidential Speechmaking, 1949–1980," *American Political Science Review* 78 (1984): 971–84.

70. Hogan, "The Rhetoric of Presidential Approval," 278.

71. Edwards, *On Deaf Ears,* 28–29.

72. Edwards, *On Deaf Ears,* 15.

73. For the most recent contribution to this literature, see Brian Newman, "Integrity and Presidential Approval, 1980–2000," *Public Opinion Quarterly* 67 (2003): 335–67.

74. Wheeler, *Lies, Damn Lies, and Statistics,* 17.

75. In 1966, reporter William Honan drew this conclusion in a report that caused considerable controversy by exposing Oliver Quayle's private polling for the president. See William H. Honan, "Johnson May Not Have Poll Fever, but He Has a 'Good Case of the Poll Sniffles,'" *New York Times Magazine,* August 21, 1966, 34–69. See also Bruce E. Altschuler, *LBJ and the Polls* (Gainesville: University of Florida Press, 1990).

76. See Eisinger, *The Evolution of Presidential Polling,* 122–24.

77. Eisinger, *The Evolution of Presidential Polling,* 127–34. For a more detailed look at now the Nixon Administration tried to manipulate the polls, see Lawrence R. Jacobs and

Robert Y. Shapiro, "Presidential Manipulation of Polls and Public Opinion: The Nixon Administration and the Pollsters," *Political Science Quarterly* 110 (1995–96): 519–38.

78. Herbst, *Numbered Voices*, 168.

79. David Hill, "Pundit Pollsters Blur Lines," *The Hill: The Newspaper for and about the U.S. Congress*, 4 February 2004, http://www.hillnews.com/david_hill/020404.aspx (accessed March 29, 2004).

80. Call-in and Internet "polls," of course, are not really polls at all, since respondents are self-selected rather than identified through random sampling techniques. "Overnight" polls *are* based on random samples, yet those samples are small and inherently defective. Overnight polls typically have samples of only 400–700 respondents, and they do not allow for "call-backs," or later efforts to interview hard-to-reach respondents. As a result, their samples tend to be significantly older, more female, and more Democratic than truly representative national samples. In addition, the opinion measured by overnight polls is "notoriously perishable"—that is, it has not yet jelled and stabilized in the context of public discussion. See Cantril, *The Opinion Connection*, 47–48, 100–102, 144–46.

CHAPTER 14

REPORT OF THE NATIONAL TASK FORCE ON THE ETHICAL RESPONSIBILITIES OF PRESIDENTIAL RHETORIC

Chair: Steven R. Goldzwig, Marquette University
Karrin Vasby Anderson, Colorado State University
Frederick J. Antczak, Grand Valley State University
Thomas W. Benson, Pennsylvania State University, University Park
Rita Kirk Whillock, Southern Methodist University

ON RHETORIC, ETHICS, AND THE PRESIDENCY

Part of the implicit charge of this task force is to call the presidency to its ethical obligations, most particularly with respect to its rhetorical activities. And yet as any observer of the ongoing four-year cycles of presidential campaigning has come to see, American political discourse is saturated with candidate rhetoric designed to display "character" and surrogate rhetoric designed to cast doubt on the character of rival candidates. Talk radio often excoriates the character of political opponents as a premise and primary subject of political conversation. We distract ourselves with indignation, yet have trouble finding a purchase for reflective ethical inquiry and mutually respectful policy debate. In some ways, it seems that we need a moratorium on ethics as the implicit theme of presidential and campaign discourse. And yet it is not so much that we need less focus on ethics as that we may need to refocus how we talk about ethics. The work of scholars in rhetoric has done much to encourage such a refocusing of ethical inquiry.

The rhetorical tradition has invoked ethics in three interrelated senses—rhetoric and moral outcomes as the substance of persuasion; moral character as the basis of persuasion; and ethics as implied in the relation of public deliberation.

ETHICS AND THE ENDS OF RHETORIC

The tradition tells us that we should value speakers and audiences who seek ethical ends. Of course, what counts as an ethical end is often precisely the issue that divides speakers on various sides of a question, forming the subject matter of public address; rhetoric itself can provide no infallible rule to choose among policy alternatives, in most cases—such judgments are part of the larger relations of ethics and politics. Rhetorical scholars and the public are rightly interested in how persuaders depict the ethics of policy questions. Some rhetorical scholars have warned against the danger of turning everyday policy arguments into ethical arguments prematurely, since such tactics can backfire, creating polarization, rigidity, and self-righteousness; pushing aside pragmatic considerations and mutually beneficial compromises; and creating mutually antagonistic camps both accusing the other side of moral blindness. Turning a great public question into a moral confrontation can have the effect of silencing the very deliberation that the society needs to deal with the problem; failing to acknowledge the moral dimensions of a problem can prolong evasion and injustice.

Some rhetorical scholars have asked whether certain ends are so important that the president has a moral obligation to support them. Steven R. Goldzwig and George N. Dionisopoulos argue that John F. Kennedy was right to make a moral commitment to civil rights, a position shared by Garth Pauley; Thomas W. Benson has interrogated Franklin D. Roosevelt's silence on civil rights in two speeches delivered on the Gettysburg battlefield in the 1930s.[1]

CHARACTER AS RHETORICAL PROOF

Ethics, and the perceived enactment of ethics in the performed character of the speaker, form part of the "proof" of any discourse, from the audience's point of view. This form of proof Aristotle called *ethos*.[2] To ethos (the depicted character of the speaker or implied author), contemporary rhetorical theory has added concerns with how texts represent not only their authors but also their *listeners* and *readers* (second persona; implied audience); and how the text represents *other human agents*.[3]

Listeners do and should assess the ethical character of a speaker as part of the speaker's general argument; the rhetorical text itself is a guide, though in the age of ghostwriting not always a reliable guide to presidential ethos.[4] Assessments of presidential ethics properly include a consideration of how the president depicts not only himself or herself but also other human agents.

ETHICS OF COMMUNICATION IMPLIED BY RHETORIC ITSELF

The act of engaging in rhetoric, as speaker or listener, implies ethical obligations for both. Karl Wallace wrote that "communication carries its ethics within itself," by which he meant that "public address of any kind is inseparable from the values which permeate a free and democratic community."[5] Wallace argued that in a democratic society, speakers have an implicit obligation to meet certain ethical standards—they should be well informed on the subjects they address and should acknowledge legitimate opposing views; they should be fair and accurate and should help their listeners to arrive at fair judgments by cultivating the "habit of justice"; they should reveal the sources of their motives, information, and opinion; they should make themselves publicly accountable and should prefer public to private motivations; they should "acknowledge and respect diversity of argument and opinion"; they should respect dissent.[6]

Employing Wallace's sense of the implicit ethical rules of democratic rhetoric, Christopher Lyle Johnstone argues that Ronald Reagan's 1984 campaign rhetoric was deficient in meeting "the procedural standards of intelligent public deliberation and judgment."[7]

> He has bequeathed us a vision of the political process in which the
> values and forms of democratic decision-making have been replaced
> by activities and expectations geared more to entertainment than

to wise judgment. This vision substitutes the campaign rally for the town meeting, patriotic homily for argument, spectacle for discussion and debate. It makes every public appearance by the candidate into a performance—staged, scripted, recorded, and then repackaged as press-coverage-by-soundbite and as campaign commercial. It replaces judgment with emotional satisfaction as the aim of public communicative encounters. It replaces the ideal of citizen-as-judge with that of citizen as spectator.[8]

Richard L. Johannesen has expressed similar but in some ways narrower doubts about the rhetoric of Ronald Reagan. In assessing the first two years of the Reagan presidency, Johannesen concludes that "President Reagan plays fast and loose with the facts and thus warrants ethical condemnation."[9] Having briefly catalogued representative critical practices that focus rhetorical inquiry on the ethics of presidential discourse, we next turn to a discussion of what we believe rhetorical critics can and perhaps ought to be engaged in *now*, both in fashioning a critical stance toward presidential ethics and in developing critical practices.

WHAT CRITICS CAN AND SHOULD BE DOING NOW

A conundrum of idealism vs. pragmatism hovers over presidential ethics and effectiveness and the development of a critical stance. Nearly twenty years ago, Thomas B. Farrell reflected on "rhetorical resemblance," identifying a paradox between rhetoric as an ethical-political practice and as a poetic. Farrell contended that "Aristotle gave us a double standard for appreciating and engaging the mimetic status of rhetorical discourse."[10] He continued by observing:

> My suspicion is that Aristotle conceives the qualities of rhetorical discourse quite differently from an *ethical-political* stance (employed in the *Rhetoric*) and from an aesthetic stance (employed in the *Poetics*). As many observers have noted, for instance, Aristotle believed that acting (*praxis*) was superior to making or creating (*poesis*).... But at the same time, he construes poetic "truth" to be more universal and truer than historical truth (what men have actually done). And he places credible impossibilities on a higher aesthetic plane than incredible fact. He would value myth more than, say, news.[11]

If Farrell's supposition is correct, Aristotle's choice to tie together rhetoric and poetic in an untanglable knot was deliberate. It was necessitated by the paradox of public discourse. Farrell concluded his argument by contending that "*rhetoric is the only art responsible for the imitation and expression of public thought. And nothing is more tenuous than that.*"[12]

Aristotle's "double standard" for evaluating rhetorical discourse is mirrored in discussions of the ethical responsibilities of presidential discourse. On one hand, critics attend to presidential rhetoric from an ethical-political perspective—establishing normative standards by which presidents should abide but from which most leaders (save those who agree with our political predilections) inevitably fall short. On the other hand, scholars know that presidential discourse is governed by the practitioners who take a decidedly more aesthetic approach to the crafting of political discourse. Just as "beauty" is in the "eye of the beholder," "virtue" is often determined by the popular vote. Although none would argue that a popular message is always an ethical message, many contend that in politics one cannot accomplish anything unless one is in office—thus the achievement of ethical goals is dependent on rhetoric that is persuasive and, as such, aesthetically appealing.

Hence a battle rages between idealism and pragmatism. Do we establish lofty standards for presidential discourse, knowing full well that mortal presidents will fail to abide by them? Or do we acknowledge politics as an inherently strategic activity for which the only credible measure of excellence is winning?

The solution to this problem, suggested by Farrell via Aristotle, is not to attempt to unravel the paradox but instead to recognize the strength inherent in the paradoxical form. Presidential discourse is not least ethical when it is most aesthetically appealing. Ethics lies outside the realm of aesthetics. However, where discourse is concerned the ethics of a message is entwined—knotted—to its aesthetic appeal. Critics must provide normative standards acknowledging that these two realms—rhetoric and poetic—are melded in political discourse. All our recommendations for ethical communication will be disregarded unless we acknowledge that ethical speech also needs to be persuasive.

The conundrum of ethics versus effectiveness was addressed in an episode of *The West Wing*, NBC's pop culture site for negotiating the issue of presidential ethics. Fictive Democratic campaign strategist Bruno Gianelli is debating the merits of using soft money for political advertising with White House Deputy Communications Director Sam Seaborn. Seaborn, taking the ethical high road, argues that the president cannot oppose soft money in his campaign rhetoric and then use it for political gain. Seaborn opines, "There's such a thing as leadership by example." Gianelli responds, "Yeah, it comes right before getting your ass kicked in an election." Gianelli argues for the importance of leveling the playing field—if conservatives are going to play rough and tumble with their campaign ads, then liberals have to do the same in order to continue to give voters a choice—"We're both right. We're both wrong. Let's have two parties." Communications Director Toby Ziegler weighs in with an Aristotelian solution: "Let's stick to the spirit of the law." Seaborn interrupts, "The spirit of the law means no soft money." Ziegler continues, "No, I'm saying let's do an issue ad—an actual issue ad. Let's do a bunch—health care, equal opportunity, school construction. Does anyone think that raising awareness of crumbling schools won't help us?" After outlining an issue ad strategy that both meets the ethical "spirit" of the campaign finance law and promises to be rhetorically and politically effective, campaign strategist Gianelli remarks, "This isn't bad. I like this. Why am I nervous?" Seaborn quips, "It's not amoral." Both characters chuckle.[13]

Implicit in the television narrative is at least one answer to the paradox between idealism and pragmatism in political discourse. If a president has faith in the soundness of his or her policy, in the clarity of his or her vision, then ethics need not be sublimated to strategy. Instead, all of rhetoric's aesthetic strength can be mustered to support its ethical-political purpose. Moreover, when this occurs both critical and public cynicism are apt to diminish. Attempts to mine and identify when this happens and when it decidedly does not, of course, have implications for how we go about the process of rhetorical criticism.

ENRICHING OUR CRITICAL STANCE AND CRITICAL PRACTICES

Certainly recent presidential rhetoric has presented one of the most intriguing challenges for criticism. The public spectacle of a Nixon or a Clinton clinging precariously, desperately to the bare bones of a legal defense has perhaps given us some reason to believe that no one is entirely above the law, that despite creaks and sputters, the system in some sense works. But the law is aimed, more or less, to enforce our minimum standards for behavior, and minimum standards leave a good bit unsaid. How could a legal code begin to express critically the larger ethical *disappointment* in a president using a merely legal rhetoric to wriggle away from legal responsibility—whether it is a Nixon covering up a cover-up or a Clinton clinging to the nuances of defining of "what 'is' is"—when the larger issue is a failure of moral vision and discipline? How could critical discourse examine cases where a simple up or down evaluation is less interesting than a description of what is going on—for example, the apparent capitulation of the Carter energy messages? How are we to approach mixed cases, like the valiant hubris of LBJ's declaration of a "war on poverty," or tease out shadings of ethical difference between JFK's two televised messages on civil rights?

One of the most recent trends in ethics has been the "Virtue Ethics" movement spurred by philosophers like Alasdair MacIntyre and theologians like Stanley Hauerwas.[14] Moving away from a rule-based approach to ethical judgment of ethical choices, virtue ethics seeks to frame ethical issues in terms of the character formed in community practices.

This movement has attracted a great deal of attention in philosophy, but rhetorical scholars had been moving in the direction of "character in community" for years. Wayne Booth's emphasis in his *Modern Dogma and the Rhetoric of Assent* envisioned "the self as a field of selves"—not an automatic individual making discrete rational choices and bound by unambiguous rules so much as "a social product in process of changing through interaction, sharing values with other selves."[15] Thus his ethical imperative "must always be to perform as well as possible in the same primal symbolic dance which makes us able to dance at all"; that is, the enrichment of the common stock of reasons for elevating its practice of rhetoric.[16] Booth went on to develop "an ethics of fiction" focused on the quality of relationship enacted in the inductive, deductive, and "coductive" processes of reading in *The Company We Keep*.[17] While Booth has largely focused his system of rhetorical ethics on literature, James Boyd White has taken more specifically polemical material. White's *When Words Lose Their Meaning* focused on the constitutions and reconstitutions of language, character, and community and their processes of mutual influence; in later work like *Acts of Hope* he developed an ethically charged notion of authority in literature, law, and politics.[18]

This is to say that in the ethics of rhetoric, *character counts*. But in the richness of our scholarship, character counts across a variety of dimensions: the formulation of the character of the audience has been a concern as far back as Edwin Black's "The Second Persona."[19] Concern about those excluded or effaced from audiences, and the import of that exclusion for those still included in discourses of power, was the focus of Philip Wander's introduction of "The Third Persona."[20]

While efforts to develop rules, as part of a normative code of ethics for presidential discourse, are earnest and worthy enterprises, codes (even the ones we will introduce in this report) often come to suffer the fate of campaign finance laws; loopholes will be found, ethically indeterminate new ground will eventually be plowed (email and Internet campaigning, for example, seems to have become a whole new area of campaigning in the wake of Howard Dean's improbable early emergence as a frontrunner for the 2004 Democratic nomination). And in our pluralistic diversity, agreement on any particular code is likely to be a slow process, the results of which can easily be too general or innocuous or dated to matter. By what code can we capture the ethical content of, say, threatening music accompanying a message like "there's a Bear in the woods," or golden sunshine on a backdrop banner—"Mission Accomplished!"—that elides an occasion of congratulating sailors returning from combat to an unspoken visual claim of presidential accomplishment, without ever admitting to such a shift?

In a society bound in part by rules, we must continue to hone ethical codes. The further challenge posed by ethically interesting presidential discourse is to develop supplementary approaches, like those following from the work of scholars—from MacIntyre and Hauerwas to Booth and White, and on through Black and Wander—capable of more precision and nuance in describing ethical issues, virtues, and practices. The work of ethical codes needs to be supplemented by a descriptive ethic focused on character and community.

The purpose of such a critical ethic would be to formulate—in a publicly accessible, intersubjectively testable way—critical claims about the implied author of any "text" and the audience constituted as author and audience interact. It is to describe, with some degree of intersubjectively testable precision, what sort of relation, what sort of "discursive community" is enacted between the implied author and audience as the "text" unfolds.

To do this, we will need to learn to combine some familiar questions of close reading with new questions about the world as reconstituted by the discourse. For example we already have some ways of asking:

(1) What are the text's constitutive *topoi,* and how are they built out of the text's characteristic terms of description and evaluation? How do they work to rank-order the possibilities for appeal to others, for intersections of motive?

(2) How do these terms clarify and advance some possibilities (and occlude others) for sustaining, extending, and transforming the immediate community of discourse and the wider world in which it is to operate?

(3) What modes of reasoning and proof are practiced as if they were valid, reliable, authoritative? What are the specific functions accorded

to deduction, anecdote, analogy, aphorism, appeal to authority? What is the relative force of each? Which transitions and shifts does the text treat as if they should pass without question, and which does it acknowledge the need to defend?

Such questions could enable ethical critics to begin to determine what one can and cannot say, what one can and cannot do, or even aspire to do, in the world constituted by the text. Questions could be asked, testable claims formulated about who we have to become in relation to the author, to the text in its dispositions of language and habits of persuasion, in order to belong and move appropriately and effectively in the sort of world the text establishes and enacts, and what it can mean to move that way. But such traditional questions need to be combined with new sorts of questions about presidential character and democratic community. For example:

(1) How is the discourse inclusive and exclusive? What roles does it offer or preclude for the variety of potential members of the audience, and for other parties affected but not addressed by the text? On what principles is this inclusion and exclusion done, how explicitly, and how justly, especially as readers are given to see justice?

(2) What relation exists between the discursive community constituted and enacted in the text and the culture that supplies materials from which the text is formed? How are the potential materials for discourse treated and preserved? What is discarded without explanation or afterthought, what may be pillaged, what comes with strings attached? Who may and may not interpret these materials? What parts of the past—especially discourses of the past—may be, in the words of Nixon press secretary Ron Ziegler, "rendered inoperative"?

(3) How is the discursive community constituted in the text committed to maintaining and extending, or transforming, or demoting and destroying these cultural resources? How is that community committed to a recognition or admission or celebration of their past, or to denying it, or reshaping it? How does the act of "reading" commit the engaged reader to the promise of a particular future for its author, its audience, its materials, and any others who inhabit such communities?

What can this critical approach do that we need to do? We believe it can do at least three things:

- Assess the quality of accountability. One might, for example, assess JFK's speech on the Bay of Pigs disaster over against the subsequent practices of presidential apology and deniability.
- Elucidate the sources of comfort. For example, one might seek to elucidate the ways in which Reagan drew upon such sources in his response to the Challenger disaster.
- Examine claims about the nature and sources of evil. One might examine "the designs of evil men" and the messianism that brooks no possibility of self-judgment.

There is much work remaining for ethical critics of presidential discourse, describing who our presidents make themselves in their discourse and what kind of listeners they create—what kind of people they call us to be.

INSTITUTIONAL FORCES AND CONSTRAINTS: A BRIEF ENCOUNTER

We acknowledge that our critical work may not always proceed smoothly. There are major institutional forces and constraints that threaten to impede our efforts and those of engaged publics.

Challenging a candidate's ethical standards is one publicly accepted form of political discourse. Typically, public discourse and criticism center on what an opponent said and when, assumptions about self-interest, assessments of actions related to the public good, and communal judgments regarding the candidates' abilities to learn from past successes and failures. While these topoi are common, the 2004 presidential election campaign presented additional dilemmas. In dispute are at least three other issues: the realm for public debate, who gets to speak and who does not, and distracting public attention from critical claims.

The Realm for Public Debate

The 2004 presidential election continued a debate on where public debate resides. One clear example is the controversy occasioned by the initiatives of MoveOn.org. In 2003, MoveOn.org sponsored a television advertisement contest that was intended to attract and showcase "really creative ads that will engage and enlighten viewers and help them understand the truth about George Bush."[21] The competition generated over 1,500 submissions with over 110,000 people logging on to vote for their favorite ad from a group of finalists. People might never have known of the contest or the advertisements except that two ads comparing Bush to Hitler were posted on the site. The creator of both ads was George Soros, who claims that he was awakened in the middle of the night thinking about Bush's statement that "you're either with us or against us." Soros said the speech reminded him of Nazi slogans he read as a child in Hungary.

On January 4, 2004, chair of the Republican National Committee Ed Gillespie criticized the Hitler/Bush comparison saying that the tactics were "despicable" and that they were characteristic of "the left today." Fox News Channel began the media coverage of the story on January 5, followed by other media organizations. Concurrently, the advertisements were pulled from the MoveOn.org site. The debate raged on for a few more days, despite the fact that viewers were unable to see the advertisement that created the controversy. Essentially, the public debate ended before it began.

Who Gets to Speak and Who Does Not

Moveon.org represents another ethical issue related to who gets to speak and who does not. Two issues are illustrative of these claims. First, where should hostile speech reside in a mass-mediated society? Does the public only get to debate *reports about* the speech as opposed to exposure to the speech itself? Moveon.org pulled the ads before the eruption of media attention, yet it remained a story for several days and was even included on the RNC website.

A second issue concerns the winning advertisement of the competition. Moveon.org hoped to air the advertisement during the Super Bowl but was rejected by CBS on the grounds that the ad constituted "advocacy advertising," which is against CBS policy. The policy was established in the 1950s and is based upon a consumer entertainment model of television. Basically, people want to be entertained during programming like the Super Bowl. Divisive ads are not conducive to entertainment. Assuming for a moment that we accept the CBS policy on those grounds, where does the public debate take place? It appears that the "place" for debate is becoming more and more limited. While venues for expression are available on some media channels, it is more likely to take place on specialized Internet sites that cater to like-minded people.

This issue is critical and is certain to be the subject of contention during future presidential elections. In an effort to curb the influence of "soft money" on elections, new campaign-finance laws ban soft-money ads that use a candidate's name within thirty days of a primary and sixty days of a general election. The Supreme Court in *McConnell v. Federal Election Commission* upheld the statute in December, 2003.

On the negative side, free speech seems jeopardized. Not only is it becoming increasingly difficult to find a mass media outlet in which citizens can bring before the population issues they wish to be debated; they are now limited as to the timing of those messages. On the positive side, ads that claim to be issue ads will have to focus on the issues and not the people who represent those issues. Essentially, the only unrestricted free speech can come from people who run for office, thus ratcheting up the negative campaign style that many voters eschew.

Distracting Public Attention from Ethical Claims

In the film *Wag the Dog,* the fictitious tale is told of a campaign distracting the voters from certain issues by having them focus on the central issue of war. Although initially written as a novel regarding President George H. W. Bush, the story is typically interpreted as a parody of President Clinton. What fascinates the public, perhaps, is that it *could* be true that the public was duped by an invoked war.

In 2004, as in earlier campaigns, questions concerning what is real and what is staged in politics continued to emerge. Whether it was "Astroturf," creating the illusion that a grassroots campaign is unfolding when it is not, or the effect of tax breaks on the economy, the public will continue to try to be the arbiters of truth, and well-funded, often partisan institutional forces will seek to influence those judgments.

Significantly, voters cannot make informed decisions in a democracy unless they have *access* to information. Judging the credibility of information is critical to success in decision making. At a time when information is a commodity that both the government and the press are more than pleased to release for public consumption, the discovery and application of higher ethical standards of information use and dissemination is of primary importance.

THE RHETORIC OF WAR AND THE ETHICS OF PRESIDENTS AND PRESIDENCIES: SOME CONCERNS

Probably the most important ethical stakes impinging on presidential rhetoric have to do with the issues of war and peace. The human consequences of that discourse have inescapable moral dimensions. Rhetoricians have maintained a healthy caution about the rhetoric of war. They have noted the complex relationships between war and the presidency. They have also issued informative and telling moral judgments in their evaluations of presidential discourse over war.[22] Certainly rhetoricians have weighed in heavily over Vietnam.[23] They have demonstrated how presidents and their administrative representatives have also attempted to purge "bitter memories" and transform our interpretations of that particular war.[24] Rhetoricians continue to weigh in on other U.S. military conflicts and crises.[25]

The war in Iraq has brought home a bevy of ethical dilemmas, not least of which implicate the discourse of President George W. Bush and his administration. Many question the prudence as well as honesty of the president and his administration. Has the administration tried to link Saddam Hussein to Al Qaeda without sufficient grounds for the charge? In addition, President Bush's credibility has been impugned by his claim that Hussein had weapons of mass destruction, which was offered as a key rationale by the president for going to war with Iraq. No WMDs have been found.[26] Pentagon propaganda activities associated with this war also seem troubling. Who bears responsibility for the Pentagon's seeming willingness to "enhance" the truth about the Jessica Lynch story?[27] Who bears responsibility for the Pentagon's seeming willingness to "enhance" the truth by supplying fictitious letters to newspapers and news organizations such as the *Boston Globe* and the *Los Angeles Times* and Gannett news services, all of which uncovered duplicate letters purported to have been written by soldiers serving in Iraq?[28]

Not only do we have efforts to "enhance" the truth; we also have reports of efforts to squelch important information about the Iraq war. For example, reporters found scant information about how many troops were leaving the front lines in Iraq and returning home after sustaining life-threatening injuries and/or other physical or mental incapacities. Another example is the attempt by the Bush Administration to "stonewall" investigation into potential intelligence lapses and procedural improprieties that may have led to 9/11.[29] In addition, the Pentagon's dismay over photographs of flag-draped coffins of the returning fallen soldiers summons questions about truth telling and cover-ups, and whether such photos should be censored for the sake of the privacy of the families involved or merely to purge images said to "comfort the enemy." People in the United States and the international community have been horrified to learn that abuses of Iraqi prisoners at Abu Ghraib occurred at the hands of U.S. military personnel. Seymour Hersh, among others, has alleged that these abuses can be linked directly to the upper reaches of the command structure. New Bush Administration policies seem to have defined enemies in the "war on terror" as "unlawful combatants" and therefore not fully subject to the protections of the Geneva Conventions.[30] These events and charges beg for investigation. They implicate the moral leadership of the United States and world opinion. They make a fundamental new look at the ethics of the presidency and presidential ethics even more urgent. In sum, the war in Iraq has provided a rather large tableau for unearthing and interrogating ethical issues: Was the government unethical in its advocacy on the need to go to war and in its manipulation of the news about the war and the postwar reconstruction? This question implicates both the ethics of the president and the ethics of the presidency.[31]

ON PRESIDENTIAL ETHICS AND THE ETHICS OF THE PRESIDENCY

We cannot assess with clarity how a president is doing the job, nor can we accurately interpret the quality of presidential leadership, unless we can trust the words spoken by or for the chief executive. The president is responsible for upholding and extending the public trust.[32]

Role Model and the Public Trust

The president can be a role model who can make a difference in our national life by becoming a model of ethical behavior and by the practice of a public discourse that is both responsible and ethical. The president can encourage members of the administration to do likewise. Cynicism and lack of trust is engendered by the wanton, brazen violation of public trust over time; one way to restore it is to put guidelines in place and then follow them. There will be circumstances under which the president will not be able to be entirely truthful—and we, the public, will grant that. Certainly in times of war, when national security is at stake, or when divulging information that might threaten the life, liberty, or even property of others, then a modicum of prudent silence is in order. A "war on terror" can go on ad infinitum. If "war time" restraints and modes of propaganda also go on ad infinitum, questions as to the ultimate state of our ethics as a nation arise rather poignantly, especially as we become mired both nationally and internationally in perceived gaps between our democratic principles and practices.

The ethical questions and dilemmas posed by this brief rehearsal of current concerns, however, should not be read merely as a complaint leveled against the Bush Administration's handling of the Iraq war and its aftermath—although we might well offer such a critique in another venue. Rather, our discussion points to larger questions about our democracy and the nature of the ethics of U.S. presidents and the presidency in a post- 9/11, electronically mediated age.

Key Normative Values

What is clear at the present moment is that the president has a distinct and overriding advantage in advancing both foreign and domestic policy rhetoric. Presidents have more information and more expertise to draw upon than the American public has. Since this is the case, the president's ethical responsibilities in the public sphere are profound. Public dependence on and deference to the president in matters of war and peace, in particular, should engender a concomitantly grave presidential responsibility. The president needs both a personal and a public ethic and a set of values to draw upon, especially during crisis periods. Those ethics and values must be in conformity with the expectations of the citizenry—as diverse and disparate as those principles and normative standards might be. Thus, consensus must be built around the highest standards: respect for democratic values, human rights, the exercise of prudence, and ensuring that just policies will prevail seem minimum requirements for helping shape presidential decision making. Obviously the tension between moral idealism and *realpolitik* can and should be navigated. Principles and standards, while absolutely necessary, are certainly by no means altogether sufficient for effective governance. Political circumstances almost always call for an "idealistic pragmatism."

Fundamental normative values for informing and enacting presidential discursive acts include a demonstrated understanding, development, and exercise of prudence, courage, honesty, respect for human choice, forthrightness, a sense of humility as well as a vigilance for justice, equality, and human rights; a capacity for developing, pronouncing, and implementing short- and long-term political and social vision; and finally, when necessary, a sincere desire to search for words and policies that reflect a spirit of compromise, reconciliation, and healing in a nation too often divided and too readily prone to resort to violence and give in to hatred. Three of these values—prudence, honesty, and the spirit of compromise and conciliation—deserve further elaboration in this limited context.

Prudence

If one were to cast about for a key value or virtue necessary for this time and place, perhaps we might choose a renewed focus on the need for prudence. According to J. Patrick Dobel, in politics, "Prudent judgment identifies salient moral aspects of a political situation which a leader has a moral obligation to attend to in making a decision." Acting with prudence requires "disciplined reason and openness to experience" and "foresight and attention to the long term." Prudential modalities of statecraft that must be mastered include how to "deploy power," understanding "timing and momentum," and having a keen sense of "means and ends." Prudent political outcomes regarding the practice of statecraft would be measured by "the durability and legitimacy of [the] outcomes" and their "consequences for the community." Accordingly, as Dobel notes, "If leaders account for each aspect, they have lived up to part of their ethical responsibilities as leaders; if they fail, they are guilty of moral negligence and irresponsibility."[33]

There is no necessary, nor even advisable, division between prudential statecraft and political wordcraft. Indeed, prudential political considerations also call for prudence in rhetorical appeals. The rhetoric practiced by the president, then, must display disciplined reason, openness to experience, the understanding that words are themselves an enactment and deployment of power, that timing and momentum are not inconsiderable aspects of the rhetorical appeal, and that appropriate ends and means are called for. Thus, if the American public is to be convinced to go to war with Iraq, we need some signs of prudent political statecraft and a matching rhetoric. A president ought not to claim that Saddam Hussein has weapons of mass destruction without presenting compelling evidence. A president ought not to engage in questionable or false public charges, such as Hussein's alleged solicitation and attempted procurement of nuclear weapons grade materials from Niger. If the United States is indeed in Iraq for selfless reasons, there will come a time when we will be able to determine this by assessing "the durability and legitimacy of the outcomes" and the "consequences" for the Iraqi people.

Honesty

To hold the public trust, a president must adopt and practice rhetorical integrity. At the core of such integrity, of course, is the duty to tell the truth. When the president deceives, he or she invites negative judgments on personal character and attacks the administration. The president also risks diminished public trust, unnecessary curtailment of public dialogue, and perceived manipulation of the mass media; this in turn intensifies growing cynicism of the citizenry, which leads to disaffection and disenfranchisement. A president must avoid, then, to the greatest extent possible, lies, distortions, and /or misrepresentations of the facts. To the degree possible and under the known constraints of our constitutional system, the president should strive to maintain consistency in word and deed, trying to fill in privately and publicly any and all gaps between public promises and public performance. Under most circumstances, if the president is to err in matters of public disclosure, those efforts should be to err on the side of full disclosure.

Compromise, Reconciliation, and Healing

The divisiveness and inveterate partisanship attending public political life today in the United States demands that we look deeper than at present to processes and products that have been arrived at through non-zero-sum activities. President Bush came into office without a popular mandate and embarked upon a controversial war and reconstruction effort. In addition, the nation now seems divided between Red and Blue states where values are fundamentally different.[34] Thus we ask those in power to explore compromise where possible, to reconcile where necessary, and to bind up and heal past political wounds so that we can move on to new and better and more capacious public policies and programs. The president has the task of shouldering this burden and taking up this cause. Thus prudence, honesty, compromise, reconciliation, and healing are valuable as virtues, and when exercised judiciously, serve as invaluable tools of presidential leadership.

ETHICAL STANDARDS FOR PRESIDENTIAL RHETORIC

Vietnam, Watergate, and the most recent Clinton scandals are progenitors of today's ethical dilemmas. The experience of each has made trust in public officials and in the governments and policies they represent questionable. Rhetoricians have played a key role in examining each of these national crises.[35] Under present rhetorical circumstances, a case can and should be made for a renewed focus on presidential ethics and the ethics of the presidency. We need specific criteria and normative standards for both politicians and public alike. It is the convergence of a variety of new circumstances and changes in both policy and perspective that have created what we perceive as a need for special vigilance. While we have recommended personal virtues for presidential consideration and while virtue ethics have their place, we see the need for additional ethical guidelines. Indeed, in the post-9/11 rhetorical and political environment, we are entering new, uncharted territory. Presidential discourse issued on both foreign and domestic policy has even more pronounced and even more complex ethical implications. Foreign policy in the age of the war on terrorism has direct implications for freedoms and responsibilities on the domestic front. The Department of Defense now works in tandem with the new Department of Homeland Security. In addition, in a world marked by instantaneous electronic communication, where globalized information networks carry signals of war and peace, action and inaction, good and evil, it is especially incumbent on U.S. presidents to communicate clearly, effectively, and ethically. To do so, it is important to have in mind (and perhaps even more important, in place) a set of ethical guidelines equal to the complex challenges of national and international political cultures. Both presidents and citizenry alike must be able to draw upon a set of shared normative criteria that will ensure ethical rhetorical efforts and rhetorical accountability.

RECOMMENDATIONS

1. The president should adhere to the highest standards of integrity in public address.
2. To the greatest extent allowed by national security, the sensibilities of the president's party, and those of the American people, a president should not lie or distort the truth in public statements. Thus, the president should make every effort to excise from presidential discourse any claim of fact or piece of evidentiary material known to be false or misleading and should support claims with verifiable evidence, avoiding unverified, distorted, misleading, inexact, vague, or in any way otherwise untenable forms of rhetorical support. The same holds true for presidential surrogates speaking on behalf of the administration.
3. The president and his or her subordinates should not make derogatory public statements about other agencies or operatives or branches of government that are functioning as required by the Constitution, law, or legal precedent.
4. In debates of public policy, the president and subordinates should not misrepresent the opinions of others with whom they disagree. This would include any direct communications with the public in the form

of printed reading materials, public speeches, radio addresses, print and electronic political campaign advertisements, and the like.

Since the practice of ethical rhetoric is meant to promote, protect, and defend the people's sovereign right to fair and accurate knowledge about their government and its operations, it is crucial to protect and defend the free flow of information in society. We view this as a serious ethical obligation to ensure a vibrant democracy. Thus, we further recommend:

5. The president should promote the free flow of information. The president should not seek to classify public documents for the purpose of deceiving the public nor attempt to cover up activities that might be perceived as unethical or embarrassing.
6. The president and surrogates should make every effort to engage in dialogue with the American people on substantive foreign and domestic policy issues. This means exploring and inaugurating ample opportunities for news conferences, town hall meetings, and open debates on important public policy issues.
7. The president must explain policies clearly and effectively and refrain from obfuscating, squelching, or otherwise banning from the press or the public the potentially negative or deleterious effects of policies and proposals. This norm also applies to presidential advisers and representatives in the administration charged with advancing the president's agenda.
8. To foster responsible public policy debate and implementation, the president ought to be willing to engage opponents openly and directly. In addition, the president should be willing to compromise, without undermining his or her principles, when both prudence and the public good demand it. Here compromise is viewed as a public act of healing and political efficacy.[36]

The virtues, ethical norms, and the recommendations offered here are not only emblematic of those needed to develop and sustain presidential character but also components of presidential leadership that take on the order of moral necessity. Thus, to lead well and truly, the president must have these virtues as an individual, must set out to incorporate these normative criteria in public discourse, and must extend them to others (subordinates and public alike) through modeling behavior. We strongly believe in and appreciate the direct link between public discourse and public policy.[37] Submitting presidential public discourse to ethical analysis will improve candidates, presidents, policies, and programs. Under the crucible of informed, normatively based criteria, public scrutiny of presidential rhetorical discourse can improve, and so can the quality of the citizenry (and their decision-making capacities) whose obligation is to hold their presidents accountable. This mutual check and balance, in turn, can pave the way for a better society. Having been measured by normative values and scrutinized under the microscope of substantive and relevant ethical criteria and standards, presidential performance has not only the potential, but the obligation, to live up to its promise.

Notes

1. Steven R. Goldzwig and George N. Dionisopoulos, "John F. Kennedy's Civil Rights Discourse: The Evolution from 'Principled Bystander' to Public Advocate," *Communication Monographs* 56 (1989): 179–98; Garth E. Pauley, *The Modern Presidency and Civil Rights: Rhetoric on Race from Roosevelt to Nixon* (College Station: Texas A&M University Press, 2001); Thomas W. Benson, "FDR at Gettysburg: The New Deal and the Rhetoric of Presidential Leadership," in *The Presidency and Rhetorical Leadership*, ed. Leroy G. Dorsey (College Station: Texas A&M University Press, 2002), 145–83.

2. "[There is persuasion] through character whenever the speech is spoken in such a way as to make the speaker worthy of credence; . . . character is almost, so to speak, the controlling factor in persuasion." Aristotle, *On Rhetoric*, trans. George A. Kennedy (New York: Oxford University Press, 1991), 38.

3. See Wayne C. Booth, *The Company We Keep: An Ethics of Fiction* (Berkeley: University of California Press, 1988); Wayne C. Booth, *The Rhetoric of Fiction*, 2nd ed. (Chicago: University of Chicago Press, 1983); Thomas W. Benson, "Rhetoric as a Way of Being," in *American Rhetoric: Context and Criticism*, ed. Thomas W. Benson (Carbondale: Southern Illinois University Press, 1989), 293–322; Thomas W. Benson, *Writing JFK: Presidential Rhetoric and the Press in the Bay of Pigs Crisis* (College Station: Texas A&M University Press, 2004); Stephen Howard Browne, *Angelina Grimke: Rhetoric, Identity, and the Radical Imagination* (East Lansing: Michigan State University Press, 1999); Stephen H. Browne, *Edmund Burke and the Discourse of Virtue* (Tuscaloosa: University of Alabama Press, 1993); Stephen Howard Browne, *Jefferson's Call for Nationhood: The First Inaugural Address* (College Station: Texas A&M University Press, 2003); Edwin Black, "Gettysburg and Silence," *Quarterly Journal of Speech* 80 (1994): 21–36; Edwin Black, "The Second Persona." *Quarterly Journal of Speech* 16 (1970): 109–19; James Darsey, "The Legend of Eugene Debs: Prophetic Ethos as Radical Argument," *Quarterly Journal of Speech* 74 (1988): 434–53; Eugene Garver, "The Ethical Criticism of Reasoning," *Philosophy and Rhetoric* 31 (1998): 107–30; J. Michael Hogan and Glen Williams, "Republican Charisma and the American Revolution: The Textual Persona of Thomas Paine's *Common Sense*." *Quarterly Journal of Speech* 86 (2000): 1–17; Charles E. Morris III, "Pink Herring and the Fourth Persona: J. Edgar Hoover's Sex Crime Panic," *Quarterly Journal of Speech* (2002): 228–44; David L. Rarick, Mary B. Duncan, David G. Lee, and Laurinda W. Porter, "The Carter Persona: An Empirical Analysis of the

Rhetorical Visions of Campaign '76," *Quarterly Journal of Speech* 63 (1977): 258-73; Philip Wander, "The Third Persona: An Ideological Turn in Rhetorical Theory," *Central States Speech Journal* 35 (1984): 197-216; B. L. Ware and Wil A. Linkugel, "The Rhetorical Persona: Marcus Garvey as a Black Moses," *Communication Monographs* 49 (1982): 50-62.

4. There are a number of ethical dilemmas associated with presidential speechwriting. A president's team of ghostwriters can have significant influence. For example, Davis Houck's book on FDR's first Inaugural Address challenges notions of FDR's ethos and agency by claiming that Raymond Moley was the primary author. Peggy Noonan's account of her construction of Reagan's ethos in the Normandy speech unwillingly confesses to the break between the speaker's ethos and the speechwriter's phronesis (she maintains her admiration for Reagan). See Davis Houck, *FDR and Fear Itself: The First Inaugural Address* (College Station: Texas A & M University Press, 2002); Peggy Noonan, *What I Saw at the Revolution: A Political Life in the Reagan Era* (New York: Random House, 1990). For further discussion on the ethics of ghostwritten speeches see Ernest G. Bormann, "The Ethics of Ghostwritten Speeches," *Quarterly Journal of Speech* 47 (1961): 262-67; Lois J. Einhorn, "The Ghosts Unmasked: A Review of Literature on Speechwriting," *Communication Quarterly* 30 (1982): 41-47; Lois J. Einhorn, "The Ghosts Talk: Personal Interviews with Three Former Speechwriters," *Communication Quarterly* 36 (1988): 94-108.

5. Karl Wallace, "An Ethical Basis of Communication," *Speech Teacher* 4 (1955): 1-9.

6. Wallace, "An Ethical Basis," 6-9.

7. Christopher Lyle Johnstone, "Reagan, Rhetoric, and the Public Philosophy: Ethics and Politics in the 1984 Campaign," *Southern Communication Journal* 60 (1995): 93-108.

8. Johnstone, "Reagan," 103.

9. Richard L. Johannesen, *Ethics in Human Communication*, 5th ed. (Prospect Heights, Ill.: Waveland, 2002), 263.

10. Thomas B. Farrell, "Rhetorical Resemblance: Paradoxes of a Practical Art," *Quarterly Journal of Speech* 72 (1986): 1-19; quotation, 14.

11. Farrell, "Rhetorical Resemblance," 14.

12. Farrell, "Rhetorical Resemblance," 17 (italics in original).

13. "Gone Quiet," *The West Wing*, season 3, episode 227207 (NBC: airdate November 14, 2001), personal videotape.

14. See Aladair MacIntyre, *After Virtue* (Notre Dame, Ind.: University of Notre Dame Press, 1981); Alasdair MacIntyre, *Whose Justice? Which Rationality?* (Notre Dame: University of Notre Dame Press, 1988); Stanley Hauerwas, *Vision and Virtue* (Notre Dame, Ind.: Fides Press, 1974); Stanley Hauerwas, *A Community of Character: Toward a Constructive Christian Social Ethic* (Notre Dame, Ind.: University of Notre Dame Press, 1981).

15. Wayne C. Booth, *Modern Dogma and the Rhetoric of Assent* (Chicago: University of Chicago Press, 1974), 126.

16. Booth, *Modern Dogma*, 137.

17. Booth, *The Company We Keep*.

18. James Boyd White, *When Words Lose Their Meaning* (Chicago: University of Chicago Press, 1984); James Boyd White, *Acts of Hope* (Chicago: University of Chicago Press, 1994).

19. Black, "The Second Persona."

20. Wander, "The Third Persona."

21. Cited at http://www.bushin30seconds.org/rules.html.

22. See, for example, Robert L. Ivie, "Presidential Motives for War," *Quarterly Journal of Speech* 51 (1974): 337–45; Robert L. Ivie, "Images of Savagery in American Justifications for War," *Communication Monographs* 47 (1980): 279–94.

23. See Robert P. Newman, "Under the Veneer: Nixon's Vietnam Speech of November 3, 1969," *Quarterly Journal of Speech* 56 (1970): 168–78; Hermann G. Stelzner, "The Quest Story and Nixon's November 3, 1969 Address," *Quarterly Journal of Speech* 57 (1971): 163–72; Forbes I. Hill, "Conventional Wisdom-Traditional Form: The President's Message of November 3, 1969," *Quarterly Journal of Speech* 58 (1972): 373–86; Richard A. Cherwitz, "Lyndon Johnson and the 'Crisis' of Tonkin Gulf: A President's Justification of War," *Western Journal of Speech Communication* 42 (1978): 93–104; Richard A. Cherwitz, "Making Inconsistency: The Tonkin Gulf Crisis," *Communication Quarterly* 28 (1980): 27–37; Lee Sigelman and Lawrence Miller, "Understanding Presidential Rhetoric: The Vietnam Statements of Lyndon Johnson, *Communication Research* 5 (1978): 25–56; Robert A. Vartabedian, "Nixon's Vietnam Rhetoric: A Case Study of Apologia as Generic Paradox, *Southern Speech Communication Journal* 50 (1984): 366–81.

24. See Kenneth S. Zagacki, "Rhetoric, Failure, and the Presidency: The Case of Vietnam," *Communication Studies* 43 (1992): 42–55; George N. Dionisopoulos and Steven R. Goldzwig, "'The Meaning of Vietnam': Political Rhetoric as Revisionist Cultural History," *Quarterly Journal of Speech* 78 (1992): 61–79.

25. Rhetoricians have studied a number of other U.S. involvements in conflict and wars including Somalia, the Persian Gulf War, and Granada. See John R. Butler, "Somalia and the Imperial Savage: Continuities in the Rhetoric of War," *Western Journal of Communication,* 66 (2002): 1–24; Robert L. Ivie, "Tragic Fear and the Rhetorical Presidency: Combating Evil in the Persian Gulf," in *Beyond the Rhetorical Presidency,* ed. Martin J. Medhurst (College Station: Texas A&M University Press, 1996), 153–78; Kathleen M. German, "Invoking the Glorious War: Framing the Persian Gulf Conflict through Directive Language," *Southern Communication Journal* 60 (1995): 292–302; Ralph E. Dowling and Gabrielle Marraro, "Grenada and the Great Communicator: A Study in Democratic Ethics," *Western Journal of Speech Communication* 50 (1986): 350–67.

26. Dana Priest and Walter Pincus, "U.S. 'Almost All Wrong' on Weapons: Report on Iraq Contradicts Bush Administration Claims," *Washington Post,* October 7, 2004, A1, at www.washingtonpost.com/ wp-dyn/articles/A12115–20040ct6.html.

27. Nancy Gibbs, "The Private Jessica Lynch," *Time,* November 17, 2003, 24–29, 31, 33.

28. Eugene Kane, "U.S. Troops Blindly Used as PR for War in Iraq," *Milwaukee Journal Sentinel,* October 16, 2003, B1.

29. Report by Daniel Zwerdling, Senior Reporter, National Public Radio, WUWM Radio, Milwaukee, WI, January 7, 2004; Arizona Republican Senator John McCain charges that the Bush Administration has "slow-walked and stonewalled" House and Senate inquiries into 9/11. See "9/11 Probe: Aiming High," *Time,* February 3, 2003, 16.

30. See John Barry, Michael Hirsh, and Michael Isikof, "The Roots of Torture," *Newsweek,* May 24, 2004, 28–34.

31. Following Stuart C. Gilman's helpful observation, in analyzing the ethics of the arguments for and against war (or any other issue of ethical import) and in trying to come to terms with questionable actions by the president, administration advisers, cabinet members, representatives, or any other surrogates, there must be concern for both presidential ethics (the ethics of the individual officeholder and his or her personal behavior) and the ethics of

the presidency (defined here for present purposes as words and actions formed and enacted by a particular presidential administration, including those institutional initiatives and actions which might be constitutive of oral, written, and/or visual communication that seeks to influence multiple audiences by issuing explanations and/or accusations and defenses undertaken by the president, his or her aides, speechwriters, cabinet personnel, agency heads and directors, or other surrogates involved in rhetorical efforts to enact, execute, enforce, or reinforce executive branch-led statements, orders, policies, procedures, programs, legislative initiatives, and the like). See Stuart C. Gilman, "Presidential Ethics and the Ethics of the Presidency," *Annals of the American Academy of Political Science* 537 (1995): 58–75.

32. In employing the term *public trust* we invoke the work of Max Weber. As elected officials in a democracy, government employees should be regarded as public servants. A breach of trust by a public official means that he or she has neglected or betrayed his or her public responsibilities. A helpful discussion of Weber's views can be found in Bryan R. Fry, *Mastering Public Administration* (Chatham, N.J.: Chatham House Publishers, 1989), esp. 31.

33. J. Patrick Dobel, "Political Prudence and the Ethics of Leadership," *Public Administration Review* 58 (1998): 74–81; quotations, 76, 80.

34. The 2000 election left us deeply divided. Al Gore won the popular vote; George W. Bush won the electoral college and the national election but only after a disputed vote process in Florida and a Supreme Court decision. During the 2004 election the nation seemed equally divided. As pollster John Zogby noted, the United States seemed to be "slowly cleaving into two separate nations culturally." John F. Dickerson and Karen Tumulty, "The Love Him, Hate Him President," *Time*, December 1, 2003, 28–36, 38–40; Sheryl Gay Stolberg, "The High Costs of Rising Incivility on Capitol Hill," *New York Times,* November 30, 2003, 10; Katherine M. Skiba, "U.S. States Remain Divided, Poll Shows," *Milwaukee Journal Sentinel,* January 7, 2004, 9A.

35. Studies on Vietnam are cited in footnotes 1 and 2. On Watergate, see Jackson Harrell, B. L. Ware, and Wil A. Linkugel, "Failure of Apology in American Politics: Nixon on Watergate," *Communication Monographs* 42 (1975): 245–61; Dennis S. Gouran, "The Watergate Cover-Up: Its Dynamics and Implications, " *Communication Monographs* 42 (1976): 176–86. On Clinton, see Michael R. Kramer and Kathryn M. Olson, "The Strategic Potential of Sequencing Apologia Stases: President Clinton's Self-Defense in the Monica Lewinsky Scandal," *Western Journal of Communication* 66 (2002): 347–68; Robert E. Denton Jr. and Rachel L. Holloway, eds., *Images, Scandal, and Communication Strategies of the Clinton Presidency* (Westport, Conn.: Praeger, 2003); Joseph R. Blaney and William L. Benoit, *The Clinton Scandals and the Politics of Image Restoration* (Westport, Conn.: Praeger, 2001).

36. These principles are drawn from our own work and that of others. Others responsible for informing our thinking here include direct adaptations of the work of Ed Perley and Dennis Gouran. Perley's guidelines include Numbers 1–4. Gouran's insight can be found in Number 5. See "Presidential Ethics—Seven Principles," at http://www.nfinity.com/~exile/pres.htm; Gouran is cited in Johannesen, *Ethics in Human Communication,* 32–33. The original citation for this work can be found in Dennis Gouran, "Guidelines for the Analysis of Responsibility in Governmental Communication," in *Teaching about Doublespeak,* ed. Daniel Dietrich (Urbana, Ill.: National Council of Teachers of English, 1976), 20–31.

37. See Kurt Ritter and Martin J. Medhurst, eds., *Presidential Speechwriting: From the New Deal to the Reagan Revolution and Beyond* (College Station: Texas A&M University Press, 2003).

CHAPTER 15

REPORT OF THE NATIONAL TASK FORCE ON THE THEORY AND PRACTICE OF THE RHETORICAL PRESIDENCY

Chair: David Henry, University of Nevada, Las Vegas
Philip Abbott, Wayne State University
Davis W. Houck, Florida State University
Mel Laracey, University of Texas at San Antonio
Stephen E. Lucas, University of Wisconsin, Madison
Shawn J. Parry-Giles, University of Maryland

The processes and goals that guided participants in the 1970 National Developmental Project on Rhetoric served as the starting point for the task force's work. In January and May meetings that year, "scholars from several fields considered rhetoric's past and future, identified the problems in contemporary life which require applications of rhetorical concepts and methods, and recommended lines of research and educational programs needed to bring an effective rhetoric into relation to current and future needs."[1] In parallel fashion, the task force's charge was to consider a series of critical *topoi* as a starting point for theorizing a rhetorical presidency for the twenty-first century. Relevant questions posed for the group's work included: What are the fundamental questions or issues? Which issues have dominated recent debate? Which are likely to become even more important in the future? What are the ten most important works currently written on the topic? Are the methodological options currently available adequate to the challenges of the topic? What should be the research agenda of the next ten years, and how should it be pursued?

Discussion generated by these questions led to a focus on four issues that may inform the theory and practice of the rhetorical presidency in the twenty-first century. First, before we can project "what ought to be" in future research, it is essential to take stock of "what is." Thus, we begin with a brief synthesis both of what may be taken as conventional wisdom about the rhetorical presidency and of challenges to that conventional wisdom, which we believe is in evolution. Next, we consider the nature of theory building generally, then posit the prospective utility of theory construction in relation to presidential rhetoric. Third, we explore topic areas and criteria for future scholarship, research that may simultaneously contribute to theory development and avoid the pitfalls of current challenges to conventional wisdom. And finally, in the manner of participants at the National Developmental Project on Rhetoric, we advance a series of recommendations.

Taking Stock of the Rhetorical Presidency

We do not intend to rehearse the entire history of research on presidential rhetoric, but it is essential to establish key markers of extant scholarship before we can project what may follow. To do so, we first offer a working definition of the rhetorical presidency, then attend to three challenges to current scholarship, scholarship grounded largely in the examination of case studies.

Conventional wisdom holds that the rhetorical presidency is a product of the twentieth century generally and of the media age in particular. As James Ceaser, Glen E. Thurow, Jeffrey Tulis, and Joseph Bessette have it, three factors merged to transform the president's role from "head of the government" to "leader of the people": (1) during Woodrow Wilson's presidency, exhortation replaced "calm and deliberate discussion" as the dominant mode of political discourse; (2) with simultaneous developments in mass communication, aphorism surpassed argument as the primary content of presidential speech; and (3) campaigning for office became an almost continuous process. In combination, according to Ceaser and his colleagues, these features yield a circumstance in which "presidential speech and action increasingly reflect the opinion that speaking *is* governing."[2]

As Mary E. Stuckey and Frederick J. Antczak explain, following formulation of this construct, research on the presidency divided often into two categories. Studies of the president's institutional roles within the government and research on the president's increased public functions, they maintain, suggest the value of research on rhetoric's instrumental and constitutive functions alike. They laud Roderick Hart's research, in part for delineating how the presidency "has been transferred from a formal, print-oriented world into an electronic environment specializing in the spoken word and rewarding casual, interpersonally adept politicians." Presidents use the spoken word, J. Michael Hogan adds, to "set the agenda and to define the terms of debate" in policy deliberations. And as David Zarefsky reminds us, the power to set the terms of debate is often accompanied by an advantage to win the debate.[3] On this collective view, then, rhetorical presidents are interpersonally adept orators who elevate narrative or aphorism to argument in mass communicated messages.

However, despite considerable scholarship that certifies implicitly if not explicitly the force of the rhetorical presidency, the concept is not without its critics. In combination the critical commentary results in at least three challenges to theorizing a rhetorical presidency. Three challenges with which we dealt in our deliberations are (1) the charge that the rhetorical presidency is a myth, (2) difficulties in differentiating between the "rhetorical presidency" and "presidential rhetoric," and (3) responding to critics who question the utility of scholarship grounded in evidence not derived from social scientific research.

Consider, first, David Nichols's provocative charges in *The Myth of the Modern Presidency*.[4] Nichols's book constitutes an important rejoinder to Tulis and others insofar as he argues that Tulis does not have the constitutional arguments right. That is, Nichols maintains that Tulis erroneously attributes the origin of the rhetorical presidency to Theodore Roosevelt and Woodrow Wilson. The rhetorical presidency begins only in the early twentieth century, Tulis contends, and only by subverting the Founders' intent vis-à-vis presidential speech. Nichols demonstrates, though, that there are ample constitutional grounds for a rhetorical president, starting as early as George Washington. Stephen E. Lucas has made much the same point, arguing that there are in fact two rhetorical presidencies—the twentieth-century rhetorical presidency described by Tulis and colleagues, and a nineteenth-century rhetorical presidency that was considerably different from its successor. Such a conclusion, Lucas maintains, allows us to "acknowledge the broad gulf between the rhetorical practices of nineteenth- and twentieth-century presidents and, at the same time, takes cognizance of the fact that a substantial number of nineteenth-century presidents did indeed use rhetorical means to present their policies to the public and to develop support for those policies."⁵ Recent research by Mel Laracey, Richard Ellis, and others further documents the power of presidential discourse in the eighteenth and nineteenth centuries to shape the political agenda and influence policy debate.⁶ Few doubt the significance of Tulis's work in framing debate on the rhetorical presidency, but there is a growing body of scholarship that illustrates the dangers of privileging any single conceptualization of the rhetorical presidency.

A second challenge to future scholarship is establishing a common ground from which research is to progress, particularly in differentiating between a rhetorical presidency and presidential rhetoric. In an attempt to discern differences in the assumptions that political scientists and communication scholars make about the rhetorical presidency, Martin J. Medhurst contends in *Beyond the Rhetorical Presidency* that those who study the rhetorical presidency often find their institutional homes in departments of political science. He locates their central concern in the "nature, scope, and function of the presidency as a constitutional office." Conversely, Medhurst contends, communication scholars are more interested in presidential rhetoric and the "human capacity to see what is most likely to be persuasive to a given audience on a given occasion."⁷ In working to integrate these two perspectives—an institutional conception of the presidency with a sensitivity to rhetorical purpose—Karlyn Kohrs Campbell and Kathleen Hall Jamieson help us to refine the study of presidential rhetoric. They "look at the presidency as an institution in which rhetoric plays a major role, asking what can be discovered if we assume that the character of presidential rhetoric has been created, sustained, and altered through time by the nature of the presidency as an institution."⁸

Zarefsky takes us even further in suggesting how occupants of the office alter the nature of that institution. In reviewing the work of Richard Neustadt, Stephen Skowronek, James MacGregor Burns, and Bruce Miroff, Zarefsky concludes that such scholars recognize a need for presidents to promote "transformative change," which links to an ability to discover and use the "available means of persuasion in any given case." Although Zarefsky concludes that it "is probably going too far to assert that all presidential leadership is rhetorical," he believes we can conclude that "rhetoric is intimately involved in its exercise." While he offers numerous examples of rhetoric's force in the nation's earliest decades, he highlights the idea that "nowhere does the Constitution require that the president deliver an inaugural address. George Washington nevertheless initiated the practice, modeling it on British custom, and it was quickly established as the norm."⁹ Furthermore, Zarefsky holds that the exercise of the presidency goes beyond persuasive speech, for "going public" entails the earliest presidents' use of newspapers during campaigns and while in office, particularly for such leaders as Washington, Jefferson, Madison, Monroe, and Jackson.[10]

A final challenge that constituted a recurring thread in our discussions was how best to respond to critics who argue that research not based in the findings of social scientific investigation merits little credence. Inevitably, this brought us to George Edwards's *On Deaf Ears: The Limits of the Bully Pulpit*. Edwards's major claims appear to be two: (1) that presidential rhetoric lacks any grounding in material audiences, and (2) that even when one looks at those audiences, influence is negligible. In contrast to Samuel Kernell's emphasis on "going public," Edwards urges presidents to "stay private." In doing so, he seems to hold, most of our political problems would be solved. Staying private, Edwards maintains, "is likely to contribute to reducing gridlock, incivility, and, thus, public cynicism, and deserves a more prominent role in the president's strategic arsenal."[11] Not public debate. Not public deliberation. And certainly not public speeches. Such rhetoric, in Edwards's view, merely obstructs productive presidential-congressional private negotiations. Armed with empirical polling results, Edwards takes issue with Dick Morris, Karl Rove, and Lee Atwater as well as with the presidents who followed their advice en route to the White House. His message for each: public persuasion is vastly overrated.

Two impressions, finally, define our response to Edwards's antirhetorical theme. First, while we may question the bifurcated view of public discourse implicit in Edwards's argument, we also note the strength of the rhetorical technique that defines much of his analysis. We actually came away from *On Deaf Ears*, authorial intentions notwithstanding, seeing it as a pro-presidential rhetoric book. The rhetoric that Edwards studies, and so often appears to eschew, did nevertheless move the response needle, did change views of the president, and did make a difference to policy deliberations, however minimal according to statistical measures. What this suggests to us is that research based both on Edwards's preferred social science model and on that produced by rhetorical-critical-humanistic scholarship need not be in opposition, with survival of one dominant means of investigation as the only acceptable result. We would argue, rather, that rhetorical studies of sustained persuasive transactions have the potential—and in important instances an already realized capacity—to reveal enlightening consequences of discursive encounters, even if we cannot point to cause-effect relationships at statistically significant levels of influence.[12] We believe, moreover, that scholarship in presidential rhetoric can contribute significantly to the development of useful theory about the rhetorical presidency.

Theorizing the Rhetorical Presidency

Case studies of rhetorical practice comprise a substantial amount, if not a majority, of the research done by communication scholars on presidential discourse. Our definition of case studies is broad, including research on single presidents, on specific rhetorical acts or campaigns, on multiple presidents addressing a common subject, or on common features of presidential discourse in similar contexts or situations. What defines the scholarship as a case study rather than a contribution to theory is the writer's attention to the individual president, to the single subject, to the discreet address, or to the thread that runs through a common situation. The concern is not, primarily, with examination of the discursive experience for what the case might reveal about a more general or abstract concept, principle, or theme.[13] Although some communication scholarship—Campbell and Jamieson's *Deeds Done in Words* comes to mind—seeks to isolate generalizable principles, our attention as a field remains centrally on the case. Are there, though, ways that rhetorical-critical works might parallel Stephen Skowronek's *The Politics Presidents Make*, Mel Laracey's *Presidents and the People*, and Richard Neustadt's *Presidential Power and Modern Presidents* to yield principles-concepts-precepts with import-interest-value beyond the inherent interest of the case?[14]

In relation to theory development, we believe that the presidency is an important site for two reasons. First, it allows researchers to focus on classification problems in relation to the rhetorical presidency. To date, researchers have tended to rely on bifurcation, which, as Laracey and Nichols illustrate, may be more complex than the categories suggest. Second, a focus on the presidency allows researchers to explore the relationship between presidential power and rhetoric. A view posed by Harvey Mansfield in *Taming the Prince*, a view perhaps shared by George Edwards and others, is that there is an element of executive power existing independently from persuasion, and since it is considered the "essence" of executive power, it tends to make rhetorical efforts marginal or inconsequential.[15] Such a view may be too simple.

Theorizing about these phenomena involves examination of the categories—such as rhetorical/prerhetorical, modern/premodern, modern/postmodern—as well as clarification by the genres that are employed in comparing and analyzing administrations or clusters of administrations. The following questions are frequently asked by philosophers of science and could be helpful in evaluating models of the rhetorical presidency:

1. Are the categories too broad?
2. Are the standards for the categories clear?
3. Do the entries readily fit?
4. Is there too much variation in the categories?
5. Are the entries transferable to other categories?
6. What does the classification illuminate?
7. Are important entries not classified?
8. Are there numerous "hard/transitional" cases?
9. Is the classification too simple or too complex?
10. Can new cases be readily added?
11. Does the classification explain some phenomena better than others?
12. Does the classification predict some phenomena better than others?
14. Is the classification based upon theory?
15. Are the categories complete?

For example, consider item 2—how clear are the standards for categories in presidential classification? Clarity, of course, is itself a standard that cannot be applied with precision, but major departures can still be identified. Jeffrey Tulis's classification system in *The Rhetorical Presidency* suggests one possible problem. His two presidencies rest upon a demarcation based upon the proscription of rhetoric by subject, object, and form.[16] When he approaches the presidency of Theodore Roosevelt, however, Tulis notes that these restrictions were discarded. Roosevelt initiated a series of "swings around the circle" in defense of the Hepburn Act that prominently featured oral discourse directed to the public in support of policy recommendations. All of these actions constituted a break with presidential precedent that for Tulis is both extreme and decisive. Was TR then the first rhetorical president? No, concludes Tulis, since Roosevelt's actions were characterized by "moderation." Moderate "use of popular rhetoric," he writes, "moderate appeals for moderate reform . . . and most importantly, an appeal to moderate disputes" might entail "several ironies" but nevertheless constituted a "middle way" rather than a "new" one.[17]

Was "moderation" an unanticipated or unstated aspect of the Founders' prohibition on rhetoric? This interpretation can be questioned since the Founders' proscriptions of subject, form, and object were designed to produce rhetorical moderation and were not designed to be ends in themselves. If moderation were added as part of the categorical definition, what would be the status of presidents who, in Tulis's classification, followed the proscriptions with regard to form, object, and subject but *not* moderation? Jackson's rhetoric could conceivably fit this alteration, especially in regard to his statements on the bank veto. If Jackson was fomenting class conflict (hard demagoguery), which his critics suggested, was he a (kind of) rhetorical president even though he obeyed other proscriptions? Could Tulis's classification then be reformulated as "presidents can be divided into those who governed rhetorically, those who did not, and those who did in some respects but not in others"? If this is the case, the contention that there are two identifiable constitutions, one overlaid on the other, raises classification questions (item 9). On the other hand, Tulis's categories may be adequate and he has instead made an entry error (item 3), or more seriously, his classification exhibits multiple entry problems (items 3, 4, 10).

Perhaps, then, a problem with Tulis's classification system lies with the breadth of his two categories (item 1) rather than their clarity. There is considerable support for the preceding reformulation that reorders presidents and expands the category bifurcation. Indeed, it was Washington who began the practice of touring the country, and as Lucas has shown, the first president was in some ways more transparent in his rhetorical practices than were most of his nineteenth-century successors.[18] Moreover, as Laracey demonstrates, as early as Jefferson presidents used party newspapers to advance their views.[19] Thus, while presidents might have appeared to be honoring rhetorical restrictions, it was an open secret that their papers spoke for them. Tulis himself also notes that "there was a substantial increase in speechmaking after the Civil War, which raises questions about treating the century as a unit."[20] If several patterns of combinations among rhetorical form, object, subject, and content in the nineteenth-century presidency can be identified, then his classification system must be revised.

If there are, in fact, more rhetorical styles before the rhetorical presidency, perhaps also there are more after it as well. Are the categories Tulis advances complete (item 15)? Is there, for example, a new postmodern rhetoric that alters the form, object, and subject of presidential address? Tulis does not classify rhetorical styles despite the fact that there are major variations across time in most genres of presidential speech. However, since these styles may have no bearing on presidential performance, especially in regard to the formation of new constitutional forms, he can safely ignore these variations. What if, though, new forms of rhetoric have emerged that *do* suggest constitutional transformations like the one that Tulis identifies as having been created by the rhetorical presidency?

The existence of a postmodern presidency is certainly a contested category. But if its components included new proscriptions on rhetorical content such as those implied by the thesis of the "loss of grand narrative," or new forms such as those offered by communication technology that may alter the relation between rhetorical performance and action, as in "virtual reality," then questions necessarily arise. For example, Bruce Miroff has suggested that presidents now use the new media to create "spectacles" for the public that often have little relation to actual events. The spectacle, he argues, is more like a wrestling match than a boxing match, in which the only point of the event is the gesture and the performance. Miroff contends that President Clinton is the first president to employ the postmodern spectacle, in which "fleeting images and fractured continuity, surfaces without depth, personae rather than personality" are the main features of his presidency.[21] If a postmodern rhetorical presidency does exist, or is in the process of formation as Miroff suggests, then this form is likely to have as much impact on rhetorical performance as did Wilson's departure from nineteenth-century presidencies. The rhetorical presidency classification would be revised as: "Presidents can be divided into those who governed rhetorically in either a modern or postmodern sense, and those who did not."

We believe this extensive attention to one theory of the rhetorical presidency and its implications for premodern, modern, and postmodern conditions is instructive not so much for the questions it raises about a single book as for the broader questions one might ask—criteria one might apply—in attempting to develop a comprehensive theoretical construct. We realize such a task is a long-term project, but we believe the eventual utility of such an enterprise merits the required investment of time and thought. To aid in that process, in the final section of our report we offer recommendations of research projects that may move us toward productive theory development.

Considerations for Future Research

After hearing an early draft of this report, David Zarefsky suggested that we focus on what he termed "the next generation of scholarship on presidential rhetoric." It might be more constructive, Zarefsky proposed, to ask in the next stage of scholarship: "What does it mean to think about the presidency as an institution, rhetorically?" We agree that such a focus has utility, and we have the question in mind as we suggest five areas of scholarship that could contribute to answering it adequately.

The great majority of scholarship on the rhetorical presidency attends to post-Wilson administrations. We are convinced much is to be learned about presidential rhetoric and/or the rhetorical presidency with more research on eighteenth- and nineteenth-century presidential discourse. Research is in progress, to be sure. The Texas A&M Conference "Before the Rhetorical Presidency," the forthcoming volume from the conference, Laracey's *Presidents and the People,* and several essays in *The Presidency and Rhetorical Leadership* illuminate the research program's potential. But much more needs to be done to delineate the salient features of eighteenth- and nineteenth-century presidential rhetoric. Attending to pre-FDR studies, Laracey writes, reveals the complexity of the rhetorical presidency, a complexity missed with a focus predominantly on mass-mediated presidential discourse.

Closely related to our belief that research on presidents prior to Wilson is potentially bountiful is our conviction that we should conduct much more archival research. Such scholarship, we are confident, will allow us to understand more fully how the rhetorical presidency functioned throughout U.S. history. Thomas W. Benson's article on Gerald Ford's farm bureau speech, for instance, merits close reading for any number of reasons. Not least of these is the evidence Benson's analysis provides of the politicization surrounding the speechwriting process. Such studies inform our understanding of a president's public discourse as well as the behind-the-scenes machinations from which the public presentation grew. Further evidence for this claim is readily available in most, if not all, of the contributors' work in *Presidential Speechwriting: From the New Deal to the Reagan Revolution and Beyond.* Particularly instructive on this count are Moya Ann Ball on LBJ's renunciation speech, Charles J. G. Griffin on Eisenhower's 1954 State of the Union address, and Theodore Windt on presidential speechwriting as collaboration in the Kennedy Administration.[22]

Similarly, Fred Greenstein's *Hidden-Hand Presidency* illustrates the productivity of combining the study of a president's public statements with an analysis of primary papers pertinent to the statements' planning and presentation. Building on Greenstein's work, Shawn Parry-Giles demonstrates that by studying development of the U.S. propaganda program under Presidents Truman and Eisenhower, we can see the ways in which "covert actions expand, supplement, and supplant the bully pulpit, transforming and enhancing the presidential-rhetorical paradigm." Even though presidential surrogates delivered key messages, these speakers frequently worked for government agencies such as the Voice of America. The surrogates' themes were coordinated with larger presidential initiatives, particularly Truman's Campaign of Truth and Eisenhower's Chance for Peace and Atoms for Peace campaigns. As Parry-Giles concludes, these messages "reinforced the bully pulpit themes that Truman and Eisenhower promulgated" and expanded the chief executive's power to manage impressions of administration policy.[23] Such case studies illustrate the value of presidential papers in understanding and evaluating the inner workings of the rhetorical presidency.

As a final note on archival research, one twenty-first-century issue that commends itself is how electronic access to archival material may affect the process of scholarship based in primary data. In what ways, if any, will the capacity to conduct research from one's own office affect scholarship grounded in archival documents? More crucially, how will the generation of electronic documents that are inherently ephemeral affect what is left to be researched?

Our call for more scholarship on the eighteenth- and nineteenth-century chief executives, as well as for more archival research on presidential speech in all eras, should not be taken to diminish the importance of mediated presidential rhetoric. For we believe, third, that in this era of the image, one fruitful line of inquiry regards how presidents use pictures and images to supplement or even supplant their words. Perhaps this aspect of going public should be called "going visual." Examples include George W. Bush landing on the aircraft carrier and serving Thanksgiving dinner in Baghdad. An author of a recent book on Karl Rove reports that Rove views political advertising as a silent movie. As previously noted, Miroff explains the significance of the visual in "The Presidency and the Public: Leadership as Spectacle," an essential essay for appreciating how the presidential practice of projecting images to shape public understanding and gain popular support is accomplished.

Fourth, in addition to refining visual image strategies, technology has enhanced the ability of presidents to target carefully defined groups of voters and to reach them instantly. Mass e-mail, as Howard Dean's candidacy for the 2004 Democratic presidential nomination demonstrated, has the capacity to deliver finely tuned messages to select groups and to mobilize and energize target audiences. This new form of presidential communication has aspects of "going private" as well as going public. Benson's essay in *Beyond the Rhetorical Presidency* foreshadowed a good deal of this new emphasis. Undoubtedly this form of communication will grow in importance as the Internet, instant messaging, and other aspects of direct electronic communication become more pervasive. Some possible research questions are: How specifically are these tools of mass communication being used by presidents? How useful are the tools? Are the messages delivered in these ways different from the traditional forms of going public?

And finally, whether research focuses on new technology or old, on the eighteenth century or the twenty-first, we urge expansion of scholarship on the presidency and national identity. Two excellent examples of the kind of research we envision are Mary E. Stuckey's *Defining Americans: The Presidency and National Identity*, and Vanessa B. Beasley's *You the People: American National Identity in Presidential Rhetoric*. Beasley acknowledges in her introduction that questions "about the creation and maintenance of American national identity are not new, to be sure." Social scientists and humanists have examined political tracts, literary texts, published lectures, and additional documents in an effort to explain how "diverse American people have somehow imagined themselves" to be united. Beasley adds to this body of work by exploring how presidential Inaugural addresses and State of the Union messages between 1885 and 2000 shaped perceptions of a common identity on issues of immigration, gender, and race.[24]

Similar issues occupy Stuckey, albeit in a different fashion, as she examines the complex interplay between a "national identity" and the nation's diversity. Stuckey focuses on three recurring topoi in presidential speech on diversity: balance, citizenship, and visibility. Attending to seven nineteenth- and twentieth-century case studies, from Andrew Jackson to George H. W. Bush, she demonstrates the "constitutive capacities and the conservative tendencies" of presidential rhetoric.[25] Although these works approach a common topic in diverse ways, or perhaps *because* their approaches are so different, both warrant attention for the instruction and direction they offer. For despite the differences that characterize America in the twenty-first century, appeals to the "we" and "us" that define our national identity continue to pervade arguments in political persuasion. That the president's role is central to the process of definition is undeniable. That scholarship in presidential rhetoric should help to delineate that role is equally clear and compelling.

Recommendations

1. Scholars should devote greater attention to presidential rhetoric in the age of the Internet. With presidents able to communicate directly with interested parties and to maintain their own web sites, scholars must consider how—or whether—they will have access to key twenty-first-century documents.
2. The Internet's role in presidential communication also suggests important questions on archival research. Is there any mechanism, for example, for periodically preserving the content of the White House web site, or of the links to other sites to which the White House has access? If so, are disinterested/impartial persons overseeing the preservation, so as to ensure the integrity and completeness of the records?

3. Our support for archival research extends beyond an interest in new technology. For we recommend additional projects based in archival study that examine the rhetorical motives at work in eighteenth- and nineteenth-century presidential discourse.
4. Revelations about the Bush Administration's use of surrogates to issue pseudo–media "reports" raise issues that merit scholarly attention. What are the implications for research on the rhetorical presidency, for instance, of White House efforts to co-opt media opinion and/or to create media content?
5. Visual rhetoric in presidential communication demands closer attention. Ronald Reagan's first Inaugural Address, for example, was a very different speech for television viewers who followed coverage on CBS or NBC or ABC. The task force thus endorses Miroff's call for close study of "presidential spectacle" and strongly encourages more scholarly inquiry into how presidents use pictures and images to supplement or supplant their words.

Notes

1. Edwin Black and Lloyd F. Bitzer, "Foreword," *The Prospect of Rhetoric: Report of the National Developmental Project,* ed. Lloyd F. Bitzer and Edwin Black (Englewood Cliffs, N.J.: Prentice-Hall, 1971), v.

2. James W. Ceaser, Glenn E. Thurow, Jeffrey Tulis, and Joseph M. Bessette, "The Rise of the Rhetorical Presidency," *Presidential Studies Quarterly* 11 (1981): 158–71. Jeffrey Tulis develops the argument further in *The Rhetorical Presidency* (Princeton: Princeton University Press, 1987).

3. Mary E. Stuckey and Frederick J. Antczak, "The Rhetorical Presidency: Deepening Vision, Widening Exchange," in *Communication Yearbook 21,* ed. Michael E. Roloff (Thousand Oaks, Calif.: Sage Publications, 1998), 405–407; Roderick P. Hart, *The Sound of Leadership: Presidential Communication in the Modern Age* (Chicago: University of Chicago Press, 1987), 14; J. Michael Hogan, *The Panama Canal in American Politics: Domestic Advocacy and the Evolution of Policy* (Carbondale: Southern Illinois University Press, 1986), 10; David Zarefsky, *President Johnson's War on Poverty: Rhetoric and History* (Tuscaloosa: University of Alabama Press, 1986), 8–11. This synopsis of the origins and dimensions of the rhetorical presidency is adapted from David Henry, "Ronald Reagan and Aid to the *Contras:* An Analysis of the Rhetorical Presidency," in *Rhetorical Dimensions in Media: A Critical Casebook,* 2nd edition, ed. Martin J. Medhurst and Thomas W. Benson (Dubuque, Iowa: Kendall/Hunt, 1991), 73–75.

4. David K. Nichols, *The Myth of the Modern Presidency* (University Park: Penn State University Press, 1994).

5. Stephen E. Lucas, "Present at the Founding: The Rhetorical Presidency in Historical

Perspective," in *Before the Rhetorical Presidency,* ed. Martin J. Medhurst (College Station: Texas A&M Press, forthcoming).

6. Illustrative are Stephen E. Lucas, "George Washington and the Rhetoric of Presidential Leadership," in *The Presidency and Rhetorical Leadership,* ed. Leroy G. Dorsey (College Station: Texas A&M University Press, 2002), 42–72; Stephen Howard Browne, *Jefferson's Call for Nationhood* (College Station: Texas A&M University Press, 2003); and Mel Laracey, *Presidents and the People: The Partisan Story of Going Public* (College Station: Texas A&M University Press, 2002). On the link between varied levels of leadership success and presidential discourse prior to Wilson, see also Philip Abbott, *Strong Presidents: A Theory of Leadership* (Knoxville: University of Tennessee Press, 1996), especially chapters 1 on Washington, 2 on Lincoln, 4 on Jackson, and 7 on Jefferson.

7. Martin J. Medhurst, "Introduction: A Tale of Two Constructs—The Rhetorical Presidency Versus Presidential Rhetoric," in *Beyond the Rhetorical Presidency,* ed. Martin J. Medhurst (College Station: Texas A&M University Press, 1996), xi–xiv.

8. Karlyn Kohrs Campbell and Kathleen Hall Jamieson, *Deeds Done in Words: Presidential Rhetoric and the Genres of Governance* (Chicago: University of Chicago Press, 1990), 3.

9. David Zarefsky, "The Presidency Has Always Been a Place for Rhetorical Leadership," in *The Presidency and Rhetorical Leadership,* 21–24.

10. Zarefsky, "The Presidency Has Always Been a Place for Rhetorical Leadership," 31.

11. George C. Edwards III, *On Deaf Ears: The Limits of the Bully Pulpit* (New Haven: Yale University Press, 2003), 254.

12. Examples of studies that illustrate a "consequential relationship," though perhaps not cause-effect, between presidential advocacy and public policy include Hogan, *The Panama Canal in American Politics;* Zarefsky, *President Johnson's War on Poverty;* Campbell and Jamieson, *Deeds Done in Words;* Garth E. Pauley, *The Modern Presidency and Civil Rights: Rhetoric on Race from Roosevelt to Nixon* (College Station: Texas A&M University Press, 2001); Moya Ann Ball, *Vietnam-on-the-Potomac* (New York: Praeger, 1992); multiple chapters in Martin J. Medhurst, ed., *Eisenhower's War of Words: Rhetoric and Leadership* (East Lansing: Michigan State University Press, 1994), and Davis Houck, *FDR and Fear Itself: The First Inaugural Address* (College Station: Texas A&M University Press, 2002).

13. Exemplary of the range of the "case study" approach to presidential rhetoric are Thomas W. Benson, *Writing JFK: Presidential Rhetoric and the Press in the Bay of Pigs* (College Station: Texas A&M University Press, 2004); Denise M. Bostdorff, *The Presidency and the Rhetoric of Foreign Crisis* (Columbia: University of South Carolina Press, 1994); Browne, *Jefferson's Call for Nationhood;* Davis W. Houck, *Rhetoric as Currency: Hoover, Roosevelt, and the Great Depression* (College Station: Texas A&M University Press, 2001); Pauley, *The Modern Presidency and Civil Rights;* Kimber Charles Pearce, *Rostow, Kennedy, and the Rhetoric of Foreign Aid* (East Lansing: Michigan State University Press, 2001); Kathleen J. Turner, *Lyndon Johnson's Dual War: Vietnam and the Press* (Chicago: University of Chicago Press, 1985); and Michael Weiler and W. Barnett Pearce, eds., *Reagan and Public Discourse in America* (Tuscaloosa: University of Alabama Press, 1992).

14. Rick Vallely articulates the value of theory, particularly of Skowronek's *The Politics Presidents Make,* in "An Overlooked Theory of Presidential Politics," *Chronicle of Higher Education,* October 31, 2003, B10–B12. See also Laracey, *Presidents and the People,* and Richard E. Neustadt, *Presidential Power and the Modern Presidents: The Politics of Leadership from Roosevelt to Reagan* (New York: Maxwell Macmillan, 1990).

15. Harvey C. Mansfield Jr., *Taming the Prince: The Ambivalence of Modern Executive Power* (New York: Free Press, 1989).

16. Tulis, *The Rhetorical Presidency,* 17–23.

17. Tulis, *The Rhetorical* Presidency, 96–97.

18. See Lucas, "George Washington and the Rhetoric of Presidential Leadership."

19. Mel Laracey, "The Presidential Newspaper: The Forgotten Way of Going Public," in *Speaking to the People: The Rhetorical Presidency in Historical Perspective*, ed. Richard J. Ellis (Amherst: University of Massachusetts Press, 1998), 66–67. See also Laracey, *Presidents and the People.*

20. Tulis, *The Rhetorical Presidency,* 65.

21. Bruce Miroff, "The Presidency and the Public: Leadership as Spectacle," in *The Presidency and the Political System*, ed. Michael Nelson (Washington, D.C.: Congressional Quarterly, 1998), 316.

22. Thomas W. Benson, "To Lend a Hand: Gerald Ford, Watergate, and the White House Speechwriters," *Rhetoric & Public Affairs* 1 (1998): 201–25. The representative essays—all in Kurt Ritter and Martin J. Medhurst, eds., *Presidential Speechwriting: From the New Deal to the Reagan Revolution and Beyond* (College Station: Texas A&M University Press, 2003)—include Moya Ann Ball, "Lyndon B. Johnson: From Private Deliberations to Public Declaration—The Making of LBJ's Renunciation Speech"; Charles J. G. Griffin, "Dwight D. Eisenhower: The 1954 State of the Union Address as a Case Study in Presidential Speechwriting"; and Theodore Otto Windt Jr., "John F. Kennedy: Presidential Speechwriting as Rhetorical Collaboration."

23. Fred I. Greenstein, *The Hidden-Hand Presidency: Eisenhower as Leader* (New York: Basic Books, 1982), and Shawn J. Parry-Giles, *The Rhetorical Presidency, Propaganda, and the Cold War, 1945–1955* (Westport, Conn.: Praeger, 2002), 185.

24. Vanessa B. Beasley, *You the People: American National Identity in Presidential Rhetoric* (College Station: Texas A&M University Press, 2004), 7–23.

25. Mary E. Stuckey, *Defining Americans: The Presidency and National Identity* (Lawrence: University Press of Kansas, 2004), 3–7.

CHAPTER 16

REPORT OF THE NATIONAL TASK FORCE ON PRESIDENTIAL RHETORIC IN TIMES OF CRISIS

Chair: Denise M. Bostdorff, College of Wooster
Martin Carcasson, Colorado State University
James M. Farrell, University of New Hampshire
Robert L. Ivie, Indiana University, Bloomington
Amos Kiewe, Syracuse University
Kathleen B. Smith, Wake Forest University

Presidential crises are rhetorical constructs, transacted and mediated between the president and the public. According to Murray Edelman, "The word 'crisis' connotes a development that is unique and threatening."[1] To call a set of events a crisis, he argued, is to imply that a given event is different from routine political and social issues, that the event came about for reasons beyond the control of leaders, and that the solution to this different situation will require sacrifice, although we may assume that *others* will sacrifice, rather than ourselves.[2] Crisis is more powerful than other political terms because it suggests the need for unity in the face of a common threat. And although crisis terminology may be invoked in arbitrary ways—whether that terminology originated with the president, the media, or others—Edelman noted that "mass acceptance of the label is necessary even if the acceptance is ambivalent" for a crisis to be said to exist.[3] The term *crisis* has been applied to a variety of contexts, as well, such as foreign policy, economics, drugs, and even the state of the polity's confidence. Hence, crisis is an example of what Charles Stevenson referred to as a persuasive definition, one in which the denotation of a word varies, while the connotation stays the same.[4]

If managed well, crises can increase levels of personal credibility and replenish presidents' symbolic reserves by providing them with successes through which they can distribute symbolic reassurance to the populace in the future. Presidents also may use crisis rhetoric to accrue more power, to justify policies that they have already enacted, to legitimize policies that they desire, or to distract attention from troublesome issues and focus it upon their successes instead. Because of these temptations, presidents have increasingly resorted to the "crisis tool" since the end of World War II, particularly in the realm of foreign affairs.[5]

At the same time, presidents have not always found crisis to be a quick means to political success. Presidents may prove unable to solve a crisis and thereby appear ineffectual, undermining perceptions of their leadership. Or, as Lyndon Johnson found, crises may compete, with one crisis (Vietnam) diverting resources desperately needed to succeed in another crisis (the war on poverty). Just as the Chinese character for crisis has the dual connotation of "threat" and "opportunity," presidents have used the threats implied by crisis as opportunities to strengthen public perceptions of their political leadership, and they have also sometimes discovered that crises can threaten those perceptions, as well.[6]

Because presidents have demonstrated such a predilection for crisis, rhetorical scholars have likewise shown an interest in how presidents have talked about such issues. James Pratt published the first essay focusing on crisis speeches as a type of rhetoric, but it was Theodore O. Windt's 1973 essay, "The Presidency and Speeches on International Crises: Repeating the Rhetorical Past," that laid the foundation for much of the research that would follow.[7] It was not until 1994, however, that books devoted to the phenomenon of presidential crisis rhetoric appeared with Denise Bostdorff's *The Presidency and the Rhetoric of Foreign Crisis* and Amos Kiewe's edited volume, *The Modern Presidency and Crisis Rhetoric*.[8] As this report outlines, a plethora of rhetorical research has been done and continues to be done, all focused on how presidents have spoken about crises.

In the pages that follow, we draw upon this research to pose four challenges for scholars of presidential crisis rhetoric: (1) the challenge of expanding the historical/rhetorical record of presidential crisis discourse; (2) the challenge of examining the relationship between media coverage and presidential crisis rhetoric; (3) the challenge of analyzing how presidents attempt to maintain or to deflate perceptions of crisis; and (4) the challenge of critiquing the use of presidential crisis rhetoric and exploring its implications.

Expanding the Historical/Rhetorical Record of Presidential Crisis Discourse

One task for rhetorical analysts is to provide a more complete understanding of the historical/rhetorical record of presidential crisis discourse. According to David Zarefsky, the term *rhetorical history* may embrace four different kinds of scholarly endeavors, one of which is simply the history of the development of rhetorical concepts.[9] More germane to the study of presidential crisis rhetoric are the other three forms of inquiry that Zarefsky delineates. The first is what he terms ideological because it recognizes that historians and policy makers "not only argue *about* history; they also argue *from* it, using historical premises to justify current actions and beliefs."[10] A great deal of research on presidential crisis rhetoric, for instance, has revealed the extent to which circa–World War II arguments about appeasement have influenced the perceptions and public policy discourse of later presidents. Likewise, much of Robert L. Ivie's work has traced the ways in which presidential rhetors have relied upon established premises about order and about democracy.[11] Another kind of research pursuing rhetorical history is what Zarefsky describes as "the historical study of rhetorical events." Such research may take one of several forms, such as examining the ways in which a message changed public discourse; following the historical evolution of particular key arguments or terms; or ascertaining patterns in sets of messages about a particular issue.[12] Garry Wills's analysis of the Gettysburg Address, for example, demonstrated how Lincoln used his speech to redefine the Declaration of Independence as the nation's founding document and, hence, to redefine Americans as a people dedicated to a single proposition of equality.[13] Finally, a third form of rhetorical history takes place when scholars study history but, in Zarefsky's words, from the perspective that history is "a series of rhetorical problems, situations that call for public persuasion to advance a cause or overcome an impasse. The focus of the study would be on how, and how well, people invented and deployed messages in response to the situation."[14] Perhaps the lion's share of presidential crisis studies dealing with rhetorical history have taken this perspective. Zarefsky's analysis of Johnson's war on poverty, Windt's examination of Kennedy's foreign policy and civil rights crisis rhetoric, and Kiewe's study of George H. W. Bush's abandonment of his "no new taxes" pledge all exemplify this approach.[15]

While past presidential crisis research has often dealt with one or more of these approaches, rhetorical history has not been the sole focus of such scholarship, nor are we arguing that it should be. Case studies in rhetorical history are still very much needed in the area of presidential crisis rhetoric, however, and even rhetorical analysts of a different bent would be well advised to keep rhetorical history in mind. As Martin J. Medhurst observed, "rhetoric and history must be studied together, because both are complicated matters that directly impinge upon one another."[16] Moreover, when presidents know they must speak about crises, often the first step that they or their speechwriters take is to look at what presidents have said in past, similar crisis situations. Presidential crisis rhetoric, then, is influenced by perceptions that a situation is critical, the unique problem and constraints that a situation poses, the characteristics of the particular presidential rhetor, the president's and/or speechwriters' awareness of history and past responses, the audience or audiences that the president must address, and the rhetorical premises, handed down from culture and history, that have currency in the situation. By looking to the past, we may better understand not only those cases but also the presidential rhetoric that followed.

To provide a clearer direction to scholars, it might be good to begin with what we know. That is, what crisis rhetoric do we know a fair amount about? Past research has looked most extensively at presidential foreign crisis rhetoric.[17] Specifically, Cold War rhetoric has received a great deal of attention, including the rhetoric of Truman, Eisenhower, Kennedy, Johnson, Nixon, Ford, Carter, and Reagan.[18] The post–Cold War discourse of the Bushes and Bill Clinton has also been examined, albeit not to the same degree, given the recentness of their presidencies.[19]

Conversely, we still know relatively little about how U.S. presidents have spoken about other foreign policy crises. Aside from Stelzner's close textual analysis of FDR's declaration of war, a computer-based analysis of the fireside chats, Hikins's study of the doctrine of unconditional surrender, and a few early and/or relatively brief examinations of Roosevelt's rhetoric, scholars still have not studied FDR's speeches during the war years to any great extent, an especially surprising fact given the length of his tenure and his presumed impact on the presidents who followed.[20] Likewise, Wilson's speeches during World War I have received little attention—Herbert L. Carson has provided a brief comparison of Wilson and FDR, and Ivie has examined Wilson's motives in his 1917 war address as part of a larger group of presidential messages—while Wilson's speeches on behalf of the League of Nations have been studied in more depth.[21] Presidential crisis rhetoric of the eighteenth and nineteenth centuries has been even more overlooked. Although Laracey's *Presidents and the People: The Partisan Story of Going Public* has made a major contribution by showing how presidents of these eras relied on newspapers to make their case, relatively little has been done to examine the presidential use of public address, either in tandem with partisan papers or alone, during foreign policy crises. We do have scholarship on Lincoln.[22] That aside, rhetorical research on presidential war rhetoric during the eighteenth and nineteenth centuries appears to be limited to James M. Farrell's study of John Adams's discourse in the Franco-American crisis, Ivie's analysis of Polk's rhetoric justifying war with Mexico, and the inclusion of such speeches within larger samples studied by Karlyn Kohrs Campbell and Kathleen Hall Jamieson, and by Ivie.[23] As yet, no published work has provided an in-depth case study of presidential crisis rhetoric about the War of 1812 or the Spanish-American War.

In regard to so-called "domestic" crises, scholars have made a great deal of progress in studying contemporary presidential rhetoric about civil rights, but the discourse of earlier presidents remains largely unexamined.[24] Economic crisis rhetoric has also garnered a fair amount of attention.[25] Much of it has focused on Kennedy's management of the steel crisis and Johnson's war on poverty.[26] Left unexamined are Van Buren's responses to the financial panic of 1837, Grant's efforts to restore order in the panic of 1873, Cleveland's discourse on the panic of 1893, Reagan's reaction to the 1987 stock market crash, and Bush's efforts to bolster the market in the wake of September 11. For the most part, rhetorical critics have also not analyzed presidential crisis rhetoric dealing with labor—how, for example, did Cleveland justify his decision to call in federal troops to end the Pullman strike?—nor have we given appropriate attention to the many presidential wars on drugs.[27] Scholars have studied Reagan's response to the explosion of the space shuttle but have not examined Lyndon Johnson's or George W. Bush's rhetoric in similar circumstances.[28] In regard to the crisis rhetoric of succession, Kurt Ritter and, earlier, Campbell and Jamieson have analyzed the words of vice presidents ascending to the presidency, particularly those of Lyndon Johnson.[29] Likewise, scandal and corruption have received ample attention.[30] The hands-down favorite topic has been Nixon in the era of Watergate.[31] Nevertheless, well-known scandals, like those that both Grant and Harding endured at the hands of their associates, have remained unexamined.

This quick review of past research may suggest that crisis rhetoric falls into one of two categories—foreign or domestic—but increasingly those lines are less distinct. In an age of globalism, foreign policy and economic policy quickly become intertwined, as demonstrated by Bush's rhetoric about the war on terrorism. Even when these realms were more discrete, they clearly impacted one another, as studies on Eisenhower's response to the Sputnik crisis, Kennedy and Johnson's national security justifications for domestic reforms, and the competing demands of Vietnam and the war on poverty on Johnson's discourse demonstrate.[32] Future crisis research should recognize that the distinctions between the foreign and the domestic have now blurred. Just as Melvin Small has traced how domestic politics have historically influenced foreign policy, rhetorical scholars might explore how and when these concerns have both been addressed in past presidential crisis discourse as well as track how they have become more entangled over time.[33]

The historical tracing of the use of the term *crisis* itself might also prove informative. In his Inaugural Address in 1789, George Washington became the first president of the United States to use the word *crisis* when he referred to the crisis of confidence and authority associated with the Articles of Confederation that resulted in the drafting and ratification of the new Federal Constitution.[34] His usage suggested a momentous event, the outcome of which was uncertain and which required human deliberation as well as providential intercession. Washington did not refer to "crisis" again until 1794 in his Sixth Annual Message, when he remarked on the Whiskey Rebellion in Pennsylvania.[35] Although he was not yet president in 1858, Lincoln also treated crisis as a deliberative moment in his "House Divided" speech when he stated: "We are now far into the fifth year since a policy was initiated with the avowed object and confident promise of putting an end to slavery agitation. Under the operation of that policy, that agitation has not only not ceased, but has constantly augmented. In my opinion, it will not cease until a crisis shall have been reached and passed."[36] By contrast, contemporary presidents—at least as early as the Truman Doctrine speech—have spoken of crisis as an urgent situation demanding immediate action.[37]

Studies of the historical evolution of *crisis* may shed greater light on what this term has meant over time, how often it has been used during the course of the American presidency, and under what conditions it has been employed. According to the *Oxford English Dictionary,* the word *crisis* refers to "the turning-point of a disease for better or worse" and also "a state of affairs in which a decisive change for better or worse is imminent." The volume also mentions an obsolete usage of "judgment" or "decision." Indeed, *crisis* derives from the Greek κρισις, meaning a choosing, a dispute, an issue, or a decision.[38] Future research might explore at what point presidents began treating crisis no longer as an occasion for careful and reasonable deliberation about possible courses of action but as an urgent event of national peril that requires an immediate exercise of authoritative presidential power—and an event, we might add, that may be integrally linked to a president's image of leadership and enduring legacy. Furthermore, research along this line also may begin to uncover some of the collective assumptions regarding the intellectual and emotional resonance of crisis rhetoric among the American people, leading us to understand better the relationship between rhetoric that actually employs the term *crisis* and discourse that treats a matter as extremely urgent but does not name it as a crisis per se. In addition, such research might examine how the term *crisis* today is often accompanied by one adjective or another: "domestic crisis," "international crisis," "political crisis," "economic crisis." The emergence of such constructions in presidential discourse may indicate one dimension of the evolution of crisis rhetoric. And, since most adjectives are typically rooted in and emerge from a particular historical and political context, we are encouraged once more to investigate the range of rhetorical situations in which crisis rhetoric could be anticipated. As the example of Washington demonstrates, contemporary presidents have also used *crisis* far more frequently.

Nevertheless, as scholars undertake this form of historical research, they need to be cautious about distinguishing between those moments when presidents themselves or others—for example, the media, the political opposition, and/or the public—discussed an event or issue as a crisis, and those many instances in which historians and critics have retroactively defined the moments of crucial decision in the past, lest we impose our own frameworks in ways that decontextualize past rhetoric.[39]

Examining the Relationship between Media Coverage and Presidential Crisis Rhetoric

A second challenge remaining for rhetorical critics is to examine the relationship between media coverage and presidential crisis rhetoric. As Laracey has demonstrated, presidents in the nineteenth century used newspapers to shape public perceptions of issues such as the Mexican-American War and the Civil War.[40] The twentieth century brought Teddy Roosevelt, who persistently used press coverage to advance his agenda, and Woodrow Wilson, who counted on press coverage of his speaking tour to build public support for the League of Nations. Later, Calvin Coolidge created the device of "the White House spokesman," to whom journalists were to attribute messages that Coolidge did not want directly attributed to himself, while Franklin Roosevelt regularly planted newspaper stories aimed at strengthening his position and undermining his critics.[41] Kennedy and the presidents who followed him turned news management into an art form. While not all efforts to shape media coverage of crises were successful—or at least successful in the long term—presidents proved particularly adept at managing news about foreign policy crises.[42]

Once the Cold War ended, the president's ability to shape news coverage seemed to diminish. President Clinton found it more difficult to control media messages about foreign crises without the meta-narrative of the Cold War.[43] Moreover, his efforts to win supportive coverage of his proposed policies for the health care crisis also failed, albeit primarily due to the ineptness of the administration's messages and the slow pace at which Clinton worked to resolve what he had defined as a crisis.[44]

Changes in the media have also led observers to predict the dwindling power of the president to influence public opinion. According to Matthew Baum and Samuel Kernell, the expansion of cable channels has significantly decreased the exposure that presidents receive on television. Gone are the days when the president could appear on the three major networks and be watched by 59 percent of households in the United States, a viewership that Nixon's prime-time press conferences enjoyed.[45] In addition, research shows that the networks themselves are more reluctant to give presidents time, and even the length of sound bites during the evening news has decreased significantly.[46] In other words, the president is no longer guaranteed a direct audience; thus, if a message makes it to the public, it will likely be filtered through the media even more than in the past. A number of observers have also argued that media coverage is increasingly cynical in that it assumes politicians are always acting in their own self-interest. The ideological nature of many developing media outlets, the failure to provide a useful context for political events in media coverage, and the focus upon conflict and strategy, rather than policy, in the political coverage of even "mainstream" news organizations in turn activate the cynicism of the public.[47] Finally, young people are more likely to get their political news not from regular news coverage but from late-night comedians and political satire, sources not likely to present the president and his policies in the most positive way.[48]

All these developments point to a diminished presidential ability to shape media and public perceptions of crises, but one must also add several caveats.

While, at face value, more media voices appear to exist, more and more of those voices are owned by the same small group of companies seeking to improve their bottom lines, which can lead to two market-driven, often inadvertent forms of censorship. The first is an appeal to the broadest common denominator in order to guarantee the highest amount of consumption. When large media companies own a high number of media outlets, it is simply more cost efficient to have uniform programming that will appeal to as many individuals as possible.[49] This means that popular presidents who provide interesting and entertaining messages are more likely to be heard—even if only in sound bite form—whereas less captivating presidential rhetors may find themselves shut out. Second, the media may engage in targeted messages to reach very specific audiences more efficiently but do so in a way that pushes different groups or "image tribes" away from each other.[50] Amazon.com, for example, informs customers returning to its web site of new books that might interest them, based upon their past preferences. If a customer previously purchased a book by Al Franken, then he or she is directed to books by Molly Ivins, Jim Hightower, and Michael Moore. In so doing, the company encourages readers to attend to mediated messages with which they are already somewhat familiar and with which they are presumed to agree.

In such an atmosphere, presidents may need to rely upon their unofficial surrogates in the ideological media to help convey their crisis messages, just as presidents of an earlier time relied upon partisan newspapers. This reliance brings advantages to presidents—they can appear to be above the fray and can mobilize those groups most likely to support them—but may lead to problems, too, since presidents are unable to control their partisan surrogates' messages completely, and the existence of partisans on both ends of the political continuum feeds public polarization. In today's media, censorship may also be quite intentional at times, with both political and market forces playing a role, as in CBS's decision to drop a miniseries about Ronald Reagan and to refuse to show a political spot critical of George W. Bush at the same time that it agreed to air White House ads promoting the president's controversial Medicare program.[51] Presidents who are able to win the allegiance of media companies are likely to find their crisis messages conveyed in a manner more to their liking.

Along with market changes, another transformation that has impacted presidents' ability to control media coverage while engaging in crisis rhetoric is journalists' loss of skepticism concerning the information that political leaders provide them.[52] James Fallows attributes this change to a number of different factors: journalists who are now more likely to be college-educated, upper class, and therefore more likely to identify with the governmental leaders that they cover; news organizations' reliance on easy, inexpensive, convenient news gathering that primarily summarizes statements from official sources rather than investigates issues; and a compressed news cycle that means reporters are constantly in need of stories and thus are more likely to swallow the "line of the day" provided by an administration's representatives.[53]

Because journalists have become more cynical about politicians' motives and, simultaneously, less skeptical or willing to question facts, presidents may find crisis rhetoric a double-edged sword.[54] Reporters may accept their presentation of facts at face value—even when healthy skepticism would raise questions—but still focus upon the strategic advantages and disadvantages of the president's words. As a result, presidents may hesitate before engaging in crisis talk unless (a) they have a compelling crisis definition and efficacious solution that they can easily enact; (b) they are forced to engage in such discourse by public sentiment (promulgated by the public, the media, and/or political opponents) that a crisis exists and must be addressed; and/or (c) the crisis in question is a crisis in which the nation's institutions appear to be threatened *and* the president has come to represent the nation.

Recent research by Jamieson and Paul Waldman found that "journalists may express cynicism toward the *individuals* who seek and hold power, but they are reverent toward the *institutions* of power" because they themselves "have an investment in the legitimacy of the system, more so during a crisis." Media coverage of the Supreme Court decision in the 2000 presidential election, for example, tended to emphasize that the system had worked.[55] When a crisis threatens the nation's institutions *and* the president comes to represent the nation, as in foreign crises where citizens tend (at least initially) to rally around the flag, journalists cede an incredible degree of control over media coverage to White House officials. Jamieson and Waldman's analysis of media coverage after September 11 found the threat posed by the terrorist attacks catapulted journalists into the role of patriots who spoke with the inclusive language of "we," depicted Bush in an exceedingly positive fashion even when his statements were undeserving of such praise, adopted the frames provided by the administration, and failed to offer critiques of White House policy. According to Jamieson and Waldman, journalists in the patriot role exhibit "a heightened consciousness of being part of the nation, and in the process set skepticism and cynicism aside and adopt a reassuring tone about the well-being of democratic institutions and the dexterity of the country's leaders."[56] Given all of the constraints that presidents face, foreign crises and their attendant military interventions may offer particularly tempting opportunities for presidents since military engagement with a foreign enemy can provide a compelling narrative in which U.S. institutions appear to be threatened.

We also should be mindful that George W. Bush's rhetoric about September 11 and the war on terror has transformed the Cold War dualism of freedom versus communism into freedom versus terrorism, once again providing a compelling unified meta-narrative that may be applied not only to what we typically think of as the domain of foreign affairs (e.g., the wars in Afghanistan and Iraq) but also to what we usually identify as the domain of domestic issues (e.g., the privatization of airport security and budget deficits).[57] The overwhelmingly positive coverage of the administration in the period leading up to the war in Iraq and during the early months of the war again points to the White House's ability to shape news coverage during a crisis in which the nation appears threatened and the president appears to represent the nation. As Michael Massing asked in February 2004, after examining all of the *post hoc* media criticism of the administration's claims about weapons of mass destruction and rush to war, "Where were you all before the war?" Although the dissension within the intelligence community over weapons of mass destruction was clearly visible to reporters as early as the summer of 2002, Knight Ridder was the only national news organization to raise serious questions about the administration's rationale for war with Iraq.[58] Still, the fact that the media coverage shifted to become critical of the Bush Administration's claims in early 2004 demonstrates that even patriotic coverage is unlikely to continue indefinitely if a president begins to face significant criticism from other political elites, thereby triggering a return to cynical coverage that emphasizes strategy and conflict.[59] The shift in coverage of the Bush White House and Iraq also makes clear the "pack mentality" that encourages journalists not "to diverge too sharply from what everyone else is writing" and accentuates the need presidents have to sway significant media outlets to adopt their point of view when engaging in crisis rhetoric.[60]

While we know a fair amount about the trends of media coverage in general, a number of questions specifically focused on crisis coverage remain. How long, how well, and under what conditions are presidents able to convey their crisis messages through the media today? To what degree does media coverage respond to presidential crisis rhetoric with messages that make partisan statements, messages that focus on presidential political strategy, and/or messages that simply repeat—or even provide patriotic embellishments of—what the president has said? What are the circumstances associated with particular kinds of crisis coverage? To what degree does presidential rhetoric appear to influence media coverage and vice versa? How do different types of media outlets tend to treat presidential crisis discourse? How do presidents make use of partisan surrogates in their efforts to control crisis media coverage? As noted previously, the domestic and the foreign are more intertwined today than they have been in the past, but to what degree do the media discuss these dimensions of crises in terms of one another versus separately? We must also take care not to assume that everything we experience today is completely different than it was in the past. For that reason, scholars should examine case studies of media coverage and presidential crisis rhetoric far removed from our own experience as well as case studies that are not so distant, to ascertain commonalties and differences over time.

Analyzing How Presidents Attempt to Maintain or to Deflate Perceptions of Crisis

A third, related task awaiting scholars of presidential crisis rhetoric is examining how presidents attempt to maintain or deflate perceptions of crisis. Although a White House administration may be firmly convinced of the continuing nature of a crisis, the president will lose both authority and power if unable to transmit that frame clearly to the citizenry. The task of maintaining a sense of crisis is made even more difficult given the fleeting attention span of the media and the public. To maintain public concern for a perceived crisis, the president needs to address the constraints that Galtung and Ruge highlighted in their essay on the structure of news. Among the more pertinent of the thirteen attributes that they discussed are the need to make an event unambiguous and easily understood, personalized, unpredictable, and relevant.[61] To ensure citizen support, presidents need to keep their crisis explanations simple. Too much complexity can overwhelm the public; moreover, complicated crisis definitions are less likely to be conveyed accurately by media coverage, which tends to simplify and polarize issues.[62]

To maintain a sense of crisis, presidents also must use personification in crisis discussions, come up with unexpected events or highlights to spark the flames of interest, and show how the crisis continues to be of immediate relevance to the audience. As Galtung and Ruge explained, personification is particularly useful for maintaining newsworthiness because events are easier to understand when shown through people rather than social forces.[63] Presidential crisis rhetoric can depict an ongoing morality play between good and evil, represented by actors on each side, while a future goal of conquering the villains can motivate support for presidential policies. Through personification, presidents can deflect criticism (by focusing on U.S. soldiers as representative of foreign policy), stir pity (by pointing to a hungry child as the victim of poverty), and focus anger (by blaming the leader of another nation or greedy health insurance executives for an ongoing crisis). The pragmatic challenge, of course, is to cast roles in believable ways. To maintain a climate of crisis, presidents also must provide new material for the ongoing, old story by using multiple administration speakers on varied platforms to promote news coverage as well as media coverage on television and radio talk shows. The president may link the initial crisis event to other events, locations, or people so that the crisis story can appear to move as in a text, from one chapter to the next. Moreover, the president may provide shifting milestones to measure what has been accomplished, but also what remains to be done, and may construct levels of crisis concern to reduce monotony and keep the issue alive—the current five levels of terrorist alert, coded by color, come to mind here. Future research needs to examine how presidents may have used these and other strategies to maintain an ongoing sense of crisis as well as the degree to which presidents prior to the modern mass media have attempted to maintain perceptions of crisis and how they may have done so.

Presidents, of course, do not welcome crises that they cannot easily control or solve. When the *Maine* sank in 1898, for example, President William McKinley initially said nothing about it because he hoped to resolve the matter diplomatically, rather than having to escalate to other means.[64] Even if presidents initially promote a crisis, however—as Jimmy Carter did in the early months of the Iranian hostage crisis—they may quickly find that the ongoing perception of crisis is damaging politically if they are unable to resolve the crisis or at least demonstrate that progress is being made. Situations such as these point to the need for additional research on how presidents have attempted to deflate perceptions of crisis. While presidents may ignore the crisis claims of others or deny them, these strategies have their costs as well, since opponents are only too happy fill the media void created by presidential silence with their own assertions and—as Bill Clinton discovered—since emphatic denials of facts that are later revealed can seriously undermine a president's credibility. Presidents intent on deflating perceptions of crisis must also be concerned with the structure of news, but their personifications will likely depict them as innocent victims and others—usually journalists and critics—as unreliable or politically motivated. Because unexpected events spark interest, the president must distract attention from them or use language to characterize them as routine occurrences that are not unusual or cause for alarm. Likewise, the president must convey the sense that claims of crisis or events that point to crisis are irrelevant. Research on how presidents have attempted to deflate perceptions of crisis will provide a better understanding of the phenomenon of presidential crisis rhetoric in its entirety. Since efforts to deflate perceptions of crisis can distract the populace from problems in need of resolution, scholars should also concern themselves with the ethical implications of presidential crisis deflation.

Critiquing the Use of Presidential Crisis Rhetoric and Exploring Its Implications

Because crisis rhetoric can be a tempting tool to achieve political leverage, a fourth challenge that awaits scholars of presidential crisis rhetoric is the need to critique its use and explore its implications.[65] This challenge assumes even more importance in light of a post-9/11 presidency that has transformed crisis rhetoric. Indeed, a phenomenon that had been extraordinary and distinct from routine modes of governance now has become the ubiquitous shadow constituting presidential leadership and a threat to democratic rule. When terrorism exploded into the forefront of national consciousness on September 11, a previously floundering Bush Administration suddenly found its *raison d'être*. The nation collectively experienced a disorienting sense of chaos and looked immediately to the office of the presidency for reassurance and direction. Constitutional mandate and political habit privileged executive authority in the moment of crisis, and no other voice than that of the nation's supreme leader could have been heard over the din of disaster. This was an occasion requiring executive leadership in which the president would be measured by his response to the exigency at hand just as the exigency itself created a widespread presumption, motivated by both fear and desire, that President Bush was measuring up well. At that formative moment, by executive fiat, terrorism articulated a permanent and pervasive state of warfare that penetrated all walks of life and redefined every political issue. The rhetorical presidency, which already had evolved throughout the twentieth century by expanding executive presence into a presidential republic, poised itself to govern by crisis.[66] Everything domestic and foreign was tainted by the sign of terrorism and framed by the trope of war; furthermore, this perpetual and universal condition of institutionalized fear constrained democratic practice and, in the view of some scholars, undermined the nation's democratic culture.[67]

The current reign of presidential governance by crisis suggests a corresponding agenda for rhetorical scholarship, an agenda that ranges from assessing the impact of presidential governance by crisis on democratic culture and practices—both domestically and globally—to examining its confluence with political economy and the ideology of globalization. Our current presidential governance by crisis brings into focus the rhetorical agency of new media in an information age that, as noted earlier, radically compresses diversity. In addition, it also demonstrates the ways in which democratic practices are threatened by the opposing impulses of empire—on the one hand, corporate globalization that seeks to universalize markets and that increasingly bypasses or browbeats efforts at governmental intervention; on the other hand, tribalism, whereby groups threatened by globalization reject democratic practices in favor of recreating "ancient subnational and ethnic borders from within."[68] President Bush's crisis rhetoric privileges a hyperinflated discourse of American exceptionalism, mission, and empire, a policy of preemption and a project of universal democratization that promotes war in the name of peace, utilizes a polarizing rhetoric of evil, and risks a "blowback" of unintended consequences in what Jonathan Schell calls an "unconquerable world."[69] Governing by a continuous discourse of crisis also raises questions of how to deliberate the full range of issues (such as those related to the environment, education, welfare, and taxation policies) without subsuming everything under a patriot call to arms. By extension, presidential governance by crisis should intensify our concern for preserving civil liberties, which are often curtailed in the name of "crisis" conditions. The Patriot Act is one example, passed in a context of continuous war and terror, a war justified ironically as a defense of freedom.[70] Even more fundamentally, the troublesome regime of presidential crisis rhetoric is reinforced by a seeming lack of confidence in democracy itself and warranted by a foundational discourse that caricatures the *demos* as diseased.[71]

The rise of an increasingly rhetorical presidency, which scholars warned would diminish rather than enrich democratic deliberation, has morphed since 9/11 into a republic of fear and a state of executive preeminence that should remind rhetorical scholars of their calling to criticism.[72] The current case of the war on terror and the Patriot Act calls for our scrutiny. Indeed, even past cases of crisis rhetoric that have threatened democratic processes—Adams and the Alien and Sedition Acts, Lincoln and the suspension of habeas corpus, and FDR's internment of Japanese Americans, to name a few—have not yet been scrutinized carefully. As Kenneth Burke warned at the beginning of his critique of the rhetoric of Hitler's "Battle," we must do all that we can to forestall "the concocting of a similar medicine in America."[73] Governance through the discursive construction of perpetual crisis is just such a devilish brew that requires the critical engagement of rhetorical scholarship in order to meet the challenges of our time by enriching rather than degrading democratic culture. And, even more important, that engagement needs to be shared with the public at large if we are to fulfill our responsibilities not only as scholars but as citizens, as well.

THREAT AND OPPORTUNITY

In this report, we have presented four challenges for scholars of presidential crisis rhetoric: (1) the challenge of expanding the historical/rhetorical record of presidential crisis discourse; (2) the challenge of examining the relationship between media coverage and presidential crisis rhetoric; (3) the challenge of analyzing how presidents attempt to maintain or to deflate perceptions of crisis; and (4) the challenge of critiquing the use of presidential crisis rhetoric and exploring its implications. Just as the term *crisis* suggests both threat and opportunity, future research examining how presidents have talked about threats may provide an opportunity to shed light on the rhetoric of the presidency as a whole.

RECOMMENDATIONS

1. Presidential crisis rhetoric should be subjected to increasing scrutiny by the press, public, and academy.
2. Any law, executive order, or proclamation that curtails or has the effect of curtailing civil liberties needs to be subjected to thorough analysis and critique by the judiciary, the Congress, the news media, the academy, and all other organs of public opinion.
3. Use of the rhetoric of "crisis" should be limited to those situations where an immediate and imminent threat to the health and safety of the republic is at hand.
4. Presidents who manufacture "crises" for purely political ends should be held accountable for such misuse by the media, the academy, and the electorate.
5. Journalists who facilitate the presidential manufacturing of "crises" for purely political ends likewise need to be held accountable for their actions by their peers, the academy, and the public.
6. "Crisis" rhetoric appealing to fear, vengeance, retribution, hate, or expediency should be rejected in favor of informed public discussion and debate.

NOTES

1. Murray Edelman, *Political Language: Words That Succeed and Policies That Fail* (New York: Academic Press, 1977), 43.
2. Edelman, *Political Language*, 44; Murray Edelman, *Constructing the Political Spectacle* (Chicago: University of Chicago Press, 1988), 31.
3. Edelman, *Political Language*, 45–46.
4. Charles L. Stevenson, *Ethics and Language* (New Haven: Yale University Press, 1944), 206–26.
5. Amos Kiewe, "The Crisis Tool in American Political Discourse," *Politically Speaking: A Worldwide Examination of Language Used in the Public Sphere*, ed. Ofer Feldman and Christ'l De Landtsheer (Westport, Conn.: Praeger, 1998), 80–81; Denise M. Bostdorff, "'An Endless Series of Hobgoblins': The Rhetoric and Politics of Crisis from John Kennedy to George Bush and Beyond," in *The Presidency and the Rhetoric of Foreign Crisis* (Columbia: University of South Carolina Press, 1994), 237–40.
6. Meaning of the Chinese character is from Alexander L. George, *Managing U.S.-Soviet Rivalry* (Boulder, Colo.: Westview Press, 1983), 1, quoted in Bostdorff, *The Presidency and the Rhetoric of Foreign Crisis*, 239.
7. James W. Pratt, "An Analysis of Three Crisis Speeches," *Western Journal of Speech Communication* 34 (1970): 194–203; Theodore Otto Windt Jr., "The Presidency and Speeches on International Crises: Repeating the Rhetorical Past," *Speaker and Gavel* 11 (1973): 6–14.
8. Bostdorff, *The Presidency and the Rhetoric of Foreign Crisis*, and Amos Kiewe, ed., *The Modern Presidency and Crisis Rhetoric* (Westport, Conn.: Praeger, 1994).
9. David Zarefsky, "Four Senses of Rhetorical History," in *Doing Rhetorical History: Concepts and Cases*, ed. Kathleen J. Turner (Tuscaloosa: University of Alabama Press, 1998), 26.
10. Zarefsky, "Four Senses," 28.
11. See, for example: Robert L. Ivie, "Presidential Motives for War," *Quarterly Journal of Speech* 60 (1974): 337–45; Robert L. Ivie, "Tragic Fear and the Rhetorical Presidency: Combating Evil in the Persian Gulf," in *Beyond the Rhetorical Presidency*, ed. Martin J. Medhurst (College Station: Texas A&M University Press, 1996), 153–78; Robert L. Ivie, "A New Democratic World Order?" in *Critical Reflections on the Cold War: Linking Rhetoric and History*, ed. Martin J. Medhurst and H. W. Brands (College Station: Texas A&M University Press, 2000), 247–65.
12. Zarefsky, "Four Senses," 29.
13. Garry Wills, *Lincoln at Gettysburg: The Words That Remade America* (New York: Simon and Schuster, 1992), 121–47.
14. Zarefsky, "Four Senses," 30.
15. David Zarefsky, *President Johnson's War on Poverty: Rhetoric and History* (Tuscaloosa: University of Alabama Press, 1986); Theodore Otto Windt Jr., *Presidents and Protesters: Political Rhetoric in the 1960s* (Tuscaloosa: University of Alabama Press, 1990), 25–84; Amos Kiewe, "From a Rhetorical Trap to Capitulation and Obviation: The Crisis Rhetoric of George Bush's 'Read My Lips: No New Taxes,'" in *The Modern Presidency*, 179–202.
16. Martin J. Medhurst, "Afterword: Rhetorical Perspectives on the Cold War," in *Critical Reflections*, 266.

17. In *Deeds Done in Words,* Campbell and Jamieson focus on the generic characteristics of presidential war rhetoric, based on their analysis of speeches from Washington through Reagan that justified sending troops into imminent or actual hostilities (101–26). Hence, the point of their work is not to provide in-depth case studies of specific speeches—although they do provide thoughtful analysis of particular passages—but rather to discern overarching themes and significant differences among the speeches included. See Karlyn Kohrs Campbell and Kathleen Hall Jamieson, *Deeds Done in Words: Presidential Rhetoric and the Genres of Governance* (Chicago: University of Chicago Press, 1990).

18. See Martin J. Medhurst, Robert L. Ivie, Philip Wander, and Robert L. Scott, *Cold War Rhetoric: Strategy, Metaphor, and Ideology,* rev. ed. (East Lansing: Michigan State University Press, 1997). On Truman, see William R. Underhill, "Harry S. Truman: Spokesman for Containment," *Quarterly Journal of Speech* 47 (1961): 268–74; Wayne Brockriede and Robert L. Scott, *Moments in the Rhetoric of the Cold War* (New York: Random House, 1970), 27–35; Ivie, "Presidential Motives"; Ray E. McKerrow, "Truman and Korea: Rhetoric in the Pursuit of Victory," *Central States Speech Journal* 28 (1977): 1–12; Robert L. Ivie, "Literalizing the Metaphor of Soviet Savagery: President Truman's Plain Style," *Southern Communication Journal* 51 (1986): 91–105; Martin J. Medhurst, "Truman's Rhetorical Reticence, 1945–1947: An Interpretive Essay," *Quarterly Journal of Speech* 74 (1988): 52–70; Lynn Boyd Hinds and Theodore Otto Windt Jr., *The Cold War as Rhetoric: The Beginnings, 1945–1950* (New York: Praeger, 1991), 129–63; Robert L. Ivie, "Declaring a National Emergency: Truman's Rhetorical Crisis and the Great Debate of 1951," in *The Modern Presidency,* 1–18; Robert L. Ivie, "Fire, Flood, and Red Fever: Motivating Metaphors of Global Emergency in the Truman Doctrine Speech," *Presidential Studies Quarterly* 29 (1999): 570–91.

For Eisenhower, see Pratt, "Three Crisis Speeches"; David E. Procter, "The Rescue Mission: Assigning Guilt to a Chaotic Scene," *Western Journal of Speech Communication* 51 (1987): 245–55; Robert L. Ivie, "Eisenhower as Cold Warrior," in *Eisenhower's War of Words: Rhetoric and Leadership,* ed. Martin J. Medhurst (Lansing: Michigan State University Press, 1994), 7–25; Richard B. Gregg, "The Rhetoric of Distancing: Eisenhower's Suez Crisis Speech, 31 October 1956," in *Eisenhower's War of Words,* 157–87; Lawrence W. Haapanen, "The Missed Opportunity: The U-2 and Paris," in *Eisenhower's War of Words,* 251–71; Medhurst, "Eisenhower, Little Rock, and the Rhetoric of Crisis," in *The Modern Presidency,* 19–46. For Kennedy, see Brockriede and Scott, *Moments,* 79–117; Pratt, "Three Crisis Speeches"; Windt, "The Presidency"; Richard A. Cherwitz and Kenneth S. Zagacki, "Consummatory versus Justificatory Crisis Rhetoric," *Western Journal of Speech Communication* 50 (1986): 307–24; Windt, *Presidents and Protesters,* 25–59; Moya Ball, *Vietnam-on-the-Potomac* (New York: Praeger, 1992), 67–107; Denise M. Bostdorff, "The Rhetoric of Deflection: John F. Kennedy and the Cuban Missile Crisis of 1962," in *The Presidency,* 25–55; Denise M. Bostdorff and Steven R. Goldzwig, "Idealism and Pragmatism in American Foreign Policy Rhetoric: The Case of John F. Kennedy and Vietnam," *Presidential Studies Quarterly* 24 (1994): 515–30; Enrico Pucci Jr., "Crisis as Pretext: John F. Kennedy and the Rhetorical Construction of the Berlin Crisis," in *The Modern Presidency,* 47–72; Thomas W. Benson, *Writing JFK: Presidential Rhetoric and the Press in the Bay of Pigs Crisis* (College Station: Texas A&M University Press, 2004).

For Johnson, see Pratt, "Three Crisis Speeches"; Ivie, "Presidential Motives"; Richard A. Cherwitz, "Lyndon Johnson and the 'Crisis' of Tonkin Gulf: A President's Justification of War," *Western Journal of Speech Communication* 42 (1978): 93–104; Robert L. Ivie, "Images of Savagery in American Justifications for War," *Communication Monographs* 47 (1980): 279–94; Kathleen J. Turner, *Lyndon Johnson's Dual War: Vietnam and the Press* (Chicago: University of Chicago Press, 1985); Cherwitz and Zagacki, "Consummatory versus Justificatory Crisis Rhetoric"; Procter, "The Rescue Mission"; Robert L. Ivie, "Metaphor and Motive in the Johnson Administration's Vietnam War Rhetoric," in *Texts in Context: Critical Dialogues on Significant Episodes in American Political Rhetoric*, ed. Michael C. Leff and Fred J. Kauffeld (Davis, Calif.: Hermagoras Press, 1989), 121–48; Windt, *Presidents and Protesters*, 96–105; Ball, *Vietnam,* 107–86; Jeff D. Bass, "The Appeal to Efficiency as Narrative Closure: Lyndon Johnson and the Dominican Crisis, 1965," *Southern Speech Communication Journal* 50 (1985): 103–20; Denise M. Bostdorff, "LBJ Balances Strength and Restraint: The 1964 Gulf of Tonkin Crisis and the Danger of the Middle Ground," in *The Presidency,* 56–91.

For Nixon, see Robert P. Newman, "Under the Veneer: Nixon's Vietnam Speech of November 3, 1969," *Quarterly Journal of Speech* 56 (1970): 168–78; Pratt, "Three Crisis Speeches"; Hermann G. Stelzner, "The Quest Story and Nixon's November 3, 1969 Address," *Quarterly Journal of Speech* 57 (1971): 163–72; Forbes I. Hill, "Conventional Wisdom—Traditional Form: The President's Message of November 3, 1969," *Quarterly Journal of Speech* 58 (1972): 373–86; Karlyn Kohrs Campbell, "An Exercise in the Rhetoric of Mythical America," *Critiques of Contemporary Rhetoric* (Belmont: Wadsworth, 1972), 39–58; Windt, "The Presidency"; Richard B. Gregg and Gerard A. Hauser, "Richard Nixon's April 30, 1970 Address on Cambodia: The 'Ceremony' of Confrontation," *Speech Monographs* 40 (1973): 167–81; Denise M. Bostdorff, "Richard M. Nixon and the Grotesque: The 1970 Invasion of Cambodia," in *The Presidency,* 92–122; Carole Blair and Davis W. Houck, "Richard Nixon and the Personalization of Crisis," in *The Modern Presidency,* 91–118. For Ford, see Dan F. Hahn, "Corrupt Rhetoric: President Ford and the *Mayaguez* Affair," *Communication Quarterly* 28 (1980): 38–43; Cherwitz and Zagacki, "Consummatory versus Justificatory Crisis Rhetoric"; Denise M. Bostdorff, "The Quiet Man: Ford's Portrayal of Leadership during the *Mayaguez* Crisis," in *The Presidency,* 123–43. For Carter, see Cherwitz and Zagacki, "Consummatory versus Justificatory Crisis Rhetoric"; Gerard A. Hauser, "Administrative Rhetoric and Public Opinion: Discussing the Iranian Hostages in the Public Sphere," *American Rhetoric: Context and Criticism*, ed. Thomas W. Benson (Carbondale: Southern Illinois University Press, 1989), 323–83; Denise M. Bostdorff, "Idealism Held Hostage: Jimmy Carter's Rhetoric on the Crisis in Iran," *Communication Studies* 43 (1992): 14–28; Denise M. Bostdorff, "Idealism Held Hostage: Jimmy Carter and the Crisis in Iran," in *The Presidency,* 144–74; Charles J. G. Griffin, "Narrative Character in Presidential Crisis Rhetoric: Jimmy Carter and the Iranian Hostage Crisis," *The Modern Presidency,* 137–54.

For Reagan, see Procter; Robert L. Ivie, "Speaking 'Common Sense' about the Soviet Threat: Reagan's Rhetorical Stance," *Western Journal of Speech Communication* 48 (1984): 39–50; Cherwitz and Zagacki, "Consummatory versus Justificatory Crisis Rhetoric"; David C. Klope, "Defusing a Foreign Policy Crisis: Myth and Victimage in Reagan's 1983 Lebanon/Grenada Address," *Western Journal of Speech Communication* 50 (1986): 336–49; Procter, "The Rescue Mission"; David S. Birdsell, "Ronald Reagan on Lebanon and Grenada: Flexibility and Interpretation in the Application of Kenneth Burke's Pentad," *Quarterly Journal of Speech* 73 (1987): 267–79; Bonnie J. Dow, "The Function of Epideictic and Deliberative Strategies in Presidential Crisis Rhetoric," *Western Journal of Speech Communication* 53 (1989): 294–310; Marilyn J. Young and Michael K. Launer, "KAL 007 and the Superpowers: An International Argument," *Quarterly Journal of Speech* 74 (1988): 271–95; Denise M. Bostdorff, "The Presidency and Promoted Crisis: Reagan, Grenada, and Issue Management," *Presidential Studies Quarterly* 21 (1991): 737–50; Kathryn M. Olson, "Constraining Open Deliberation in Times of War: Presidential War Justifications for Grenada and the Persian Gulf," *Argumentation and Advocacy* 28 (1991): 64–79; Denise M. Bostdorff, "Mission and Manifest Destiny in Grenada: Ronald Reagan Rallies the American Faithful," in *The Presidency,* 175–204; Greg Dickinson, "Creating His Own Constraint: Ronald Reagan and the Iran-Contra Crisis," in *The Modern Presidency,* 155–78; Craig Allen Smith and Kathy B. Smith, *The White House Speaks: Presidential Leadership as Persuasion* (Westport, Conn.: Praeger, 1994), 210–21.

19. See, for example, Olson, "Constraining Open Deliberation"; Mark A. Pollock, "The Battle for the Past: George Bush and the Gulf Crisis," in *The Modern Presidency,* 203–24; Mary E. Stuckey, "Competing Foreign Policy Visions: Rhetorical Hybrids after the Cold War," *Western Journal of Communication* 59 (1995): 214–227; Kathleen M. German, "Invoking the Glorious War: Framing the Persian Gulf Conflict through Directive Language," *Southern Communication Journal,* 60 (1995): 292–302; Robert L. Ivie, "Tragic Fear and the Rhetorical Presidency: Combating Evil in the Persian Gulf," in *Beyond the Rhetorical Presidency,* 153–78; Ivie, "A New"; Denise M. Bostdorff, "George W. Bush's Post–September 11 Rhetoric of Covenant Renewal: Upholding the Faith of the Greatest Generation," *Quarterly Journal of Speech* 89 (2003): 293–319; John M. Murphy, "'Our Mission and Our Moment': George W. Bush and September 11th," *Rhetoric & Public Affairs* 6 (2003): 607–32; Robert L. Ivie, "Evil Enemy v. Agonistic Other: Rhetorical Constructions of Terrorism," *Review of Education, Pedagogy, and Cultural Studies* 25 (2003), 181–200.

20. Hermann G. Stelzner, "'War Message,' December 8, 1941: An Approach to Language," *Communication Monographs* 23 (1966): 419–37; James W. Hikins, "The Rhetoric of 'Unconditional Surrender' and the Decision to Drop the Atomic Bomb," *Quarterly Journal of Speech* 69 (1983): 379–400; Elvin T. Lim, "The Lion and the Lamb: De-Mythologizing Franklin Roosevelt's Fireside Chats," *Rhetoric & Public Affairs* 6 (2003): 437–64; and, Ivie, "Presidential Motives."

21. Herbert L. Carson, "War Requested; Wilson and Roosevelt," *Central States Speech Journal* 19 (1958): 28–32; Ivie, "Presidential Motives"; Jeffrey K. Tulis, *The Rhetorical Presidency* (Princeton, N.J.: Princeton University Press, 1987), 147–61; Leroy G. Dorsey, "Woodrow Wilson's Fight for the League of Nations: A Reexamination," *Rhetoric & Public Affairs* 2 (1999): 107–35.

22. Wills, *Lincoln at Gettysburg;* and several works in *Rhetoric & Public Affairs* 3 (2000): David Zarefsky, "Lincoln's 1862 Annual Message: A Paradigm of Rhetorical Leadership," 5–14; Kirt H. Wilson, "The Paradox of Lincoln's Rhetorical Leadership," 15–32; Martha Watson, "Ordeal by Fire: The Transformative Rhetoric of Abraham Lincoln," 33–49; Edwin Black, "The Ultimate Voice of Lincoln," 49–57.

23. James M. Farrell, "Classical Virtue and Presidential Fame: John Adams, Leadership, and the Franco-American Crisis," *The Presidency and Rhetorical Leadership,* ed. Leroy G. Dorsey (College Station: Texas A&M University Press, 2002), 73–94; Robert L. Ivie, "Progressive Form and Mexican Culpability in Polk's Justification for War," *Communication Studies* 30 (1979): 311–20; Campbell and Jamieson, *Deeds;* Ivie, "Presidential Motives."

24. See David Zarefsky, "Lyndon Johnson Redefines 'Equal Opportunity': The Beginnings of Affirmative Action," *Central States Speech Journal* 31 (1980): 85–94; Steven R. Goldzwig and George N. Dionisopoulos, "John F. Kennedy's Civil Rights Discourse: The Evolution from 'Principled Bystander' to Public Advocate," *Communication Monographs* 56 (1989): 179–98; Windt, *Presidents and Protesters*, 78–84; Medhurst, "Eisenhower, Little Rock, and the Rhetoric of Crisis," in *The Modern Presidency*, 19–46; Garth E. Pauley, *The Modern Presidency and Civil Rights: Rhetoric on Race from Roosevelt to Nixon* (College Station: Texas A&M University Press, 2001); Steven R. Goldzwig, "LBJ, the Rhetoric of Transcendence, and the Civil Rights Act of 1968," *Rhetoric & Public Affairs* 6 (2003): 25–54.

25. See Hermann G. Stelzner, "Ford's War on Inflation: A Metaphor That Did Not Cross," *Communication Monographs* 44 (1977): 284–97; Kiewe, "From a Rhetorical"; Davis W. Houck, *Rhetoric as Currency: Hoover, Roosevelt, and the Great Depression* (College Station: Texas A&M University Press, 2001).

26. See Windt, *Presidents and Protesters*, 44–52; Denise M. Bostdorff and Daniel J. O'Rourke, "The Presidency and the Promotion of Domestic Crisis: John Kennedy's Management of the 1962 Steel Crisis," *Presidential Studies Quarterly* 27 (1997): 343–61; and David Zarefsky, "President Johnson's War on Poverty: The Rhetoric of Three 'Establishment' Movements," *Communication Monographs* 44 (1977): 352–73; David Zarefsky, "The Great Society as a Rhetorical Proposition," *Quarterly Journal of Speech* 65 (1979): 364–78; Zarefsky, *President Johnson's War on Poverty*; Tulis, *The Rhetorical Presidency*, 161–72.

27. Elwood does a brief analysis of Reagan's and George H. W. Bush's declarations (27–28), but he does not look at Nixon's war on drugs. Elwood's book focuses mainly on media messages like those of Partnership for a Drug-Free America. See William N. Elwood, *Rhetoric of the War on Drugs: The Triumphs and Tragedies of Public Relations* (Westport, Conn.: Praeger, 1994).

28. Steven M. Mister, "Reagan's Challenger Tribute: Combining Generic Constraints and Situational Demands," *Central States Speech Journal* 37 (1986): 158–65.

29. Kurt Ritter, "Lyndon B. Johnson's Crisis Rhetoric after the Assassination of John F. Kennedy: Securing Legitimacy and Leadership," in *The Modern Presidency*, 73–90; Campbell and Jamieson, *Deeds* 37–51; Kathleen Hall Jamieson and Karlyn Kohrs Campbell, "Rhetorical Hybrids: Fusions of Generic Elements," *Quarterly Journal of Speech* 68 (1982): 146–57.

30. See James F. Kumpp and Thomas A. Hollihan, "Debunking the Resignation of Earl Butz: Sacrificing an Official Racist," *Quarterly Journal of Speech* 65 (1979): 1–11; Amos Kiewe, "The Public vs. the Private: Bill Clinton's Speech of August 17, 1998," *American Communication Journal* (1999), available from http://www.americancomm.org/~aca/acj; Joseph R. Blaney and William L. Benoit, *The Clinton Scandals and the Politics of Image Restoration* (Westport, Conn.: Praeger, 2001); Robert E. Denton Jr. and Rachel L. Holloway, *Images, Scandal, and Communication Strategies of the Clinton Presidency* (Westport, Conn.: Praeger, 2003).

31. See Barry Brummett, "Presidential Substance: The Address of August 15, 1973," *Western Journal of Speech Communication* 39 (1975): 249–59; Jackson Harrell, B. L. Ware, and Wil A. Linkugel, "Failure of Apology in American Politics: Nixon on Watergate," *Communication Monographs* 42 (1975): 245–61; Carol J. Jablonski, "Richard Nixon's Irish Wake: A Case Study of Generic Transference," *Communication Studies* 30 (1979): 164–73;

William L. Benoit, "Richard M. Nixon's Rhetorical Strategies in his Public Statements on Watergate," *Southern States Communication Journal* 47 (1982): 192–211; Blair and Houck, "Richard Nixon and the Personalization of Crisis"; Smith and Smith, *The White House Speaks*, 191–227.

32. David Henry, "Eisenhower and Sputnik: The Irony of Failed Leadership," in *Eisenhower's War of Words*, 223–49; H. W. Brands, "Liberals All! Politics and Rhetoric in Cold War America," in *Critical Reflections*, 169–86; Turner, *Lyndon Johnson's Dual War*; Zarefsky, *President Johnson's War on Poverty*.

33. Melvin Small, *Democracy and Diplomacy: The Impact of Domestic Politics on U.S. Foreign Policy, 1789–1994* (Baltimore: Johns Hopkins University Press, 1996).

34. First Inaugural Address of George Washington, April 30, 1789, in *A Compilation of the Messages and Papers of the Presidents*, ed. James D. Richardson (New York: Bureau of National Literature, 1897), vol. 1:44. In his own Inaugural Address, John Adams referred to the same "crisis" in American history. See Inaugural Address of John Adams, March 4, 1797, in *A Compilation of the Messages and Papers of the Presidents*, ed. James D. Richardson (New York: Bureau of National Literature, 1897), 1:218.

35. Sixth Annual Message of George Washington, November 19, 1794, in *A Compilation of the Messages and Papers of the Presidents*, ed. James D. Richardson (New York: Bureau of National Literature, 1897), 1:156.

36. Abraham Lincoln, "House Divided," in *The Essential Abraham Lincoln* (New York: Gramercy Books, 1993), 115.

37. Harry S. Truman, "Special Message to the Congress on Greece and Turkey: The Truman Doctrine," March 12, 1947, in *The Public Papers of the Presidents of the United States* (Washington, D.C.: United States Government Printing Office, 1963), 177.

38. "Crisis," *The Compact Edition of the Oxford English Dictionary* (New York: Oxford University Press, 1971); "κρισις," *Liddell and Scott's Greek-English Lexicon*, 1977 abridged ed., cited in Bostdorff, *The Presidency*, 5.

39. Even as early as the 1830s, there was a tendency in the public press to look back on how the nation had navigated or survived this or that "crisis." See "Life of Henry Clay," *North American Review* 33 (October 1831): 372; "Memoir of Mr. Justice Story," *New England Magazine* 3 (December 1832): 440; "Mr. Everett's Address," *New England Magazine* 5 (August 1833): 144.

40. Mel Laracey, *Presidents and the People: The Partisan Story of Going Public* (College Station: Texas A&M University Press, 2002), 88–89, 107–12.

41. Arthur Krock, "Mr. Kennedy's Management of the News," *Fortune*, March 1963, 202; John Tebbel and Sarah Miles Watts, *The Press and the Presidency: From George Washington to Ronald Reagan* (New York: Oxford University Press, 1985), 441; and B. H. Winfield, "The New Deal Publicity Operation: Foundation for the Modern Presidency," *Journalism Quarterly* 61 (1984): 45. All cited in Bostdorff, "The Rhetoric of Deflection," 33.

42. Bostdorff, "An Endless Series," 234–37.

43. Jim A. Kuypers, *Presidential Crisis Rhetoric and the Press in the Post–Cold War World* (Westport, Conn.: Praeger, 1997), 9, 197–99.

44. Rachel L. Holloway, "The Clintons and the Health Care Crisis: Opportunity Lost, Promise Unfulfilled," in *The Clinton Presidency: Images, Issues, and Communication Strategies*, ed. Robert E. Denton Jr. and Rachel L. Holloway (Westport, Conn.; Praeger, 1996), 159–87.

45. Mathew A. Baum and Samuel Kernell, "Has Cable Ended the Golden Age of Presidential Television?" *American Political Science Review* 93 (1999): 99.

46. Center for Media and Public Affairs, "The Incredible Shrinking Sound Bite," September 28, 2000, available from http://www.cmpa.com/perssrel/electpr5.htm.

47. Larry Sabato, *Feeding Frenzy: How Attack Journalism Has Transformed American Politics* (New York: Free Press, 1991); Thomas E. Patterson, *Out of Order* (New York: Vintage Books, 1993); Joseph N. Cappella and Kathleen Hall Jamieson, *Spiral of Cynicism: The Press and the Public Good* (New York: Oxford University Press, 1997), particularly 19–21, 139–69; James Fallows, *Breaking the News: How the Media Undermine American Democracy* (New York: Pantheon Books, 1996), 131–43, 146–52, 161–65.

48. See, for example, Gloria Goodale, "Politics as Punch Line," *Christian Science Monitor*, January 30, 2004, available at http://www.csmonitor.com/2004/0130.

49. Benjamin R. Barber, *Jihad vs. McWorld: Terrorism's Challenge to Democracy* (New York: Ballantine Books, 1995), 150, 220–22.

50. Joseph Turow, *Breaking up America: Advertisers and the New Media World* (Chicago: University of Chicago Press, 1997), 5, 125–56, 199–200.

51. "Medicare Ad Riles Bush Critics," *CBSNEWS.com*, February 6, 2004, available at http://www.cbsnews.com/stories/2004/02/06.

52. Cappella and Jamieson, *Spiral of Cynicism*, 26.

53. Fallows, *Breaking the News* 49, 75–80, 144–46, 182–83, 191–92; Mark Hertsgaard, *On Bended Knee: The Press and the Reagan Presidency* (New York: Farrar Straus Giroux, 1988), 34–53.

54. Cappella and Jamieson, *Spiral of Cynicism*, 26.

55. Kathleen Hall Jamieson and Paul Waldman, *The Press Effect: Politicians, Journalists, and the Stories That Shape the Political World* (New York: Oxford University Press, 2003), 136.

56. Jamieson and Waldman, *The Press Effect*, 137–64, 138.

57. Bostdorff, "George W. Bush's," 303–305.

58. Michael Massing, "Now They Tell Us," editorial, *New York Review of Books*, February 26, 2004, 1, 3, available at http://www.nybooks.com/articles/16922.

59. Jamieson and Waldman found domestic coverage reverted to a more cynical focus on conflict and strategy once the president began facing criticism from other elites, both in his own party and in the Democratic Party, over issues like finance reform (161–62).

60. Massing, "Now They Tell Us," 16.

61. J. Galtung and M. H. Ruge, "The Structure of Foreign News," *Journal of International Peace Research* 1 (1965): 64–80.

62. Steven L. Vibbert and Denise M. Bostdorff, "Issue Management in the 'Lawsuit Crisis,'" in *The Ethical Nexus*, ed. Charles Conrad (Norwood, N.J.: Ablex, 1993), 108–10.

63. Galtung and Ruge, "The Structure of Foreign News," 64–80.

64. Laracey, *Presidents and the People*, 137.

65. Tulis, *The Rhetorical Presidency*, 178; Bostdorff, "An Endless Series," 237–40; Kiewe, "The Crisis Tool," 81–82.

66. Tulis, *The Rhetorical Presidency*; Gary L. Greg, II, *The Presidential Republic: Executive Representation and Deliberative Democracy* (Lanham, Md.: Rowman and Littlefield, 1997), 1–4, 9, 198–99, 207.

67. Benjamin R. Barber, *Fear's Empire: War, Terrorism, and Democracy* (New York: W. W. Norton and Company, 2003), 32, 90, 92, 132, 138–41, 215–17.

68. Barber, *Jihad vs. McWorld*, 6; also 5–7, 48–49, 103, 116–20, 150, 209, 215, 236–46, 268–92.

69. Andrew J. Bacevich, *American Empire: The Realities and Consequence of U.S. Diplomacy* (Cambridge, Mass.: Harvard University Press, 2002); Clyde Prestowitz, *Rogue Nation: American Unilateralism and the Failure of Good Intentions* (New York: Basic Books, 2003), 19–49; Robert L. Ivie, "Democratizing for Peace," *Rhetoric & Public Affairs* 4 (2001): 309–22; Robert L. Ivie, "Evil Enemy," 181–200; Bostdorff, "George W. Bush's": 303–305; Chalmers Johnson, *Blowback: The Costs and Consequences of American Empire* (New York: Henry Holt and Company, 2000), 5–10, 33, 223–29; Jonathan Schell, *The Unconquerable World: Power, Nonviolence, and the Will of the People* (New York: Metropolitan Books, 2003), 6–8, 339–52, 386–88.

70. David Cole and James X. Dempsey, eds., *Terrorism and the Constitution: Sacrificing Civil Liberties in the Name of National Security* (New York: New Press, 2002); Richard C. Leone and Greg Anrig Jr., eds., *The War on Our Freedoms: Civil Liberties in an Age of Terrorism* (New York: Public Affairs, 2003).

71. Robert L. Ivie, "Distempered Demos: Myth, Metaphor, and U.S. Political Culture," in *Myth: A New Symposium*, eds. Gregory A. Schrempp and William F. Hansen (Bloomington: Indiana University Press, 2002), 165–79.

72. On the republic of fear, see Robert L. Ivie, *Democracy and America's War on Terror* (Tuscaloosa: University of Alabama Press, 2005), chapter 1.

73. Kenneth Burke, *The Philosophy of Literary Form*, 3d ed. (1941; Berkeley: University of California Press, 1967), 191.

CONTRIBUTORS

James Arnt Aune is professor of communication at Texas A&M University. He is the author of *Rhetoric and Marxism* (1994) and *Selling the Free Market* (2001), which won the 2003 National Communication Association Diamond Anniversary Award as the best book published in communication in a two-year period. He coedited (with Rick Rigsby) *Civil Rights Rhetoric and the American Presidency* (2005). He studies public controversy about legal and economic issues. He is currently working on a project titled *Millhands and Marxists: Competing Narratives of the 1929 Gastonia Textile Strike*.

Roderick P. Hart is dean of the College of Communication at the University of Texas at Austin and holds the Shivers Chair in Communication and Government. He is also director of the Annette Strauss Institute for Civic Participation. He is the author or editor of twelve books, including *Campaign Talk: Why Elections Are Good for Us* (Princeton, 2000) and most recently *Political Keywords: Using Language That Uses Us* (Oxford, 2004). He has received grants from the Ford, Carnegie, Exxon, Annenberg, Gates and Hatton Sumners foundations and the Pew Charitable Trusts. He has been named a research fellow by the International Communication Association and a distinguished scholar by the National Communication Association, and he has received the Edelman Career Award from the American Political Science Association. He has also been elected to the Academy of Distinguished Teachers at the University of Texas.

Marouf Hasian Jr. is a professor in the Department of Communication at the University of Utah. He received his J.D. in 1984 from Campbell Law School and his Ph.D. in speech communication from the University of Georgia in 1993. His scholarly areas of interest include contemporary public address, law and rhetoric, freedom of expression, postcolonial studies, and critical memory studies.

Martin J. Medhurst is Distinguished Professor of Rhetoric and Communication at Baylor University in Waco, Texas. He is the author or editor of eleven books, including *Dwight D. Eisenhower: Strategic Communicator, Beyond the Rhetorical Presidency,* and *The Rhetorical Presidency of George H. W. Bush.*

John M. Murphy (Ph.D., University of Kansas, 1986) is an associate professor and graduate coordinator of speech communication at the University of Georgia. His research interests focus on contemporary American public address, the rhetorical presidency, and rhetorical criticism and theory. His work examines the ways in which enduring political languages take form in particular public debates and influence policy decisions. He has published essays in journals such as the *Quarterly Journal of Speech, Rhetoric & Public Affairs, Communication Monographs, Presidential Studies Quarterly,* and *Rhetoric Review.*

Trevor Parry-Giles is an associate professor in the Department of Communication at the University of Maryland, where he is also an affiliated scholar with the Center for American Politics and Citizenship. Parry-Giles is the coauthor of *Constructing Clinton: Hyperreality and Presidential Image-Making in Postmodern Politics* (Peter Lang, 2000) and *The Prime-Time Presidency: The West Wing and U.S. Nationalism* (University of Illinois Press, 2006) and the author of *The Character of Justice: Rhetoric, Law and Politics in the Supreme Court Confirmation Process* (Michigan State University Press, 2006), an expanded version of his chapter in this volume.

Marilyn J. Young is the Wayne C. Minnick Professor of Communication emerita at Florida State University. She has published four books, including *Nuclear Energy and Security in the Former Soviet Union* (with David Marples) and *Flights of Fancy, Flight of Doom: KAL 007 and Soviet-American Rhetoric* (with Michael K. Launer). Dr. Young is the author of numerous scholarly essays and book chapters, including "Non-Rational Assessment of Risk and the Development of Civilian Nuclear Power"; "Not in Our Names: The Bush Administration's Private Construction of the War in Iraq" (with Kathleen Farrell); "Composite Narrative, Authoritarian Discourse, and the Soviet Response to the Destruction of Iran Air Flight 655" (with Jim A. Kuypers and Michael K. Launer); and "The Situational Perspective." Dr. Young continues to be an active scholar in retirement and regularly attends academic conferences.

INDEX

9/11, 69–71, 73, 74, 75, 78, 80–81, 84, 87, 88, 90, 149, 163, 171, 173, 175–76, 195–96, 217, 282, 331, 365, 368, 369

Adams, John, 280
Adams, John Quincy: 7, 255; speeches of, 280
"advice and consent" *See* Senate, US
Al Qaeda, 70, 71, 74, 77, 84, 195–96, 202, 329
American Dream, The: 130–33, 134–52; George W. Bush and, 133, 149–52; Ronald Reagan and, 133, 137, 143–49, 152; Theodore Roosevelt and, 133, 137, 138, 139–43, 152
anti-semitism, 61–62
Arendt, Hannah, 29–30, 32, 34
Aristotle, 319, 320–21
Ashcroft, John, 85
author, 31–32, 324
authority: 29–35, 36, 41, 282; moral, 210, 219, 295, 318, 322; power and, 31, 32, 33, 282; rhetoric and, 30, 31, 34, 36, 43, 282

Baird, A. Craig, 7, 8
Bauer, Marvin, 5
Berry, Mildred Freburg, 6–7, 8, 16
Black, Edwin: 10, 323, 324; *Rhetorical Criticism, A Study in Method*, 10
Bitzer, Lloyd, 13
Booth, Wayne, 323, 324
Brandenburg, Earnest, 7, 9, 16
Brandeis, Louis, 111–12
bully pulpit, 101, 139, 239, 281, 295, 296, 344, 349
Burke, Edmund, 42–43, 199
Burke, Kenneth, 30, 31, 369
Bush, George (H. W.), 54, 62, 171, 186–87, 193–95, 200–201, 301
Bush, George W.: 20, 29, 35–36, 56, 63, 69, 87, 115, 118, 119, 120, 149, 152, 153, 163, 166, 172, 173–74, 182, 212, 214–16, 225, 232–33, 278, 282, 284, 285, 301, 350, 368–69; and 9/11, 70–71, 74–75, 149, 187, 195; and Christianity, 217–28, 230–33, 245; Military Order of Nov. 13, 2001, 70, 80, 81, 84, 86–88, 90, 91; speeches of, 35–42, 149–52, 175–77, 187–88, 195–96, 218, 229–30, 329, 365; First Inaugural, 29, 35–42, 150, 218; Second Inaugural, 176–77; State of the Union (2002), 75; State of the Union (2003), 175, 176, 218–19; State of the Union (2004), 226–28

campaign, presidential, 6, 9, 12, 15
Campbell, Karlyn Kohrs, 15, 34, 37, 279, 343, 345
Carter, James, 52–53, 144, 162, 169–70, 301, 367
Chertoff, Michael, 76
"chosen people," Americans as, 36, 38, 134–35, 148, 153, 196–97
Christianity: 134, 198, 201, 217–20; as civil faith, 38–43, 135, 136, 143, 153, 197, 219, 220–24, 226–27, 230

Churchill, Winston, 160
Cleveland, Grover, 110–11, 258
Clinton, William Jefferson: 55–56, 82, 115, 117, 118, 120, 172, 212, 266, 283, 284, 301, 304–305, 322, 362; speeches of, 348; State of the Union (1996), 264
communism, 161, 164, 165–66, 167, 182–84, 188–89, 191–92, 196, 197
Connolly, William, 30
constituency: 34; as rhetorical construction, 34, 37, 39, 40, 41, 324
Constitution, U.S.: 103–104, 105, 254; separation of powers (Article II), 103, 107–108, 112, 115, 117, 119, 272
Coolidge, Calvin, 135, 362
crisis: 355–56, 360–62, 366–70; rhetoric and, 356–57, 368–70
Crowell, Laura, 7, 9, 16

debate, presidential, 9, 258, 260
Declaration of Independence, The, 134–35, 165, 357
Defense of Marriage Act, 213, 229, 230, 231
democratic deliberation: 252, 254–67; the presidency and, 252, 253, 254, 256, 257–58, 260–63, 264, 266–67
discourse, presidential: 12, 273–74, 279, 282, 285–86, 294–96, 326–28, 331, 332–34, 343, 345, 350, 357–66; crisis and, 357–70; ethics and, 319–20, 321–24, 325–30, 332–33; Inaugural Address, 15, 35, 36–37, 41, 254, 257, 262, 279–80, 343; State of the Union Address, 257, 262, 279–81; to Congress, 272–86, 294

Eisenhower, Dwight D., 50, 169, 265, 349
epideictic rhetoric: 35–37; Inaugural Address as, 35, 36–37, 41; purpose of, 35

ethics: 317–22, 323–33; presidency, the and, 330–33; rhetoric and, 318–21, 323–26
ethos, 319
ex parte Milligan, 70, 73, 86–87, 88, 90
ex parte Quirin, 69, 73, 78, 85, 86, 87, 88, 91

Farrell, Thomas, 34, 320–21
Federal Open Markets Committee (FOMC), 47, 48–49, 51, 59
Federal Reserve, The: 46–47, 49–50, 51, 52, 53, 55, 57–61; conspiracy, 61–63, 65; and democracy, 63; and presidents, 49–56, 57, 58
Federalist Papers, The, 82, 104–105, 254
Ford, Gerald, 51, 261, 301, 349
Foucault, Michel: 31, 32; "author-function," 32

Gag Rule, the, 255
Geneva Conventions, 74, 86, 87, 89, 330
Gonzales, Alberto, 85
Goodridge et al v Department of Public Health, 212, 217, 224
Graham, Gladys Murphy, 5–6, 8
Grant, Ulysses S., 110
Gunderson, Robert G., 10

Habermas, Jurgen, 64
habeas corpus, 78, 81, 87, 369
Hamdan v. Rumsfeld (2006), 74, 80–81, 89
Hamilton, Alexander, 104–105, 294
Harding, Harold, 9
Harding, Warren G., 135
Hart, Roderick P., 4, 13, 36, 342
Hayworth, Donald, 6, 9
historical method *See rhetorical studies*
A History and Criticism of American Public Address, 7
Hoover, Herbert, 112, 135, 265

immigration, 130–31, 138, 151, 152
imperial presidency, 70–72

Jackson, Andrew, 107–108, 294, 344, 346–47
Jamieson, Kathleen Hall, 4, 13, 15, 34, 37, 279, 303–304, 343, 345, 364
Jefferson, Thomas, 7, 10, 82, 347; speeches of, 7, 10
Johnson, Andrew: 258, 283, 294; speeches of, 9–10
Johnson, Lyndon: 50–51, 73, 113, 169, 183, 184, 190, 197, 261, 263, 265, 301, 303, 306, 356; speeches of, 10, 184, 197, 265; "Great Society," 135

Kennedy, John F.: 50, 169, 182–83, 188, 261, 265, 300, 301, 318, 362; speeches of, 10, 349; Inaugural, 174
King, Martin Luther Jr., 131, 265

law, 74, 76–77, 100, 119, 120, 228, 231
Lawrence v. Texas, 212, 221–22, 228
Lincoln, Abraham: 5, 7, 81, 135, 258, 282; speeches of, 5, 6, 7, 360; "Emancipation Proclamation," 135, 257; "Gettysburg Address," 357

Madison, James, 7, 82, 107, 119, 254, 255, 344
Malcolm X, 131–32
Masons, The, 62–63
McKean, Dayton David, 6–7, 8, 16
McKinley, William, 81, 259, 367
Milligan. *See ex parte Milligan*
Monroe, James, 344
Murphy, John M., 20
myth, 135–37, 139–40, 145–46, 148, 149, 152, 153–54, 170, 246

neo-Aristotelianism, 10
Nixon, Richard M.: 51–52, 72–73, 79, 113–16, 169, 183, 184, 261, 274, 284, 305–306, 322, 362; speeches of, 184, 263–64
Nuremberg Trial, 73, 76

Olson, Lester, 15

Paget, Edwin, 6
Parry-Giles, Trevor and Shawn, 33–34, 349
Patriot Act, The, 70, 75, 79, 90, 149, 368
Phifer, Gregg, 9–10
Pierce, Franklin: 257; "Proclamation" (11 Feb 1856), 257
Polk, James K., 109–10
Postmodernity, 29, 31, 32, 63
Presidential Studies Quarterly, 19
public address, 3, 4, 12, 318
public opinion: 293–309; polling, 297–300, 301–305; presidency, the and, 294–97, 300–309
Puritans, The, 133, 134, 136–37, 140–41, 142, 143, 148–49, 153

Quarterly Journal of Speech, 5, 9
Quirin *See ex parte Quirin*

Reagan, Ronald: 53, 54, 56, 82, 85, 115, 116–17, 133, 143–49, 150, 151, 152, 153, 162, 168, 170–71, 185–86, 189–91, 197–200, 264, 277, 284, 296, 301, 304; speeches of, 143–49, 184–85, 191–93, 199, 281, 319–20; "Farewell," 148–49; First Inaugural, 144, 263; Second Inaugural, 148; State of the Union (1982), 146; State of the Union (1984), 143, 146
religion, 30–31
rhetoric: 251–52, 317–21, 340–48; as mode of inquiry, 4, 5–6, 10–11, 12, 102; authority and (*see* authority);

rhetoric (cont.)
    ideology and, 33–34, 102;
    presidency, the and, 19–20, 132,
      319–21, 341–48
Rhetoric and Public Affairs, 19
*Rhetorical Criticism, A Study in
    Method,* 10–11
rhetorical studies: 3, 11–12; critical
    pluralism, 10–11, 12; historical
    method, 6, 7–9, 10, 12, 101; publi-
    cation of, 16–17
Robertson, Pat, 62–63
Roosevelt, Franklin Delano: 6, 7, 82,
    85, 112–13, 261, 285, 301, 318,
    362; speeches of, 6, 7, 9; First Fire-
    side Chat of 1935, 263; "Four Free-
    doms," 135; Second Inaugural, 6
Roosevelt, Theodore: 7, 57, 82, 83,
    133, 138–43, 149, 151, 152, 153,
    264–65, 282, 295, 342, 346, 361;
    speeches of, 138–39, 140–42,
    295; First Annual Message, 142;
    "Square Deal," 138

Senate: US, 99–100, 105–106, 108–
    109, 118; "advice and consent," 99–
    101, 102, 103, 104–105, 106–108,
    109–110, 111, 114–17, 118–19
Skowronek, Steven, 33, 34, 343, 345
Soviet Union, 160, 161
Speech Criticism, 7
Speech Monographs, 9
Stuckey, Mary E., 20, 33, 351
Supreme Court, U.S.: 74, 83, 86, 89,
    113, 114, 116, 278, 284, 364;
    nominations to, 99–100, 102–13,
    149, 276–78, 287

Taft, William, 259
telos, 30
Toryism, 73, 80, 88–89
Truman, Harry S.: 7, 9, 46, 82, 165,
    168, 265, 285, 301, 349; speeches
    of, 9, 10, 197, 360
Tulis, Jeffrey, 33, 57, 260, 275,
    294–95, 346–47
Tyler, John, 108–109

Underhill, Robert, 13

Wallace, Karl, 319
Wander, Phillip, 16, 323, 324
War Powers Act of 1973, The, 72,
    73
Washington, George: 168, 255, 282,
    285, 342, 344, 347; speeches of,
    280, 360; "Farewell," 135, 160;
    Sixth Annual Message, 360
Whiggism, 73, 77, 79–80, 88–89, 108
White, James Boyd, 34, 42, 101, 323,
    324
Wiley, Earl W., 6–7, 8, 16
Wilkie, Wendell L., 9
Wilson, Woodrow: 5–6, 7, 57, 58, 82,
    111–12, 259, 260–61, 265, 308,
    342, 361–62; speeches of, 5–6, 7,
    10, 259, 280, 295; First Inaugural,
    6; "Lawyer and the Community,
    The," 6
Windt, Theodore Otto Jr., 3, 13, 177,
    282, 349, 356, 358

Zarefsky, David, 4 , 15, 342, 343–44,
    348, 357–58